When it was founded in 1824, the A

Unlike other pre-eminent clubs, members were chosen on the basis of their achievements rather than their background or political affiliation. Public rather than private life dominated the agenda. With its tradition of hospitality to conflicting views, the club attracted leading scientists, writers, artists and intellectuals – Charles Darwin and Matthew Arnold, Edward Burne-Jones and Yehudi Menuhin, Winston Churchill and Gore Vidal.

This book is not presented in the traditional, insular style of club histories, but devotes attention to the influence of Athenians on the scientific, creative and official life of the nation.

From the unwitting recruitment of a Cold War spy to the welcome admittance of women, this lively and original account explores the corridors and characters of the club, its wider political, intellectual and cultural influence, and its recent reinvention.

# THE ATHENÆUM

# THE ATHENÆUM

More Than Just Another London Club

MICHAEL WHEELER

YALE UNIVERSITY PRESS
NEW HAVEN AND LONDON

For information about this and other Yale University Press publications, please contact:
U.S. Office: sales.press@yale.edu      yalebooks.com
Europe Office: sales@yaleup.co.uk      yalebooks.co.uk

Set in Adobe Garamond Pro by IDSUK (DataConnection) Ltd
Printed in Great Britain by Gomer Press Ltd, Llandysul, Ceredigion, Wales

Library of Congress Control Number: 2020941219

ISBN 978-0-300-24677-3

A catalogue record for this book is available from the British Library.

10 9 8 7 6 5 4 3 2 1

*To the members of the Athenæum,*
*past, present and future*

# CONTENTS

# CONTENTS

ﭖ

# ILLUSTRATIONS

*Owner and copyright holder is the Athenæum unless otherwise stated.*

### In text

p. xviii: Walter Wilson, *Ballot Day 1892*, with key.

p. 73: 'The Athenæum Club, London: Ground and First Floor Plans',
*Architectural Review*, 1905.

### Plates

1. Sir Thomas Lawrence, *Portrait of John Wilson Croker*, 1825, NGI 300.
   © National Gallery of Ireland.
2. Thomas Hosmer Shepherd, *Waterloo Place, and Part of Regent Street*, 1828.
3. William Miller after Hugh William Williams, 'Part of the Temple of
   Minerva in the Acropolis of Athens', in *Select Views in Greece*, 1829.
   © British Museum.
4. Sir Thomas Lawrence, design for the club seal, 1824.
5. Charles Wild, 'The Crimson Drawing Room, Carlton House', in
   W.H. Pyne, *The History of the Royal Residences*, 1819.
6. Decimus Burton, *Design Elevation for a Public Building*, early 1820s.
   Hastings Museum and Art Gallery.
7. James Basire, *Plan of the Proposed Improvements at Charing Cross*, 1826.
   City of Westminster Archives.

# STYLE, REFERENCES AND ABBREVIATIONS

Middle names were often used in the nineteenth century and the convention has usually been followed here. The names of members of staff are provided wherever possible. In the notes, the place of publication is London unless otherwise stated and privately printed books are indicated as 'p.p.'.

Athenæum archive sources referred to most frequently in endnotes are indicated by catalogue numbers only:

| | |
|---|---|
| BUI 1/ | Building Committee papers |
| CAT 4/ | Menus |
| COL /1/1/ | Scrapbooks |
| COM 1/ | General Committee minutes |
| COM 7/ | Library Committee minutes |
| COM 13/ | Executive Committee minutes |
| COM 20/ | Annual Reports |
| MEM 1/ | Ballot Books |
| MEM 1/1/ | Candidates Books |
| SEC 1/ | Letter Books |

Where typescripts of Executive Committee minutes, printed annual reports and minutes of AGMs are inserted in General Committee minute books post-1945, the reader is directed to these insertions for ease of reference.

The following printed sources are referred to most frequently in the main text and endnotes:

Cowell    Frank Richard Cowell, *The Athenaeum: Club and social life in London, 1824–1974* (Heinemann, 1975)

Fernández-Armesto    *Armchair Athenians: Essays from Athenæum life*, ed. Filipe Fernández-Armesto (Athenæum, 2001)

*ODNB*    *Oxford Dictionary of National Biography*, ed. H.C.G. Matthew and Brian Harrison, 60 vols (Oxford: Oxford University Press, 2004; updated online, ed. David Cannadine)

*OED*    *Oxford English Dictionary* (online)

Tait    Hugh Tait and Richard Walker et al., *The Athenæum Collection* (Athenæum, 2000)

Ward    Humphry Ward, *History of the Athenæum, 1824–1925* (Athenæum, 1926)

Waugh    Francis Gledstanes Waugh, *The Athenæum Club and its Associations*, p.p., *c.* 1897; reprinted 1968

# PREFACE

Members of the older private clubs in London's West End look out on the passing world and the passing world peers in at the members. One particular bow-window at the top of St James's Street has long symbolised White's, London's oldest and most exclusive gentleman's club, historically the haunt of the landed and the titled. This window separates a peaceful interior from a noisy thoroughfare, as do the windows of Brooks's, the Whiggish rival club just across the street.

By contrast the Athenæum is symbolised, not by its large plate-glass windows that look onto Pall Mall and that were smashed from time to time by the London mob and the Luftwaffe, but by the steps and portico of its entrance on Waterloo Place, features to which reference has been made throughout the club's history. For it is in the traffic between the interior, with its unique facilities for reading and informed conversation, and the exterior, where members of the Athenæum have been influential, that the genius of the club is defined. National trends are reflected in the club's formation, its later development and its recent reinvention, while many of its members have helped to shape the institutional and public life of Britain through their contributions in a wide variety of fields.

In the decades that followed victory over the French at Waterloo, in 1815, Britain became a reformed, industrialised and expansive superpower. The Athenæum was founded in 1824 as a meeting place for the leading artists, writers and scientists of the day, along with cabinet ministers, bishops and judges. Its founder, John Wilson Croker, was a true blue Tory who ensured that a majority of Whigs served on the inaugural committee, and that members of this new kind of non-partisan club, with its close connections to the learned societies, were elected on the basis of achievements rather than birth. From its origins in the years before the First Reform Act through to its current existence in the twenty-first century, the Athenæum has adhered to the values that shape the liberal arts and sciences: it has always been hospitable to competing or indeed conflicting ideas, for example. In 1928 it was described in the *Graphic* as 'the brainiest club in the world': it certainly was a hundred years earlier and probably still is today.

*The Athenæum* is not cast in the traditional, insular mould of club histories, but devotes attention to the influence – the sometimes decisive influence – of Athenians on the intellectual, scientific, creative and official life of the nation. So more space than is usual in club histories is devoted to public affairs outside the clubhouse. The book also reflects a revival of interest in Clubland itself among social, cultural and political historians over the past couple of decades, as in Amy Milne-Smith's *London Clubland: A cultural history of gender and class in late Victorian Britain* (2011), for example, Barbara Black's *A Room of His Own: A literary-cultural study of Victorian Clubland* (2012) and Seth Thévoz's *Club Government: How the early Victorian world was ruled from London clubs* (2018).

I have divided my time over six years of research and writing between exploring the broad savannahs of the club's political, intellectual and cultural hinterland and the narrow defiles of its wonderfully preserved archive, which has yielded huge amounts of hitherto unpublished information about its aspirations and policies, its financial crises and intellectual triumphs, and its mundane day-to-day housekeeping. Writing the book has been an enriching experience, so many and varied are the former members whose eminence makes them worthy of close attention. The aim, however, has been to avoid duplicating material that is easily available in the *Oxford Dictionary of National Biography* or *Who's Who*, and instead to focus upon the membership's shared preoccupations from generation to generation, and their contribution to national life. The area treated most lightly is the Athenæum's collection of art works, as this is documented so effectively by Hugh Tait and Richard Walker in a book, published in 2000, to which reference is occasionally made. Unlike the library, which was built up by the club's first sub-committee on the basis of agreed criteria, the Athenæum Collection was acquired in a rather haphazard way and largely through private donations. The fact that the priority for wall space has always been given to bookcases rather than framed works of art underlines the Athenæum's main purpose and predilections.

I am grateful for the cheerful support of all the staff at the Athenæum during the preparation of this book. In particular I wish to thank: the secretary, Jonathan Ford, who was always a strong supporter of the project; the archivist, Jennie de Protani, who provided me with archival material and offered much help and advice; the librarian, Kay Walters, who provided books, along with her assistants Annette Rockall and Laura Doran; and Tia Cox, committee secretary, who supported the work of the History Committee. Simon Reeve photographed items from the club's own collection. Thanks are also due to the staff of the British Library, the City of London Archive, Gladstone's Library, the London Library, the London Metropolitan Archive and the Royal Institution.

Many members of the club have offered advice and support. I am particularly grateful to Brian Gilmore, who initiated the project and chaired the committee charged with its oversight, to Dr Richard Davenport-Hines, who read chapters as they were written, greatly to their advantage, and to four members who read the whole book: Professor Sir David Cannadine, Jenny Uglow, Michael Shaw, who nursed the book and its author throughout, and Bruce Hunter, consummate drafter of contracts and sterling supporter. Malcolm Bishop scoured the internet for references to the club and kindly shared his findings with me. Further thanks are due to Professor Michael Alexander, Len Berkowitz, Professor Jeremy Black, Rabbi Professor Dan Cohn-Sherbock, Dr Yolande Hodson, Dr Henry Kinloch, Professor Roger Knight, Hazhir Teimourian, Sir David Wilson and John Wilson. Also to Rosalind Gilmore and Professor Richard Shannon, both of whom were members of the advisory History Committee. Jane Barker, who became chairman of the General Committee in 2018, warmly supported a project inherited from three of her predecessors.

Since starting work on this book I have been asked the same question by many fellow members: 'How's it going?' Some have wondered whether it would be published in their lifetime and, alas, I have failed a few of them. Moral support was generously offered, especially by David Cooper, Sir Roland Jackson, Graham

Nicholson, David Thomson, Patience Thomson, Dr Christopher Wright and four late lamented members: Christopher Barker, Dr Andrew Brown, Sir Alcon Copisarow and Eliot Levin.

Of the friends and colleagues outside the club who have been supportive, I thank particularly Graham Beck, Greg Gardner, the Revd Terry Hemming, Professor Frank James and Professor Sharon Ruston. Chief friend and supporter was my beloved, Susan Woodhead.

At Yale University Press I want to thank Heather McCallum for her warm support and expert guidance throughout the process of publication, and also Heather Nathan, Marika Lysandrou, Clarissa Sutherland, Sophie Richmond, Lucy Buchan, Rachael Lonsdale, Percie Edgeler and Katie Urquhart for their kind and highly professional contributions.

A final note. I completed the main text of this book in August 2017.

MDW, Hampshire, June 2020

1. Lord Justice Denman
2. Bishop of London
3. Duke of Argyll
4. Mr. Lecky
5. Canon Farrar
6. Sir Arthur Sullivan
7. Dr. Quain
8. Professor Seeley
9. Bishop of Winchester
10. Bishop of Gloucester
11. Dr. Stainer
12. Lord Hannon
13. Dean Bradley
14. Sir F. Burton
15. Lord Justice Fry
16. Sir Charles Hallé
17. Lord Esher
18. Justice North
19. Justice Chitty
20. Lord Dufferi

21. Lord Knutsford
22. Rt. Hon. Hugh Childers
23. Mr. Speaker Peel
24. Professor Huxley
25. Archbishop of Canterbury
26. Lord Lorne
27. Bishop of Oxford
28. Lord Playfair
29. Bishop of Manchester
30. Justice Hawkins
31. Mr. John Evans
32. Lord Chief Justice
33. Bishop of Newcastle
34. Lord Northbrook
35. Professor Stokes
36. Mr. H. R. Tedder (Secretary)
37. Canon Duckworth
38. Dr. Vaughan
39. Sir John Gilbert
40. Sir John Lubbock

41. Mr. John Morley
42. Mr. Alma-Tadema
43. Sir Theodore Martin
44. Lord Kelvin
45. Mr. G. J. Goschen
46. Sir Henry Rawlinson
47. Sir F. Leighton
48. Baron Pollock
49. Bishop of Chichester
50. Sir Rutherford Alcock
51. Mr. Shaw-Lefevre
52. Lord Carlingford
53. Lord Selborne
54. Mr. Herbert Spencer
55. Sir Joseph Lister
56. Sir F. Abel
57. Lord Sherbrooke
58. Archbishop of York
59. Mr. Andrew Lang

*Walter Wilson*, Ballot Day 1892

# PROLOGUE

A large number of gentlemen, most of them standing, are crowded together in a stately reception room. There may be a ghost of a smile on a few faces, but the general impression is of earnest members of the liberal professions, and perhaps one or two noblemen and gentlemen of leisure, in conversation or at ease. The late-Victorian dress code is formal: frock coats and waistcoats prevail. Several clerical collars are in evidence, but only one Norfolk jacket. We are in the drawing room of the Athenæum, with its high bookcases and heavy furniture, much of which is still in use today. We are looking north. In the northeast corner of the room (at the back on the right) members are casting their votes for or against candidates, whose signed certificates can just be made out, sticking up above individual ballot boxes, which are out of sight. Most of the ten or so candidates have been on the waiting list – currently running at a staggering sixteen hundred names, or thereabouts – for at least fifteen years.

Before the advent of photography, large group portraits with explanatory keys could present to the viewer a combination of individuals who had never been simultaneously in the same place together. This particular image is neither an oil painting nor a photograph, but a worked-up drawing by J. Walter Wilson, an artist who specialised in group or crowd scenes such as parliamentary debates, coronations, public meetings or even battles. When *Ballot Day 1892* was published on 11 March 1893, as a large double-page pull-out supplement to an article on the Athenæum, the *Illustrated London News* was on the cusp of printing more photographs than drawings. For fifty years the world's first illustrated weekly newspaper had provided its readers – over 300,000 of them latterly – with celebrity portraits and on-the-spot sketches of newsworthy events and places. Its artists had visited parts of the British Empire which most readers would never see for themselves, and now Wilson had gained entry to four of the grander private clubs in London (the Carlton, the Reform, the Athenæum and the United Service Club), in Pall Mall, an elegant street in St James's, the area between Mayfair and St James's Park. The third article in a series entitled 'In Clubland' was illustrated with further sketches by Wilson. It was written by a member of the Athenæum, the Revd Francis Gledstanes Waugh, whose name was proposed to the editor by the club itself, indicating a desire to control the way in which it was presented to the world.[1]

The decision to allow the artist access to each club would have been made by its committee; but who had the unenviable task of choosing the luminaries among the membership who were to appear in each group portrait? Perhaps it was decided by the chairman – at the Athenæum in 1890–93 alternately Lord Aberdare, who is not portrayed here, and Sir Frederick Abel (56), seated on the right – in consultation with the secretary, in this case Henry Tedder (36), librarian since 1875 and secretary since 1889. Eminence was clearly the first criterion: eighteen of the fifty-nine members portrayed here are 'Rule II' members, who were specially invited to join without being balloted; fifty have titles of some kind; and of the other nine only three will go to their graves as plain 'Mr', two being knighted later and four raised to the peerage. Involvement in the governance of the club also seems to have counted: twenty-six have served on the General Committee; the commanding figure on the extreme left, Lord Denman (1), and the seated figures shown in profile in the foreground, William Lecky (4) and Lord Leighton (47), were all on the Committee in 1891–92. But there may also have been a more practical reason for inclusion. Images of most of the individuals represented had been in the public domain for some time. Portraits of those who had already appeared in the *Illustrated London News* would have been on file there; no fewer than forty-one of them had been caricatured in *Vanity Fair* and about half that number in *Punch*.[2] So actual drawing from life, in the clubhouse, was probably limited.

The selection of members and the way in which they are portrayed offer clues to the composition and ethos of the Athenæum in the 1890s, and provide a reference point in the discussion which follows in this book, where continuities and changes in the club are related to the society in which it has operated from its foundation in 1824 to the present day. *Ballot Day 1892* presents to the viewer figures from the intellectual stratum of what we would now call the 'British Establishment'. Comfortably seated in the centre, and with a respectful space around him, is the aproned figure of the Most Revd Edward White Benson (25), Archbishop of Canterbury, second only to Queen Victoria constitutionally and one of the eighteen Privy Counsellors in the drawing. (Eighty-six of Victoria's privy counsellors had been Athenians when she ascended the throne in 1837.)[3] The new Archbishop of York, William Dalrymple Maclagan (58), is also here, over on the right, as are eleven other senior clergy, including, on the left, Anthony Thorold (9), Bishop of Winchester, who is chatting to Charles Ellicott (10), Bishop of Gloucester. Bishops' distinctive dress leads to their presence in the Athenæum being exaggerated by certain lay members from time to time. A survey of 1884 does reveal, however, that of the 1,500 or so members, 37 were bishops and 132 were clergy ('including 41 Dignitaries').[4]

In contrast, the 56 judges blended in sartorially in 1884, as did the 30 QCs and 161 barristers. The founder of the club, John Wilson Croker, felt that judges and bishops should be eligible for consideration as they were, '*par état*, literary men'. The most prominent of the ten judges in the drawing is standing in the centre foreground, thus partially concealing Archbishop Benson: John Duke Coleridge (32), the Lord Chief Justice, has been in office since 1880 and is to die in 1894. He is holding forth to a group on his left. The seated figure reading a document is the president of the Royal Society, William Thomson, 1st baron Kelvin (44), who has developed some of the discoveries of Michael Faraday, the club's first secretary. The artist Lawrence Alma-Tadema (42), who has recently made designs for the redecoration of the hall and grand staircase, looks over Lord Kelvin's shoulder, while John Morley (41), formerly a leading political journalist, leans forward in order to catch Coleridge's conversation. August 1892 sees the defeat of the Conservative government led by Lord Salisbury (a member who is not shown here) by the Grand Old Man of British politics, William Ewart Gladstone, a frequenter of the club who never joins it, and the absent *eminence grise* of *Ballot Day 1892*. Morley is not only Gladstone's Chief Secretary for Ireland, but will later be his biographer. And in front of Morley is George Joachim Goschen (45), now in opposition, having formerly been a member of Gladstone's first administration before defecting to the Liberal Unionists and becoming Salisbury's Chancellor of the Exchequer. Goschen, Morley and fifteen others depicted here have held political posts. Sixteen of them have been Liberal parliamentarians; seven have then broken with Gladstone over home rule for Ireland.

One of the seven is the hirsute Mr Speaker Peel (23), younger son of Sir Robert (an 'original' member).[5] In the House of Commons, Peel has to be politically impartial, yet even this former Liberal MP has declared his opposition to Gladstone by becoming a Liberal Unionist. He is conversing with Lord Knutsford (21) – Henry Thurstan Holland – until recently Colonial Secretary under Salisbury. The Hollands, like the Darwins and several other families, are creating an Athenian dynasty.[6] Lord Knutsford's father, Sir Henry Holland, and Sir Henry Halford issued the death certificate for Sir Thomas Lawrence, president of the Royal Academy, in 1830: all three were original members. The elegant figure standing in front of Lord Knutsford is the marquess of Dufferin and Ava (20), ambassador to France and formerly viceroy of India, governor-general of Canada and quondam ambassador to Russia, Turkey and Italy. It was while in Naples, two years ago, that the Dufferins were visited by Rudyard Kipling, who knows them well. Kipling, later a member of the club, had published a Browningesque monologue entitled 'One Viceroy resigns', which reflects the interconnectedness of diplomatic, military and educational activity in the subcontinent under the British Raj. While handing over to his successor, the 5th marquess of Lansdowne, Dufferin refers in the course of the poem to Lord Ripon, his predecessor, Sir William Wilson Hunter, a leading historian of India, General 'Bobs' Roberts, formerly Commander-in-Chief, India, and Sir Garnet Wolseley, who distinguished himself at the relief of Lucknow in 1857: all were members.

In the Gladstonian age of the polymath, many of the top lawyers and politicians in the Athenæum have literary and/or scientific interests. The standing figure on the right, who inclines towards the Lord Chief Justice, is Sir Charles Pollock (48), a justice of the High Court and a staunch member of the Royal Institution in Albemarle Street, a scientific body with which the club has close links. Behind him, and equally attentive to the Lord Chief Justice, is the bearded John George Shaw-Lefevre (51), First Commissioner of Works in Gladstone's cabinet, who enjoys learning languages – he can read fourteen with ease – and

4

translating foreign literatures into English. Among the clutch of judges on the left-hand side of the picture, are the Master of the Rolls Lord Esher (17), Justice North (18) and Justice Chitty (19), as well as Lord Justice Fry FRS (fellow of the Royal Society; 15), a Quaker judge in the Court of Appeal, who is later to publish two zoological studies on bryophytes.

Membership of the Athenæum and a fellowship of a learned society often go together: in 1884, 290 Athenians were fellows, mainly of the Royal Society, in whose rooms the Athenæum's first committee meeting was held sixty years earlier. In the picture there are eleven 'scientists' – a term coined only in 1840 by the Revd William Whewell, an original member, and which Charles Darwin never applied to himself – and yet there are seventeen FRSs, reflecting the fact that the Royal Society still has fellows who are enthusiasts and potential sponsors of scientific work rather than practitioners. Over on the right, for example, is the lawyer and politician Roundell Palmer FRS, 1st earl of Selborne (53), a former Lord Chancellor under Gladstone who reorganised the judiciary and broke with his chief over Irish home rule. Near Lord Selborne is the alternating chairman of the club's General Committee, Sir Frederick Abel FRS (56), a professional scientist, Faraday's successor as professor of chemistry at the Royal Military Academy and co-inventor of cordite with James (later Sir James) Dewar, also a member: they are soon to be successful in defending a legal action brought against them by Alfred Nobel. Sir Frederick was the founding director of the Imperial Institute, at the opening of which Sir Arthur Sullivan (6) conducted his 'Imperial Ode' in the presence of the queen. Standing next to the chairman is Sir Joseph Lister (55), the pioneer of sterile surgery. The number of medical men among the membership is high throughout the club's history: in 1884 the count stood at seventy-one. One of the best known is in the picture: Sir Richard Quain (7).[7]

The most famous scientist in the room is at the centre. As a young man, Professor Thomas Huxley FRS (24) served as naturalist to the British Geological Survey, a project which involved several original members of the Athenæum and many of their successors, including Lord Playfair (28).[8] Huxley has been known as 'Darwin's bulldog' ever since his disagreement with Samuel Wilberforce, then Bishop of Oxford, on the *Origin of Species* in 1860. ('Soapy Sam' Wilberforce, himself a prominent member of the club, died twenty years ago.) With impish humour, Walter Wilson shows the inventor of the term 'agnostic' moving towards

Archbishop Benson with a piece of paper in his hand. In 1864 Professor Huxley founded the X Club with eight other liberal thinkers who shared scientific interests, all of whom were members of the Athenæum. Two other X Club members are in the picture: the banker, archaeologist and naturalist Sir John Lubbock (40), one of Darwin's pall-bearers and a former president of the Linnaean Society, and Herbert Spencer (54), philosopher, biologist, sociologist and political theorist, who virtually lives in the clubhouse.

Whereas some of the juxtapositions in *Ballot Day 1892* accentuate a shared profession or calling (bishop speaks to bishop), the most telling are those that cross boundaries of profession or discipline. Lord Justice Fry is in conversation with the musician Sir Charles Hallé (16), for instance. The web of connections between figures who are not visually juxtaposed is equally significant, reflecting the way in which social relationships develop at the Athenæum. Consider, for example, the three figures standing by the fireplace on the left. The caricature of Lord Justice Denman (1) in *Vanity Fair* (19 November 1892), marking his retirement as a High Court judge, bears the legend, 'He was an ornament of the bench'. Facing us is the Right Revd Frederick Temple (2), whom Gladstone marked down early as a Liberal, worthy of preferment, and controversially recommended to the Crown as bishop first of Exeter and then of London. (Following Benson's sudden death in Hawarden church, Temple will become Archbishop of Canterbury in three years' time and later crown Edward VII.) Temple is what we would now call an Anglican Liberal Catholic. Four years ago, in 1889, during the St Paul's reredos case, he clashed with Lord Coleridge, his old friend from their time up at Balliol and later in Exeter, when the Lord Chief Justice was an MP for the city. In fact three of the judges involved in the case are portrayed in *Ballot Day 1892*: Temple's appeal against Coleridge was supported by Sir Charles Pollock, and the Master of the Rolls, Lord Esher, upheld the appeal.

The third figure near the fireplace, the ubiquitous duke of Argyll (3), was formerly Secretary of State for India in Gladstone's first administration and Lord Privy Seal in his second, but parted from him over home rule. In the scientific debates of the 1860s he led the opposition to Darwin, and thus to Huxley. The duke has his back to the company, and thus to his son, Lord Lorne (26), who is talking to the Bishop of Oxford (27). It was unfortunate that *Vanity Fair* accompanied its celebratory caricature of the marquess, on the occasion of his engagement to the queen's fourth daughter, Princess Louise, with the legend, 'If everywhere as successful as in love a great destiny awaits him' (19 November 1870). The couple often live apart and the first marriage of a commoner to a princess for three centuries is childless. Having been the fourth governor-general of Canada, he is now governor and constable of Windsor Castle. Lord Lorne's homosexuality is the subject of open society gossip.[9]

Under the unwritten rules of the Athenæum, however, public rather than private life dominates the agenda. Even those engaged in the arts tend to have some kind of public role as well as a more private creative life. When the Athenæum was founded as a 'literary' club, literature was broadly interpreted: the judges, bishops and cabinet ministers were all assumed to be literary, or highly educated and involved in the world of books. As the Revd Henry Hart Milman, an original member, said in 1837, literature 'in its widest acceptation, may properly comprehend everything which is recorded in written language'.[10] Only one figure in *Ballot Day 1892* is strictly a 'man of letters', in the sense that writing is his profession.[11] Andrew Lang (59), the anthropologist, folklorist, reviewer and poet, is seated on the right and, yes, sports the one Norfolk jacket: he has a high public profile at present, not least as a frequent contributor to the *Illustrated London News*. But then there is also his fellow Scot, Sir Theodore Martin (43), who was a solicitor by training and a parliamentary agent by profession, specialising in facilitating the passing of private bills: he is the co-author of the 'Bon Gaultier' ballads (1845) and of the official biography of the prince consort, and is now a trusted guest of the queen's. Canon Farrar (5), chaplain to the House of Commons, is the author of two novels as well as numerous theological works, and John Morley is a biographer. In the heyday of narrative history, we should perhaps also add to our list of authors William Lecky (4), the historian of eighteenth-century England, who will soon become MP for Trinity College Dublin and later a Privy Counsellor; John Seeley (8), Regius Professor of History at Cambridge and author of *Ecce Homo* (1866); and the Right Revd William Stubbs (27), Seeley's opposite number at Oxford until he became bishop there four years ago.

The musicians in the club are represented by three knights: Sir Arthur Sullivan, Sir Charles Hallé and Sir John Stainer (11), organist, professor of music at Oxford and composer of *The Crucifixion* (1887), who was described by Sullivan as a genius. Similarly the artists, who as a professional body were specifically identified as suitable candidates for membership by the founder, have their pre-eminent figures on show. Sir Frederic Leighton (47), president of the Royal Academy, is prominently seated in the foreground with a cup of tea and a newspaper to hand: he is one of the most influential members of the club and an active proposer or seconder of new members. The other major public office relating to art, the directorship of the National Gallery, is currently held by Sir Frederic William Burton (14), who is also active in the club and also seems to be fond of tea (available gratis on ballot days). Criticised for preferring his chair at the Athenæum to travelling in search of acquisitions,[12] Burton nevertheless manages to purchase for the nation Leonardo's *Virgin of the Rocks*, Raphael's *Ansidei Madonna*, Van Dyck's *Equestrian Portrait of Charles I*, Holbein the Younger's *Ambassadors* and many early Italian works. Sir John Gilbert RA (39) is both an artist and an illustrator, who is best known for his almost thirty thousand illustrations for the *Illustrated London News*.

Some of these illustrious members of the Athenæum, selected for public display in a popular weekly newspaper, will figure again in later chapters, as the story of the club and its political, intellectual and cultural hinterland unfolds, and as the themes that have been prefigured here are developed. The history of a club is the history of its members and their interactions, its constitution and function, its buildings and collections, and its external relations and profile, all of which change over time. In the case of the Athenæum the hall of fame is second to none, and the less eminent members – the body of the kirk – nevertheless have to have made a distinctive contribution in some field or other, as well as being 'clubbable', in order to be elected. The clubhouse is a noble example of its kind and is deserving of detailed treatment in terms of its architecture and its later adaptations. The library is the finest in Clubland, providing compelling evidence of a continued commitment to erudition over two centuries. This book identifies and describes the club's ethos and 'aura', demonstrating the persistent continuities, even as the club adapts to irresistible change, and showing how its members, amenities and values relate to British society and its evolution, up to the present day. In order, however, to understand the club's founding purpose and early identity as a 'literary' club, we must turn back to the beginning.

# Part I
# 'EVERYTHING MUST HAVE A BEGINNING'

## (1823–30)

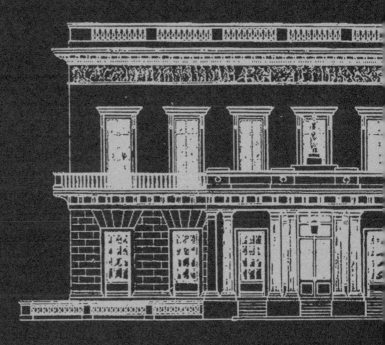

# 1

## CROKER'S LONDON

Pasted into the first minute book of the Athenæum's Committee are copies of letters from John Wilson Croker, the founder of the club, to Sir Humphry Davy, its first chairman. In the course of the first letter, dated 12 March 1823, Croker reminds Davy of an earlier conversation or letter:

> I will take this opportunity of repeating the proposition I have before made to you about a Club for literary and scientific men, and followers of the fine arts. The fashionable and military clubs not only absorb a great portion of society, but have spoiled all the Coffee Houses and Taverns, so that the artist, or mere literary man, neither of whom are members of the established clubs, are in a much worse situation, both comparatively and positively, than they were. – I am therefore satisfied that a Club for their accommodation is desirable, and would be very successful.[1]

Croker was well placed to make such a confident statement: he was a member of White's, the oldest 'fashionable' club; he was deeply involved in the governance of the Union Club, the first of the new 'members' clubs'; and he knew that there was now a gap in the market for a literary club (Plate 1). Taverns had provided meeting places for writers and intellectuals in Shakespeare's day, and coffee houses in Dr Johnson's. Of the two thousand coffee houses in London in the early eighteenth century, 122 were located in St James's, the area in which some coffee houses were to become subscription clubs, thus creating 'Clubland'.[2] Serving officers and veterans of the French

11

wars had their military clubs, and the upper classes had their fashionable clubs. The 'literary and scientific men' had access to the many learned societies that flourished in early nineteenth-century London, but no club of their own. In rectifying this situation, Croker created a new kind of club, which had no political affiliation, which chose its members on the basis of achievements rather than birth and which was to benefit from the rapid rise of an expanding middle class.

Croker knew about clubs, and he also knew literary, scientific and artistic London better than most. Many of the Athenæum's 'original' members, as those elected in the first year or so were called,[3] moved in the same political and intellectual circles, in the House of Commons and the Admiralty, at John Murray's publishing house and the Royal Institution (both in Albemarle Street), among the book shops of St James's (by the end of the eighteenth century the centre of the London retail book trade),[4] at the learned societies in Somerset House off the Strand, at soirées in private houses, or at the Union Club in Waterloo Place. In this chapter we shall visit these centres of activity in the years after Wellington's victory at Waterloo in 1815, a victory that estab-lished Great Britain as the leading European power which ruled over the largest empire the world had ever known.[5] In this way we can see what Croker meant when he referred to 'these times' as being propitious for the formation of a new London club, in his second letter to Davy: 'All that is necessary to create a Club in these times is a Circular Letter of invitation.'

These letters were sent from the Admiralty, where Croker served as first secretary. (His most illustrious predecessor, Samuel Pepys, had gone 'clubbing' at Wood's in Pall Mall back in 1660.)[6] When Croker took up his appointment in the autumn of 1809 he was only twenty-eight years old.[7] An Irish Protestant from Galway, and thus a member of a ruling minority, he had been educated at Trinity College Dublin and then been called to the Irish bar. His strong literary interests led to the publication of verse satires and a friendship with the poet Thomas Moore which was to continue after they both became original members of the Athenæum. Croker found the polarisation of Irish politics and religion unattractive: later he supported Catholic Emancipation while remaining a pragmatic and unsentimental member of the Church of England. In the summer of 1807 he took his seat in the Commons as the member for

Downpatrick.[8] Croker's success in deputising for Sir Arthur Wellesley as Chief Secretary for Ireland during the peninsular campaign led to the post at the Admiralty. Brought up in an environment of patronage and close family ties, Croker placed great emphasis upon personal loyalties and party allegiance.

Over a period of twenty-two years, Croker was a member of four Tory administrations in a highly paid senior post outside the cabinet. An outstanding administrator, accustomed to making difficult decisions and to explaining his position trenchantly, he said that he felt as guilty as a 'truant boy' when not at his desk.[9] He and his wife had apartments in both the U-shaped three-storey building in Whitehall and Kensington Palace. On top of the Admiralty building was a semaphore through which messages could be received from the ports. So the first person in London to hear how the war was going, at sea and on the Continent, was often John Wilson Croker, a man relied upon by monarchs and premiers, colleagues at the Admiralty, and wealthy friends and patrons. These included Lord Hertford, a notorious rake,[10] Viscount Lowther, whose political role was to prove helpful during the club's building programme, and Sir Robert Peel, who wrote 620 letters to Croker between 1810 and 1846:[11] all three were original members of the Athenæum.

By the time he wanted to establish a new literary club, Croker could call upon some of the many personal and political allies he had made at the Admiralty and in the Commons. The biggest prize of all was Arthur Wellesley, the duke of Wellington, who had effectively been Croker's patron in 1807, supplying his election expenses in the general election of that year, and to whom Croker naturally felt a strong allegiance. The duke presented the cloak that he had worn at Waterloo to Croker, who wrote his wife a vivid account of a visit to the battle-field. At the Royal Academy summer exhibition of 1822 a protective rail had to be placed around *Chelsea Pensioners receiving the Gazette announcing the Battle of Waterloo* by Sir David Wilkie RA, the fee for which was negotiated upwards by the sculptor, Francis Chantrey.[12] The historian Henry Hallam celebrated the peace and prosperity which followed the battle as 'the most beautiful phenomenon in the history of mankind'.[13] Hallam, Chantrey, Wilkie and Wellington were all to be original members of the Athenæum, as were Robert Dundas, 2nd viscount Melville, First Lord of the Admiralty from 1812,[14] and Captain (later Rear-Admiral Sir Francis) Beaufort, creator of the wind force scale. Beaufort's description of near drowning in a letter to a fellow original member, the wealthy scientist William Hyde Wollaston, was of special interest to another, the royal physician Henry Halford, who was researching the nature of the death agony and owned half of the severed fourth cervical vertebra of King Charles I.[15]

Working at the Admiralty and in parliament, at the centre of an extensive web of professional and social intelligence, Croker exercised power in his office and influence at private dinner tables. During a visit to London in November 1826, Sir Walter Scott, an original member, recorded a number of dinners at which Croker was present. On the 14th Scott 'dined at Croker's, at Kensington, with his family, the Speaker [Sir Charles Manners Sutton], and the facetious Theodore Hook'; on the 15th with Wellington, where the party included the Peels and Croker; on the 16th as the guest of Croker at the Admiralty, when 'no less than five Cabinet Ministers were present – Canning, Huskisson, Melville, Peel, and Wellington, with sub-secretaries by the bushel'; and on the 18th 'at Mr. Peel's with Lord Liverpool, Duke of Wellington, Croker, etc.'[16] Known by everybody who was anybody, Croker involved himself in a range of projects which he deemed to be in the national interest. He was, for example, the MP who argued most strongly in support of the arts, and who campaigned for the acquisition of the Elgin Marbles by the British Museum.[17] Croker was often abrasive in style, both in his speeches and his published articles, and as a result made as many enemies as friends.[18] In the first two chapters of Benjamin Disraeli's political novel, *Coningsby* (1844), the portrayal of the odious Mr Digby reveals how Croker was regarded by an ambitious politician who believed himself to be thwarted by him.[19] In reality Croker was politically loyal and administratively dynamic, never pushing himself forward for further promotion and always refusing honours. He preferred to play a supporting rather than a starring role, and his contribution to British political history has been underestimated as a result.

In his letter of 12 March 1823, Croker envisaged a club for 'literary and scientific men, and followers of the fine arts'. The letter's recipient, Sir Humphry Davy, was president of the Royal Society and had been a poet before he was a scientist. He had walked the fells with his friend Samuel Taylor Coleridge, and with Sir Walter Scott and William Wordsworth, who asked him to correct the proofs of the second edition of *Lyrical Ballads* (1800).[20] Today, 'literary' and 'scientific' are often opposing or contradictory terms. Not so in the first half of the nineteenth century, when scientific papers were written in polished English prose, often embellished with classical allusions, and when scientific discovery and literary work often went hand in hand.[21] Sir John Barrow, who served at the Admiralty even longer than Croker did, as second secretary, was awarded an LLD by Edinburgh University in 1821 as a 'proof of their respect' for his 'literary talents' and for his 'effective zeal in promoting the progress of science'.[22] Barrow published accounts of voyages of discovery, including in the Arctic, and considered that nothing was of more interest 'among the literary and scientific world' (rather than worlds) than Captain Parry's 'late Expedition' to discover the North-West Passage.[23] In 1852 the Royal Institution's aim of furthering 'scientific research' was broadened to that of promoting 'Science and Literary Research' – literary in the sense of 'relating to letters or learning'.[24] Many of what Croker describes as 'followers of the fine arts' in his day were also engaged in an important dialogue with the scientists.[25]

By 1823, Croker and Davy had witnessed the rapid expansion of learned societies and institutions in London. During the French wars, the Royal Institution had been established (1799) and three new learned societies founded – the Horticultural Society of London (1804), the Medical and Chirurgical Society (1805) and the Geological Society of London (1807). After Waterloo came the Institution of Civil Engineers (1818), the Astronomical Society of London (1820, later the Royal Astronomical Society), the Royal Asiatic Society (1823) and the Royal Society of Literature (1823). During the 1820s six of these new learned societies were to have a present or future member of the Athenæum as president.[26] But why this ferment of activity?

An anonymous review article of 1826 on the transactions of various provincial 'scientific institutions', in Murray's Tory *Quarterly Review*, praised the wisdom and liberality of the nation's (Tory) ministers. 'Our rapid improvement in wealth, intelligence, and civilization', argued the geologist Charles Lyell, an original member of the Athenæum, 'should not merely render indispensable successive modifications and re-modellings of our political institutions, but also call, from time to time, for some corresponding changes in our public provisions for extending the advantages of a liberal education'.[27] Along with the growth of new cities, and the 'sudden affluence to which commercial or manufacturing industry has raised districts hitherto insignificant and thinly peopled', Lyell noted the 'introduction and discovery of various arts and sciences before unknown or disregarded'.

The emergence of new kinds of knowledge was also central to the Revd Abraham Hume's explanation for the growth of learned societies. Writing in the 1840s, Hume argued that members joined in order to 'enable themselves to keep pace with the literary and scientific progress of their own times'.[28] He calculated that by 1847 over fifteen thousand members of learned societies were taking an interest, 'more or less active, in the progress of literature and science'.[29] And 'science' was as broadly defined as 'literature'. The 'modern and extended use' of the term 'science', he explained, in part accounted for the number of 'scientific' institutions which had sprung up in the country: 'for we apply it now to almost any subject which is or may be followed out upon fixed principles'.[30] The truly learned man had to be something of a polymath, and this was reflected in the subjects addressed by the learned societies: 'the Royal Astronomical embraces a class of subjects that are ranged with mathematics on the one hand, and with natural history on the other; the antiquary ought to be familiar with architecture, manufactures, costume, palæography, &c.'[31] The Athenæum was founded at a time of intellectual excitement and expansiveness, when a victorious nation was asserting itself as a liberal state which fostered liberal education and research.

The Revd Hume described members of learned societies as the 'choice spirits of the age, the intellectual men in their various localities, the ablest in their respective departments'.[32] It was the choicest Fellows of the oldest learned society whom Croker had in mind in his letter to Davy, when he went on to develop his idea of a new club:

> As every thing must have a beginning, I would propose, in the first instance, to write to each member of the Council of the Royal Society, and each Royal Academician, to propose to them to be of the Club – perhaps also a dozen letters to persons of acknowledged literary eminence might be ventured, such as Sir Walter Scott, Mr. Moore, Mr. Campbell, Mr. Rogers, Mr. Rose, &c &c.

The Royal Academy and both of the leading learned societies – the Royal Society and the Society of Antiquaries – had been accommodated in Somerset House, on the Strand, since 1780. When Davy became president of the Royal

Society in 1820 the scientific fellows were still outnumbered by the non-scientific, such as John Wilson Croker FRS. While vainly attempting to professionalise the institution, which was deeply divided after the presidency of the nepotist Sir Joseph Banks, Davy continued his predecessor's tradition of privately funding weekly soirées at which the latest scientific advances could be discussed – a tradition which Davies Gilbert, another poet and original member of the Athenæum, kept going when he took over the presidency in 1827.[33] Royal Society meetings were dull: papers were simply read aloud and there was no discussion.[34] From Davy's point of view, the new club that he and Croker were discussing could provide FRSs and members of their neighbouring learned societies with a setting for relaxed and lively exchanges of views on science and the arts, leaving the Royal Society to focus upon being a professional scientific body which could engage with government. Davy's ambitions for the Royal Society were to have a crucial influence upon his relationship with Croker and the foundation of the Athenæum.

Of the Royal Academicians elected during Benjamin West's presidency, seventeen were to be original members of the Athenæum;[35] and West's successor, Sir Thomas Lawrence, was to be a trustee of the club, *ex officio*, along with the presidents of the Royal Society and the Society of Antiquaries.[36] The artistic and intellectual elite was a tight-knit group, who often supported one another professionally. Among Lawrence's sitters were at least sixteen fellow Athenians, including the duke of York, the earl of Liverpool, Wellington, Canning, Earl Bathurst and Croker,[37] while Thomas Phillips's tally reached twenty-two.[38] Francis Chantrey's sculptures included busts of ten original members, including Croker, Wellington, Raffles, Canning, Watt, King William IV, Peel and Sir Walter Scott.[39] Royal Academy dinners were opportunities for this elite to get together. In his diary for 29 April 1820, Croker recorded sitting at a small table with, among others, the painters Thomas Phillips and William Mulready, whom he liked. HRH the duke of Sussex, president of the Society of Arts and an original member of the Athenæum, made a dreadful speech.[40]

Before the Royal Society moved out in 1837, Somerset House was the site of cross-fertilisation between the disciplines, in spite of the fact that the council of the Society of Antiquaries declined a request that meetings should not be held on the same night as the Royal Society's.[41] Several Royal Academicians who were also active in the Society of Antiquaries, including Chantrey, Sir Richard Westmacott, Thomas Phillips, Sir Thomas Lawrence and Charles Robert Cockerell, became members of the Athenæum, as did a number of FRSs who were also Antiquaries: John George Children, Sir Everard Home, Sir Humphry Davy, William Whewell and Davies Gilbert.[42]

Also at the small table with Croker at the Royal Academy dinner in 1820 was the poet Thomas Campbell, one of the dozen 'persons of acknowledged literary eminence' whom Croker had in mind in March 1823 as potential recipients of special letters of invitation. The self-aggrandising Campbell, best known for his war songs such as 'Ye mariners of England', played a leading role in the establishment of London University. William Jerdan, a prominent editor and clubman, described this as the 'great public act of Mr. Campbell's life', in one of a series of short laudatory memoirs of the 'illustrious and eminent personages' of early nineteenth-century Britain, many of them original members of the Athenæum, entitled the *National Portrait Gallery* (1830–34).[43] Like Jerdan, Croker (himself the subject of a memoir) particularly valued those literary figures who made great public acts. Scott's worldwide fame rested not only upon his poetry and fiction, but also his contributions to British public life, particularly in relation to Scotland. Croker also held in high esteem William Stewart Rose, a friend of Scott's and the verse translator of Ariosto, who served as a Whig MP for Christchurch, Dorset, and as Reading Clerk to the House of Lords. Like Scott, Thomas Moore found himself in severe financial difficulties, in his case for political rather than commercial reasons, when his deputy Admiralty registrar at Bermuda incurred huge debts. Moore was rescued by another founding member of the General Committee of the Athenæum, the 3rd marquess of Lansdowne.

Moore and Lansdowne were Whigs, members of the Holland House set which also included Thomas Babington Macaulay, historian, poet, politician and Croker's leading antagonist in politics and the higher journalism, and Samuel Rogers, poet and wealthy retired banker, best known for his patronage of friends such as Campbell and Moore, and his famous literary breakfasts. Ten of the men in John Doyle's imaginary group portrait of one of these breakfasts, dated around 1823, were to be original members of the Athenæum; Sydney Smith was to join a little later; and four of the poets mentioned in Croker's letter are among the ten. Scott wrote in his journal for 19 October 1826:

Breakfasted at Sam Rogers's with Sir Thomas Lawrence; Luttrel, the great London wit; Richard Sharp, etc. One of them made merry with some part of Rose's Ariosto; proposed that the Italian should be printed on the other side, for the sake of assisting the indolent reader to understand the English; and complained of his using more than once the phrase of a lady having 'voided her saddle,' which would certainly sound extraordinary at Apothecaries' Hall. Well, well, Rose carries a dirk too.[44]

All five poets mentioned by Croker also attended the literary gatherings at 50 Albemarle Street, where John Murray II, another original member of the Athenæum, had his publishing house.[45] Like the soirées of the learned societies, Rogers's literary breakfasts in St James's Place, and similar gatherings in Sir John Soane's house and Francis Chantrey's studio, these meetings of what Scott called Murray's 'four o'clock friends' were seedbeds from which the Athenæum grew.[46]

These informal sites of literary, artistic and scientific discussion, spiced with gossip, allowed individuals such as Thomas Moore to move between opposing political camps. In the years between the French Revolution and the first Reform Act, English letters were 'more polarised by political antagonism than ever before or since';[47] and in Clubland, White's was mainly Tory and Brooks's Whig. Most of the 'four o'clock friends' who gathered in Murray's offices were contributors to his Tory *Quarterly Review*, founded in 1809 in direct opposition to the highly successful and Whig *Edinburgh Review*, launched seven years earlier.[48] Contributors to the *Quarterly* included Scott (Murray's mainstay), John Barrow, Robert Grant, William Stewart Rose and Thomas Young. Gifford, the first editor, regarded Croker himself as 'really a treasure to us'. Croker wrote around 270 pieces, many of them articles on historical and political themes, or literary reviews, including his notorious evisceration of Keats's 'Endymion' (1818). He also advised, or rather pushed, successive editors. Indeed, Scott's future biographer and member of the Athenæum, Lockhart, complained during his editorship that he was 'Over-worked, over-hurried, / Over-Croker'd, over-Murray'd'.

Croker's letter to Davy of 12 March 1823 concludes with some vague hints about the selection of members (by 'ballot, or other wise'), a more solid suggestion about a clubhouse ('I attach great importance to a good situation, but perhaps for the first year or two we should confine ourselves to a hired house') and a reminder that the time was ripe: 'Pray think and talk over this proposition, and recollect that it is just the season at which the thing must be done, if done at all'. In his reply, written the next day, Davy came to the question of the club after two paragraphs of official business relating to the Royal Observatory:

> I am quite of your opinion as to the Club; except that I think 300 at a moderate subscription would not afford sufficient funds: – I have mentioned the idea in conversation and have found it generally well received. – I think it would be expedient to receive a certain number of names before any letters are circulated & the Founders list should contain not only the names of Men of Science Art & Literature but likewise of some of the higher patrons of these subjects. I shall have an opportunity of mentioning the subject this evening at the Royal Society & likewise on Saturday at a general meeting of the Trustees of the British Museum.[49]

Discussion on the putative club was generally interwoven with discussion on official business, and the success of the enterprise depended upon Croker's and Davy's ability to mobilise their existing professional connections.

Eight months later, on 23 November 1823, Croker had to write to Davy again from the Admiralty, and with a sense of urgency. Davy had spent the summer fishing with Wollaston in Ireland and Scotland, and had not returned to London until the end of October, when he quickly set about investigating an urgent problem relating to the copper sheathing attached to ships' hulls, a crisis that confronted the Admiralty, and thus Croker.[50] On the other pressing question of the new club, Davy and Croker had clearly established broad agreement between themselves by November 1823, so the formality of the March letter's address to 'My dear Sir' is now replaced by the greeting, 'My dear Sir Humphrey',[51] as Croker makes some specific proposals:

> Since you agree in my general proposition about a Literary Club, is it not time to set about the work? All that is necessary to create a Club in these times is a Circular Letter of invitation – our only difficulty I believe will be to

decide to whom the letters should be addressed: I will give you my ideas. In order to keep our Club, what it is intended to be, a Club of Literary men & Artists, we must lay down, <u>clearly</u> and <u>positively</u>, as our first rule, that no one shall be <u>eligible</u> into it, except Gentlemen who have either published some literary or professional work, or a paper in the Philosophical transactions – Members of the Royal Academy – Trustees (not officials) of the British Museum – Hereditary and Life Governors of the ~~Royal~~ ∧ {British} Institution: the latter will open our doors to the Patrons of the Arts – I do not see any other classes which could be admitted, unless Bishops & Judges who are, <u>par état</u>, literary men, altho' they may not have published any literary work.[52]

Croker is putting flesh on the bone. He wants, first, gentlemen who have published and, second, Royal Academicians. His third category, trustees of the British Museum, reflects the fact that this institution was rapidly growing in importance, having recently received the Elgin Marbles and now, in 1823, the King's Library. As Robert Smirke junior worked on the new buildings in Bloomsbury (he completed the King's Library in 1827), many of the museum's trustees were known to Croker and soon became members of the Athenæum, as did some of the officials Croker hoped (in vain) to keep out.[53] The arts, and patronage of the arts, were close to Croker's heart: hence his fourth category, governors of the British Institution at 52 Pall Mall (its title frequently confused with the scientific Royal Institution in Albemarle Street). 'The British Institution for Promoting the Fine Arts in the United Kingdom', to give the body its full title, was founded in 1805 with a view to exhibiting works of art – the first temporary exhibitions of Old Master paintings were held there – and enabling living artists to sell their work. Finally, Croker adds the bishops and the judges, who are assumed to be 'literary', in the broad sense that was then current.

He then moves on to the crucial question of governance:

We ought next to form, out of the above classes, a Committee of eleven, or twenty-one – suppose, Sir H. Davy, Sir Thos. Lawrence, Sir James Mackintosh, Sir Walter Scott, Sir Geo: Beaumont, Sir Charles Long, Lord Spencer, the Bishop of Carlisle, Mr. Rogers, Mr. Moore, Dr. Wollaston, Mr. Croker, Mr. Chantry [sic], Mr. Smirke, Dr. Young, &c &c. The

Committee, thus formed, should then write about 200 letters to persons whom they should consider fit Members of the proposed Club, and I have little doubt that the answers to these letters would enable us to set the Club agoing at once. The Union, which consists of 1000 Members, and which has now 600 Candidates, was formed with less machinery, and I think my experience there will be of much use in facilitating our first steps.

The choice of these men, most of whom we have encountered already, reflects the quality of Croker's strategic thinking. Several of them are leading patrons of the arts, for example: Sir George Beaumont, painter, patron to William Wordsworth and generous supporter of the fine arts; Lord Farnborough (Charles Long), one of the founders of the British Institution, an early benefactor of the National Gallery (founded in 1824), a trusted advisor of King George IV on aesthetic matters, and known to Croker as Paymaster General of the forces; and Samuel Rogers. Robert Smirke junior will be useful to have on the Committee as an architect. The inclusion of Sir James Mackintosh, a Whig MP as well as an historian and journalist, sends out the right signals about the non-partisan nature of the club. The 'scientific men' are Davy, Wollaston, Young and Samuel Goodenough, Bishop of Carlisle, who is not only a botanist but also one of the founders of the Linnæan Society, as well as being active in the running of the Royal Society and the Society of Antiquaries. Earl Spencer is president of the Royal Institution, where Faraday – said to have been Davy's greatest discovery and soon to be the temporary secretary of the Athenæum – is superintendent of the house.

Croker then argues that the next logical step is for the Committee to invite 200 individuals to become members. Here he draws on his experience at the Union Club, founded by English and Irish gentlemen in honour of the creation of the United Kingdom through the Acts of Union of 1800, and consisting of 'politicians, and professional and mercantile men, *without reference to party opinions*' (emphasis added).[54] The Union also broke new ground in being the first of the major members' clubs in which the membership 'clubbed' together in order to socialise in style, as distinct from the eighteenth-century proprietary clubs, run for a profit by individuals.[55] Its early history was troubled, however, and a resolution was taken to re-establish the club in 1821, when it was announced that:

in conformity to the plan adopted on the Establishment of the United Service Club, of considering as Original Members of the Club all Generals, Admirals and Field Officers of the Army and Navy, so, all Noblemen, Baronets, Members of Parliament, and Gentlemen of the highest respectability should have letters written to them, giving to them the same opportunity of thus becoming Original Members of the New Union Club.[56]

Clearly the cachet of being in at the beginning, as an 'original' member, was used as bait when founding or relaunching a club in the 1820s.

When, in September 1821, the committee of the Union Club decided to build their own clubhouse, it was the indefatigable Croker who had 200 copies of a road plan of the 'New Square' (later Trafalgar Square) printed 'at the press of the Admiralty' and then presented them to the committee.[57] The Union Club's first minute books are lost, but the earliest we have, those of 1823, reveal that Croker was very active in committee while Robert Smirke junior's Greek Revival clubhouse was being built on the western side of the square, then a large open space.[58] There were usually weekly committee meetings, on a Wednesday, with three or four members present and often chaired by Viscount Lowther, or by his friend Croker as a substitute. So Croker heard reports on a wide range of domestic matters, such as articles missing from the current temporary clubhouse at 12 Waterloo Place ('46 napkins, 131 rubbers, 11 teacups and 12 saucers, 4 jelly moulds (kitchen)'), the quality of the meat supplied by the splendidly named Mr Giblet and the question of compensation for two injured workmen at the new building.[59] Significantly, he was also present when the possibility of admitting a further 200 members was discussed, in the light of increased costs. Retirements from the committee by rotation, in May 1823, included two future members of the Athenæum, Sir Robert Peel and the Earl Waldegrave; and of the twelve new names, nine were future Athenians.[60] On 4 November 1823, a fortnight before writing his second letter to Davy, Croker attended a small meeting of the building committee of the Union Club to decide upon furniture.[61] The excitement associated with preparing Smirke's clubhouse for the Union, combined with a sense that new members' clubs were good prospects in the early 1820s,[62] energised Croker, encouraging him to pursue his dream of a literary club and thus filling a gap in the market.

Croker concludes his letter of 23 November 1823 by suggesting an entrance fee of 10 guineas and an annual subscription of 5 guineas, enough to provide a 'tolerable house, until we should grow rich enough to build one'.[63] If Sir Humphry agrees, Croker continues, and has found in conversation, as he has, 'a tolerably general assent to the proposition . . . Lawrence and Smirke are both <u>very</u> cordial to it' – he will prepare a prospectus. Davy replied the same day:

My Dear Sir,

We should lose no time in drawing up the 'Prospectus.' I think members of the Royal and Antiquarian Society, and of the Linnæan, ought to be admitted by ballot; for my idea is that it should be a scientific as well as a literary club. Lord Aberdeen, with whom I have had a good deal of conversation on the subject, has taken it up warmly.

I know already more than 100 persons who wish to belong to it, and many, most of their names will be attractive – Mr. Heber and Mr. Hallam, Mr. Colebrooke, Dr. Young, Mr. Chantrey, Mr. Hatchett, Mr. Brande, Mr. Herschel, and a number of other men of science, will give their names.

When I talked to Lord Spencer on the subject, he did not seem to take an interest in it; and Dr. Wollaston says he is not a man of clubs. But we are certain of success. The difficulty will be in a short name, and one not liable to any Shandean objections. We can talk of this when I have the pleasure of seeing you to-morrow.

I do not think it would be going too far to make members of the corporate scientific and literary bodies eligible by ballot. I see no reason for excluding Judges, Bishops, and Members of both Houses, none of whom can perform their high duties without a competent knowledge of literature.

Very sincerely yours,

H. Davy[64]

Davy has clearly been sounding out potential members for some time and now shares Croker's sense of urgency. Although Croker referred in March to 'a Club for literary and scientific men, and followers of the fine arts', his latest letter makes no reference to scientists. So now the most famous scientist in the land, who is past his best but whose latest experiments are still described breathlessly in *The Annual Register*,[65] reminds Croker that it should be 'a scientific as well as a literary club', and that it is this 'idea' that he has been sharing with his own circle of friends and colleagues, a circle that overlaps with Croker's and is equally eclectic. Not that Davy is uncomfortable with the idea of a literary club which also attracts 'followers of the fine arts'. He was a member of the small and exclusive literary dining club, founded by Reynolds and Johnson in 1764, and known simply as 'The Club'.[66] He recorded his impressions of a long Continental tour in 1813–15 in verse.[67] His lectures at the Royal Institution, so popular that Albemarle Street had to be made the first one-way street in London to cope with the crush of carriages, were as elegantly expressed as they were dramatic, and took place in the same rooms as lectures by Constable, Phillips and Haydon on the fine arts. In a few years' time he will be in Italy recuperating after a stroke and recording his 'visions' in a way that is reminiscent of Wordsworth and Blake.[68] Now, however, in November 1823 and as president of the Royal Society, he has consulted his opposite number at the Society of Antiquaries, the earl of Aberdeen, who has taken up the subject of the new club 'warmly' – an encouraging sign from a future prime minister who gives the impression of being cold and reserved, even at his own table.[69] Davy has also talked to the medievalist Henry Hallam, a vice-president of the Antiquaries and a member of Murray's circle, as is Richard Heber, the prodigious book collector and MP for Oxford University. The president of the Astronomical Society of London is the orientalist Henry Colebrooke, one of whose successors will be the mathematician and astronomer John Herschel, winner of the Royal Society's Copley Medal in 1822.[70] Charles Hatchett, a chemist, chaired the meeting of managers of the Royal Institution that approved the appointment of Faraday as a laboratory assistant in 1813, the year in which Davy was succeeded as professor of chemistry there by the steady William Thomas Brande. Four of the individuals mentioned in Davy's letter – Brande, Hatchett, Herschel and Wollaston – were members of the small committee of the Royal Society that he had created earlier in the year to consider the problem of the copper sheathing attached to ships' hulls.[71]

Davy and Croker planned to meet next day, and discussions continued in December 1823 when they exchanged lists of 'Committee-men': Croker's contained 'about twenty-eight names'.[72] Croker also asked Davy not to extend invitations hastily, saying that he himself had 'applied to no one but to Lord Lansdowne, Sir Walter Scott, and Thomas Moore'. As John Thomson points out in the best essay on the foundation of the Athenæum, 'Lansdowne was a Whig grandee, albeit ready to ally with moderate Tories, Scott a literary Tory and Moore a poet more inclined to the left than to the right, but friends with both': that these three men should be Croker's first choices 'speaks volumes'.[73] Thomson's argument that the bipartisan membership of the club was deliberate, and was primarily due to Croker, is supported by the evidence.[74] His case, however, that 'in the context of its time, it was an innovation which probably could not have succeeded ten years earlier' is rather more questionable: the Union Club was already re-established.

Like other commentators, Thomson focuses upon a particular source or point of departure for the Athenæum, in his case *The Edinburgh* and *The Quarterly*, the calibre and interests of which, he maintains, inspired the creation of the club. He also gives his essay some Scottish spin, suggesting that, if the Athenæum had a model, the Friday Club, established by Scott in Edinburgh in 1803, might be it.[75] Others point to Murray's 'four o'clock club' as the main source, while ignoring Samuel Rogers's breakfasts and similar gatherings of the intelligentsia; in foregrounding the learned societies and their influence, the Royal Institution can be overlooked; and so on. The various intellectual and political circles discussed in this chapter overlapped, and many of the individuals mentioned were involved in several areas of literary and scientific activity, often crossing party political lines in doing so. Interdisciplinary exchange defined the intellectual and cultural life of modern Britain in the 1820s and made the Athenæum possible, largely through Croker's perspicacity and drive. The club's original members included many of the leading figures of the age, whose interests often encompassed a range of disciplines. As we will see in the next chapter, the first Athenians were among those who, in an era of political and institutional reform, shaped early Victorian Britain. The analogy of the literary or scientific 'circle' in this context is perhaps less useful than George Eliot's analogy of the web: touch one strand and the whole web moves.[76] There were almost as many strands to the idea of the Athenæum as there were to Croker's London.

# 2

## 'A COMMITTEE HAVING BEEN FORMED'

In December 1823 John Wilson Croker shelved the problem of finding a 'short name' for the club until there was a committee to discuss the matter. He focused instead upon the wording of the prospectus which was to accompany the letters of invitation. This was a crucial moment: his ideas were about to be tested. Having been reminded by Sir Humphry Davy that it should be 'a scientific as well as a literary club', Croker gives the 'scientific' precedence over the 'literary' three times in the opening paragraphs:

> It is proposed to establish a Club for scientific and literary men and Artists, on the principles which have been so successful in the United Service, the Union and other Clubs lately instituted.
>
> It is proposed that the Club shall consist, in the first instance, of 300 Members, to be increased to 500, or more, if the Club, after it is instituted, shall think such an extension advisable.
>
> That persons eligible to this club shall be Authors known by their scientific or literary publications; Artists of eminence in any class of the fine arts; and Noblemen and Gentlemen, distinguished as liberal patrons of science, literature, or the arts.[1]

The prospectus begins as a modest proposal, with its low ceiling for numbers and a bow to recent successes in Clubland; but when it comes to the supremely important question of eligibility it becomes much more ambitious, with its references to known authorship, eminence, distinction and liberality. (Authorship was a priority for Croker, who in 1838 was to object to the election of Charles Sumner, the Massachusetts politician and lawyer, to Honorary Membership as he 'was not known as the author of any book'.[2])

Modesty prevails, however, as the prospectus continues:

> Candidates shall be admitted, in the first instance, by the Committee, to the number of 300; after which the Club shall be considered as constituted, and it will form its own resolutions as to the mode of admitting other members.
>
> The rules of the United Service, Union and University Clubs, which have been found to combine so much accommodation to their members with so much *economy* and good order, shall be the guide of the Committee in the formation of the regulations of this new club.
>
> The admission money shall be ten guineas, and the annual subscription five guineas.

It was sensible to base the rules and regulations of the new club on those that had worked for others, and it was inevitable that Croker would do the drafting in due course.

The prospectus concludes:

> The Committee will, as soon as a sufficient number of names are obtained, proceed to hire a proper house for the Club, until they shall be enabled to decide on the expediency of building a house for its accommodation.
>
> Noblemen or gentlemen belonging to any of the classes before enumerated, and who may be desirous of belonging to the Club, are requested to signify their wish by letter (post paid, or franked) addressed to 'Mr. Faraday, Royal Institution,' who has undertaken to act as temporary Secretary.
>
> COMMITTEE

Faraday, the unworldly Sandemanian who owed his first position at the Royal Institution to Davy, would have felt impelled to respond to the call of his erstwhile master. Ten years earlier, during Sir Humphry and Lady Davy's long Continental tour, he had served as both valet and research assistant. More recently, when he was proposed for a fellowship of the Royal Society, Davy's opposition hindered the electoral process.[3] Now, as Davy continues to treat him as an assistant in this new project, thus interrupting Faraday's heavy schedule of experimental work,[4] the fellowship is finally confirmed, on 8 January 1824. For the next few months, the brilliant Michael Faraday FRS will slave away as honorary secretary to a fledgling organisation which requires large amounts of paperwork to be handled quickly and efficiently.

Meanwhile Croker's covering letter to Davy, enclosing the draft prospectus, again shows that he has taken the point about scientists: the committee that he proposes includes not only Aberdeen and Chantrey among Davy's 'attractive' names, but also Colebrooke, President of the Astronomical Society of London, Hatchett, the chemist, and Dr Young, the scientific polymath. In his reply, dated 8 February and marked 'Private', Davy pointed out that they now had 'persons in every department of Science except Natural History'.[5] He therefore wished to add the name of Aylmer Bourke Lambert, a vice-president of the Linnæan Society, who would, he thought, be 'very sensible and inoffensive'.

As well as planning the new club, Croker and Davy were urgently discussing the problem of the copper sheathing attached to ships' hulls: on 17 January 1824, Davy was to report directly to Croker on progress with his experiments, believing that Croker's support would ensure that the Navy Board approved practical tests at sea.[6] In his private letter of 8 February, Davy expressed his disappointment at the board's response and asked Croker to petition their lordships at the Admiralty to allow his experiments to continue. As usual, Croker had the upper hand. While flattering Davy by suggesting that they were both 'founders' of the new club, Croker made it clear that he expected his own advice on the committee to be followed and asked Davy 'not to decide on any new names without a consultation', adding, 'My experience in these matters is considerable, and I assure you that all depends on having a Committee with a great *many* good *names* and a *few* working *hands*'.[7]

'Good names' which would attract and reassure recipients of the prospectus included both 'noblemen and gentlemen'. Peers continued to be in the majority in both Tory and Whig cabinets, and dynastic grandees still figured prominently in public life.[8] (The first three presidents of the Royal Institution were earls and the fourth and fifth were dukes.) As a politician who knew about patronage and presentation, Croker wanted a few big beasts on his committee. Alongside the earls were the presidents of the learned societies and some famous scientists and writers. The 'working hands' were expected to attend meetings and elect the club's first members, thus in effect creating the club. They are italicised here in a list drawn up by Croker and Davy, which is remarkable for its social range in terms of birth and its inclusion of political opponents: the earl of Aberdeen, the earl of Ashburnham, *Sir George Beaumont*, Lord Bexley, *Francis Chantrey* (who trained as a wood-carver, as did Davy's father), *Henry Thomas Colebrooke*, *John Wilson Croker*, Sir Humphry Davy, *Davies Gilbert*, *Sir Henry Halford*, Charles Hatchett, *Richard Heber*, *Joseph Jekyll*, Richard Payne Knight (who declined on health grounds), Aylmer Bourke Lambert, the marquess of Lansdowne, Sir Thomas Lawrence, *Edward Hawke Locker* (a watercolourist, FRS, secretary to Greenwich Hospital and friend of Sir Walter Scott's), Sir Charles Long (1st baron Farnborough in 1826), Sir James Mackintosh, Thomas Moore, Viscount Palmerston, Thomas Lister Parker, Samuel Rogers, *William Stewart Rose*, Robert Smirke junior, Earl Spencer (the Whig Chancellor who was to assist Russell in bringing in the First Reform Act, anathema to Croker) and *Dr Thomas Young*.

Of the politically active members of the proposed committee, eight were Tories and ten were Whigs. Against a background of violent radical activity in the late 1810s and early 1820s, Tories such as Croker, who was an expert on the French Revolution, and Whigs such as Lansdowne were aware that cross-party cooperation and even, *in extremis*, coalition, could be in the national interest. John Thomson suggests that, 'with the prospect of revolution so vividly before them, there was a drawing together throughout the country of the elite and the propertied': the Athenæum was, in a way, a 'product of this feeling of solidarity'.[9] He emphasises the strength of Irish and Scottish interests in the committee, and reflects upon an emerging sense of solidarity between Dublin, Edinburgh and London which was fostered by the quarterlies and the Athenæum, thus helping to create a 'new sense of Britishness'.[10]

The names agreed between Croker and Davy were duly listed by Faraday in the minutes of the inaugural meeting of the Committee on Monday 16 February 1824, truly the birthday of the club, in the apartments of the Royal Society.[11] 'A

Committee having been formed', Davy took the chair, twelve other members being present. But where was Croker? He was not at the Union Club, dealing with the practicalities involved in moving to their new building.[12] Nor was he in the House of Commons, supporting Sir George Clerk, Lord of the Admiralty, in presenting the navy estimates for the year.[13] He was ill, one imagines from a complaint brought on by exhaustion.[14] Whatever the complaint, its effect was that those who gathered in Somerset House to establish the club had to proceed without Croker.

The first resolution of the Committee was 'That the ___Club is established this day': discussion of the 'short name' presumably had to be deferred until Croker was present. It was then resolved that 'the number of Members be limited to five hundred of which four hundred are to be nominated by the Committee and the rest admitted by ballot'. Clearly the response to the prospectus had been even more positive than Croker and Davy had anticipated. Having confirmed the 'admission subscription' of 10 guineas and the 'annual contribution' of 5 guineas, and having named Messrs Drummond as bankers, the meeting resolved that the trustees should be the presidents of the three leading learned societies – Davy, Aberdeen and Lawrence – all of whom were present. A formal alliance between the club and the learned societies was forged.

Five names were then added to the 'Committee of management', which was to have a quorum of nine: the Lord Bishop of Carlisle (Samuel Goodenough, who helped to found the Linnæan Society), the Hon. George Agar-Ellis (a Whig politician and man of letters), Earl Gower (another Whig, later the 2nd duke of Sutherland), Sir Walter Scott and Sir George Staunton (a Canningite Tory MP, traveller and orientalist). Under a final constitutional resolution a sub-committee was appointed, with a quorum of three, 'for the purpose of engaging a suitable house for the temporary service of the Club of purchasing furniture hiring servants and making the necessary preparations for the accommodation of the Members' – precisely the business that Croker had undertaken for the Union Club.[15]

The Committee then turned to the list of 'Noblemen and Gentlemen' who had responded positively to the letter of invitation: they admitted so many members – a total of eighty-two – that Faraday made some slips in the minutes.[16] The best-known figures among them were the duke of Bedford, Viscount

Lowther and the prime minister, the earl of Liverpool, together with two future premiers, Peel and Russell, the geologist Revd William Buckland and Sir Astley Cooper, who was later surgeon to George IV. Less well known at the time, but characteristically Athenian in his range of interests, was Dawson Turner FRS, banker, botanist and antiquary, whose descendants make up one of the club's family dynasties.[17] The list also included the youthful John Lettson Elliot, who managed to outlive all those elected in 1824: he died in 1898.

Thus began a process of election by the Committee which took the membership to around five hundred in four months. Meetings, usually weekly, took place in Joseph Jekyll's house in New Street, Spring Gardens, only a step away from the Admiralty, with Jekyll himself in the chair, even when Croker and Davy were both present.[18] There would have been two advantages to this arrangement. Firstly, the club's founder and its first chairman would be freer to argue for or against candidates. (On 20 February Davy wrote to Croker saying that he was keen to 'pause upon any suspected bores'.)[19] Secondly, Jekyll, famous for the dreadful puns which his generation loved, would have created a convivial atmosphere in his own home. At the first of these meetings, however, on 1 March 1824, a note of caution was sounded. Having repeated the criteria for membership – 'individuals known for their scientific or literary attainments', etc. – the minutes continue with a resolution which suggests that Croker is bringing the Committee to heel when first in attendance: 'It appearing that several persons who do not strictly come under the above description have had notice of their admission. Resolved that they are Members of the Club, but that their admission shall form no Precedent for any departure from the Regulations of the Club.'[20]

Croker was also present the following week, on 8 March, when the Committee resolved that the name of the club should be 'The Society', a dull generic appellation, smacking of hubris and fraught with potential confusion, particularly as it was already applied informally to the Royal Society. He was present again on 29 March, when the twenty-three-year-old Decimus Burton, a protégé of John Nash, gave a verbal report on the house in Regent Street that the Building Committee were considering as a potential temporary home.[21] Indeed, Croker attended every meeting, applying his own style of micro-management to proceedings, until 27 April, when he was absent again. The following day Jekyll wrote him a letter which gives a vivid insight into the workings of the Committee:

Dear Croker,

We did as much yesterday at the Committee as could be done in the absence of such a *primum mobile* as yourself. Elections and nominations were expedited. We have now, I should think, 380 members, and above 100 invitations remain unanswered. Verging so closely on our 400, we suspended 50 invitations suggested by a list sent in by Heber, and containing many eligible names.

Saturday next, many of us dine with the Royal Academicians, so the Committee will meet again on Monday, May 3rd.

If our candidates overflow, Davy said the Society might extend its numbers to 600.

Burton said the house might be ready in a fortnight. By Heber's direction Chalié sent in a wine estimate. Wine and servants seem at present the principal desiderata; and except yourself, I think we have no active member for those details. Chalié's wines are high priced. If you desire to inspect his paper before Monday, I will send it to you.

Yours ever,

Joseph Jekyll.[22]

Jekyll's estimate of 380 members was 8 short of the true number, which can be calculated from the minutes and Faraday's tally of elections.[23] The Committee had elected 187 members at its first three meetings and a further 201 in the six meetings since 15 March. On 8 March, Faraday had been instructed to circulate candidates who had not yet responded to the invitation and prospectus with a reminder that they could become 'original' members if they accepted nomination by the end of the month.[24] This private circular, dispatched from 12 Albemarle Street (the address of the Royal Institution), included the first printed list of 'present members'.[25] Setting aside the Committee, more than half the remaining names of the initial 187 members had some kind of title attached to them: there were two dukes, one marquess, nine earls, five viscounts, nine lords, ten baronets, eleven knights, five right honourables (three of whom were also knights), nine honourables (one of whom was also a reverend and another two also colonels), one right reverend, thirteen reverends, two captains RN, three colonels, one major, six captains, eight MDs and one LLD (like the bishops, the lawyers seem to have been slow to reply). Most of those who simply had 'esq.' after their names were members of the learned societies – thirty-two of the 'misters' were FRSs, six were FSAs and nine were RAs – or were MPs (five of them). Only thirteen in the list had no stated title or affiliation, and they too are a distinguished group, including Sir Arthur Wellesley's predecessor as MP for Tralee, Samuel Boddington, the poet Thomas Campbell, the architects Charles Robert Cockerell and John Nash, and the young joint secretary of the Geological Society of London, Charles Lyell, later created a baronet.

Throughout the three months of The Society's nascent existence, Croker was also busy at the Union Club, dealing with what Jekyll referred to as 'wine and servants'. As the Union prepared to move into their new Grecian home, designed by Robert Smirke junior, on the western side of what became Trafalgar Square, Croker attended meetings of the building committee that took responsibility for preparing the clubhouse for occupation.[26] He was also involved in planning the Union's move out of its temporary house at 12 Waterloo Place, at the bottom of Regent Street, on 17 April (Plate 2). Croker and Smirke briefed Burton and the rest of The Society's Building Committee on the timing, thus smoothing the path for the new club to take over the house, as the Travellers Club had previously made way for the Union.[27] What is more, among the legal papers in the Athenæum's archive relating to the club's letting agreements with Mr Fielder, the leaseholder of 12 Waterloo Place, is a copy of the Union Club's own agreement of 1822. This was perhaps Croker's copy, which could be used by Clarke, the Athenæum's solicitor, when drafting the new agreement.[28]

By Monday 17 May 1824 – the day on which John Murray burnt the manuscript of Byron's memoirs at 50 Albemarle Street – the Union had moved into its new clubhouse and The Society could bring its own plans to fruition. As Croker could not attend the meeting held at Jekyll's house that day, a letter from him was read from the chair, reporting to the Committee that 'the establishment of servants was now completed and the necessary furniture plate and other articles provided and that the house in Waterloo Place would be ready to be opened in a few days'.[29] Croker's report reveals the extent to which he used his experience and connections in Clubland. In hiring the servants he was anxious to obtain 'people who had been accustomed to the peculiar business of a Club': 'I have therefore hired a Steward and a Butler, the late head waiter of the Union Club. As Housekeeper, a respectable woman who was barmaid of the United Service Club, and as Man Cook, the person who was late second cook of the latter establishment.' These 'principal servants' recommended 'inferior' ones for vetting by Croker, who then authorised their appointment.

The house, he reported, had been 'thoroughly cleaned within', and some alterations 'in the lower part' had been made under the direction of Decimus Burton. Croker had ordered from Messrs Taprell and Holland twenty dinner tables and sixty chairs of the same pattern and price as those they had furnished to the Union. Shrewdly, he had also arranged for the firm to lend the club more expensive items such as sofas, easy chairs and drawing room tables, 'until the Committee should be able to decide on its probable wants with reference to a new residence'. On the question of wines, next in importance after furniture and servants, he set out comparative prices in shillings per case of port, sherry, madeira, claret, light claret and champagne from three vintners, including Chalié & Co. As those of Messrs Durand & Blakeway were the lowest (49, 52, 71, 78–90, 56–66 and 105 shillings respectively), and as it was necessary to bottle some port, sherry and madeira immediately, he had placed an order with them. The Committee could decide on policy for the longer term once they had tasted the wines, but Croker could testify that some 'gentlemen of his acquaintance' had been well served by the firm. Coals were ordered from Messrs Feetham, glassware from Messrs Pellatt & Green, who had served the Union Club, silverware, 'plated articles' and cutlery from Messrs Thomas & Co., beds for the servants from the suppliers to the Union, along with kitchen furniture. Messrs Billings had been contracted for the servants' liveries at £4. 15s. 0d. per suit, 'viz. a fine drab coat with plated buttons, a waistcoat of the same with sleeves, and black velveteen breeches and drawers'. Croker suggested that the Committee might prefer plush to velveteen 'after half a year's trial', but that the tailor himself recommended velveteen. With his eye for detail, developed after many years considering the fitting out and victualling of ships at the Admiralty, Croker seems to have thought of everything.

The Committee duly thanked Croker *in absentia* and instructed Faraday to have the clubhouse ready to receive the Committee on Friday 28 May. In stating that those who wished to dine that evening as a Committee were to 'give in their names accordingly', there began a tradition which continues to this day. Faraday was further ordered to circulate the first four hundred or so members with a printed list and notice of a General Meeting at 12 Waterloo Place on 1 June, at which the Committee's proceedings were to be confirmed, the rules and regulations adopted and the Committee's preferred new name for the club, 'The Athenæum', discussed.[30] Faraday, who had 'afforded his gratuitous services to the Committee during the formation of the Club', was to be offered the office of secretary with a salary of £100 per annum, subject to the 'approbation of the General meeting'. Finally, fifteen new members were elected and Jekyll was thanked for his hospitality. Within a fortnight of this last meeting in Spring Gardens all but one of the Committee's resolutions had been enacted.

At 11 a.m. on Saturday 22 May 1824, the General Committee of the new club gathered at its first home, 12 Waterloo Place, by then in the final stages of preparation after the departure of the Union Club. The house was in the north-west corner of Waterloo Place and was rented by the club from Fielder for £900 per annum, including taxes.[31] The building was later demolished (the club rescued a shattered volute as a keepsake),[32] but a schedule of furniture and effects in the Union Club's indenture of 1822 indicates that the clubhouse contained a billiard room, a large drawing room, a 'Chinese Room', library, 'dining parlour', coffee room (i.e. larger dining room) and a small back parlour.[33] It was clearly a dusty house. In March 1825, Philip Duncan, keeper of the Ashmolean Museum in Oxford, wrote to Heber suggesting that 'it would be advisable to cover our dining room entirely with oil cloth like that which is now laid down at the Entrance', adding that 'the room is not fit for use for some time after it is brush'd in the morning.'[34] That the house was suitable only as a temporary home, largely because of the 'limited means of accommodation' which it afforded,[35] is evident from the fact that both the Travellers Club and the Union had moved on to purpose-built clubhouses, as the Athenæum was to do in 1830. Indeed, even before they moved into 12 Waterloo Place the Committee had passed a resolution relating to 'the house to be built'.[36]

The main purpose of the Saturday meeting was to confirm the rules and regulations that had been approved by a sub-committee the previous day. Both Davy and Croker were present, but no chairman is specified in the minutes.[37] Variations in the texts suggest that Croker, the consummate draftsman of Admiralty documents, had probably worked through the Union Club and United Service Club rules line by line and amended them where necessary.[38] Whereas the United Service had a committee of thirty-six, the Athenæum opted for twenty-four, as at the Union, although initially there were in fact thirty-three members. They were to hold weekly meetings at 1 p.m. on Tuesdays, whereas the Union, like the United Service, met on Wednesdays: so Croker could ride two horses. The Athenæum followed the Union in having five trustees, of whom two were to be elected from the Committee. All three clubs opened at 9 a.m. and closed their doors to new arrivals at 2 a.m.,[39] all banned gambling – an important feature of the older 'fashionable' clubs in St James's Street – and all were insistent that no dogs should be taken into their clubhouses.[40]

The object of the club was expressed simply and with characteristic solemnity: it was for the 'association' of its members (Rule I). For provincial members who had business or social engagements in the metropolis, the clubhouse provided a haven. Many original members of The Society lived in or around St James's, however, in houses which they owned or rented, particularly during parliamentary sessions, and this is reflected in its Rule XXVI: 'no Provisions cooked in the Club-house or Wines or other Liquors, are to be sent out of the house *on any pretence whatsoever*'. For those who lived or worked nearby, 'association' in the clubhouse could be casual and frequent. (For example, in the late 1820s and early 1830s the vicinity of Spring Gardens was inhabited not only by Jekyll, but also Decimus Burton, Sir Astley Cooper, John (later Lord) Campbell and Sir James Scarlett, all early members, and by Joseph Freeman and John Hill who joined in the 1840s. Among many other examples, John Taylor lived at 13 Waterloo Place and Henry Southern lived in Suffolk Street, Pall Mall East.) A century and a half later, amendments to the wording of Rule I were to reflect changes in the living and working patterns of members, and were to signal the reinvention of the club for a different age.[41]

A number of other matters associated with the rules and regulations needed to be settled at the Saturday meeting. Most significantly, the club's new name, the 'Athenæum', was confirmed and adopted for use at the head of notices. Derived from the temple in Athens where poets, philosophers and orators met to share their ideas, the name of the new 'literary' club announced its commitment to intellectual exchange – a significant aspect of 'association' for its species of member – under the auspices of Athena, the goddess of wisdom in the ancient world, also known as Minerva by the Romans. (Athena/Minerva's association with owls is illustrated in William Miller's engraving of 1829, Plate 3.) A representation of Athena's temple figured on the cover of the magazine entitled *The Athenæum* (1828–1921), many of whose contributors would be members of the club. An earlier monthly magazine of the same name, offering 'literary and miscellaneous information', was edited by the Unitarian John Aikin MD. This journal epitomised the spirit of rational enquiry and the defence of civil and religious liberty that was fostered by Joseph Priestley and his circle, of which Aikin was a member, in the late eighteenth century. The term 'Athenæum' had a particular resonance in the north of England. The Liverpool Athenæum, founded in 1797 as a library and news room for 'the acquisition of knowledge', was visited by an approving Washington Irving, an original member of the St James's Athenæum, in the mid-nineteenth century.[42] Manchester's Athenæum was established in 1835 for the 'advancement and diffusion of knowledge', and numerous smaller Athenæums with similar aims sprang up around Britain. The Boston Athenæum, founded in 1807, still flourishes today as a membership library; the founding of the Athenaeum Club of Melbourne in 1868 fulfilled colonial aspirations; and there are numerous other examples overseas.

In St James's in 1824 the new name expressed the club's classical ideals and thus its non-sectarian and non-partisan identity. It also made a statement about the quality of its membership. Sir Thomas Lawrence designed a handsome seal, based on the goddess's helmeted head, which was engraved by William Wyon RA: it remains the club's emblem today (Plate 4).[43] At a more mundane level, the club's change of name was later to come to the attention of London's Central Criminal Court during a case relating to stolen linen. Over the weeks leading up to the occupation of 12 Waterloo Place, the newly acquired linen had been marked with the name of The Society, and some of this remained in use for the first five years of the club's existence. We know this because Martha Geary, the housekeeper during those years, was accused of stealing '2 sheets, value 8s.;

8 napkins, value 7s., and 22 table-cloths, value 6l., the goods of the Earl of Aberdeen and others', and in October 1829 the club's representative had to explain to an Old Bailey jury that some of the club's linen was marked 'The Society' and some 'The Athenæum'.[44] Although found not guilty, Geary was less fortunate when also indicted on the same day for stealing linen from General Stapylton's house.

The temporary clubhouse was duly opened on Monday 31 May 1824. Next day Croker took the chair for the first regular Tuesday meeting of the General Committee, at which a further twenty-four new members were elected.[45] Davy was present at the meeting, and it soon became apparent why he was not chairing it: Faraday announced that he would not be accepting the Committee's offer of the post of secretary, due to pressure of work elsewhere. By offering him a salaried position, which he could decline, the Committee had freed him from Davy's control. As a mark of their gratitude to Faraday, who had served in an honorary capacity during the club's gestation, the Committee made him an honorary member and waived his entrance fee and his subscription for the current year. They also accepted his recommendation of Edward Magrath as his successor, and on the same terms.[46]

Once settled at 12 Waterloo Place, the General Committee dealt with numerous practical matters associated with establishing and running a club-house, while also taking advice from the Building Committee, which was to meet numerous obstacles on the road to establishing a permanent home – the subject of the next chapter. The new clubhouse could not be afforded unless the membership grew. On Saturday 22 May the General Committee had decided that the membership was to be increased by 200, half of whom would be chosen by the Committee and half elected by ballot. A further extraordinary meeting was held the following Wednesday, 26 May, primarily to start the process of electing a further 100 members.[47] This was a young club in a hurry: with Jekyll in the chair, and with both Davy and Croker present, they elected thirty-two new members. They directed that a letter of invitation be sent to 'all the Judges not already members', all English archbishops and bishops, the four Irish archbishops and the bishops of Limerick, Raphoe and Dromore. This covered an important point formerly agreed between Croker and Davy during the planning phase. They also resolved to maintain the pace of elections by establishing a House Committee which would meet for an hour before each regular weekly meeting 'until the fifth hundred of the members be filled'.

After only four meetings the House Committee had filled its quota of one hundred, at which point the General Committee decided that they should nominate a further fifty.[48] This incremental process continued throughout 1824, with the result that the great majority of the 990 members listed in January 1825 had been elected by the General Committee. A Candidates Book, opened on 30 June 1824 for the use of the general membership, yielded only thirty-one new balloted members by the same date.[49] The General Committee's earlier decision to have half the candidates balloted had been quietly set aside.[50] The upshot was that control remained firmly in the hands of the Committee. From the beginning, membership of the club signified either recognised distinction or potential. In an age, however, in which patronage or personal support was needed in any transaction or appointment, it was taken for granted that individuals also had to know at least one member of the Committee, and preferably several. Each Committee member was expected to propose names, and, if he wished, could exercise considerable influence by attending meetings and speaking for or against candidates. In his letter of 28 April 1824, quoted earlier, Jekyll informed Croker that Richard Heber had sent in a list of at least fifty names.[51] The fact that Committee members submitted batches of names helps to explain why those elected at a particular meeting sometimes included a high proportion of one profession or calling. On 31 August 1824, for example, eight of the nineteen members elected were doctors of divinity, including the 'high and dry' Revd Henry Phillpotts, who was later to be a combative Bishop of Exeter.[52]

In choosing virtually the whole of the foundation membership, the Committee, steered strongly by Croker, set the tone of the club for generations to come; and 215 of those elected in 1824 were still on the list of members in 1858.[53] Over the twelve months that it took to elect the one thousand original members, at an average rate of over eighty a month, a high standard was set. The ratio of noblemen to gentlemen is rather higher in the first list of 187 members (March 1824) than in later lists, where professionals such as lawyers and clergy, and gentlemen belonging to the learned societies, figure in large numbers.[54] Although all three categories in Croker's initial prospectus – 'scientific and literary men and Artists' – are represented, it is the scientists who stand out, not only in terms of their eminence but also for their contribution to the life of the club. Alongside the physicists, chemists, botanists, astronomers and geologists were pioneering engineers and inventors who helped to create a modern infrastructure for the age of steam. George and John Rennie junior were among those elected at the first meeting of the General Committee; Thomas Telford, president of the Institution of Civil Engineers, followed in March 1824 and Mark Isambard Brunel in May. These early engineer members 'carried many of the marks associated with the élite – working and residing in Westminster and often also qualified as lawyers, well-placed for promoting parliamentary bills to develop roads, bridges, canals and railways'.[55] Among the inventors who followed a less conventional route to fame was Sir William Congreve, elected in April 1824, whose successful experiments at Woolwich – Congreve rockets terrified the French, even though they did little actual damage – were followed by other inventions, some of which worked, included a hydropneumatic canal lock and sluice, a perpetual motion machine, a process of colour printing and a gas meter. A great favourite of King George IV's, he was also MP for Plymouth.

Of the original members, however, it was the geologists who had the highest profile within the club: Sir Roderick Murchison and General Sir Edward Sabine both became trustees, and Buckland and Lyell served on the General Committee. (All but Buckland, a clergyman, were later knighted.) Every president of the Geological Society from 1824 to mid-century was a member of the club.[56] Geology was the most controversial of the sciences in the 1830s, when differences between the 'catastrophist' theories of William Buckland, Canon of Christ Church and Oxford's first Reader in Geology, and the 'uniformitarian' arguments presented by his brilliant former pupil, Charles Lyell, raised difficulties for those who read the early chapters of Genesis as history.[57] Although it is true that academic disagreements could generally be separated from personal feelings 'among the clubbable' at the Athenæum,[58] it is unlikely that sensitive topics such as the fossil record never brought a flush to a clerical cheek there.

Most of the leading geologists could be described as 'compound characters', a phrase applied by William Jerdan to Lord Eldon, himself an Athenian, who was not only a lawyer and judge but also a politician and statesman.[59] Murchison could have been speaking for several of them when he recalled that, as an 'active' original member of the club, he 'had a finger in most things which were stirring among men of letters, art, and science'.[60] The Revd William Whewell DD, who published on geology (he invented the terms 'catastrophist' and 'uniformitarian'), mineralogy, philosophy, architecture, theology, physics, political economy, mathematics, education and the history of science, was perhaps the most wide-ranging among a number of early nineteenth-century polymaths who were also active in public life: Whewell was president of the Geological Society for two years and Master of Trinity College, Cambridge for a quarter of a century, actively engaged in university politics.[61] These compound characters also tended to be collaborative, as in the case of the Geological Survey, founded in 1835 by several members of the club. Similarly with the Zoological Society of London, instituted by Sir Humphry Davy in 1824 and presided over by his friend Sir Stamford Raffles, recently returned from Singapore. The institution developed its famous zoological gardens through the efforts of the marquess of Lansdowne, Joseph Sabine and Sir Robert Peel, all original members of the Athenæum, and of Lord Auckland and Nicholas Aylward Vigors, both elected in 1830. Decimus Burton, the future architect of the Athenæum's clubhouse and an original member, designed the layout for the zoo. Raffles became a member of the Athenæum in November 1824 and joined the General Committee eighteen months later.

Some of the most active members in the club were also the busiest outside it. Dr Thomas Young, for example, who attended twenty-five meetings of the General Committee in the first year of its existence, rivalled Whewell as a polymath and had even more demands upon his time in the wider world.[62] A child prodigy from a Quaker background, he mastered ten languages, studied medicine at Edinburgh, Göttingen and Cambridge, and became an effective if somewhat aloof physician at St George's hospital in London, handsome, rich (by inheritance) and happily married. He was professor of natural philosophy (1801) and a rather ineffective superintendent of the house at the Royal Institution, and became foreign secretary to the Royal Society. As a botanist, he announced new discoveries to the Linnæan Society; as a physicist, he developed theories of light, elasticity ('Young's modulus') and surface tension; and as a physiologist, he worked on the muscularity of fibres attached to the eye. He assisted in the interpretation of the hieroglyphics on the Rosetta Stone, wrote the article on Egypt for the supplement to the *Encyclopædia Britannica* (1819)[63] and contributed articles to Murray's *Quarterly Review* on a wide range of subjects. Several of the colleagues whom Young encountered on the way were later to be fellow members of the Athenæum and its General Committee.

It is Young's work on longitude, however, that best illustrates the kind of relationship that existed between professional networks and club life. The bill that consolidated early acts for rewarding the discovery of longitude, and that established a new Nautical Almanac, was introduced to the House of Commons by Croker, as Secretary to the Admiralty, in 1818.[64] It was again Croker who presided over the transfer of responsibility from the Board of Longitude to the Admiralty in 1828, four years after he founded the Athenæum. A member of the board who also 'assisted in the obsequies' was Davies Gilbert, an original member of the club who was Davy's successor as president of the Royal Society and was one of Bodmin's two MPs, the other being Croker.[65] The advisors to the Admiralty on longitude were also original members: Young, as superintendent of the Nautical Almanac, assisted by Faraday, as a chemist, and Colonel Sabine, as a 'practical observer'. Even the opposition originated within the club, in the shape of the irascible James South FRS, astronomer and original member.[66] In 1829 South published a pamphlet entitled *Refutation of the Numerous Mistatements and Fallacies contained in a Paper presented to the Admiralty by Dr. Thomas Young*, a copy of which is held in the Athenæum library.[67] Back in 1818, South reported, Croker found fifty-eight errors in the Almanac, and yet today the number remains the same; and whereas the post of superintendent was once full time, Dr Young has at least five other stipendiary positions, leaving little time for the Almanac, which should now be reformed.[68] South was knighted two years later.

Although Croker's concept of a 'literary' club was broad, it is surprising to see how few creative writers there were among the original members. Keats, Shelley and Byron had died, and in any case would have been considered no more clubbable than Wordsworth, the great philosophical poet of the 'egotistical sublime', and Coleridge, who held court in Highgate. Scott and Moore were both on the first General Committee, although neither attended meetings. George Crabbe and Thomas Campbell were also original members, as were a string of authors whose poetry is little known today, including the Revd Henry Hart Milman, Thomas Babington Macaulay, Samuel Rogers and Francis

Palgrave. The fine arts were rather better represented: among the Academicians were Lawrence, Chantrey, Mulready, Phillips, Soane, Turner and Wilkie.

Whereas documentary material relating to elections at the Athenæum is plentiful, evidence of attendance at the clubhouse is harder to come by, and accounts of conversations harder still, as an unwritten rule of confidentiality has generally prevailed. Some raw data are available from 1830 in the form of selected dinner bills, preserved by a miracle of archival retentiveness, which have members' comments on the food and wine scribbled on the back. Many past members who attended the clubhouse on a particular day did not dine, however, and in order to discover more we have to draw upon anecdotal evidence in the biographies, journals and letters of members in each generation. Three examples from the early years of the club will suffice to indicate the scattered nature of such evidence.

In a century of religious revival and intense sectarian controversy, some of the most voluminous 'lives and letters' are by and about clergymen. Joseph Blanco White's long journey from Seville, where he was brought up and trained for the Catholic priesthood, to Liverpool and Unitarianism, via Oxford, Anglican orders and Dublin, is the subject of the once widely read *Life, written by Himself, with Portions of his Correspondence*, edited by his friend John Hamilton Thom, a Unitarian minister, in three substantial volumes (1845). Following his election to the Athenæum on 22 March 1824, White was one of the first members to donate books to the club.[69] Unique in his spiritual formation, he might also be the only member to have been awarded a degree in the clubhouse. Among the journal entries towards the end of the first volume of the *Life* are these:

> 19 April 1826: Received a letter from Dr. Coplestone [Provost of Oriel College, Oxford], telling me that the University is about to give me a Diploma of Master of Arts . . .
> 28 April 1826: To the Athenæum, – met the two Duncans, in whose presence Dr. Coplestone gave me my Diploma, with the hearty congratulations of all.[70]

Further entries record how White first wore his Master's gown in Oxford, on 3 October 1826, later preaching there and having long conversations on walks with Whately and Newman of Oriel.[71] Whereas histories of the Tractarians are enriched by quotations from letters and journals recording conversations in college rooms and on walks in Oxford, similar records from the early years of the Athenæum are not available to the historian.[72] The paucity of the evidence can be illuminating, however, as when we find only one example among Blanco White's selected letters of his writing on club paper: this was when he was a candidate for a post and presumably wanted to make a good impression.[73]

Connop Thirlwall, the highly literary Bishop of St David's, was described by Gladstone as 'one of the most masculine, powerful, and luminous intellects that have for generations been known among the bishops of England'.[74] Thirlwall's work on the *History of Greece* and his deep involvement in a series of ecclesiastical controversies are described in his letters and *Remains*, published posthumously in five octavo volumes. When the Committee elected him, on 2 November 1824, they were adding to the membership, not a clergyman but a barrister: the 'great change in his life', when he 'abandoned the legal for the clerical profession', occurred in 1827.[75] It was said, hyperbolically, that only Thirlwall and Julius Hare (elected in 1825) had enough German to read Schleiermacher in the early 1820s. On 1 November 1824, the day before his election, Thirlwall wrote to Hare from 52 Lincoln's Inn Fields: 'The plan of the *Athenæum* is very tempting, though I am afraid I shall not be able to make much use of it. Still I think I can hardly decline so flattering an offer.'[76] It is likely that many other original members felt equally flattered and accepted the club's invitation in the knowledge that they would make little use of the clubhouse: it was membership that mattered. Thirlwall himself went on to Cambridge and ordination, eventually becoming a bishop who, on visits to London, wrote from 1 Regent Street. Evidence of his dropping into the clubhouse is not to be found in the five volumes.

Our third example is the diarist Henry Crabb Robinson, barrister, German scholar and a friend of Blake, Wordsworth and Coleridge, who were to figure prominently in his famous *Reminiscences*, again published posthumously. When he first visited 12 Waterloo Place, on 1 July 1824, he recorded that it was 'a genteel establishment' and added: 'I foresee that it will not answer my purpose as a dining-place, and, if not, I gain nothing by it as a lounge for papers, &c.'[77] He was to change his mind, however, and in 1851 appended to this entry a reminiscence in which he stated that the club constituted one of the 'great elements' of his 'ordinary life'. In fact his becoming a member had proved to be an 'epoch' in his life: 'I had a place of resort at all times, and my circle of acquaintance was greatly increased.'[78]

In Robinson's diary entry of 4 May 1825 we get a rare glimpse of a private social event at Waterloo Place, probably held in the 'Dining Parlour', with a narrowly professional *dramatis personae*:

> A house dinner at the Athenæum set on foot by me. It went off very well indeed. I took the bottom of the table. We had Edward Littledale at the top. The rest barristers, or coming to the Bar, viz: – F. Pollock, Storks, Wightman, L. Adolphus, Wood, and Amos, Dodd and his pupil, Lloyd – not an unpleasant man of the party. The conversation not at all professional or pedantic. We broke up early. I remained at the place till late. After my nap, Sir Thomas Lawrence came in, Dawson Turner, &c. The President and Turner talked of the present Exhibition, Turner asserting it to be superior to the Exhibitions in the days of Sir Joshua. This Sir Thomas denied.[79]

Professional networking, followed by a nap (on a sofa or deep armchair) and concluding with a chat with friends who drop in: the kind of evening which modern members would recognise. Again, however, we have to rely on scraps of evidence rather than a solid body of material relating to life at no. 12.

Like most of the original members, White, Thirlwall and Robinson were elected by the Committee. There had been some balloting for new members since the summer of 1824, but this became a more significant aspect of club life only after the original members had been listed in March 1825. As the Committee had resolved that the number of members would 'not on any pretence exceed one thousand',[80] it was now only through vacancies caused by death, resignation or expulsion that it was possible to join the club. Again the hand of Croker can be detected in the shaping of policy. Davy may have signed the first Annual Report of 1825, but it was Croker who drafted it, at the request of the General Committee. There is much justifiable trumpeting of the first year's achievements, especially in the paragraph on membership. A reference to politics strikes a new note, reflecting satisfaction that no fewer than

100 MPs, including Huskisson, Palmerston, Peel and Russell, were among the original members:

> The estimation, in which the Club and its objects are held, may be best appreciated, by observing that the List of Members includes the names of the most distinguished Literary, Scientific, and Political characters, and of the most eminent and successful Artists of the present day. And the Committee have the pleasure of adding, that the desire of being associated to this Institution is by no means diminished, and that there are numerous Candidates of great respectability, who, as it has been thought necessary to limit the Members to One Thousand, must await the occurrence of vacancies.[81]

In the months that followed, a number of problems associated with balloting came to light. On 15 June 1825, several members 'declared their belief that they had not voted as they intended in consequence of a misapprehension arising from the marks on the Boxes'.[82] Heber and Rose, as members of the General Committee, declared the ballot void and ordered Magrath to remove the balls from the boxes 'without making himself acquainted with the results'. The following month another ballot was declared void as only six members voted.[83] This was probably unusual, although there is no hard evidence, the earliest balloting certificates having been lost. The first surviving certificates indicate that one of the candidates whose names were entered in the book in mid-January 1825 and who went into the ballot thirteen months later was elected (51 yes, 2 no), and another was rejected (45 yes, 6 no).[84] 'Blackballing' meant placing a cork ball on the black 'no' side of the wooden divider inside the box: more than one 'black ball' to ten balls on the white 'yes' side led to rejection. Clerks were stationed at the ballot boxes to take the names of members, in an attempt to prevent them from voting early and voting often.[85] Feelings could run high as ballot days approached, as a minute of the General Committee meeting on 24 January 1826 reveals:

> Ordered That the names of Parties proposed for Ballot be hung up as usual and that the Secretary be directed to provide a Glass Frame to prevent their

being disfigured. The same to be kept under Lock and Key and that members who think proper be allowed to add their names to those of the proposer and seconder certifying their acquaintance with the Candidate either personal or from a knowledge of his works.[86]

This distinction between personal acquaintance with the candidate and 'a knowledge of his works' (note the plural) is retained in the Candidates Book of the Athenæum to this day. Evidence of both clubbability and a substantial contribution to science, literature or the fine arts was required for success in elections which became increasingly testing later in the nineteenth century, as both the list of candidates and the years of waiting lengthened, and the bar was raised to one black ball to fifteen white.[87]

While attempting to limit the abuses associated with ballot boxes and cork balls, the General Committee also retained as much power as possible in the selection of members. In February 1826 they 'abrogated' their own self-denying ordinance, thus enabling members of the Committee to propose or second candidates in the book: their status in the club ensured a good number of signatures on a certificate and votes in a ballot.[88] At the AGM in May 1827 they proposed electing a further 200 members themselves, 'in the manner in which the election of Members was conducted up to the period when the present number of the Club was completed'.[89] A year later they proposed to the AGM that they should elect one-third of the candidates for vacancies without ballot in any one year, but this too was rejected by the membership.[90] After a further two years, in 1830, they succeeded in introducing the famous 'Rule II', whereby the Committee could elect no more than nine particularly distinguished members without ballot each year.[91] Meanwhile membership of the General Committee, which was to rotate on a regular basis, was itself balloted for, thus making the group rather more representative than formerly. Trustees, however, including Croker, remained on the committee.

Once settled into 12 Waterloo Place, the General Committee began its weekly meetings with housekeeping: approving bills, getting cheques signed by trustees and making decisions on a wide range of practical matters which the secretary and senior servants brought to their attention. In August 1824, for example, with Croker in the chair, the Committee ordered that 'the Servants be supplied with working Jackets, Trousers and Hats', presumably to save those fine liveries.[92] During 1825 the Committee ordered that green cloth be provided for the coffee room tables, approved the wording for a form letter which the steward could send to debtors, ordered that fires be lit when the temperature fell below 62° F or on demand, and stipulated that 'the Green Grocery be purchased from Covent Garden Market'.[93] Disciplinary matters arose from time to time. In December 1846 it was reported that the barrister Charles Edward Dodd, a member of Henry Crabb Robinson's party the previous year, had brought a 'stranger' into the clubhouse and had dinner with him in the coffee room. The secretary was instructed to write, warning him against repeating 'so manifest an offence against the fundamental constitution of the Society', lest steps be taken to expel him.[94]

Having dispatched the immediate business of the day, the Committee would then turn to more general matters of policy. Perhaps the most significant innovation was agreed at a meeting on 2 November 1824, with Davy in the chair: 'Resolved that from the commencement of the sittings of the Royal Society until the rising of Parliament a conversazione be held every Monday evening at nine o' Clock.'[95] Fine-tuning was required at subsequent meetings to make these occasions more attractive to members and to strengthen still further the club's connection with the learned societies: tea was to be served at the club's expense (7 December) and the three presidents were to be 'privileged to introduce five Visitors each at the Monday evening parties' (14 December). Even as the ceiling of 1,000 members was reached, the committee was seeking a means of introducing strong candidates to the club who might later fill any vacancies.

The administrative work associated with these meetings was handled by the first salaried secretary, Edward Magrath. In his 1926 history of the Athenæum, Humphry Ward simply states that Magrath had a keen sense of humour, was friendly with Jekyll and Faraday, served well for many years and was a serious loss to the club when he retired in 1855, shortly before his death.[96] F.R. Cowell does not even mention Magrath's thirty-one years of service in his 1975 history, although he makes much of the fact that some eminent early *members* of the club came from humble origins: Faraday and Chantrey (1824), Daniel Maclise RA (1841), John Gould FRS (1854), Richard Cobden (1858) and W.P. Frith

RA (1859), for example.[97] Cowell's defensiveness on questions relating to class and Ward's Olympian approach to the question reflect the attitudes of earlier generations. The appointment of a good secretary, crucial to any club's well-being, was awkward in terms of the rigid social hierarchy of the day. Like a governess in a private house, who was neither servant nor family, a club secretary operated in a liminal position between classes. In 1829 Magrath, for it was he at the Old Bailey, answered to Lord Aberdeen, a trustee of the Athenæum, and also managed the light-fingered housekeeper, Martha Geary. Earlier, in the first years of his secretaryship, class had been a factor in Magrath's troubled relationship with the Committee.

Little is known about Magrath, even though he served for three decades at the Athenæum and was of sufficient standing to be portrayed in oils by a well-known artist.[98] Some light was shed by Faraday's first biographer, Henry Bence Jones, who cited memoranda of Faraday's in which he explained how Magrath, as secretary of the City Philosophical Society, had introduced him as a member in 1813.[99] The society, he went on, 'consisted of thirty or forty individuals, perhaps all in the humble or moderate rank of life', who met every Wednesday evening 'for mutual instruction'. That spring, Faraday and Magrath established a 'mutual-improvement plan' and met either at the former's rooms in the attics of the Royal Institution or at the latter's place of work, a ribbon warehouse in Wood Street: 'It consisted perhaps of half-a-dozen persons, chiefly from the City Philosophical Society, who met of an evening to read together, and to criticise, correct, and improve each other's pronunciation and construction of language. The discipline was very sturdy, the remarks very plain and open, and the results most valuable. This continued for several years.'[100]

In September 1826 Faraday, by now director of the laboratory at the Royal Institution, wrote from there to Magrath, secretary of the Athenæum, who was in France, with some reassuring news: 'I was at the Athenæum nearly two whole days looking over the Journals all seemed right there. I have not been lately. There is nobody in town.'[101] The following year Faraday added a postscript to another letter from the Royal Institution, asking Magrath how much he paid his 'waiting man' per night for attendance at the club: 'he charges us 5/- which we think rather high'.[102] These letters are from one professional gentleman to another. The servant side of Magrath's story emerges from his commonplace book, referred to obliquely by Ward but hitherto largely ignored.[103] As in his thousands of official minutes of meetings, there are spelling mistakes. Many of the entries record comments, particularly witticisms, made by Committee members. Occasionally, however, when Magrath feels aggrieved in his lonely position as the senior member of staff at the Athenæum, he writes private minutes in his commonplace book. A scribbled entry misleadingly dated 30 August 1826 reveals not only the source of Magrath's unhappiness but also something of club life at 12 Waterloo Place:

Lord Guilford's Secretary Mr Robertson was here taking Coffee this afternoon. On stating to him the hard bargain made with me as Secretary of the Athenæum he encourage [sic] me by stating that his outset in Official Life he received a hundred Guineas a year only from his Patron but that he soon was employed by Lord Guilford and that he is now well provided for. I requested him to bear me in mind because my remuneration of £200 a year with the obligations to keep up appearances and a residence in the house is not adequate. It is scarcely credible that a body like the Committee of the Athenæum could have descended to the paltry saving of Thirty pounds a year after having requested as a favour that I would come to reside in the house. Perhaps such a proceeding was never heard of and I will therefore record it. After having procured my assent to reside in the house – Sir H Davy said – You will save your Lodging – We shall charge you Twenty Pounds. I enquired what I was to do for Breakfast as I could not afford to pay eighteen pence a morning and one shilling an Evening for Tea to the Coffee Room keeper. On which he of course with the consent of the Committee deducted me another Ten pounds – Leaving me £170 a year with the privilege of paying for Dinners at the Coffee Room prices – Adding a stipulation that I should confine my services exclusively to the Athenæum – The members of the committee as written under the direction of Mr Locker are curious and will be found amongst my Papers. The members present were – Sir H Davy – H T Colebrooke Charles Hatchett Richard Heber E H Locker W S Rose and Dr Young – After the Committee broke up Mr Heber asked me if I was satisfied I asked him how it was possible to be so. On which he said Mr Locker and I fought a hard-battle [sic] for you Sir H D strove hard to confine you to a £100 a year.[104]

The waspish Croker was far from universally popular at the Athenæum, and here is Sir Humphry Davy being betrayed by Heber, a fellow trustee. It seems that Faraday's departure had only hardened Davy's attitude towards the secretaryship. Davy had taken the chair when Magrath's case was discussed by the General Committee for the second time, on 14 June 1826.[105] The unminuted meeting with Magrath must have taken place on or around that day, as by 25 June Scott was lamenting the fact that Heber had resigned as MP for Oxford and gone abroad, long after rumours of homosexual activity had begun circulating in London.[106]

The dispute between Magrath and the club remained unresolved for months. Various compromises were suggested by the Committee on 12 December 1826, but Magrath was far from satisfied.[107] He wrote in his commonplace book:

> It will scarcely be credited that the representatives of such a body as the Athenæum could condescend to deal in a style with an acknowledged important Officer which would disgrace an inferior merchant or Tradesman. I have still the privilege of paying for my Dinners because say they I might choose to be extragavant [sic]; thus putting me on a worse footing than their upper Servants who have unlimited command of the Provisions . . .

Magrath's request was met in due course: his salary was raised from £200 to £250 in 1830 and to £300 in 1835, and for the rest of his career he enjoyed his life at the club, according to his niece.[108]

A happier aspect of the General Committee's work was its gradual building of a library.[109] A number of bibliophiles were available to advise them, including the 2nd earl Spencer, president of the Roxburghe Club in 1812; Viscount Morpeth, soon to be the 6th earl of Carlisle; the antiquary James Heywood Markland; Earl Gower, later the 2nd duke of Sutherland; Heber, the collector who filled eight houses with books, and who believed that a gentleman should own three copies of every title, one for show, one for use and one for borrowers; and, initially, the Revd Thomas Frognall Dibdin, an obsessive bibliographer whose catalogue of Earl Spencer's library at Althorp was unreliable, but whose charming accounts of bibliographical tours of the libraries of Europe and whose book, *Bibliomania*, first published in 1809, made him famous. Later in life, Dibdin recorded that he was pleased to have 'contributed, in conjunction with the late Sir Humphry Davy and Mr. Heber, to the establishment of the Athenæum'.[110] Of the thirty-one members of the Roxburghe Club who subscribed to its first publication, no fewer than twenty were future members of the Athenæum, six of them serving on its General Committee.[111]

To begin with, the library was formed largely through donations, a process that was strongly encouraged by the Committee. On the cover sheet of a printed list of the first 506 members, dated 22 June 1824, 12 Waterloo Place, and intended to attract more members, were these words: 'All members of the Club are invited to present copies of their published works, for the purpose of forming a Library for the use of the Club.'[112] The first donations of books – they were charmingly called 'presents' – were from William Stewart Rose, a member of the General Committee, who in June 1824 gave copies of his *Letters from the North of Italy* (1819), addressed to fellow Committee member Henry Hallam, and his translations of Casti's *Gli Animali Parlanti* (1819) and Ariosto's *Orlando Furioso* (the first two volumes of four, 1823).[113] The Committee ordered Magrath to write and thank the donor – a courtesy which is still maintained – and at its next meeting further decreed that 'a Copper Plate similar to that used by the Royal Society be prepared for a Letter of thanks for presents received by the Club', and that a bookplate be made for presents. William Tooke FRS, a founding member of the University of London, donated his *Lucian of Samosata: works from the Greek* (1820); the Revd Blanco White gave eight volumes of *El Espanol*, the journal that he edited, and his *Letters from Spain* (1822), under the pseudonym of Doblado; the businessman John Taylor presented selections from the Baron de Humboldt relating to Mexico (1824); Sharon Turner gave his *History of the Anglo-Saxons* (1820); and James Mill his *History of British India* (1818) and *Elements of Political Economy* (2nd edn 1824).[114]

So significant were donations in the early days that an additional request for 'any other useful publications, more especially works of reference', was inserted in a new printed list of members in January 1825. Reference books, the core of what was always a working library, were also purchased by the club: in October 1824 the 'Booksellers Bill to this time amounting to £40. 7s. 1d. was presented and ordered for payment'.[115] Equally important were periodicals, such as the

*Classical Journal*, to which the club subscribed liberally from early on.[116] Back in December 1823, when Davy was responding to Croker's draft of the first prospectus for the new club, he recommended adding words to the effect that, in addition to the comforts of the most popular clubs, this one would provide 'periodical publications foreign or domestic on the subjects of letters'.[117] Davy believed that this 'would offer a temptation to persons not caring for french cookery, or even good Society, I mean some of the retiring philosophers whom it is always desirable to bring into the living world.' Again, an emphasis upon the importance of periodicals offers a clue to the usage of the library. Many of the founding members, and not only the retiring philosophers, were engaged in research and writing, and they needed to keep in touch with the latest findings in the scholarly journals to which they themselves contributed. And the quarterlies, particularly the Whig *Edinburgh Review* and Murray's Tory *Quarterly Review*, were not only read by members but, in the case of the *Quarterly*, largely written by them.

Unfortunately, by November 1825 several newspapers and books, including presents, were missing from the Reading Room at no. 12, and a reminder of the rules had to be posted up there.[118] Three months later, the committee room was converted into a 'Reading Room for Newspapers'.[119] In January 1830, just before the move to the new clubhouse, Croker chaired a meeting of the General Committee, at which the wording of another circular was discussed. It was to include yet more guidance on 'presents', with a view to the club's new accommodation. 'It is not necessary', the circular reads, 'for the Committee to offer to the members any particular suggestions for the selection of Books to be presented by them but they may be permitted to observe that Maps, Plans and Works of local information collected during their Travels, as well as Engravings of every description, more particularly the Portraits of Individuals belonging to the Club would fall in conveniently and usefully with the arrangement in contemplation.'[120] The number of acquisitions – donations and purchases – would rise, and at a phenomenal rate, once a permanent clubhouse had been built which could accommodate a large collection of books. In 1824 the General Committee hoped that they would be able to move within about three years. In the end it took six.

# 3

## 'THEY HAVE BUILT A PERFECT PALACE'

Why did it take the Athenæum so long to build a clubhouse of its own? First, a potential site considered by the Committee in 1824 failed to meet their requirements. Then another site proved to be less attractive than a third option, which in turn remained unavailable until 1826. Planning complications associated with this excellent site on Pall Mall delayed the approval of Decimus Burton's proposed elevations, which later had to be changed as a result of skulduggery outside the club. Negotiations with the owners of properties that stood on the site caused further delays. What is more, all three sites, and an existing clubhouse that was offered for purchase but declined, were located in an area that was being redeveloped as part of the most comprehensive building programme that London had seen since the Great Fire of 1666. This programme was the responsibility of the Office of Works, the Land Revenue Office and the Office of Woods and Forests, three departments that would be combined in 1832. In pursuit of its goal, the club's Committee frequently had to negotiate with the Commissioners of His Majesty's Woods, Forests and Revenues. The result of all this was that members could not take possession of their 'perfect palace' until February 1830.

Even before the triumph of Waterloo, the prince regent (King George IV from 1820) had dreamed of creating an imperial city that would outshine Paris.[1] John Nash, soon to be appointed the royal architect, began to execute his plan for the Regent's Park in 1812, collaborating with his young protégé Decimus Burton and with builders such as Burton's father James.[2] Following the passage of the New Street Act in 1813, work also began on Nash's plan to break through a number of cross streets to the south of the park, in order to create a royal mile, later named Regent Street, that terminated at Carlton House, the prince's residence immediately to the north of another royal park, St James's.[3] By 1815–16 James Burton, one of the most successful developers in London, was building Waterloo Place at the bottom of what is now Regent Street St James's and facing Carlton House.[4] In practice, this ambitious programme was subject to compromises, with the result that it was quite unlike the kind of Gallic planning that produced modern Paris.[5] In principle, however, it was coherent, and in style it was Greek. If Waterloo was Britain's Marathon, could not the prince regent be compared to Pericles?[6]

The Greek Revival in architecture, which was to peak in 1820, was the product of a passion for all things Hellenic after Lord Elgin had displayed the Marbles that he had brought back from the Parthenon in a makeshift museum on Park Lane. Whereas the 'artists', such as Haydon, Chantrey, Lawrence, Westmacott and Keats, were enchanted by their naturalism, the 'connoisseurs', including Payne Knight, Wilkins and the earl of Aberdeen, considered that they fell short of the classical ideals expounded by Sir Joshua Reynolds and the Royal Academy, and embodied in the Townley Marbles at the British Museum.[7] With opinion sharply divided, it was not until 1816 that the government finally agreed to accept the Marbles for the nation and to pay Elgin less than half his expenses in acquiring them, which he had done with the support of William Richard Hamilton in Greece and John Wilson Croker in London. In Croker's article of that year in the *Quarterly Review* he described the Temple of Minerva in the Acropolis (Plate 3) in detail, praised Pericles and Phidias to the skies, and sympathised with Lord Elgin, who, like most benefactors of mankind, had been 'traduced by ignorance, by envy, and by malice'.[8] He particularly admired the 'fabulous Minerva, whose story the eloquent chissel of Phidias recorded', and the frieze.[9] Those of his readers who had access to *The Antiquities of Athens*, whose subscribers included Decimus Burton, could see engravings of the frieze, based on drawings of the Marbles, in the fourth volume (1816).[10]

Several future members of the Athenæum visited Athens in the early years of the century and enthused about it on their return to London. Colonel W.M. Leake, the topographer of the Levant, was there in 1802 and sailed with William Richard Hamilton that year in the very boat in which many of the Elgin Marbles

were sunk off Cythera.[11] Like other travellers at that time, Robert Smirke junior
and the earl of Aberdeen brought home antique fragments, and Byron's 'travell'd
thane, Athenian Aberdeen' established the short-lived Athenian Club.[12] Thomas
Hope, who travelled in Greece in 1799–1800, had a powerful influence upon the
reinterpretation of antiquity in Regency design, opening his eclectic Duchess
Street house-museum to Royal Academicians in 1802 and later to other insiders,
and publishing *Household Furniture and Interior Decoration* in 1807. Other visitors to Athens included William Haygarth, William Walker, Sir Charles Monck,
John Galt, Gally Knight, Lord Sligo and the earl of Guilford.

Among several works by these future Athenians that were later to be
acquired by their library, one is pre-eminent as an index of the cultural milieu
in which both the club and its new house were conceived. Lord Aberdeen's
*Inquiry into the Principles of Beauty in Grecian Architecture* was published (inevitably by John Murray) in 1822, just two years before the earl became a trustee
of the Athenæum – *ex officio*, as president of the Society of Antiquaries – and
a member of its first Building Committee.[13] George Hamilton Gordon assumes
that his reader shares his ideals of civilised taste and values. He states that 'all
nations in the most advanced state of civilization, have been unanimous in
their admiration of Grecian architecture', and that 'such admiration appears to
have been generally considered as inseparable from the existence of real taste
and knowledge in the art'.[14] His 'endeavour to trace the causes of this unanimity,
and to ascertain the principles on which it is founded', may therefore 'form the
subject of an interesting inquiry'.

Although the *Inquiry* proves to be less interesting than its subject matter, it
is significant here, being written in the same spirit that inspired the new classical clubhouses in London, such as Robert Smirke junior's Union Club (1824)
and United Service Club (1819).[15] In his concluding remarks, for example,
Lord Aberdeen comments on the value of studying the 'precious remains of
Grecian art', so long neglected but now available to the architect who 'aspires
to permanent reputation':

Other modes are transitory and uncertain, but the essential qualities of
Grecian excellence, as they are founded on reason, and are consistent with
fitness and propriety, will ever continue to deserve his first care. These

models should be imitated however, – not with the timid and servile hand of a copyist; but their beauties should be transferred to our soil, preserving, at the same time, a due regard to the changes of customs and manners, to the difference of our climate, and to the condition of modern society.[16]

'Reason', 'fitness' and 'propriety' were to be key principles for Aberdeen, Croker and their colleagues as they considered the design of a house for literary and scientific men, and followers of the fine arts, who were leaders of 'modern society'.

In 1822, the year of the *Inquiry*, the radical philhellene Percy Bysshe Shelley proclaimed in his preface to *Hellas* that 'We are all Greeks'.[17] 'Our laws', he argued, 'our literature, our religion, our arts have their root in Greece. But for Greece – Rome, the instructor, the conqueror, or the metropolis of our ancestors, would have spread no illumination with her arms.' Most of Croker's generation did not share Shelley's republican views, and for them Rome was more closely associated with Napoleon and France, the vanquished enemy, than with Wellington and England. Nevertheless, like Athens and Pericles, Rome and Augustus could be invoked as classical models. In June 1826, a reviewer in Murray's *Quarterly* cited a popular facetious epigram that ironically compared Augustus with Nash, also 'a very great master': 'He finds us all brick and he leaves us all plaster'.[18] The following month, Nash's royal patron was compared to Augustus without irony in James Elmes's oleaginous dedication of his *Metropolitan Improvements*.[19] Some Roman sources were to be in Decimus Burton's mind as he designed and then redesigned his Grecian clubhouse for the Athenæum.

Nobody had more influence over Burton and the process of securing a good site for the house than Croker, who ensured that a powerful group of architects, connoisseurs, politicians and administrators could provide support at crucial moments during the planning stages. No fewer than ten of the witnesses before the House of Commons select committee on the Elgin Marbles in 1816 would later be original members of the Athenæum: Croker would have ensured that they were recruited.[20] John Nash, the king's architect, Sir John Soane and Robert Smirke junior were the three 'attached architects' to the Board of Works, and thus responsible for public buildings in London. All three men were to be original members of the club, as were James and Decimus Burton. Smirke was to serve on both the General and Building Committees. Sir Charles Long, another future member of both committees, was said to have been the spectacles through which the king viewed architecture and interior decoration: he became Lord Farnborough in 1826, the year in which he published his *Short Remarks* on Nash's 'improvements'.[21] The five successive First Commissioners of Woods and Forests, with whom Croker and Farnborough negotiated between 1824 and 1830, were all original members of the club, and all but one served on the General Committee.[22] Croker himself was one of the ministers who presided over the 'metropolitan improvements' of the 1820s, along with figures such as Lord Farnborough and Lord Liverpool, another original member.[23]

Croker was also an insider at court. He had become a member of the Carlton House set in 1813, the year in which the prince regent appointed Nash. Croker was a regular guest, at one period, dining there as often as twice a week.[24] The house had been acquired from Richard Boyle, the earl of Burlington, in 1732 for Frederick, Prince of Wales, and William Kent had improved the grounds. When the prince regent took it over and commissioned Henry Holland to make improvements in 1783, Horace Walpole was astonished by the 'august simplicity' of this 'chaste palace', with its tastefully arranged ornaments.[25] The Prince's initial delight abated, however, and, inspired by the Bourbon splendours of Paris and Versailles, he commissioned Walsh Porter and others to embellish Carlton House. A permanent record of the sumptuous rooms that Croker knew, such as the crimson drawing room, is provided in Pyne's *History of the Royal Residences* (1819; see Plate 5).[26] In 1826 Carlton House was demolished, creating the space for the southern continuation of Waterloo Place on which Nash's United Service Club and the 'new' Athenæum, as it was called,[27] were to be built.

Members of the Athenæum could observe these activities from the south-facing windows of their temporary clubhouse at 12 Waterloo Place (Plate 2). Even before they moved in there, back in May 1824, their Committee, meeting in Joseph Jekyll's house, had made resolutions relating to the 'house to be built': the precocious Decimus Burton, aged only twenty-three, was to join the Committee and its preparatory sub-committee; and a financial arrangement proposed by his brother-in-law, the banker Edmund Hopkinson, was accepted in principle.[28] Within two months of that move a Building Committee had been formally established with authority to settle 'all matters relating to building the house and furnishing and completing it for the Reception of the Club'.[29] The three *ex officio* trustees – Davy, Lawrence and Aberdeen – were to serve, together with Croker, Heber, Hatchett, Jekyll and Robert Smirke junior. Croker called Smirke the 'Dr Baillie of architects', after the author of *Morbid Anatomy* (1793): he was a safe pair of hands and was adept at correcting the mistakes of others.[30] His Covent Garden (1808–9), perhaps the most significant building of Britain's Greek Revival, has been described as 'ruthlessly simple', the product of an 'austere and cerebral approach to the whole business of architectural design'.[31] As his British Museum rose in Bloomsbury, Smirke would have spoken with most authority on the Building Committee as they discussed Burton's drawings for the Athenæum.

The first potential site that they considered in the summer of 1824 was on the north side of the newly constructed Pall Mall East, where other significant building developments were already under way: on the corner with Suffolk Street was the United University Club, designed by William Wilkins, another original member, and opened in 1826; Smirke's College of Physicians, with its high entrance portico of six Ionic columns, was on the opposite side of the street, attached to his new Union Club, and was opened in 1825. At their first meeting, chaired by Jekyll and with Croker and Heber present, the Building Committee discussed Hopkinson's proposed heads of agreement for 'a Club House to be erected according to the design and elevation of Mr Decimus Burton, upon ground on the north side of Pall Mall East containing sixty two feet of frontage towards the street and of various depths to thirty eight feet, the extreme depth, held from the Crown by Mr Hopkinson. – Mr Hopkinson to pay to the extent of but not exceeding five thousand Pounds towards the amount of the contract'.[32] The club's solicitor, who was in attendance, was asked to negotiate with Hopkinson, and Burton was asked to let the committee know when he could present drawings.

At first all went well and at a rapid pace. Only two days later, on 23 July 1824, Burton was instructed to consult Smirke – nineteen years his senior – on his drawings and specifications before the next meeting. By 18 August the Building Committee, chaired by Davy and with Croker, Heber, Lawrence and Smirke present, could discuss drawings and a model. Whereas the plan was approved, with 'one or two alterations marked thereon', the front elevation was to be revised: 'Order'd that the Architect do make his plans elevation and spec-ification in such way as to separate the ornamental front and to substitute a plainer one and that Mr Burton be requested to push this matter on with all possible celerity.'[33] It may well have been Smirke who argued for a plainer front, supported by Croker and Lawrence, a great admirer of Smirke's Covent Garden. Or was it a question of costs rather than aesthetics? Although Burton's final elevations for the Athenæum cannot be traced, one of his unidentified elevations that has survived may be a design for the Pall Mall East site (Plate 6). Presented in a domestic idiom that is appropriate to its scale, it is simple, self-assured and elegant.[34] In the ensuing months, arguments for and against plainness were to become political counters, pragmatically handled by Croker and his colleagues, some of whom were experienced 'improvers', as they strove to build the club a house that was both affordable and handsome.

In November 1824, Magrath was ordered to write to Fielder, the leaseholder of 12 Waterloo Place, enquiring whether the club could continue to occupy the house until midsummer 1826.[35] Meanwhile, the Pall Mall East proposal was running into trouble. While tenders from contractors were coming in, Burton tried and failed to persuade Sir Richard Birnie to sell or let the plot behind the site of the proposed clubhouse, on which a kitchen and coffee room could be added to a building with a narrow frontage.[36] Moreover, the proposed 'projection' of 9 or 10 feet beyond the building line was turned down by the Commissioners of Woods and Forests. On 14 December, when the Building Committee heard both pieces of bad news, the draft agreement with Hopkinson was immediately dropped.[37] Characteristically, however, Croker was ready with a better alterna-tive, and could report to the meeting that there was 'a disposition on the part of the Commissioners to place at the disposal of the Club a piece of Ground on the eastern side of Union Square'.[38] Burton was therefore instructed to prepare 'a suitable plan for a House on that ground', and Croker was asked to continue the negotiations with Woods and Forests. With the membership now standing at around a thousand, they could work on this second, more ambitious option with confidence.

Whereas the first proposed site had been cramped, this one provided twice the frontage and a commanding position in Nash's ambitious scheme for what is now Trafalgar Square, in the spot where South Africa House stands today.[39]

Nash's 'improvements' to the former site of the King's Mews involved the demolition of numerous properties in order to create the most impressive square in London, and thus make a grand imperial statement. On a plan dated 12 May 1826, a site for the Royal Academy is shown at the centre, surrounded by regal statues (Plate 7).[40] (In the end the Academy had to share Wilkins's building on the northern side of the square with the National Gallery.) The proposed site for the Athenæum is shown on the eastern side, with a portico of five pillars, between the Royal Academy of Literature and the 'Vicar's House' for St Martin in the Fields, and with extensive stabling behind, serving the new Golden Cross inn to be built on the Strand.

Having rapidly produced a plan, Burton was asked to prepare an estimate below £12,000 and to ascertain from Woods and Forests what external elevation they would require for the proposed structure.[41] Croker's own nine-page letter to the commissioners, dated 24 January 1825, reveals his grasp of the principles involved in Nash's scheme and his attention to detail, as he weighs the arguments for and against uniformity in the square. In his closing statement he argues that the club's funds 'are too limited to allow of any considerable expenditure for mere ornament, but they also think that in point of taste, considering the materials of which the House is to be composed, too much attention to external embellishment would be out of character & might produce an appearance the very reverse of ornamental'.[42] Again, aesthetic and economic arguments are difficult to disentangle.

By 1 March 1825, Croker could report to the Building Committee, at their ninth meeting, that he had a firm offer from the commissioners of a site measuring about 130 feet by 30 feet, 'Southwards to the proposed new College of Arms'.[43] The commissioners had responded to Croker's letter, however, by insisting upon a 'very handsome and Architectural Elevation', and requesting a drawing. The committee asked Sir Charles Long and Croker to continue negotiations. It was also agreed that the rent must be reduced 'towards defraying the expences [sic] of the extra decorations'. Burton produced a new plan and elevation that were approved and forwarded to the commissioners. Another unidentified 'Design elevation of a public building' by Burton would have provided a frontage of about 130 feet (Plate 8). Written at the bottom of the sheet are the words, 'N.B. The panels are proposed to receive the Elgin Frieze'.

The Panathenaic frieze, based on the Elgin Marbles, is the most famous external feature of the built clubhouse in Pall Mall. The note strengthens the case for this drawing being an early proposed elevation of the clubhouse for Union Square, with 'extra decorations', albeit with six columns to the portico.[44]

The first annual meeting of the club, held at 12 Waterloo Place on 9 May 1825, had before it a report, signed by Davy but drafted by Croker, in which the details of current negotiations were veiled behind vague references to 'the neighbourhood of Union Square, Cockspur-street', and the 'detailed plans of the Government for the buildings in that quarter of the town not being yet finally arranged'.[45] Assurance was given, however, that the clubhouse would be 'conducive to the general convenience of its Members, and the ornamental appearance of the neighbourhood in which it is to be placed'. A 'considerable degree of external decoration' would probably be 'insisted upon by Government', but the additional expense was manageable: it was hoped that by the end of 1825 there would be between £13,000 and £14,000 'applicable to the erection of the house'. Having formerly argued for plainness, partly on economic grounds, Croker could now blame the commissioners for insisting upon 'mere decoration'.

But the house was not to be in Union Square: an even better option was coming into view. The foundations of Carlton House having been declared to be 'absolutely unsafe',[46] early bids for the space it occupied were lodged in the summer of 1825, twelve months before parliament authorised the commissioners to demolish the house.[47] The Athenæum entered the ring in December, when Croker and Long reported on progress with the commissioners.[48] In deciding against the site 'in the neighbourhood of the Mews', Croker and his colleagues saved the club from having extensive stabling to the rear of their clubhouse and the hubbub of Trafalgar Square on their doorstep. They also rejected a suggestion from the United Service Club (USC) that the Athenæum might buy their former clubhouse on Charles Street (now Charles II Street), designed by Smirke and now outgrown. Burton quickly proved that 'it would cost less to build a more appropriate building', and the Building Committee moved on, their ranks reinforced by the addition of Lord Lansdowne, the Whig power-broker, and Sir Charles Long, the king's spectacles.[49] Future generations were to thank them for securing a site on the corner of Pall Mall and the southern continuation of Waterloo Place, with gardens to the south. (Charles

Barry's Travellers Club – an Italian Renaissance *palazzo*, with a plan on the *cortile* model – was completed next door on Pall Mall in 1833.) Croker in particular deserves their thanks, as he applied much of his time, as well as his exceptional gifts, to the housing of the club.[50]

He also exercised patience. By the summer of 1826 another year had passed, and Croker had to explain in his second Annual Report that the Carlton House site was preferable to Union Square; that he recognised members' 'just anxiety' about the delay, caused by the fact that parliament had yet to pass the necessary legislation; but that they 'may be in possession' of their new house early in 1828.[51] When the USC and the Athenæum were allocated sites on opposite sides of the new section of Waterloo Place, the commissioners and their pre-eminent architect, John Nash, insisted that the two houses should be uniform in design. Nash, full of years and of his own importance, was also architect to the USC. He therefore had ample opportunity to play both sides against each other, and thus to outmanoeuvre the Athenæum, of which he was a member, and Decimus Burton, his junior colleague, when it suited him, which was often.

The Athenæum's request for a copy of Nash's plan for the USC was promptly granted by the commissioners in July 1826.[52] In drawing his own plan, Burton clearly had to pay close attention to Nash's. He also had Smirke monitoring progress. The result was a plan which followed in a tradition that began with Smirke and his original USC – the first of the post-Waterloo clubhouses – and continued with Wilkins's University Club, with a central hall from which spacious rooms were accessible on the ground floor, and a grand staircase leading to a landing which gave onto the rooms on the *piano nobile*.[53] As we will see when we come to the interior, Burton's clubhouse met the particular needs of a club for literary and scientific men, and followers of the fine arts, with its large coffee room and drawing room, and its generous allocation of space for the library. The main problem, however, was not with the internal but the external design.

In June 1826 the commissioners informed the Building Committee that the elevations of their east and north fronts must correspond with those of the USC's west and north fronts, a condition which they accepted.[54] Nash then informed them that the designs for the USC had been 'long since settled' and that therefore no changes could be made to them. This was untrue, but the Athenæum took the statement at face value and asked for copies of the elevations.[55] When these finally arrived, four months later, the Building Committee pointed out that there was an inconsistency between them and the notification that the two houses should be uniform.[56] Nash had his main façade on the Pall Mall side, which was longer than that of the Athenæum. As the two frontages onto Waterloo Place were both about 105 feet in length, would it not seem natural to have the main façades facing each other? In their reply, the commissioners indicated that uniformity could be achieved by adopting 'a style, of which the plainness would render the inevitable difference with extent of the frontage the least observable', and by having windows and doors of the same size and in similar positions.[57] Having previously argued for plainness themselves in discussions on the Union Square option, and then prepared the membership for extra costs associated with the decorations imposed by the commissioners, the Building Committee was now having plainness thrust upon them. Once again they accepted the commissioners' conditions, and in December an agreement was signed by the Athenæum and the USC, subject to both sides making a number of modifications.[58] Nash, however, and the building committee of the USC were to renege on the agreement.

As discussions with both the commissioners and the USC dragged on, the Building Committee of the Athenæum accepted a tender from Messrs Bennett and Hunt, an experienced and 'very respectable' firm, who in May 1827 presented by far the lowest estimate at £26,715.[59] That month each member of the General Committee was presented with a 'Lithographic Plan and Elevation of the intended new Athenæum'.[60] At the third annual meeting of the club, the General Committee was pleased to announce that they had secured the splendid new site, but regretted that circumstances beyond their control had led to an increase in cost and a delay. The piece of ground that they had been granted, they said, 'is perhaps larger than the Committee would have thought absolutely necessary for the accommodation of the present number of members, but as the exterior which they were bound to adopt is in a plain though handsome style, the Committee hoped that the increase of expense will not be so great, as the increase of accommodation to be derived from the greater space'.[61] Once again, external pressure, whether for plainness or for decoration, is used to justify an increase in the cost involved in building a better clubhouse. The Committee also reported that 'some difficulties, which the Commissioners of His Majesty's Woods Forests and Land Revenues met with in obtaining possession of two private houses, which occupy part of the site of the Athenæum, have prevented the obtaining as early possession as they could have wished, and this has necessarily postponed the commencement, and ultimately, the completion of the House'. It was still possible, however, that the new house would be ready in eighteen or twenty-four months' time.

In July 1827 it was agreed that the ground should be staked out with a view to building as much of the house as possible, while waiting for the commissioners to arrange for the demolition of number 109 Pall Mall. The Crown lease was not due to expire until May 1829, however, and the owner refused to go to arbitration, declining generous offers from the commissioners, supplemented by extra funds from the club, until finally agreeing terms in March 1828.[62] Lord Farnborough, Croker's colleague in discussions with the commissioners, now replaced the absent Heber as a trustee, after legal advice had been taken.[63] He also chaired the meeting of the Building Committee, in February 1828, at which it was reported that Nash had failed to report that he had not implemented the modifications to the USC's house. Whereas the Committee had 'sacrificed their own intentions' in order to 'accommodate the other parties', as they stated in an aggrieved letter to the commissioners, the USC's deviations from the agreed scheme 'must tend to throw a shade of inferiority over the Edifice of the Athenæum'.[64] Moreover, the 'hardship upon them' was 'very much aggravated' by the fact that the only notice they had received of these deviations was 'by seeing from the Street the erections actually completed': Nash had retained an upper portico on the Pall Mall façade and a 'colonnade' facing south, and had not added a continuous balcony. Claiming the moral high ground, the committee added that they were now willing to make their own balcony 'as little conspicuous as possible', again for the sake of uniformity, and to 'give up the idea of forming it with a stone parapet and Balustrade, as was prescribed to them by the Commissioners'.

Meanwhile much time had been lost: by March 1828 the contractors were submitting bills to cover the cost of delays, as well as for work completed.[65] Soon the General Committee were preparing for yet another AGM, at which they were to announce that the building should be 'covered in' during the autumn and ready for the 'accommodation of members' twelve months later.[66] In June the Building Committee's concerns about the proposed height of the Travellers clubhouse, to be built next door on Pall Mall, and the question of a party wall were amicably resolved in discussions between Burton and Barry.[67] John Brady, a labourer, was injured in a fall: the General Committee awarded him 5 guineas 'towards the support of his family during his confinement in the Hospital'.[68] (Following an injury to John Burton six months later, the club was to compensate him until the clubhouse opened, when they employed him as a messenger.)[69] A group of members presented a 'memorial' to the General Committee asking for baths to be incorporated in the building, a request which was turned down on the advice of the architect: quite apart from the expense of making such a late addition, 'steam and effluvia' would be 'felt in the apartments on the principal story'.[70] Potentially far more serious had been the matter of the foundations, to which reference was made at a meeting of the General Committee on 8 July. Receipts from the builders included an additional '£367. 13s. 5. being the cost of the Artificial Foundation'.[71] No explanation is minuted, but ten months later, at the fifth AGM held at 12 Waterloo Place, Croker told the membership that it was 'in consequence of the substratum of the ground appearing, on being opened, to consist of a shifting sand, with pits from which sand had been excavated'.[72] It was the 'absolutely unsafe' condition of the foundations of Carlton House that had justified its demolition, and the footprint of the clubhouse overlapped that of Carlton House. Although the problem had now been addressed by constructing an 'artificial foundation', Croker's enemies must have relished the thought that his house was built upon the sand.

Later in July 1828 the commissioners wrote to the USC, rebuking its committee and Nash for failing to make the agreed modifications, and to the Athenæum, thanking them for their forbearance and releasing them from the agreement of December 1826. This allowed the club to make significant enhancements. The commissioners immediately agreed to a request for the addition of a Panathenaic frieze, designed by John Henning junior, who started work in the autumn of 1828.[73] Jekyll's much quoted epigram, in which Croker is said to have given the members a frieze when they wanted an ice-house, has no basis in fact.[74] Like the balcony, the entrance portico and the large statue by Edward Hodges Baily based on the Pallas Athena of Velletri in the Louvre, the frieze was not only a beautiful addition to a building that would have been plain indeed, but also ensured that its lavishly porticoed neighbour cast no 'shade of inferiority' over it (Plate 9). Indeed, Nash's USC was described in the anonymous *London Interiors* (1841–44) as 'singularly plain, and unimposing'.[75] The supreme irony is that the late additions to the Athenæum's clubhouse were what Croker had much earlier described as 'mere decoration'.

Croker was ever the pragmatist and micromanager. As work proceeded on both the exterior and interior of the clubhouse, the architect consulted him personally on matters both great and small. Burton and the secretary, Magrath, called on him 'respecting the Balustrade & Balcony', for example, a matter that led to long-drawn-out discussions.[76] Burton designed many of the fittings, such as pendant light fixtures and even small items such as clock-cases; and much of the best furniture in the house is his, including massive library tables and more delicate desks, large and small armchairs, upholstered in dark green and much of it in use today.[77] *The Gentleman's Magazine* reported that 'the furniture of the whole is at once classical and elegant; the carpets are of the utmost beauty, and strength of fabric'.[78] As at 12 Waterloo Place, everything passed under Croker's critical eye, as well as those of Smirke and Lawrence.

In May 1829, Croker, as chairman, could report good progress with the building in his Annual Report, using terms which were reminiscent of Lord Aberdeen's Hellenist principles of 'reason', 'fitness' and 'propriety', adapted to 'the condition of modern society'.[79] The new house, Croker suggested, was 'suitable to the rank and the character of this Society'.[80] In order to match the enhanced USC, the Committee had agreed to additions to their clubhouse which 'could give sufficient dignity to the external appearance of their elevation', including the balustrade and cornice, and the frieze, which together cost £2,165. 1s. 10d. There had been 'no hesitation', however, in selecting the Panathenaic procession which formed the frieze of the Parthenon, as 'the most appropriate, as well as the most beautiful specimen of sculpture which could be adopted':

> To an edifice which borrows its name from Athens, intended for the reception of a Society professedly connected with Literature and the Fine Arts, they flatter themselves that the celebrated production of Athenian taste, restored, as it here is, to a degree of perfection in which it had never been seen in modern times, would not be inappropriate, and they were glad to have an opportunity of exhibiting such an admirable specimen of ancient

art in, as nearly as circumstances would permit, the position in which the original was employed.[81]

What Croker did not mention was the portico, the very feature that would later come to symbolise the club itself. On the morning of the AGM, Henry Crabb Robinson was told that the Committee had 'meant to have a neat portico of four columns – the one actually erected – but that Croker had arbitrarily changed the plan, and the foundations were then digging for a portico of two columns, not at all becoming so broad a space as the front comprises'.[82] When members gathered at one o'clock, with Croker in the chair, his report was read out and discussion invited. Dr John Henderson, presumably with the frieze in mind, reproached the committee for their 'lavish expenditure'.[83] This gave Robinson the perfect opportunity to tackle the chairman, whom he describes in his reminiscence as the 'officious manager and despot' of the club, 'according to common report'. Far from being lavish, Robinson argued, the Committee was making a false economy:

A mistaken desire to be economical had, I believed, betrayed them into an act which I thought the body of the proprietors would not approve, and on which I would take their opinion. I then began to state the point about the portico, when Mr. Croker interrupted me, saying I was under a great mistake – that there never was any intention to have any other portico than the one now preparing. This for a moment perplexed me, but I said, 'Of course the chairman meant that no other portico had been resolved on, which might well be. Individual men might be deterred by his opposition, but I knew,' raising my voice, 'that there were other designs, for I had seen them.' Then Mr. Croker requested me, as an act of politeness, to abstain from a motion which would be an affront to the Committee. This roused me, and I said that if any other gentleman would say he thought my motion an affront, I would not make it; but I meant otherwise. And then I added expressions which forced him to say that I had certainly expressed myself most handsomely, but it would be much better to leave the matter in the hands of the Committee. 'That,' I said, 'is the question which you will, in fact, by my motion, submit to the meeting.' There was then a cry of 'Move,

move,' and a very large number of hands were held up for the motion. So it passed by acclamation. I was thanked by the architect, and everybody was pleased with what I had done.[84]

In his three-volume selection from Robinson's diaries and reminiscences, Thomas Sadler omitted the damning words that follow this extract: 'A few days afterwards, seeing . . . one of the Committee, I said to him: "What could Mr. Croker mean by lying so?" He smiled: "You show your ignorance, Mr. Croker always lies." '[85] Nash was not alone in his deviousness, although it is impossible to ascertain how decisions over this particular matter had been made. There is, however, a letter from the commissioners on the subject, dated 21 April 1829, saying that they would be grateful if the Building Committee were to give instructions to the builders, who were ready to put up the portico, as soon as possible.[86] Scrawled on a corner of the letter in Burton's hand are the inscrutable words, 'Ap 23 Direct the Architect to proceed with the portico as originally designed'.

Stylistically, Burton had little choice but to follow the USC in the design of his entrance portico, although connoisseurs could see that he distanced himself from Nash's Roman emphasis by introducing a deeper entablature, in the manner of the Parthenon. This was complemented by the statue of Pallas Athena and the Panathenaic frieze, then uncoloured, above.[87] In 1858–59, Burton was to be retained by the USC to extend and augment their clubhouse. By enriching the Pall Mall front, altering the fenestration and adding a bold frieze, he sharpened the contrast between his beautiful and coolly Greek Athenæum, presided over by the goddess of wisdom, originally spearless,[88] and the assertively Roman USC, decorated with battle honours – Theodore Hook's 'mental' and 'regimental'.[89]

Meanwhile, in the summer of 1829, the pace was quickening. On 21 July, the General Committee, chaired by the 6th earl of Shaftesbury (Cropley Ashley-Cooper, father of the social reformer), ordered Magrath to write to the commissioners requesting them to 'grant the Lease of the House erected in Waterloo Place without delay'.[90] It was then reported that an agreement had been made with the Phoenix Fire Office for the loan of £16,000 at 4½ per cent, 'to be secured by a Mortgage on the Building to be repaid by Annual Instalments of £1000'. By 27 October, when the General Committee was chaired by Lord Farnborough, it was agreed that preparations for the move to the new clubhouse should be made by a sub-committee. Yet again Croker took charge, supported by Edward Hawkins, keeper of antiquities at the British Museum, and Richard Penn of the Colonial Office.[91] Having reviewed the 'Domestic Establishment', the 'duties of the Upper Servants and the management of the Accounts', they reported to the General Committee three weeks later. When salaries were compared with those of the USC, the Junior USC and the Union Club it was agreed that Magrath's £200 per annum should rise to £250 in the new club-house, increasing to £300 after five years.[92] The steward's £180 would be increased to £200 and the cook's £100 to £120. At the other end of the scale, a scullery maid would receive £12.

On their arrival at the new clubhouse to prepare for its opening in early February 1830, the non-resident staff would have first gone down long flights of back stairs into a labyrinth of vaulted basement offices, kitchens and storerooms, with exten-sive wine cellars the other side of an area and beneath Waterloo Place.[93] Members, on the other hand, passed through both sets of tall glazed double doors into the spacious hall, with the central grand staircase facing the entrance (Plate 10).[94] *London Interiors* recorded that the spectator was 'immediately struck by the classic taste, the refined feeling of the design': 'Once conceived, its clear and symmetrically defined outline never quits the mind; the plan, its arrangement, and accessories, impress and confirm the impression of unity, harmony, simplicity, proportion.'[95] Although today's members would agree with much of this state-ment, some of the most prominent 'accessories' are different from those of 1830 and the floor of the hall is a shiny modern addition.[96] A small sample of the orig-inal 'Venetian pavement' can be seen in the bag room, usually covered with pieces of luggage and hitherto unidentified: it is constructed of 'particles of marble set in hard cement, or scagliola resembling Sienna marble, rubbed down and polished'. The 'warm and carpeted effect' of this delicately coloured Venetian floor comple-mented the scagliola columns, imitating white marble, that support a Roman barrel-vaulted ceiling, richly coffered. The capitals of these columns were modelled on the Tower of the Winds, a famous structure from antiquity which was illus-trated in the first volume of *The Antiquities of Athens* (chapter III, plate III).[97]

The introduction of statues and the absence of pictures in the hall in the 1830s intensified the aura of academic classicism. In April 1832 William

Sotheby, one of the first members to be elected, donated a cast of Samson slaying the Philistines by John Graham Lough, who himself donated a Milo.[98] These were mounted on large plinths, but were later removed in order to accommodate a system of 'Warming and Ventilation'.[99] Burton's elegant treatment of the niches above the marble fireplaces, in which casts of Roman statues from the Louvre are displayed – on the east wall the 'Figure of Diana Dressing', as the supplier Peter Sarti described it, and on the west wall 'Ditto Venus Victorious' – is reminiscent of Carlton House and the house-museums of Hope and Soane.[100] (Sir Thomas Lawrence seems to have chosen these and other casts in the last months of his life.)[101] *London Interiors* reported that 'objections' had been made to the decoration of the hall and staircase: the walls were described as 'cold and naked, over which the eye wanders unexcited and unrelieved'.[102] The story of Alma-Tadema's opulent redecoration of the 1890s, and its jettisoning in 1956, with a partial return to something closer to the original scheme, must wait until later chapters.[103] In 1830, Burton's muted colours and syncretic classical references in the hall suited a space in which 'literary' Whig and Tory members of a non-partisan club mingled under the aegis of Athena / Minerva.[104] By 1841 the hall was said to be the club's 'EXCHANGE, the LOUNGE': 'Here the politicians, the men of literature, and those "about town" assemble. Often have we heard the hum of earnest debate, the laughter provoked by wit or sarcasm, mingled with the ebb and flow of topics afforded by the butterfly existence of a London season, arise in fitful gusts, and startle the more sober solemnity of the rooms we have described.'[105]

The main rooms adjacent to the hall – the morning room and the large coffee room – are both thought to have been 'equally straightforward' in their decorative schemes, originally executed in oil paint, with 'contrasting fawnish off-whites for the walls and ceiling'.[106] Ranged along the north (Pall Mall) side of the clubhouse were the morning room, where 'all the English and Foreign newspapers of any interest' were and still are supplied;[107] the writing room, also used as a 'Private Dinner Room' for parties and as a 'strangers' room', until three o'clock;[108] and the lavatories, with seats of Spanish mahogany,[109] which were later to feature in a number of myths and legends. Extending the whole length of the south side is the coffee room, which overlooks gardens. Appropriately, the south-eastern corner of this hospitable room sits above part of the footprint of the crimson

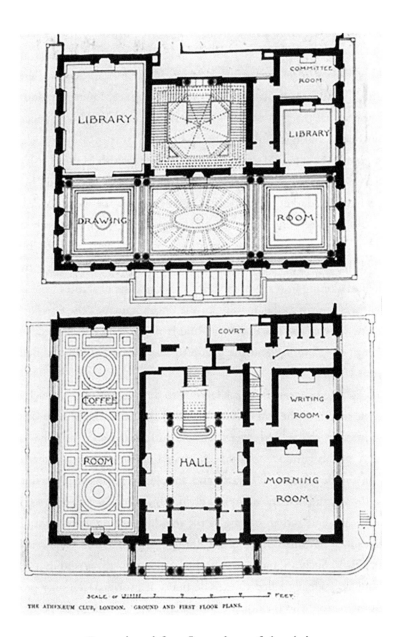

THE ATHENÆUM CLUB, LONDON. GROUND AND FIRST FLOOR PLANS.

*Ground and first floor plans of the club*

drawing room in the demolished Carlton House (Plate 5). The delicate plaster panelling on the walls was characteristic of the 1820s. Later generations wrongly assumed that these large panels defined spaces in which to hang pictures. As early as the 1830s a plan was afoot to hang paintings, 'the subjects of which should be drawn from memorable incidents in the lives of deceased members, who [had] eminently contributed to promote Science, Literature, and Art'.[110] Some hoped that the plan would not only be executed but also extended to the morning room, but mercifully it came to nothing.

Originally the splendid staircase, with its 'best spanish Mahogany hand rail' and classical detailing,[111] was naturally lit from a large skylight – an invitation upward from the darker hall under its Roman ceiling. The stairs divide beneath a large cast of the Apollo Belvedere by George Rennie RA, gratefully donated by Burton.[112] Installation of the Apollo was difficult: Sarti's bill for 'busts etc' included the sum of £3. 10s. 0d., 'For taken down [sic] & putting twice the Apollo and altering four times the leaf'.[113] More casts of statues were installed on what was known as the 'landing of the Great Staircase': the *Grecian Archer*, by Rennie, one of the first batch of Rule II members to be elected, in 1831, and *Eve at the Fountain* and the group of *Poetry and Painting* by Baily, who joined in 1830.[114]

Two doors give access from the landing to the drawing room, which extends the whole length of the east (Waterloo Place) side of the clubhouse. It was the 'grand, massive, chaste, and severely simple outline, the unity and the harmony of design' of this famous room that impressed *London Interiors*, rather than its detailing and decoration.[115] 'Chaste' and 'simple' were positive terms during the Greek Revival, and here the room was divided into three harmonious sections – a square at each end and an oblong in the middle – with a grand central dome, reminiscent of Burton's version of the Roman Pantheon at his Colosseum in the Regent's Park. Such a long room also had a practical advantage in a club that tried, but occasionally failed to exclude bores: it provided 'the only protection against the person who is eloquent upon affairs, either Foreign or Domestic, the member who sleeps and snores, the man descended from John de *Bore*ham, or the victim afflicted with the complaint called the "Grumbler"'.[116]

The development of the original decorative scheme for the drawing room can be traced by comparing Burton's coloured drawings of 1829 (Plate 11) – the only ones to survive – and James Holland's charming watercolour of *c.* 1836 (Plate 12). Burton's drawing labelled 'Athenæum', and endorsed as 'Approved by the Committee / E Magrath Secty – / 25 June 1829', shows scagliola pillars with capitals based on the Choragic Monument of Lysicrates, another familiar source which was illustrated in the first volume of *The Antiquities of Athens* (chapter IV, plate III). The larger Lysicrates pillars were adopted at the corner of each section of the room, but not the proposed shorter ones flanking the fireplaces and mirrors, where pilasters and capitals inspired by the temple of Apollo at Miletus were substituted.[117] The palmette, a decorative motif from antiquity beloved of late-Georgian architects, features throughout the room. Had Burton's proposed classical motifs above the windows and laurel wreaths in the intermediate spaces been adopted, the room would have continued the antiquarian theme of the hall and landing even more clearly. Although these classical features were dropped, however, possibly for financial reasons, the Building Committee again opted for sculptures rather than pictures, and for a unifying colour scheme, in this case fashionable puce.

Labelled the 'Library' by Burton in 1829, and described as the 'Great Room' by the General Committee as late as August 1848,[118] the drawing room as depicted by Holland contained taller bookcases than the architect had originally proposed, reflecting the fact that the club's collection of books and pamphlets was growing rapidly.[119] In 1833, Burton was asked to design these larger classical bookcases, which were topped with plaster busts of famous literary, scientific and artistic figures – a fitting pantheon for a British 'Athenæum'.[120] Three years earlier, when the club moved from 12 Waterloo Place, the whole collection could be housed in their new holy of holies, now known as the south library, which is accessible through glazed doors at the south end of the drawing room and via another door off the landing.[121] In 1832, Burton was asked to design a gallery on one side of the 'Library and Reading Room' to accommodate more books. This gallery was described in *London Interiors* as being 'of peculiar elegance' and 'constructed of mahogany, supported by ten bronze cantilevers'.[122] Characteristically, Burton ornamented the sixteen steps up to the gallery with 'elaborate scroll brackets of the same material'. Above the marble fireplace in the library was a space reserved for the large portrait of George IV on which Sir Thomas Lawrence was working at the time of his death, on 7 January 1830, and which was intended to be a gift to the club. His executors contested this, however, and it cost the club £115 to purchase the picture at a sale in June 1831.[123]

Through a door at the north end of the drawing room was the 'small library', known today as the north library: its densely packed bookshelves can be glimpsed in Holland's drawing. To the west of the small library was the committee room, now the west library. Beyond that room and above it (at a mezzanine level) were various offices and accommodation for servants. An inventory of rooms and their contents in the 1830s reveals the pecking order among the staff: the librarian's room and his bedroom (with a 'Four post bedstead'), the secretary's room (with six mahogany chairs and two 'sets of furniture') and his bedroom, the 'Old Newspaper Room', two men's bedrooms (with five iron bedsteads in each), the hall porters' bedroom (two iron bedsteads), man cook's bedroom (four poster), woman cook's bedroom (one iron bedstead), housekeeper's bedroom (four poster), kitchen maids' bedroom (four iron bedsteads), still room maids' bedroom (two iron bedsteads), housemaids' bedroom (five iron bedsteads) and their sitting room (six painted chairs).

Some of the staff were on hand to serve a group of leading members who gathered to dine there on Saturday 6 February 1830, six years after the inaugural meeting of the Committee in the Royal Society's rooms at Somerset House. Croker's old friend and colleague, Thomas Moore, wrote in his diary: 'dined at the Athenaeum – a grand dinner for the opening of the Club consisting of all those members that had belonged to Committees – Croker in the Chair, supported by Lords Lansdowne, Gower, Lowther & Bexley – Bishop of London, Agar Ellis &c. &c. to the amount of about thirty – sat next Chauntrey [sic]'.[124] Grand company, a grand setting and, presumably, food and wine to match – a combination which the club has tried to emulate on special occasions ever since. This bipartisan list of luminaries – Lansdowne, Gower, Agar-Ellis and Moore were Whigs – combines wealth, power, connoisseurship and creativity. Earl Gower is soon to be the richest man in Britain as the 2nd duke of Sutherland; the marquess of Lansdowne's house in Berkeley Square contains a superb collection of marbles purchased in Italy; Viscount Lowther, currently First Commissioner of Woods and Forests, Lord Bexley, who helped to found King's College London, Agar-Ellis, who campaigned for the creation of the National Gallery, and Croker are all FRSs; one of the most popular poets writing in English sits next to a sculptor who is to be knighted in five years' time.[125] In January 1830, Francis Chantrey described the club-house as a 'superb building' and looked forward to having a 'peep into the shop'.[126] He had heard that it was 'so fine' that statues and busts would be 'mere dirt'. What he thought on 6 February 1830 is not recorded.

Two days later the clubhouse was finally open to members. First impressions were positive: Sir Walter Scott's son, Charles, who worked at the Foreign Office, was not the only member to describe the house as a 'palace'.[127] The Athenæum was one of the 'gentlemen's clubs', of course, until a successful transition to mixed membership was made in the early twenty-first century.[128] In 1830 the admission of ladies simply to view the place was regarded as a special privilege. In an enthusiastic letter to his sister on the subject, dated 26 February, Charles Lyell throws light on ballot evenings and members' use of particular rooms:

> I wish you had been in town at the opening of our new club, the Athenæum, which is reckoned the most elegant turn-out of all, and for a fortnight gay soirées were given to the ladies between nine and twelve o'clock, and it still continues to do so every Wednesday, which I hear is to go on for months. It is really worth seeing, and fitted up in a style which I must say would be ridiculous, except for receiving ladies. There has been a great deal of fun about it, verses innumerable. Some of our members grumble at the invasion, and retreated into the library, which was respected at first, but now the women fill it every Wednesday evening, as well as the newspaper room, and seem to examine every corner with something of the curiosity with which we should like to pry into a harem. They all say it is good for bachelors, and makes married men keep away from home, and talk of a ladies' club, &c. As the house was much admired, the number of candidates increased prodigiously. The ballot, which in a smaller house was a nuisance, is now an agreeable muster.[129]

One of the misogynistic grumblers, probably a crusty bachelor, is worth quoting for his passing references to the learned peace which the female invasion disturbed:

We are now really in our new palace, and we throw open its gates every Wednesday evening to whomsoever, among your gentler sex, are disposed to enter. . . . I, who am a hermit in my own way, and by no means too inclined to sociality, must confess that I never felt a more melancholy pang than when, for the first time, I beheld, from the large chair in which I was 'quietly inurned,' a party of invading Amazons, with bare necks and yellow gowns, sweep across the chamber I had hoped would have been for ever sacred to frock coats and the modest virtue of cravats . . . true, that Wednesday is only one day in the week, but, then, that one day unsettles us for the six others . . . Besides, what mischief to the *tone* of our society! Instead of the learned silence hitherto breathing around, or the murmurs of scientific discussion or literary dispute, we hear the *suaves susurri* of 'Last night – charming woman – beautiful eyes – good bust – pretty ankle!'[130]

According to the Revd Waugh, however, these 'reunions' were 'highly appreciated by others'.

By February 1830 the USC clubhouse across the square had been open for sixteen months, and Nash's grand Carlton House Terrace was under construction. In March the General Committee was presented with a petition to the House of Commons regarding an opening from Waterloo Place to St James's Park, with a request that it be placed on the morning room table for signature.[131] This was agreed, but only as a special case, as the matter was considered to be of 'immediate and local interest'. A lithograph of the scheme shows a roadway sloping down between Nash's terraces to an ironwork screen at the level of the park. This arrangement, which was not adopted by the government, would have allowed carriages to pass through and thus alleviate the dreadful traffic jams in Charing Cross.

Instead, only pedestrian access to the Mall was provided via a handsome set of steps, at the top of which was a flat area large enough to accommodate the base of a column of Scottish granite, 124 feet high, designed by Benjamin Dean Wyatt. This was erected by public subscription, to be surmounted by a bronze statue of Frederick, duke of York – the second son of George III and a member of the club, who had died in 1827 – by an original member, Sir Richard Westmacott.[132] The General Committee was consulted by the managing committee of the project on

22 March 1831. Lord Farnborough, an authority on such matters, sent his apologies, adding that 'he did not apprehend there could be any objection on their part having understood the other inhabitants of Carlton Gardens had consented'.[133] The Committee acquiesced. At 12 Waterloo Place, members had watched their new house rising to the south. Between April 1831 and April 1834, their new southerly outlook was dominated by the scaffolding surrounding this monument – a constant reminder that their clubhouse was built on the site of a royal palace and that theirs was a Crown lease.

The clubhouse had been designed and built in the reign of George IV, who died on 26 June 1830. The king was dead, long live the king! Exuberant expressions of the club's loyalty to William IV proved to be costly, however. The contractors had to be called in to 'secure the Ballustrade in consequence of the Accident by which a part was destroyed by the Crowd at the proclamation of the King' on 28 June.[134] On 3 August, Decimus Burton was asked to 'take measures with Mr Edge for illuminating the House at the approaching Birth Day of the King', on the 21st, at 'an expence not exceeding Ten Pounds exclusive of the Frame Works'.[135] A week later the General Committee received a letter from Mr W. Smith, 'requesting to be employed to illuminate the house on the Birth day of the Queen on the 13 Instant'.[136] A design was also submitted from Mr Edge to 'illuminate with Gas at an expence of £25 which was approved and ordered to be executed provided it can be ascertained to be the intention of the USC to light on that night'. Burton reported that the frameworks for Arthur's Club and the USC cost £112 and £150 respectively, and that work on the Athenæum was in hand. The General Committee clearly wished to hold its own with other clubs, and on 17 August ordered that 'the letters for the King's birthday be 'WR'.[137]

The year 1830, one of revolutions on the Continent, marked a turning-point for both the nation, with its new monarch, and the Athenæum, with its new clubhouse. In both cases the old guard was changing. The Iron Duke's opposition to reform brought to an end two decades of Tory hegemony, when Earl Grey became prime minister on 22 November. Croker's long rule at the Admiralty ended, and he turned his formidable energies to attacking the Reform Bill in opposition; he also proposed 'Conservative' as the new name for the Tory party. Some of his most influential colleagues on the founding

Committee had already died: Sir Humphry Davy and Dr Thomas Young in 1829, and Sir Thomas Lawrence the following January. Although Croker now attended far fewer committee meetings, he remained a trustee and ensured that the club's founding principles were followed in the 1830s, a period of rapid political change and technological development, during which the Athenæum flourished, with an ever lengthening waiting list and an expanded membership, which included many of the brightest talents in science, literature and the arts.

# Part II
# VICTORIAN GRANDEUR
## (1830–90)

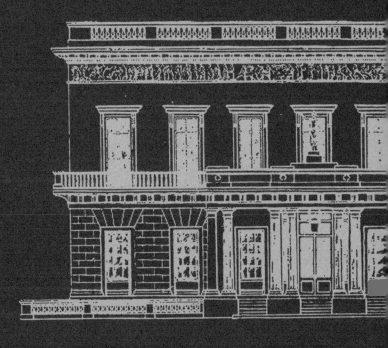

# 4

## 'THE MOST EMINENT PERSONS IN THE LAND'

Thomas Walker, police magistrate and author, considered the 'present system of clubs' to be 'one of the greatest and most important modern changes in society'.[1] His comments on his own club were no less fulsome. Among the 1,200 members of the Athenæum, he believed, 'are to be reckoned a large proportion of the most eminent persons in the land in every line, civil, military, and ecclesiastical, peers spiritual and temporal, commoners, men of the learned professions, those connected with science, the arts, and commerce in all its principal branches, as well as the distinguished who do not belong to any particular class'. Eminence 'in every line' might seem improbable, but a similar point was made eight decades later by a non-member, Thomas Escott, who stated that the Athenæum 'numbers from time to time as many famous soldiers and sailors as its nearest Pall Mall neighbour' (the United Service Club), is 'as well supplied with ambassadors as the Travellers' and with the 'makers and unmakers of administrations' as Brooks's or White's, the Carlton or the Reform, and through the nineteenth century was 'the only London home of his spiritual lordship, Samuel Wilberforce'.[2]

These claims will be tested in Part II, covering the years from 1830 to 1890, a timespan defined by the contours of British political and cultural history. By 1890, the year in which the club happened to change its administrative structure and refurbish its clubhouse, the Athenæum had achieved worldwide fame and was often invoked as the archetypal gentleman's club, the subject of Walter Wilson's *Ballot Day 1892*, discussed in the Prologue, and of the Revd Francis Waugh's short history, where he proudly announced some remarkable figures:

120 members were represented in the National Portrait Gallery, 67 were buried in Westminster Abbey and 25 in St Paul's.[3] In this chapter, which takes the story of the membership to 1860, we will consider how, as numbers increased to 1,200, the standard of new entrants, far from falling off, actually rose, not only as a result of fresh interest in a new clubhouse, but also through a series of interventions by the General Committee. By examining the special elections held by the committee in 1830 and 1838, and the introduction of 'Rule II' membership in 1830, we can see how the club defined itself for an elite on the cusp of the Victorian era, when political economists, scientists and explorers were creating an intellectual environment imbued with what Edward Bulwer Lytton described as 'the spirit of examination and questioning'.[4]

At the first AGM to be held in the new clubhouse, on 10 May 1830, it was fitting that Croker should take the chair, and that the General Committee's report should begin with its congratulations to 'the Club at large on having a Residence not inferior in beauty and convenience to that of any other Society'.[5] There was a cost, however, and the Committee earnestly appealed to the membership to tackle a debt of £3,612 (on top of mortgage repayments), either by levying a contribution from each member or by increasing the membership by 200, as previously recommended. Although the Committee made this proposition 'chiefly as a financial arrangement', they felt 'bound to state it as their opinion, that if this addition were to be made with more particular reference to the original objects of this institution, by the selection of *persons eminent in Science, Literature, or the Arts*, it would be highly advantageous to the general interests and credit of the Society'. The voice of Croker, ever vigilant in defence of the club's founding principles, is unmistakeable.

The members, always resistant to proposed levies or increases in subscriptions, agreed to the Committee's proposal, as they had done previously in 1824, when they moved into 12 Waterloo Place. But how to implement it? Rather than leaving half the elections to the General Committee, the membership preferred to create a special committee for the purpose. A second General Meeting, convened a fortnight later, ratified the proposal that '100 of the said members be selected by a Committee', and that 'the other 100 be elected by printed Lists' by the general membership.[6] The Irish poet Thomas Moore recorded in his journal that members of the selection committee were 'so

chosen as to represent different classes': 'for instance, the representative of the
Peerage is Lord Farnborough – of the Commons, Croker – of the Clergy, the
Bishop of Llandaff [Copleston], – of the Law, *Chief Justice* Park – of the Army
& Navy, Napier – of the arts, Chantrey, of Science, Davies Gilbert & Professor
Sedgwick – of General Literature, Thomas Moore, and so on'.[7] (Croker came
a lowly eighth in the ballot.)

Forty years later, Sir Henry Holland, the physician and travel writer, could
safely publish an account of the committee's confidential work.[8] They were to
'select, by unanimity of vote, one hundred out of the many hundred candidates on the books, to be immediately admitted as members'.[9] Achieving
unanimity, he went on, proved to be 'laborious, litigious and encumbered with
much correspondence'. Inevitably, Croker took the chair, and his 'astute but
despotic energy, well known to all who knew the man, was shown in the way
in which he carried the selection of any person for whom he was interested',
although in one case he failed. The admission of another person of 'some
public note' was so strongly contested that Holland received letters from four
cabinet ministers canvassing him warmly. The candidate was elected.

As soon as Thomas Moore was chosen for the selection committee he
received thirty letters from 'canvassers for the Club', one of them for a candidate
whose claim was based on having written about the Siamese twins.[10] Moore's
journal entry for Saturday 12 June 1830 is particularly revealing: 'Meeting of
Committee – got through our business – had resolved to stand by Ellis in his
general veto, in case the Bishop opposed Barnes – but all was right & unanimous.'[11] Since becoming editor of *The Times* in 1817, Thomas Barnes had
transformed it into the campaigning newspaper that in 1831 would encourage
its readers to 'thunder' for parliamentary reform. In October 1831, all but two
of the bishops were to vote against the Reform Bill in the Lords. Agar-Ellis's
'general veto' may have been against blackballing on political grounds – Edward
Copleston, Bishop of Llandaff, was a comparatively liberal Tory who strongly
opposed the Reform Bill – or possibly on the basis of candidates' private lives:
Barnes lived with a common-law wife.

Moore then refers to Colonel (later Sir) William Napier, hero and historian
of the Peninsular War: 'Napier protested against Theodore Hook, which, though
quite right, I rather regretted, on account of our Chairman Croker, who had set

his heart on getting the fellow in, and was himself most conceding & accommo-dating to the wishes of every body.' The facetious Hook was a man of letters, practical joker (he was behind the famous Berners Street hoax of 1809), debtor (he was imprisoned in the 1820s), and another common-law husband. He was supported by Scott and Croker in his literary career and was loathed by Macaulay, Croker's arch-enemy. As one of Croker's oldest friends, Moore was concerned for the chairman's feelings rather than those of the candidate, who was also a friend. There was a constant struggle between personal loyalties and objective standards in the election process. 'I could not indeed have anticipated', Moore concluded, 'that 13 men should have got on together, at once so conscientiously & smoothly, & our list tells well, I think, for the conscientious part of the business – George Villiers even withdrew his brother (whom we were all willing, for *his* sake, to elect) saying that his claims by no means came up to the point at which we had fixed our standard'. Moore 'left them nearly finished at a quarter before 7'.

Once the committee's list was settled, the general membership elected a further 100, and by 13 July the process was completed: 200 new members – technically 'supernumerary' – had been chosen from about 1,100 names in the Candidates Book.[12] As Holland pointed out, 'the distinction between the two modes of admission was keenly appreciated; and the eager struggle to be among the *select*, curiously illustrated a common form of human foible'.[13] There had been a rush to the Candidates Book, with members of the General Committee and of the selection committee prominent among the proposers and seconders of promising candidates, with the result that 44 of the 102 whom they finally elected were entered in the book between 24 May 1830 and the deadline of 1 June.[14] The 'select' 102 included luminaries such as Isambard Kingdom Brunel, Macaulay, John Stuart Mill, Edwin Landseer and Lord Ashley (later the philanthropic 7th earl of Shaftesbury). But then there were also outstanding individuals among the second group, such as Charles Austin, the brilliant lawyer who made a fortune during the railway mania, Charles Buller, the popular barrister and reforming MP, Sir Francis Goldsmid, another barrister and later a QC and MP, and Sir Moses Montefiore, the philanthropist and President of the Board of Deputies.

The second group also included two well-known raconteurs: Charles Cavendish Greville, Clerk of the Council in Ordinary since 1821 and famous for his published diaries (in which conversations at the Athenæum are unrecorded), and Theodore Hook (earlier turned down by the committee) who was to be an habitué of the clubhouse.[15] Indeed, Hook became a kind of club mascot, entertaining members and staff with his witticisms as he dined with friends, including Thomas Moore and Abraham Hayward, at his favourite table in the north-east corner of the coffee room.[16] This became known as 'Temperance Corner', as in order to avoid scandal he invented innocuous code names for the strong drinks that he ordered from the waiters in large quantities. It was easier for a colourful and controversial figure like Hook to be elected through the members' ballot than by a unanimous vote in the selection committee.

In 1836 Hook recorded that it was the 'custom with certain of the present Ministers' to have 'house-dinners' at the Athenæum – hosted affairs in the private dining room – each Wednesday.[17] It is in the political arena that the list of 200 supernumerary members proves to be most revealing. Top of the national agenda between July 1830 and June 1832 was the 'perilous question' of Reform.[18] Among the new members elected to the non-partisan club in the summer of 1830 were a number of Whigs who were to play a part in the ensuing struggle for reform: Macaulay (the *wunderkind* MP, poet and historian), Buller (a genial Radical) and 'Honest Jack' Althorp (Viscount Althorp, leader of the Whigs in the Commons and Chancellor of the Exchequer), whose name had been placed in the Candidates Book only a week before the deadline, and whose seconder was none other than Croker, one of his main political opponents. Althorp was one of the Committee of Four, who met in secret in 1830 to frame the Reform Bill. Two of the others were already members of the club: Lord Durham ('Radical Jack' Lambton, subsequently the originator of the Reform Club)[19] and Lord John Russell, who introduced the bill in the Commons.[20] Among the new Tory Athenians of 1830 were George Spencer-Churchill, marquess of Blandford, an Ultra Tory who was pro-Reform for his own reasons,[21] and Lord Wharncliffe, later a trustee, who in effect led the opposition to the second Reform Bill in the Lords in 1831, but then became a 'waverer'. They joined a club which included among its Tory members Croker, who locked horns with Viscount Althorp in the Commons,[22] Sir Robert Peel, the duke of Wellington, Viscount Mahon (later Earl Stanhope) and Henry Phillpotts, Bishop of Exeter, who was burnt in effigy in Exeter on 5 November 1831, shortly after the devastating Bristol riots.

Outside the clubhouse there was widespread hardship and political agita-tion among the 'labouring classes', sometimes breaking out into riots. Following the dissolution of parliament in April 1831, the Lord Mayor circulated hand-bills inviting citizens to illuminate their houses, thus endangering those that remained dark. Apsley House was attacked, with the Iron Duke's dead wife Kitty still lying inside, and forty-seven of the Athenæum's panes of glass were smashed by a mob.[23] Inside the clubhouse the perilous question was weighed cerebrally, through the reading and writing of pamphlets. Of the more than one hundred pamphlets on the subject of reform published between 1830 and 1832, and still in the club's library, at least seventeen were written by members, including Blandford and Buller; Henry Pelham, duke of Newcastle (an Ultra Tory); George 'Pamphlet' Scrope (a Whig geologist and social reformer); and George Grote (Radical MP, banker and historian of Greece). Many pamphlets on this inflammatory topic were anonymous or pseudonymous, as authors wished to protect themselves from verbal or physical attack, or to avoid diffi-culties with professional superiors. We shall never know how many members published as 'Country Clergyman', 'Whig Commoner', 'Barrister', 'Junius' or 'One of the Old School'. We can, however, be sure that this group of pamphlets engaged the interest of a wide range of members, some of whom were leading protagonists inside and outside parliament.

When the third Reform Bill was finally passed, the General Committee addressed the ticklish question of how 'the Club at large' was to respond. On 5 June 1832, two days before the bill received the Royal Assent, they ordered that, 'in case of an illumination being called for', the clubhouse was to be lit with 'Candles in the lower Windows and Flambeaux on the Balcony'.[24] Candles were lit throughout London, and darkened windows might have invited further atten-tion from those celebrating outside. Flambeaux, however, were expensive and more exuberantly celebratory: they were used by the club to mark major royal events.[25] On this occasion they must have been the subject of debate within the Committee, as at the next weekly meeting the minutes were approved, subject to a single alteration being made: 'That White Lamps be substituted for Flambeaux on the Balcony'.[26] The Athenæum could not, or would not be seen to exult.

In the cramped old Houses of Parliament, the 'great heat, the crowd, and the prolonged attention' were 'very fatiguing' for Tory and Whig parliamentarians alike, and some of those who belonged to the Athenæum would escape to the clubhouse.[27] The duke of Newcastle was later to describe the south library as a haven for those in high political office.[28] The long drawing room and private dining room facilitated private discussions, out of earshot and, ostensibly, off the record. The club's non-political status, established in 1824, was reinforced in subsequent decades, thus setting it apart from much of Clubland. In May 1848, only a few weeks after the great Chartist meeting on Kennington Common, the General Committee decided not to subscribe to House of Commons dispatches, as the cost would be prohibitive for a facility which few members were likely to use.[29] Magrath, the club's secretary, who had visited the Commons and several clubs in order to research the matter, reported that the Union, the United University, the United Service, the Junior United Service, the Travellers, the Reform, the Carlton and the Conservative Club each paid between £27 and £50 to receive dispatches several times per evening – eight times at the Carlton. For politicians, the neutrality of the Athenæum as a 'literary' club added to its attraction.[30]

Ralph Waldo Emerson, a distinguished outsider, gave a first-hand account of club life on his election to honorary membership, under Rule XIII, in 1848.[31] He focused upon two MPs, Macaulay and Emerson's friend and supporter, Richard Monckton Milnes, poet and Tory politician. Milnes had visited France to witness the revolution and had been satirised in Mr Punch's 'Dream of the future' as Citizen Monckton Milnes.[32] Emerson wrote home to his wife:

> I was honoured with an election into the Athenæum Club 'during my temporary residence in England,' a privilege one must prize, not because only ten foreigners are eligible at any one time, but because it gives all the rights of a member in a magnificent library, reading-room, a home to sit in & see the best company, and a coffee room, if you like it, where you eat at cost. Milnes & other good men are always to be found there. Milnes is the most goodnatured man in England, made of sugar; he is everywhere & knows every thing; his speeches in the house of Commons are always unlucky, & a signal for emptying the house, a topic of great mirth to himself & all his friends. He is so entirely at home everywhere, & takes all so quietly that Sidney [sic] Smith called him 'the cool of the evening.' They address

him now as 'Citoyen Milnes,' since Punch's, that is Thackeray's, late list of
the Ministry . . . Macaulay is the king of diners-out. I do not know when I
have seen such wonderful vivacity. He has the strength of ten men; immense
memory, fun, fire, learning, politics manners, & pride, – talks all the time
in a steady torrent. You would say, he was the best type of England. Yet, I
am told, & it was pathetic to hear; that this most fashionable orator, scholar,
poet, statesman, gentleman, is, in some companies of highest fashion, voted
a bore. Sidney Smith [sic], you know, said 'he (Macaulay) had improved, he
has flashes of silence.' Hallam is quiet & affable & courteous.[33]

The exchanges overheard by Emerson are characterised by affable banter and
good 'politics manners'.

About 10 per cent of the original members of the Athenæum were MPs,
more than the number in several of the smaller political clubs combined,[34] and
in the club's first Annual Report (1825), Croker added 'Political characters' to
his categories of the 'most distinguished'.[35] The decline in the number of MPs
from over 100 to 78 by 1838 can be explained partly by the redistribution of
seats at the first general election after the passing of the Reform Act, and partly
by the availability very nearby of Barry's Reform Club, founded in 1836 (Plate
13).[36] Nevertheless, the Athenæum's staffing levels were adjusted in accordance
with the parliamentary year. George John Shaw Lefevre, an eminent barrister
and Whig politician, was another of the new supernumerary members of 1830.
He was soon elected to the General Committee, where he presided over a
meeting in 1831 at which it was ordered that the steward 'be allowed an Extra
Man to carry up the Dinners and an Extra Waiter, both to be discharged at the
end of the Session of Parliament'.[37] Similarly, extra evening papers were ordered
while parliament was sitting, cleaning and repairs were carried out during the
summer recess, and by the 1860s meetings of the General Committee were
suspended for a few weeks during recesses.[38]

Cabinet ministers, like judges and bishops, were invited to join the club
without ballot under Rule XII, and many accepted. Eleven of the fifteen 'political characters' portrayed by John Gilbert in a painting entitled *The Aberdeen
Cabinet deciding on the Expedition to the Crimea* (1854; Plate 14) were members
of the Athenæum: Lord Aberdeen (Byron's 'travell'd thane'), Charles Wood, Sir

William Molesworth, the duke of Argyll, Lord Clarendon, Lord Lansdowne, Lord John Russell, Lord Granville, Lord Palmerston, Sir George Grey and the duke of Newcastle, who spent a 'great deal' of time in the clubhouse, 'constantly dining there'.[39]

Leaks were a serious problem for this coalition. According to George Douglas, 8th duke of Argyll, Molesworth was well named:

> Our Cabinet at that time was rather leaky. Things got out, we did not quite know how, and reports, not very correct, were circulated as to the part taken by individual members. . . . Molesworth had a habit of taking down in a pocket-book notes of what passed in Cabinet discussions. . . . If the note-books were accessible to anyone, their contents may have reached the ears of Charles Villiers, of Kinglake, and of Hayward, through whom they would have a wide circulation in the press and in the clubs of London. This I believe to have been the source of a great deal of the small-talk, full of misrepresentation, which was embalmed in the history of the Crimean War, which we owe to the clever but not very scrupulous pen of the author of 'Eothen'.[40]

The evidence points to the Athenæum as the prime suspect among the clubs referred to here. Molesworth was the only Radical member of the cabinet: early in his career his acquaintances included Buller, Grote and James and John Stuart Mill, all members of the Athenæum, to which he was elected in 1853. Argyll was elected the same year, as was the Whig barrister and MP Alexander Kinglake, best known for *Eothen* (1844), a lively account of travels in the East, and his *Invasion of the Crimea* in eight volumes (1863–87). The Hon. Charles Pelham Villiers, brother of the earl of Clarendon, had been a member since 1825: he was an MP for sixty-three years and a member of the club for seventy-three. On the death of Theodore Hook in 1841, Abraham Hayward QC, reviewer, leader-writer and advisor to cabinet ministers, had inherited his famous table in the coffee room, soon renamed 'Abraham's Bosom', and developed his own coterie, known as 'the Society'.[41]

The duke of Argyll's memoirs also provide an example of the kind of chance encounter with fellow members that is characteristic of club life. During the Crimean War he set off for a cabinet meeting:

I walked down to it, as I often did, from the Athenæum Club, and on my way I recognised the square form and sturdy step of Palmerston approaching the top of the steps leading down from the Duke of York's column. Hastening my own pace, I soon overtook him, just as he had crossed the Mall and was walking down the Esplanade. Putting my arm under his, and joining his walk, I said: 'Well, Lord Palmerston, I feel sure we have done the right thing in ordering an attack upon Sebastopol . . . and yet I cannot help feeling a little nervous about it . . .' On which Palmerston replied in his most cheery and jaunty tones: 'Oh, you need not be in the least anxious. With our combined fleet and our combined armies we are certain to succeed.'[42]

Many of the diplomats who were either appointed by Palmerston, or had to deal with him over a long political career, were also members of the Athenæum, including Sir Woodbine Parish, chargé d'affaires at Buenos Aires, Sir John Bowring, the fourth governor of Hong Kong, and Sir Harry Parkes, a controversial figure in the Second Opium War.

When Palmerston lost the general election of 1858, Richard Cobden celebrated what he hoped would be the demise of the Liberal Party by resigning from the Reform Club, the very name of which he considered to be a 'swindle', and joining the Athenæum.[43] Cobden was elected under what came to be known as 'Rule II', a means of electing particularly distinguished members which had been established in 1830. Having raised the question of adding 200 supernumerary members, the Annual Report of that year went on to argue that the club's founding principles could best be preserved by introducing 'a certain number of persons of distinguished eminence in Science Literature or the Arts' each year.[44] Rule II members would be fast-tracked into the club, rather than waiting for a decade and a half to be entered in the ballot. Here was another opportunity for the Committee to enhance the club's standing. The new rule would also enable them to bring in individuals who could be useful, and at short notice.[45] The limited scope, however, of Rule II – no more than nine candidates could be elected each year – reflected the membership's unwillingness to allow the General Committee to control the election of new candidates, as it had done in 1824–25. Members of the Committee served for only three years, apart from the five trustees, one of whom was Croker.

A quorum of nine members of the Committee was necessary when Rule II proposals were considered, and a trustee took the chair.[46] The names of the first successful candidates, who had to be elected unanimously, were listed in the Annual Report presented to the 1831 AGM, chaired by Martin Archer Shee, president of the Royal Academy:

> H.W. Pickersgill, Esq. R.A.; the Rev. Dr. Maltby, Reader to Lincoln's Inn; Dr. Christie, author of several valuable works, and now engaged in the prosecution of an overland journey to India, with the view of making a series of observations on Geological Phenomena, under the patronage of the President and Council of the Geological Society; Sharon Turner, Esq., author of the History of the Anglo-Saxons, and of other works; the Right Hon. Sir George Murray, G.C.B., late Quarter-Master-General to His Majesty's Forces; and George Rennie, Esq., Sculptor.[47]

The list provides useful clues to some of the club's priorities and predilections.

Pickersgill, the portrait painter, and Rennie, whose most widely known sculpture, *The Archer*, was on the landing of the grand staircase of the Athenæum, represented the arts. Only one other sculptor, John Foley, was elected under Rule II before 1860. Painters were much more successful: not only did they have a higher public profile, as their exhibited works were widely reviewed, but successive presidents of the Royal Academy, and thus influential trustees of the Athenæum, *ex officio* – Martin Shee, Charles Eastlake and Francis Grant – were all painters themselves. The club's Establishment leanings are reflected in the choice of artists who received royal commissions or portrayed monarchs: *The Opening of the New London Bridge* was commissioned by William IV in 1832, the year of Clarkson Stanfield's election; Francis Grant, elected in 1853, had painted several portraits of Queen Victoria; and William Frith's *Ramsgate Sands* (1854) was purchased by her five years before his election. Several of the other artists of the period elected under Rule II were household names: John Martin (1833), Daniel Maclise (1841), David Roberts (1845), John Rogers Herbert (1849), Richard Redgrave (1854), John Frederick Lewis (1856) and George

Richmond (1856), whose sitters included Athenians such as Faraday, Hallam, Macaulay, Lyell, Ruskin and Lord Lyndhurst. Three of these Rule II painters went on to serve on the General Committee, as did the architect Charles Barry, elected in 1836.

The election of John Ruskin, the most celebrated art critic of the day, illustrates the process through which a Rule II candidate passed. A first attempt to admit him by this means proved to be unsuccessful, in January 1847.[48] His proposer was the Dean of Westminster, Dr Buckland, an original member of the club and Ruskin's former tutor at Christ Church, famed for his private ambition to consume the entire bestiary. In the public realm he had been Oxford's first Reader in Geology and in London the founding president of the Geological Society, of which Ruskin had been a fellow since 1840. In a club in which there was a large contingent of distinguished scientists, including Lyell, who was present when Ruskin was discussed, Buckland would have regarded Ruskin as a promising geologist, as well as a brilliant young art critic: Ruskin's early notebooks are crammed with geological observations. Two years later, on 23 January 1849, Ruskin's name was placed in the Candidates Book by a prominent and popular member of the club, Canon Henry Hart Milman, Rector of St Margaret's Westminster, and soon to be Dean of St Paul's.[49] Ruskin, author of 'a very distinguished work on Modern Painters', was due to be considered as a Rule II candidate that day, and although Buckland, his proposer, was absent, Milman was present at the General Committee meeting.[50] It was decided, however, to postpone discussion of the eleven candidates until the next weekly meeting, which Buckland attended. Ruskin was not elected then, nor at meetings in February and early March: only thirty years of age, he was already a controversial figure. But then, on 27 March, when Buckland was present and Viscount Mahon, president of the Society of Antiquaries, was in the chair, John Ruskin, 'private gentleman', was unanimously elected to membership of the club 'under the 2nd rule'.[51] Although it is true that 'key figures were co-opted as soon as their celebrity demanded it' by means of Rule II,[52] the process itself could take two or more years.[53] Ruskin used the clubhouse, the classical design of which he always disparaged in print, and donated copies of his books to the library; but he was too shy to change for dinner there in the evenings, in case the servants did not recognise him.

As well as bringing in younger men of great potential, successive General Committees had a happy knack of anticipating preferments or promotions in their choices of older candidates under Rule II, as in the case of the Revd Dr Edward Maltby, 'Reader to Lincoln's Inn', elected in April 1831. A fine scholar and a liberal Churchman, born in 1770, Maltby was to become Bishop of Chichester in September 1831, and thus the only Whig on the bench of bishops at a crucial point in Earl Grey's struggle for Reform; he was eventually Bishop of Durham. Other clerics elected under Rule II included the legendary Sydney Smith (1832), Canon of St Paul's, whose correspondence after his election reveals friendships that were possibly made or renewed in the clubhouse;[54] Richard Chenevix Trench (1858), poet, philologist and Dean of Westminster, later Archbishop of Dublin; and Charles Vaughan (1857), New Testament scholar and headmaster of Harrow School. In terms of preferment, however, the club backed a loser in Vaughan, whose sudden resignation from Harrow in 1859 and later withdrawal of his acceptance of the see of Rochester may have been precipitated by the threat of his affair with a boy at the school being exposed: the evidence, which is ambiguous, was suppressed until 1964.[55] Within the club he was regarded sufficiently highly to figure in *Ballot Day 1892*.[56]

These clergymen joined bishops of the Established Church who had also been invited into the club without being balloted, under Rule XII. John Bird Sumner, who became Archbishop of Canterbury in 1848, was an original member. His successors, Charles Longley and Archibald Tait, also joined before their translation to Canterbury, in 1857 and 1856 respectively. Like bishops Phillpotts of Exeter, Shuttleworth of Chichester, Wilberforce of Oxford and Wordsworth of Lincoln, the archbishops held varying ecclesiastical and doctrinal positions, in a period that witnessed fierce controversies over matters relating to Church politics and to new scientific approaches to scripture and the creation. All the clerical members could be accommodated in the Athenæum, under the aegis of a pagan goddess, because their shared classical education and the range of their interests and attainments offered scope for 'association' which avoided confrontation. Several senior clergy also became involved in the governance of the club. In the mid-1850s, for example, many meetings of the General Committee were chaired by the Dean of St Paul's (Milman) or the Bishop of Oxford (Wilberforce), the latter also chairing the AGM in May 1857.[57]

The first scientist to be elected under Rule II, at the same meeting as Pickersgill and Maltby, was virtually bound to be a geologist, in a club which included Murchison, Sabine, Buckland, Lyell and Whewell among its members, and which chose the Revd Adam Sedgwick as one of the two scientists to sit on the supernumeraries committee in 1830.[58] The wordy description of Dr Christie, however, in the Annual Report of 1831, only underlines his obscurity; and Humphry Ward, who filled more than half of his 1926 history of the club with potted biographies of Rule II members, could offer no details on him. This was because he died in 1832. Another young man with great potential (he was born in 1801), Alexander Turnbull Christie wrote a treatise on epidemic cholera, served as an assistant surgeon for the East India Company in Madras and sailed back to Scotland in 1828, where he developed his interest in geology and meteorology.[59] He was appointed as a geological surveyor by the government of Madras, to which he returned in 1831 with the support of the great scientific polymath, Baron Alexander von Humboldt, who was a foreign member of the Geological Society.[60] Christie, a 'compound character', was characteristically Athenian in engaging in three areas: science, medicine and empire.

In an age of the gentleman amateur expert, when several of the most senior members of the Geological Society were clergy, geology was the most controversial of the sciences, with the highest public profile. Among the rich crop of Rule II members chosen by the General Committee in 1840 – the year of Robert Stephenson and Samuel Wilberforce – was Gideon Mantell, 'Author of various works on Geology, Founder of a large collection of Fossils recently purchased by the British Museum, and well known as the discoverer of the Iguanodon and Hylœosaurus'.[61] Mantell's descriptive catalogue of the 'objects of geology' in his Brighton museum contains epigraphs from the writings of the late Sir Humphry Davy, the first chairman of the club ('If we look with wonder upon the great remains of human works . . .') and from the future Archbishop Sumner's study *On the Records of the Creation, and on the Moral Attributes of the Creator* (1833), which aimed to prove the 'unreasonableness of supposing that geological discoveries are hostile to the Mosaic account of the creation'.[62] The ability of the Athenæum to accommodate professional antagonists is exemplified by the inclusion of the highly competitive Richard Owen in the same group of Rule II members as Mantell. Described in 1831 as the Hunterian Professor at the Royal College of Surgeons, and 'at present engaged by the British Association to draw up a Memoir on Fossil Reptiles', Owen was feared by many of his fellow scientists. Following Mantell's death in 1852 from an overdose of opium – he was suffering from scoliosis following a terrible accident – Owen stored part of his spine at the Royal College; and it was Owen rather than Mantell who was then available to advise Benjamin Waterhouse on his much visited sculptures of the Crystal Palace Dinosaurs at Sydenham.

As Bulwer Lytton pointed out in 1833, the 'cultivation of science' was not a profession in England.[63] The 'higher departments of science', he argued, 'are pursued by a few who possess independent fortune, by a few more who hope to make a moderate addition to an income itself but moderate, arising from a small private fortune, and by a few who occupy the very small number of official situations, dedicated to the abstract sciences; such are the chairs at our universities'. Lytton could have named examples of all three types at his club. Having suggested ways of improving the situation, he then turned upon Davies Gilbert, president of the Royal Society, a trustee, *ex officio*, at the Athenæum, and the second member responsible for science on its supernumeraries committee. A man of 'respectable endowments' and of 'large fortune', he was 'as a child' in science. The Royal Society, Lytton added in a footnote, was 'the mimic of a fashionable club'.[64]

So much for Davy's dream of professionalising the Royal Society.[65] His aspirations for the Athenæum, however, as a place of association for fellows, were largely fulfilled, as recruitment from among their number continued. An early composite photograph of five leading Victorian scientists depicted Faraday, Huxley, Wheatstone, Brewster and Tyndall: all were Athenian FRSs.[66] Between 1827 and 1859, twenty-seven members of the club were awarded the Royal Medal of the Royal Society, and a further eight medallists joined after receiving the honour. The medallists' range of backgrounds and interests is striking. Take, for example, the first three years in which two Athenians were joint winners: 1834, the geologist Charles Lyell and John (later Sir John) William Lubbock, astronomer and banker; 1838, the chemist Thomas Graham (subsequently elected under Rule II), who discovered dialysis, and Henry Fox Talbot, inventor of the calotype process of photography; and 1840, the astronomer Sir John

Herschel, a Rule II member and medallist for the second time, and the physicist Charles Wheatstone, famous for his 'bridge'.[67]

Dr Christie was not only a scientist, but also a medical man, and here again the Athenæum excelled.[68] Of the fifteen members who figured in Thomas Pettigrew's *Medical Portrait Gallery* (1838–40), eight held positions in the royal household at various times: among the most famous of them were Sir Henry Halford and Sir Benjamin Brodie, both original members, and Sir William Lawrence, elected in 1830.[69] Two other well-known figures elected that year were characteristically Athenian in their professional interests. 'Mummy Pee' Pettigrew, who was persuaded to include an entry on himself, entertained his friends by carrying out autopsies on mummies, and was asked by the duke of Hamilton to preserve his body after death. Bearing in mind that Halford owned half of the severed fourth cervical vertebra of King Charles I,[70] and that Richard Owen stored part of a fellow member's spine at the Royal College of Surgeons, a pattern seems to be emerging here.[71] One of the most glamorous surgeons of the day, Sir Astley Paston Cooper, exhibited another Athenian trait in his inveterate habit of note-taking: he kept a detailed journal each day, recorded geological and mineralogical observations when travelling and carefully preserved his case-notes throughout a long medical career.[72] Cooper performed a lithotomy, without anaesthetic, on a fellow original member, the courageous Sir John Leach, vice-chancellor of England, in a mere twenty-five minutes.[73]

Dr Christie applied his medical and geological skills in India, a country which for many young men of his generation was either a graveyard or a staging post in a distinguished career. Histories of British India were written by James Mill of the India Office, an original member of the club who remained firmly in Pentonville rather than travelling to the subcontinent; the Revd George Robert Gleig, a prominent Scottish military chaplain (elected in 1829); and the Hon. Mountstuart Elphinstone (1830), formerly lieutenant-governor of Bombay, who was highly regarded by the duke of Wellington.[74] Elphinstone's 'code' of the 1820s had as powerful an influence upon Indian education as did Macaulay's introduction of the English language as the medium of teaching in secondary schools in the mid-1830s, when Macaulay was a Member of the British Supreme Council in India. Many members of the club served in the East India Company and were either pupils or teachers at its college. Macaulay himself became an assistant commissioner of the board in June 1832, and within six months had become the secretary of the East India Company.[75] The Revd Thomas Malthus, an original member and one of the most influential political economists of his day, was known as 'Pop', or 'Population' Malthus at East India College, where Mahommed Mirza Ibraheem taught from 1826 to 1844, before returning to Persia. John Stuart Mill, elected in 1830, like Ibraheem, wrote in defence of Malthus and became an assistant examiner to the company. Horace Wilson, a Rule II member in 1837, held the Boden Chair of Sanskrit at Oxford and was the company's librarian. He disagreed with Macaulay on the use of the medium of English in Indian schools, and decided that it would be best to visit India when he was writing a continuation to James Mill's *History*. Henry Thoby Princep was educated at the college and travelled to Calcutta with a writership at the age of sixteen, later becoming a member of the Council of Bengal and a director of the company: when elected under Rule II in 1846, he was described as a 'distinguished Oriental Scholar & Indian Statesman';[76] and the Tory politician Edward Law, earl of Ellenborough, an original member, became governor-general of India in 1842. (In all, fifteen of the viceroys of India were members.) It is hardly surprising to find that the Athenæum was eager to benefit from a government announcement in 1859 that it was giving away certain publications printed by the now defunct East India Company.[77]

As we will see in the next chapter, books of travel and exploration were in demand at the club: many members were long-distance travellers themselves, often on East India Company vessels, and others were hungry for accounts of foreign tours.[78] The extensive journeys of Sir Joseph Dalton Hooker MD, elected under Rule II in 1851, equipped him to be the leading authority on the geographical distribution of plants, a natural successor to his father at Kew and an ideal correspondent with Darwin. Sir James Brooke, the dashing Rajah of Sarawak, 'whose merits as an enterprising Traveller are universally acknowledged', was listed in the Annual Report of 1848 alongside other Rule II members with outstanding records overseas.[79] In *Eothen* (1844), Kinglake entertained his readers with anecdotes of the Pasha of Belgrade, who announced that he understood locomotives: 'whirr! whirr! all by wheels! – whiz! whiz! all by steam'.[80] Kinglake used Clubland as a cultural reference point when exploring the modern English gentleman's response to the foreign Other. If one becomes a 'man about town' at Jerusalem, he suggests, 'your club is the great Church of the Holy Sepulchre, where everybody meets everybody every day', and 'your Pall Mall is the Via Dolorosa'.[81] A decade before Kinglake's election to the Athenæum, an encounter in the desert anticipates life in the drawing room.[82] In the middle of a 'wilderness', he passes a gentleman dressed in an 'English shooting-jacket' and riding on a camel.[83] Lifting their hands to their caps and waving their arms 'in courtesy', they pass 'quite as distantly as if we had passed in Pall Mall'. Only when their native servants fall into conversation do the two Englishmen feel constrained to address one another.

It transpires that the stranger is a military man returning home from India. Contemporary readers of *Eothen* might have imagined the 'gallant officer', once back in London, sitting in the United Service Club, or perhaps the Travellers. If, however, he had been one of the more bookish officers in his regiment, he might well have been a member of the Athenæum. Wellington's mainstay in the Peninsular War, Sir George Murray, described as 'late Quarter-Master-General to His Majesty's Forces' in the first Rule II list of 1830, was educated at the University of Edinburgh, held an honorary degree from Oxford and was a fellow of the Royal Society. Murray was to leave maps among his voluminous papers. Other officers were authors. Colonel Napier wrote the standard history of the Peninsular War (1828–40). Major General Sir John ('Jock') Malcolm, an original member, published *The History of Persia* (1815), *The Political History of India* (1826), *Sketches of Persia* (1828), *A Memoir of Central India* (1832) and *The Government of India* (1833), all of which were listed in the club's first printed catalogue of 1845.[84] Sir Graves Haughton, who studied oriental languages as a young army officer at Fort William College, Calcutta, and later taught at the East India College in England, donated several 'Works edited by him in Bengalee' to the library, on his election in 1830.[85] Colonel William Sykes of the Indian Army, elected in 1837, became a director of the East India Company on his return home and by 1845 had ten publications listed in the library catalogue, ranging from his study *On the Increase of Wealth and Expenditure in the various Classes of Society in the United Kingdom* (1837) to his monograph *On the Quails and Hemipodii of India* (1836).[86]

Several of the more adventurous military men and naval officers embraced by the Athenæum were as 'colourful' as they were gifted. The much fêted

Captain Alexander Burnes's election under Rule II in 1835 came the year after his *Travels into Bokhara* appeared, a book which rivalled the *Pickwick Papers* as a publishing sensation. The Afghans who killed him six years later were said to have included the male relatives of women with whom he had slept. Major Dixon Denham, an original member, and Lieutenant Hugh Clapperton RN, elected in 1827, were famed explorers of northern and central Africa, from which they returned as enemies. Neither lived to enjoy the clubhouse for long, but they outshone Eastlake in several respects, not least in achieving the remarkable feat of travelling together for 133 days without speaking. (Denham had accused Clapperton of having sexual relations with an Arab servant boy.) Following Denham's death in 1828, Clapperton made a second expedition into the interior of Africa, taking care to contradict Denham's version of the first expedition in his own account of the second.[87]

Clapperton had been proposed for membership of the club by Sir John Barrow, second secretary at the Admiralty.[88] Barrow sponsored a number of polar expeditions of the period which seized the popular imagination. Rear-Admiral Sir John Ross and his nephew, Rear-Admiral Sir James Clark Ross, were both elected under Rule II in 1834. (John Ross had sailed to the Arctic in 1818 with Edward Sabine on board; Ross's naming of the 'Croker Mountains', a great barrier to progress which proved to be a mirage, damaged his reputation.)[89] Rear-Admiral Sir John Franklin, an original member, died in 1847 in search of the North-West Passage: his statue with memorial plaques, raised 'by unanimous vote of Parliament' close to the clubhouse in 1866, was sculpted by Matthew Noble, later a member of the club.[90] Another naval officer and original member, George Lyon, was unusual in taking part in expeditions to both the Arctic and Africa.[91]

As well as looking outwards to empire, the club looked back to history, and particularly English history: the Committee's choice of Sharon Turner as their 'literary' figure among the first Rule II members in 1830 reflected the membership's interest in the subject. The year after his election, Turner donated four of his multi-volume works, on subjects ranging from the Anglo-Saxons to Queen Elizabeth.[92] Henry Hallam, a member of the club's founding Committee and later an active committee man, was a more distinguished scholar who wrote influential accounts of the history of medieval Europe and of the constitutional history of England. When he came off the General Committee by rotation, in 1839, Macaulay went on.[93] Nine years later Macaulay would become the most famous historian in the land, having published the first two volumes of his best-selling *History of England from the Accession of James II*. Another committee man, Milman, published his controversial *History of the Jews* in 1829, and then two widely read works: *The History of Early Christianity* (1840), as it was popularly known, and the *History of Latin Christianity* (1854–55). Milman's liberalism worried many of his clerical brethren, who felt that his histories seemed to rinse the miraculous out of the grand narrative of the Bible.

In proposing Ruskin for Rule II membership in 1849, Milman was supporting the future historian of Venice and of Amiens, who regarded Thomas Carlyle as his mentor. The delay in the election of Carlyle, 'Sage of Chelsea', until 1853, sixteen years after the publication of *The French Revolution*, reflects not only what might have been regarded as an 'unclubbable' personality, but also his personal circumstances. When Lord Ashburton brought him in under Rule II, however, with a promise to cover his fees, Carlyle wrote, 'You have really given me a very pretty Freehold for the rest of my life; and in a way that cannot be refused, – that can only be accepted, with a feeling which is itself a real possession to one. I do return many thanks; and will not speak another word. It is certain, except for this or some such miracle, I should never had been a member of any Club.'[94] Six years later, Carlyle's disciple and biographer, James Anthony Froude, was also elected under Rule II. It was Froude's monumental *History of England* (1856–70) that most effectively challenged Macaulay's Whig interpretation of history and Henry Buckle's 'doctrine of averages'.[95] Following the publication of his *History of Civilization in England* (vol. I), Buckle had been elected under Rule II in 1858,[96] the year before Froude – another example of the club's accommodation of intellectual combatants.

Milman and Macaulay both published historical verse, as well as prose: Milman was elected professor of poetry at Oxford in 1821, the year after his *Fall of Jerusalem* appeared; and Macaulay's *Lays of Ancient Rome*, begun in India, made his name as a writer in 1842. 'This is a great literary epoch with your nation', a German commented to Bulwer Lytton in 1833.[97] Reflecting upon 'the great books we have produced during the last twenty years', Lytton's memory reverts to 'the *chef-d'œuvres* of poets and writers of fiction' – the works of Byron,

Wordsworth, Scott, Moore, Shelley and Campbell. Scott, Moore and Campbell were all original members of the Athenæum, but the next generation of poets, including Tennyson and Browning, were too early in their careers to be elected.

An opportunity for reassessment presented itself in 1838, when the General Committee made its third intervention in the election process. With increased running costs, and with the total membership under strength at around 1,160, the club was again facing difficulties. The General Committee recommended the appointment of another special committee, chosen by the membership, as in 1830, in order to elect forty distinguished candidates at one blow. At the AGM held on 14 May 1838, with the 6th earl of Shaftesbury in the chair, the broad proposal was accepted, but the idea of a special electoral committee was rejected. It was resolved that ordinary members would be limited to 1,200, that the supernumeraries elected in 1830 who were still members would be included in that number and that the General Committee itself would choose the remaining forty from among the names already in the Candidates Book.[98] The constitution dictated, however, that the decision of the General Meeting had to be ratified at a second meeting, two weeks later. So there was a chance to smuggle new candidates into the book before it was closed on 28 May. Ten of those eventually elected were among them: hence the clever, if technically inaccurate sobriquet of the 'Forty Thieves'.[99]

Croker, who had seldom attended the General Committee's meetings since 1830, now chaired those at which the procedure for the impending election was agreed.[100] On 21 June 1838 the General Committee met in the library at noon, with Lord Shaftesbury in the chair. Among the other twenty-four members present were Croker and Shee (both trustees); William Brande (chemist and editor of a *Dictionary of Science, Literature, and Art*), Robert Brown (the first keeper of the Botanical Department of the British Museum) and Lyell; the Dean of Carlisle (Robert Hodgson), the Bishop of Hereford (Thomas Musgrave) and Milman; Augustus Callcott (painter and RA) and Eastlake; Hallam (historian); Colonel W. Gordon Macgregor; Dr John Mayo (physician); and John Parker (MP for Sheffield).

A jaundiced view of the election process, and particularly of Croker's role in it, emerges from correspondence between two of the Wilberforce brothers, both still clergy with rural livings in 1838, and both soon to become archdeacons. Robert Isaac Wilberforce had been elected in 1825, the same year as his reforming father, William.[101] Following the publication of their joint *Life of William Wilberforce* in five volumes (1838), the gifted and highly ambitious Samuel wrote to Robert, his elder brother, on 19 April, suggesting that a copy must go to the Athenæum, 'which you ought to give as a member, and I as an aspirant and so in which we both have an interest'.[102] Samuel had been in the Candidates Book since 30 January 1837,[103] and was piqued when he was not among the Forty Thieves, privately blaming Croker, whom he rightly suspected of writing the hostile review of the *Life* in the *Quarterly Review*.[104] 'I was *not* elected', he wrote to Robert on 6 July: 'Dr Hodgson told me. They must be unanimous. Any one voice postponed, put off the election . . . No question is asked or reason given. 15 out of the whole 25 who could have been present signed my recommendation – the feeling for me was strong.'[105] Croker, he continued, 'is a man who has raised himself by doing the dirty work of others – he is clever; but he owes far more to being a clever dung feeder than a clever man; few men would carry talents to *his* Master and therefore he found little competition'. In December 1839 the quick-tempered Samuel discussed with Robert how to 'silence' Croker, and even consulted Gladstone on the matter. Although Gladstone was not a member, he contacted a number of senior Athenians, pleading Samuel's cause. Samuel was elected under Rule II in 1840 and subsequently changed his mind about Croker, who was a member of his congregation at Alverstoke.[106] In 1845 'Soapy Sam' Wilberforce became Dean of Westminster in May and then Bishop of Oxford in November; Robert converted to Roman Catholicism in 1854 and died three years later.

The forty candidates who overcame all obstacles in 1838 included a number of academics, politicians, clergy, medical men and scientists, a sprinkling of the titled and landed, an interesting selection of artists, but only one writer. There were no fewer than nine FRSs in the list. Among the scientists, medical men and travellers were Viscount Adare MP, FRS (astronomer), Charles Darwin MA (secretary of the Geological Society of London), Captain John Washington RN (secretary of the Royal Geographical Society), John Royle FRS (surgeon, naturalist and professor at King's College, London), the Revd Francis Lunn FRS (naturalist), Bransby Cooper FRS (surgeon, lecturer in anatomy and Astley

Cooper's nephew; he died in the clubhouse in 1853),[107] Richard Partridge FRS (surgeon at King's College Hospital), William Henry MD, FRS (chemist and physiologist), William John Hamilton (geologist, son of William Richard Hamilton) and Lieutenant John Wellshead (India Navy and author of *Travels in Arabia*). Most were 'compound characters', in an age in which 'participation in science was often a form of economic and social upward mobility',[108] a process which was accelerated by election to the Athenæum, especially in this select group of 1838.

Darwin, the giant among them, had taken the first volume of Lyell's *Principles of Geology* on board the *Beagle* at Plymouth in 1831: volumes II and III were waiting for him in Montevideo and Valparaiso.[109] On his return to England, his work of classification and election as an honorary secretary of the Geological Society of London had been supported by Lyell, who also proposed him for membership of the Athenæum in December 1836.[110] The naturalist whose work was later to transform the sciences and social sciences, and destabilise received ideas in theology and the arts, wrote to Lyell on 9 August 1838: 'I go & dine at the Athenæum like a gentleman, or rather like a Lord, for I am sure the first evening I sat in that great drawing room, all on a sofa by myself, I felt just like a duke. – I am full of admiration at the Athenæum; one meets so many people there, that one likes to see.'[111] Darwin used the clubhouse frequently and made various suggestions about its working. In 1842, for example, he wrote to the General Committee, 'suggesting the propriety of having the lines of railways and stations, as far as completed and finally determined, laid down by hand on the Ordnance Maps in the cases; and also the addition of the stations to the several lines of railway represented on the large Map in the Newspaper room'.[112] This was approved, the cost for the thirty-two maps being estimated at £4. 0s. 0d.

The scholars among the Forty Thieves included Colonel John Briggs (historian of India and Persian scholar), the Revd R. W. Browne MA (Roman historian and professor of classical literature at King's College, London), the Revd Thomas Ormerod (divinity lecturer at Oxford), the Revd Arthur Stanley (Church historian, traveller and later Dean of Westminster) and George Grote MP.

From public and political life, and the law, were Andrew Rutherfurd (Solicitor-General for Scotland), the 2nd marquess of Northampton (president of the Royal Society in 1838 and a patron of the arts), Lord Lyttelton (Gladstone's brother-in-law and principal of the Queen's College, Birmingham), George Greenwood (barrister and historian of the Germans to AD 772), George Nicholls (Poor Law Commissioner), Edwin (later Sir Edwin) Chadwick (barrister, Poor Law Commissioner and sanitary reformer), William Crawford (philanthropist and prison inspector); and Richard Monckton Milnes MP.

Those associated with the arts, broadly defined, included Robert Vernon (self-made profiteer and patron of art, whose house was in Pall Mall), George Cattermole (artist and illustrator), William Macready (actor manager), James Harding (watercolourist), John Sheepshanks (art collector and public bene-factor), Philip Hardwick FRS (architect of public and railway buildings) and Sydney, later Sir Sydney Smirke (architect).

And then there was the one writer in the group of new members, another Charles and another giant. Charles Dickens of 48 Doughty Street was placed in the Candidates Book on 12 May, suspiciously close to the original deadline of the 14th, by his friend and proposer, Serjeant Thomas Noon Talfourd MP, lawyer and author, to whom he had dedicated the book edition of the *Pickwick Papers* the previous year. He was seconded by Serjeant Henry Storks, an orig-inal member of the club, and duly elected, aged only twenty-six. Six other candidates were also still in their twenties, and two were even younger than Dickens, one of them being Stanley, the future dean who was to bury him in the Abbey.[113] Dickens had completed only one novel: *Sketches by Boz* had been published in 1836, and *Oliver Twist* was currently appearing in *Bentley's Miscellany*. But *Pickwick Papers* was a phenomenon, bringing Dickens interna-tional celebrity. (Darwin loved it.) Nevertheless, Dickens's election in 1838 is remarkable, considering that he had started work in squalid conditions at Warren's blacking factory, Old Hungerford Stairs, on 9 February 1824, two days after his twelfth birthday and seven days before the foundation of the club. His election reflected the club's desire to attract the most promising talent in literature, art and science, irrespective of parentage and background.[114] For the young writer himself, admission to the Athenæum was a badge of respect-ability as a gentleman.

Dickens's main literary rival was Thackeray, whose election to the club followed a very different trajectory, partly because his rise to fame as a novelist was much slower: in 1838 the 'Yellowplush papers' were appearing in *Fraser's*, and the part publication of *Vanity Fair* was still nine years away. Hallam's first attempt to bring in the author of 'the Irish Sketch Books . . . . . . Journal from Cornhill to Cairo and various other popular productions' under Rule II failed, in February 1847.[115] No reference was made to Thackeray's popular series, 'The Snobs of England, by One of Themselves', then just concluding in *Punch*: when researching the section on clubs, he had inspected not only the complaints book of the Reform, of which he was a member, but also that of the Athenæum.[116] Soon after his rejection, Thackeray began his 'Travels in London' by describing the author meeting Mr Punch in St James's Park, 'under the Duke of York's Column', to discuss a commission for a foreign tour.[117] Having assured the author that 'Britons do not care a fig for foreign affairs', and told him to travel in London and bring him an account of his tour, Mr Punch turns into the Athenæum 'in company with my LORD BISHOP OF BULLOCKSMITHY, whose cob had just pulled up at the door'. They enter a clubhouse containing plentiful supplies of bishops, maps and books on 'foreign affairs'.

When Milman took up the cause of the 'Author of Vanity Fair' in 1850, Croker was in the chair – by now a rare event – and Thackeray remained unelected.[118] Milman shared his frustration with Hallam:

> There is no counting on the stubborn stupidities of men. One voice, you know, excludes, and among eighteen committee-men that there should not be one self-conceited – I must not fill up the sentence. We are bound not to reveal the secrets of our *Conciliabulum*, but I may say that it was curious to see Macaulay and Croker rowing together in my boat, with Mahon, &c. &c. If I had not thought myself sure of my success, I should not have subjected Mr. Thackeray to the chance of rejection. Pray assure him of my regret and disappointment . . . Every man whose opinion Mr Thackeray would value was with him.[119]

The candidate himself thanked Milman and Abraham Hayward for their efforts, telling Hayward that, as a satirist, he wondered that he had not made more enemies than he had, and adding: 'If you should ever know the old gentleman (for old I am sure he is, steady and respectable) who objects to me, give him my best compliments, and say I think he was quite right to exercise his judgment honestly, and to act according to that reason with wh. heaven has mercifully endowed him. But that he would be slow, I wouldn't in the least object to meet him.'[120]

Success came at last in February 1851, when Thackeray was proposed by William Broderip, the lawyer and naturalist.[121] Although he had joined the Garrick in 1833 and the Reform in 1840, Thackeray became an habitué, working in the club's 'beautiful library', seconding candidates for election and later enjoying whist and billiards.[122] Ironically, whereas he was the complete Athenian, Dickens, elected thirteen years earlier, seems to have been a restless and occasional attender, who would stand up eating a sandwich, sometimes pacing about, and who fantasised about an Athenian bore, 'Mr Prowler, of the Royal Society of Arts'.[123] Dickens did, however, enjoy the company of friends such as Cattermole and Macready, fellow Forty Thieves, and the journalist and historian John Forster, later his biographer. Forster was elected under Rule II in 1852. Thomas Walker had claimed in 1835 that the membership of the Athenæum contained 'a large proportion of the most eminent persons in the land in every line', and this could be said with even greater confidence by the 1850s.

# 5

## 'A SCORE OF GRAVE GENTLEMEN'

During Thackeray's first American lecture tour, two years after his election to the club, his thoughts turned towards 'the familiar London flag stones, and the library at the Athenæum'.[1] On his second tour, in 1855, he began his new lecture on George III with memories of returning from India as a child in 1817, 'peeping through the colonnade at Carlton House, and seeing the abode of the great Prince Regent'.[2] Today, he explained, 'where the palace once stood, a hundred little children are paddling up and down the steps to St. James's Park,' and 'a score of grave gentlemen are taking their tea at the "Athenæum Club;" as many grisly warriors are garrisoning the "United Service Club" opposite.' More subtle than Theodore Hook's ditty on the 'mental' and the 'regimental',[3] Thackeray's affectionate contrast between the 'grave' and the 'grisly' members of the two clubs is also more telling. His election to the Athenæum had been problematic, but now he was drawn there by the library and the opportunity to be a 'grave gentleman' himself.

The pleasures of club membership had been summarised by several earlier commentators. The author of the article on the Athenæum in *London Interiors* (1841–44) acknowledged the 'wealthy, comfortable, and gregarious' nature of life in the sparkling new clubhouses of St James's, but then chose a startling analogy to explain the levelling effect of membership:

It may be considered in some respects as like the grave, where the rich and the poor meet, and the mighty and the powerless are blended together: but this very diversity of caste and mind tends to the improvement of all; every one forms to himself an example; dullness finds its level; ability is acknowledged – the truly great mind is respected: and no morsel of pure moist Muscovado is so readily dissolved in water as the pompous gentleman, great by virtue of his ancestry, and his lofty opinion of his own good qualities.[4]

'Diversity of caste and mind' neatly summarises the range of backgrounds and intellectual pursuits that were represented in the Athenæum.

In 1835 Thomas Walker described Burton's clubhouse as a 'sort of palace', kept 'with the same exactness and comfort as a private dwelling', in which 'every member is a master, without any of the trouble of a master'.[5] He found it 'impossible to suppose a greater degree of liberty of living', adding that clubs in general afford 'a harmless place of resort at all hours', for married members as well as bachelors, because 'there is nothing going on but conversation, study, or a little play for the sake of amusement'. Walker reported that 17,323 dinners had been served at the Athenæum in 1832, costing on average 'two shillings and nine-pence three farthings', and that the average diner consumed 'a small fraction more than half-a-pint' of wine. He then outlined the pattern of attendance at the club:

Very few members breakfast there, and of those few the majority are generally visitors to town, who, if not at the club, would be at a coffee-house. There is a greater number to read the morning papers, who have breakfasted at home, and take the club in the way to their business. During the day there is a succession of stragglers who look in as they pass by, or have occasion to consult books or write letters. There is generally the largest assembly between the arrival of the evening papers and the hour of dinner, when people congregate on their way to their respective homes; but as it is to learn the news, and to give invitations, the ladies can be no losers by such a practice. From the number of dinners I have already mentioned to have taken place at the Athenæum in 1832, it appears the daily average of dinners was forty-seven and a fraction; and if from that number be deducted those members, who, independently of clubs, from their

avocations or their habits, or any other reason, would have been taking a
solitary meal, it cannot be said that female society was much affected; nor
is it more so at present. In those hours of the evening, which are peculiarly
dedicated to society, I should think, on an average, twenty members could
not be counted at any one time throughout the suite of rooms up stairs, the
largest of which is one hundred and three feet long, and thirty wide; indeed,
in general, when I have gone there in the evening, it has been as into a sort
of desert.[6]

Walker's figure of twenty members in the evening anticipates Thackeray's
'score of grave gentlemen'; and his reference to the desert anticipates Kinglake's
account of his encounter with a passing army officer in a 'wilderness'.[7] In 1831,
Faraday had estimated the largest attendance figures at 'from 50 to 200':
perhaps he had ballot days and AGMs in mind for the higher figure, and those
who gathered after the arrival of the evening papers for the lower.[8] Morning,
evening and foreign newspapers had been in great demand since the foundation of the club and, even after the abolition of stamp duty in 1855, signs had
to be put up in the clubhouse informing members that newspapers were not
be moved from room to room, and that 'No Member is to appropriate more
than one Newspaper at one time. By Order of the Committee.'[9] Most readers
of these newspapers had dropped into the clubhouse, as they lived or worked
nearby. The architect William Butterfield, elected in 1858, would often take a
break from work in the afternoon and stroll from the Adelphi, where he also
lived, to the clubhouse, in a tall chimneypot hat, for a dish of tea, perhaps a
conversation and occasionally a chance to write a letter on Church matters.[10]
Throughout the club's history, the majority of habitués have had a first or
second home in London. The number of 'visitors to town' was comparatively
low in the early 1830s, but increased with the coming of the railways: by the
end of the decade Sydney Smith was glorying in the fact that he could now
'beat a carrier pigeon or an eagle for a hundred miles'; in 1842 he announced
that 'distance is abolished'; and by 1861 the results of a circular indicated that
of the 794 Athenians who replied, 484 were 'Town' and 310 were 'Country'
members.[11] Overnight accommodation was not available, but members could
change for dinner in the dressing rooms.[12]

A contemporary comment on the 'legislation' of clubs is particularly apposite in the case of the Athenæum, the membership of which included several of the leading Utilitarians of the day: 'The greatest happiness, upon the fairest terms, for the greatest number, must be always a most important principle'.[13] For all its diversity of caste and mind, this high-minded 'literary' club shared an unwritten code of behaviour which was generally followed. Special occasions, however, did not always bring out the best in members. When elaborate preparations were made for members and their families to view the Coronation procession in 1838, for example, the 'first Supply for Luncheons was considered enough for 1000 Persons, and would have been ample had not members carried off whole dishes of Sandwiches, & Cakes (in spite of the orders of the Committee and remonstrances of the Servants) to different parts of the House'.[14] Afterwards, broken glasses and china were found 'in the Galleries, Balcony and Even on the Tops of the Water Closets'.

Individual breaches of the club's rules tended to be treated leniently by the General Committee. One Saturday night in 1858, Thomas Wrightson, a Carthusian and Oxonian, now in his fifties, arrived at the clubhouse 'in a state of inebriety'. In response to complaints from members, the secretary was ordered to write to him, saying that 'in the judgment of the Committee such conduct was calculated to cast obloquy upon the Club at large'.[15] The same magisterial tone was adopted the following year, when the Committee 'deeply regretted to learn' that the 'evil' had not diminished, and invited Wrightson to withdraw his name from the list of members, rather than move to 'more public proceedings'.[16] As he then stayed away from the clubhouse, it was decided to let the matter rest; but when he returned a month later and further complaints were received, a letter was delivered to his house by hand, saying that, if he presented himself again, the Committee would convene immediately to decide what action to take. A grovelling letter of apology came back, promising amendment of life, and no further action was taken.[17]

On at least one occasion, however, an order of the General Committee was carried out immediately, while the meeting was still in progress. Lord Nugent, the author and radical Whig reformer, was 'greatly respected for his honesty, consistency, and high principles, and one of the most polished and agreeable men of his day'.[18] Busy in his county and reputedly of an 'amorous disposition', he was a lightweight in Westminster who tended towards 'corpulence and financial ineptitude'. When the Committee learned that his lordship had failed to reply to a letter asking for his annual subscription, and that he was 'at this time in the house', they directed the secretary to 'remind him personally that the Committee were then sitting'. The secretary returned with 'a cheque upon Messrs Coutts for Six Guineas which he was directed to pay in the usual course to Messrs Drummond Bankers of the Club'.[19]

References to complaints in the minutes often shed light on aspects of club life that otherwise would have been unrecorded. In 1833, for example, the Committee received a complaint from two honorary members who, having started a game of chess on a Sunday evening and then gone to dinner, returned to find that the pieces had been disturbed and the board had been 'locked up by one of the servants'.[20] The Committee sent a formal letter of profound regret. Feelings ran highest on ballot days, when members could be reported to the Committee for uttering 'offensive expressions' about a candidate.[21] More commonplace were complaints about feet on the furniture.[22]

Of all domestic complaints, none troubled the Committee more than those from the coffee room. Trenchant comments, scribbled on the back of bills, were often sent to the Committee via the secretary, most frequently on the subject of fish, beer (which was made on the premises) and coffee (a problem that was said to have been finally resolved in 2013).[23] The folk memory of the club is stocked with oft-told tales of Palmerston stealing the chef on his one recorded visit to the coffee room, and of Guizot's chef despairing of ever seeing his master again when he went to dine at the Athenæum, while only two doors away the Reform Club gloried in having a celebrity chef, Alexis Soyer, in their kitchen.[24] Yet forty-seven dinners a night were consumed, and not all of them by Henry Crabb Robinson, who fasted one day a week 'in order to enjoy better his feasts here on the remaining six'.[25] In Thackeray's *Book of Snobs*, the Bishop of Bullocksmithy is happy with the mutton chops that Captain Shindy considers to be inedible.[26]

When it was discovered that the food was making a loss, a year after the clubhouse opened, a new price list was approved, including the following for luncheon:

| | |
|---|---|
| Joint with Bread & Table Beer | 1/- |
| Plate of Cold Meat with Dº | 6d |
| Mutton Chops each | 6d |
| Rump Steaks | 1/6 |
| Soups the Bason | 1/- |
| Two Eggs | 6d |
| Bread & Cheese & Table Beer | 6d |
| Bread & Butter & Dº | 6d |
| | |
| Curry made with ½ a Chicken | 4/- |
| Dº with ½ a Rabbit | 2/-[27] |

The Committee also ordered that 'no house Dinner be served, with Entrees under 10/- a head'. Members could now complain that the food was both poor and impoverishing. Bickering over the carving of joints went on for years and was behind the so-called 'Coffee Room revolt' of 1854, when the membership regained control of the carving knife that had been passed to an 'official carver', who had cut down on waste at a time when expenses were again far exceeding receipts.[28] It was some years before common sense prevailed, when staff members carved once again.

The club was afflicted with a number of staffing problems in the 1830s, when the butler died, the steward had to be dismissed, one of the hall porters was drunk on duty and a number of thefts were reported.[29] With so many complaints about the food being lodged, it is hardly surprising that the turnover of chefs was high.[30] (M. Tavenet, who had no English, and the translator with whom he shared a room, lasted less than three weeks in 1860.)[31] The kitchen and the coffee room were particularly troublesome sites. In 1835 a 'quarrel and fight' broke out behind the screen dividing the two spaces, attracting 'the notice of every one' in the coffee room: the men were severely reprimanded and warned.[32] Sometimes, however, it was the complaining member who was at fault, as on the occasion when Bulwer Lytton grumbled that the waiter would not set aside the remainder of a pint of Chateau Lafitte, of which he had taken only a glass or two: the Committee informed him that setting aside was against the regulations.[33]

At this early stage of the club's history, staff welfare tended to be addressed only when a particular case came to the attention of the Committee. Ross Mangles MP was a senior East India Company man, a Utilitarian Whig and a member of the Church Missionary Society. When the clerk of the kitchen died in 1845, Mangles wrote to the Committee pointing out that 'Mr Callcutt' had left a pregnant wife and three children in a destitute state.[34] Should a subscription should be opened for the family, he asked, and should the club insist that members of staff join a provident association? As usual in such cases, the Committee explained that neither action was allowed under the rules of the club, but that a single payment of £25 would be made in the light of William Calcutt's 'long and faithful service', and the staff would be encouraged to join an association. The retirement of Edward Magrath was handled quite differently, however. The secretary's 'unremitting assiduity and faithfulness for thirty-one years' had been recognised in the form of occasional salary increases.[35] When ill health forced him to resign in 1855, he was given a pension of £200 per annum. He died the following year, having been succeeded by (James) Claude Webster, who was to serve for thirty-four years: the Athenæum was and still is remarkable for its high staff retention rate.

Croker's death in 1857 marked the end of the beginning in the history of the Athenæum. A tradition of 'high thinking and plain living' had been firmly established in a club which prided itself on keeping its entrance fees and annual subscriptions well below the average in Clubland. As Thomas Walker commented, the 'mode of living' at the Athenæum was 'simple, rather than luxurious'; but it was even more economical in some of the other clubs, while at the Travellers, 'which is the most expensive, there is no approach, considering the class of which it is composed, and taking the average, to any thing like excessive luxury'.[36]

By the time that Walker wrote his rhapsodic description of Burton's 'palace' in 1835, two problems were posing a threat to the 'exactness and comfort' that he celebrated: shortage of shelf space for books and poor ventilation. Complaints about the quality of the air in the main rooms began soon after the opening of the clubhouse. This was a common problem in large new buildings of the period, when rooms were still ventilated by opening the windows, while stoking up the open fires in winter. 'Less care and less science' had been bestowed on the subject of ventilation than on any other,[37] which meant that attempts to improve conditions in buildings in the 1830s and 1840s were based upon scientific theory rather than engineering practice. In the case of the Athenæum, it was logical to turn to its own scientists, rather than looking outside for assistance. Now that Sir Humphry Davy was no more, Michael Faraday was the obvious choice, seven years after his resignation as honorary secretary. Faraday's experiments on the clubhouse proved to be as protracted as Davy's had been on the copper sheathing attached to ships' hulls.

Magrath was instructed to write a formal letter to his friend on 12 February 1831, posing ten questions on the relative merits of oil and gas lighting. Of Faraday's answers, sent two days later, in a winter month, the ninth is the most significant. The first cause of 'the complaint of the oppressive feeling' was as follows:

A house is built and every endeavour made to render floors, ceilings, windows, walls and doors tight & close. The rooms in it are well warmed during the day and then having brought them to such a temperature and state that the first person who enters says 'Aye this is comfortable' you put from 50 to 200 persons in and light a number of burners and when the injurious agency of these causes has been in action for 1, 2 or 3 hours complaints are made that the heat is oppressive and the odour unpleasant. You arrange things to be perfect in their effect under one set of circumstances and then changing the circumstances you expect the effect to remain the same – You make the large room & the Library quite warm enough by day light when there are only a few person there and then you light Lamps and put in many persons and must of course very soon expect an oppressive sensation.[38]

Faraday then comments on the subjective nature of complaints, before concluding that, in his opinion, 'the attempt has been to make the Athenæum house too perfect; for under the continual change of both Natural and Artificial circumstances it is I think impossible to obtain one constant effect'. A grateful Committee asked Faraday to collaborate with Burton in considering how best to implement his proposals in the 'principal rooms'.[39] Various experiments were made in the mid-1830s, none of which was wholly successful.[40]

Meanwhile a planning process for the new Houses of Parliament followed the devastating fire at the old Palace of Westminster in October 1834. The *dramatis personæ* involved there included several prominent members of the Athenæum, and the ventilation problems shared by these two quite different 'palaces' shed light on both institutions' economies. A select committee on the best methods of 'Ventilating, and Warming the New Houses' called in six witnesses of 'high scientific reputation', of whom three had been elected to the Athenæum in 1824: Professor Faraday, formerly Davy's protégé; Professor William Brande, Faraday's steady but effective colleague at the Royal Institution and a member of Davy's team working on the copper sheathing attached to ships' hulls; and the architect Robert Smirke, who had been a member of the club's Building Committee which scrutinised Burton's plans for the club-house.[41] Dr David Reid, one of the other witnesses, was particularly influential, having impressed a group of members of both Houses with his experimental ventilating arrangements when they visited his lecture rooms the previous year, during the summer meeting of the British Association for the Advancement of Science in Edinburgh. Reid was engaged to ventilate the temporary Commons chamber, and in February 1836 Charles Barry was named as the winner of the architectural competition for the new Houses of Parliament, out of ninety-seven entries.

The Athenæum wasted little time in recruiting the recipient of the most prestigious commission of the decade, if not the century: Barry's name went into the Candidates Book on 21 March 1836 and he was elected under Rule II eight days later. On the same day the Committee also brought Brande back into the fold (he had resigned in 1833 for some reason),[42] using Rule II as a mechanism.[43] The club was strengthening its forces at an anxious time: Burton had just submitted a report on the 'state and condition of the premises',[44] which was to be examined by a special sub-committee, including Faraday, Chantrey and Hamilton; and Faraday's answers to the General Committee's questions of February 1831 were reprinted for the convenience of all the committees.[45]

In June 1836 the General Committee received the sub-committee's lengthy report. This was accompanied by a letter from the re-elected Brande which would have made uncomfortable reading for Croker, who was in the chair, and for other colleagues who had been involved at the building's design stage. Brande pointed out that no system of warming or ventilation could now be introduced as effectively, or as cheaply, 'as it might have been had arrangements for the purpose been provided in the original building', incorporating flues 'for the admission of fresh air, and for the escape of foul air, and proper apertures for both those purposes, in the different rooms', as Burton had wished.[46] If the club were now to invest about £800 in major improvements, Brande suggested, the problem could be remedied. Once the rooms had been properly ventilated, they should be lit by gas rather than oil: this would assist ventilation without 'materially affecting the temperature of the rooms', each of which should be equipped with thermometers.

Although most elements of Brande's advice were followed, his comment on the club's original false economy did not prevent the Committee from imposing a cap of £600 on the works that ensued.[47] These involved adding a large 'Air Channel on the South side of the House', which required permission from the commissioners of Woods and Forests; the raising of chimneys on the Travellers' clubhouse, at the Athenæum's expense; and the installation of thermometers in the club's principal rooms, to be checked hourly by servants.[48] Meanwhile Faraday privately informed Magrath that his brother Robert and his nephew James were able gas fitters, but said that he was too nervous to put them forward officially.[49] Their appointment followed.

In September 1837, poor Burton was asked to present estimates of the cost of preventing smoke coming down the chimneys on the south and north sides of the clubhouse.[50] The health of members was one thing, but the condition of the books was quite another, and the deleterious effect of 'gaseous vapours' on the bindings was most alarming. As the precise cause of the defects was 'doubtful', and remained 'under investigation' for some time, expenditure on the library rose.[51] Reports were submitted on the state of the books and on the benefits of naphthalised gas.[52] Faraday, whose first profession had been bookbinding, was asked to attend the meeting, but sent his apologies from Brighton, where he was recovering after a nervous breakdown. He was able to report, however, that he had experimented on a variety of leather bindings in his laboratory, and could state that leather 'is by no means so Strong as it used to be in former years'.[53] With characteristic prudence he did not commit himself on the specific source of the 'evil', but pointed to the 'constant heat and extreme dryness of the room', the library's position above the coffee room, and the effect of 'sulphurous acid and ammonial salts' on the bindings, as possible contributory factors. Faraday and Brande were thanked for their continued efforts, as was the chemist Arthur Aikin, also hastily imported under Rule II, in 1838.[54] By the summer of 1842, Faraday's 'discovery of a mode of carrying off the products of combustion to the suspended Lights in the Great Room & South Library' was welcomed by the Library and General Committees, at an estimated cost of £230.[55] So confident was Faraday of success that he read a short paper entitled 'Description of a mode of obtaining the perfect ventilation of lamp-burners' at a meeting of the Institute of Civil Engineers, in June 1843, having 'transferred his right to this invention to his brother, Mr. Robert Faraday', who had 'secured it by a patent'.[56] Following the installation of the 'apparatus for ventilating the Lamp Burners' in the Drawing Room,[57] the Annual Report of 1844 recorded its 'complete success'.[58]

Michael Faraday was far from confident, however, on the broader question of ventilation. The lesson to be drawn from the parallel stories of the new Palace of Westminster and Burton's 'palace' at Waterloo Place is encapsulated in Faraday's observation that ventilation was 'an excessively difficult subject'.[59] After two decades in Burton's clubhouse, problems caused by the heat and vapour generated by artificial lighting, combined with a failure to install a ventilation system *ab initio*, had proved to be extremely costly, both in time and money,[60] and had necessitated the election of the 'Forty Thieves' in 1838.[61] Barry clearly learned from mistakes made at the Athenæum, incorporating an elaborate system of ventilation in his clubhouse for the Reform, two doors away on Pall Mall, in the late 1830s.[62] Even when the design of a building included sophisticated ventilation arrangements, however, as at the new Houses of Parliament, the experimental nature of the system made the result uncertain.

The first permanent gas lamps in London had been installed in front of the screen to Carlton House on Pall Mall during the Regency,[63] and the parish of St James was the first to have mains gas. A reduction in its use at the Athenæum during the 1850s, however, probably indicates a temporary loss of faith in interior gas lighting.[64] When a deputation of eight members, appointed by a General Meeting, discussed Burton's plans for 'altering the House' in 1855, one of their recommendations was depressingly familiar: 'Improved Ventilation of the Rooms generally; but especially of the Coffee Room.'[65] Of all the questions put to the deputation, however, the most contentious related to the introduction of smoking and billiard rooms. The answer came in a report, signed by Lord Overstone as chairman,[66] which revealed not only divisions within the club, but also a subject on which there was high-minded unanimity:

> We place these last in our enumeration. Because there exists in our Deputation, and we believe in the Club at large, a serious difference of opinion as to the propriety of introducing either a Smoking or a Billiard Room; And further, Because we all think that those Arrangements which affect the general convenience of the whole Club, and upon the necessity of which there is no difference of opinion, are entitled to the first attention. And that next to these, a full and adequate provision for all the demands of the Library is the duty incumbent upon a Club which in its original constitution was more peculiarly intended for the convenience of Members distinguished in Literature or Science or connected therewith by taste or habits.[67]

By the early 1860s, Thackeray could smoke and play billiards in the basement of the clubhouse. His first love, however, the library, remained the club's 'chief object of solicitude';[68] and the most pressing problem for the 'grave gentlemen' of the Athenæum was a shortage of shelf space for their 40,000 books.

Although Burton had allocated plenty of space for 4,000 books in 1830, the rate of growth in the library led to his having to respond to frequent demands for more bookcases. Shortly after they moved in, the General Committee indicated its commitment to growth by announcing that, as some members did not know 'exactly what works may be acceptable to the Club' and may wish to give money, a subscription was to be opened and a notice to that effect 'affixed in the Library'.[69] The 'presents' continued to flow in, however, and in June 1830 a sub-committee was formed 'for the management of the Library'.[70] It is significant that the three members of this Library Committee had a passion for travel, exploration and the history and topography of foreign countries that was widely shared in the Club.[71] First and foremost was Thomas Amyot, who was thanked for the 'great care and labour' that he had 'bestowed in the formation and arrangement of the Library': Amyot, a lawyer and antiquarian, worked in the Colonial Office, helped to found the Camden Society and amassed an excellent library of his own. William Richard Hamilton, diplomat and antiquarian, had served alongside Amyot on the General Committee since the foundation of the club. Colonel William Martin Leake was a military engineer and the most impressive topographer of ancient Greece and the Levant in the nineteenth century. These three were veterans of earlier shared projects. In 1802, Leake had been in Athens, and in September of that year sailed with Hamilton in the boat in which many of the Elgin Marbles were sunk off the shores of Cythera; and later it was Amyot who had arranged the transportation of the Marbles to London, along with Croker. Organising the Athenæum library later in life must have seemed light work in comparison.[72]

In 1835 the historian Henry Hallam, by now a member of the Library Committee, set out the principles upon which they operated. 'It has been their object,' he wrote, 'to form a collection of useful works in the different provinces of Literature and Science, without giving any other preference to particular subjects than popular taste, and what they conceived to be the inclination of the Members, appeared to prescribe.'[73] Although it was difficult, Hallam continued, to keep up with all fields for a membership such as the Athenæum's, that of English history was 'the most complete, and in the strict sense of the word contains almost every standard work of reference'. Much was wanting in Scottish and Irish history, he acknowledged, as well as in general biography, moral philosophy, 'miscellaneous polite literature' and certain areas of theology.

One of the most pleasant tasks for the Library Committee would have been dealing with donations. Several prominent early members of the club had attended the literary gatherings at 50 Albemarle Street, where John Murray II, himself an original member, had his publishing house; and many members published with him, or contributed to the *Quarterly Review*. In 1830 Amyot reported to the General Committee a 'most liberal and munificent offer from

Mr Murray of copies of all the Works comprised in his present publication List': this was passed back to the Library Committee for them to make their selection.[74] The letter of thanks to Murray was signed by every member of the General Committee, and the first list of volumes covers over three pages of the minute book. Captain Basil Hall donated an 'extensive and valuable collection of Publications relating to the United States of America' in 1831.[75] Further gifts from Hall followed, and a large donation from Captain Christopher Clarke, Royal Artillery.[76] In 1832 it was decided that these and other donors deserved recognition: a notice was put up in the hall on the first day of every month,[77] and Annual Reports began to include a list of the year's donations, which soon took up several pages of small type. The quality of some of the presents is as impressive as the quantity: indeed, the majority of the club's more valuable books were donations.[78]

A library does not grow at the pace of the Athenæum's – over eight hundred volumes per annum – on the basis of donations alone. Funding for acquisitions was formalised in January 1832, when the General Committee ordered that £250 be placed at the disposal of the Library Committee,[79] an order that was subsequently repeated twice a year. These grants were occasionally supplemented by ancillary income, such as receipts from the sale of waste paper.[80] Frequent adjustments were made to the interior of the clubhouse as the collection grew. As early as May 1831, Burton was instructed to create a gallery on one side of the south library, in response to the 'rapid increase of the Library of the Club'.[81] (Some members seem to have felt insecure on the gallery: an additional bar was added 'from Pillar to Pillar' in 1832 and, after twenty years' use, Burton had to strengthen its staircase, 'counteracting the Elasticity of the wrought Iron Carriage'.)[82] By 1834 several new bookcases had been installed in the drawing room, 'for the reception of recent acquisitions' (Plate 12), and in 1838 the Library Committee was congratulated 'on the advanced and improving state of the Library', the beneficial effects of which were 'evidenced by an increase in the number of readers'.[83] A proud General Committee concluded that 'the social enjoyments of a Club are here united with the means of intellectual gratification and improvement in a degree enjoyed, it is presumed by no similar Association'.

The library of one similar association, the Travellers Club next door, was neglected for many years;[84] but it was only through the courageous action of one of its servants, who warned his colleagues at the Athenæum of a fire in 1850, that the destruction of the club's library was averted.[85] Three years later a fire broke out in the north library, a favourite haunt of the painter James Hall, who was a bachelor habitué of the clubhouse. James was as generous as his brother, Basil: he donated the autograph manuscript of Scott's *Waverley* to the Advocates' Library in Edinburgh in 1850. He could also be careless, and his habit of creating makeshift shades for candles had previously led to a minor fire in the clubhouse. This time the conflagration damaged 262 books.[86] Hall narrowly escaped expulsion from the club in 1853, on the understanding that he would be vigilant and not read beyond 11.30 p.m. He died suddenly the following year after a short illness.

In the mid-1850s the main problem remained that of space. The situation was becoming critical, with limited access to about one-third of the books, distributed perforce around a number of 'private rooms'.[87] In 1853–54, Burton produced numerous alternative plans and elevations in response to the General Committee's request for 'greater accommodation' for the library and morning room.[88] Most of these involved 'an Upper Story or Attic being placed in the external walls, so as to provide additional accommodation for the Library and Servants' Sleeping Rooms' (Plate 15).[89] On the question of shelving, a range of suggestions came in from individual members, including Captain William Allen's proposal to house over five thousand volumes on either side of the grand staircase, where, 'in the place of the now useless ventilating aperture, there should be raised a large Doric column, (Grecian) forming a book-case'.[90] Burton criticised the club for its lack of clarity in this regard – no two suggestions coincided, he grumbled – and was frustrated when a proposed special General Meeting was postponed to the following year (1855).[91] This meeting elected its 'deputation' of eight members, including Sir Charles Barry, to consider various options and estimates, and the General Committee elected an advisory sub-committee of its own.[92] After further extensive discussion, two alternative plans were eventually put before the membership in March 1856 and promptly turned down.[93]

Back in the General Committee, Edward Bunbury, the author and classical scholar, insisted that the question of library provision had to be resolved.[94] Milman moved that the Library Committee 'be requested to Examine the Library and to ascertain what books being duplicated or of no value may be eliminated without loss or disadvantage' – a process that has been repeated from time to time ever since, occasionally with disastrous results when precious items have been lost.[95] Then the chairman, Earl Stanhope, established yet another advisory sub-committee, which included Bunbury. Two months later a further Extraordinary General Meeting finally accepted an estimate of £6,942 for general repairs, to include £1,120 for 'A New Gallery, with Spiral Staircase, in the South Library, including additional Bookcases, continuing the present Gallery across the Folding Doors, altering the latter, removing the Door Architrave, Cornice, &c., and substituting Book-shelves'.[96] The result is an impressive three-tiered arrangement of galleried bookcases which in later years has enchanted visitors – they can view it from the drawing room through the glazed doors – and has terrified members who suffer from vertigo: the latter rely upon the intrepid library staff to fetch books from the galleries (Plate 16).

Staffing the library was a rather haphazard affair in the early days. In November 1830, however, the Library Committee recommended that Charles Daly be employed as house clerk and librarian.[97] Unfortunately Daly's gambling led to a deficit of £200 in library funds.[98] In January 1833 he was replaced by Spencer Hall, who served for many years, producing the first printed catalogues and retiring in 1874, by which time the library contained about forty thousand items. The General Committee was no doubt gratified when Hall celebrated his appointment by donating a couple of books to the library, the act of a gentleman.[99] Even the estimable Hall, however, found himself in trouble when he was absent without leave,[100] and later failed to persuade the committee to change his terms of employment on several occasions.[101]

When members decided to spend a whole day in the clubhouse it tended to be in order to work in the south library, where members kept the librarian and other staff busy at all hours. In July 1831, Captain Richard Cook, Royal Artillery, complained of 'a great deficiency in the attendance of the Library in the Evenings'.[102] If the librarian was not in the clubhouse, the drawing room butler was expected to bring books to members.[103] In 1843 there was sufficient demand in the evening for 'Mummy Pee' Pettigrew to recommend that 'such assistance should be afforded to John Weaver after Mr Hall the Librarian leaves at 8 o'clock as would enable him to give his whole attention to members frequenting the Library and also that a notice be affixed requesting silence in the Library'.[104] (A few years later, having read the club's complaints book, Thackeray described Tiggs of the Sarcophagus ringing the bell and causing 'the library-waiter to walk about a quarter of a mile in order to give him Vol. II, which lies on the next table'.[105]) In June 1850, when the excitable Edward Bunbury complained that he rang the bell in vain at 11 p.m., the matter was carefully investigated.[106] Spencer Hall reported that this occurred on one of the two nights a week on which Wagstaffe, the 'Principal Servant on the floor', was allowed to leave at 9 p.m. rather than the usual 11 p.m. Robert Earle therefore took his place and gave Bunbury the books.[107]

The club also provided a servants' library and a subscription to a circulating library for the membership, an arrangement which caused frequent problems, as members forgot to return books, especially French novels.[108] Losses from the main library were regarded as an 'evil'.[109] A notebook recording losses 1830–41, mainly of illustrated books, contains an inscription in pencil: 'The Hand Book & Memorial of Literary Plagiary from 1830 to . . . Thou shalt not steal'.[110] In 1840 William Ballard, a Bow Street Runner, was informed, and reward notices printed, when it was discovered that a number of valuable books had disappeared, including Rogers's *Poems*, 'Illustrated, octavo, brown calf, gilt back, grained sides, marble leaves', and a 'Pictorial Shakspere, royal octavo, Vol. I, red cloth, gilt label'.[111] Being mainly association copies, such books were precious. Security was now improved and books were stamped.[112]

Looking back at the development of Clubland in his *Recollections of Past Life* (1870), Sir Henry Holland wrote this about clubs in general:

The growth of the last forty years as regards the number and palatial magnificence of their buildings, they mark a particular phase of society, and one in which good and evil are doubtfully blended. Ephemeral reading, with frequent interludes of sleep on well-cushioned arm-chairs, and the τί καινόν? question ['what's new?'] and talk of the day, will probably be admitted by those conversant with Clubs as a fair general picture of their interior life, exclusively of what belongs to the business of the dining-rooms.[113]

Some of the reading at the Athenæum has always been ephemeral, and in the nineteenth century there were frequent requests for still more home and foreign newspapers to be provided, morning and evening. But the question 'what's new?' was also answered by the transactions of the learned societies, where club members had influence. Amyot, for example, reported to the General Committee in February 1832, with Hamilton in the chair, that 'the Council of the Society of Antiquaries had acceded to his request by ordering that the Athenæum Library should be furnished with copies of all their publications not at present in that Library and with their future publications as soon as they are ready for delivery'.[114] Other transactions were donated by members, who also gave offprints from scholarly journals: Faraday, for example, and Whewell of Trinity College, Cambridge gave copies of their papers as they were published.

Only a club whose members needed to absorb the latest ideas and findings in a wide range of disciplines would have built up such a large collection of pamphlets, or 'Tracts' as they are called in Spencer Hall's first printed catalogue (1845), where they take up almost half the number of pages devoted to books.[115] The most telling adaptation to the south library was introduced as early as January 1831, when current periodicals and pamphlets were made more accessible by dividing the west end – the wall facing the glazed doors – into thirty sections of shelving for the purpose.[116] Members of a non-partisan club, who habitually exchanged ideas in 'the spirit of examination and questioning', could thus have immediate access to pamphlet wars of the kind discussed earlier – on longitude or on parliamentary Reform – in which their fellow Athenians were often the chief combatants.[117] Papers relating to particular themes were bound up together, as in the sixteen volumes on the 'Tractarian Controversy', for example, concerning the controversial *Tracts for the Times* (1833–41) by leading members of the Oxford Movement. These were shelved near pamphlets by Utilitarian economists and statisticians – anathema to the Tractarians – on subjects such as 'the Poor', population and prison reform.

A randomly selected volume of 'Miscellaneous pamphlets', bound in the 1830s, illustrates the wide range of subjects represented in the collection. Volume IV of the set includes a *Supplement to Captain Sir John Ross's Narrative of a Second Voyage in the* Victory, *in Search of a North-West passage, containing the Suppressed Facts necessary to a proper Understanding of the Causes of the Failure of the Steam Machinery of the* Victory *and a just Appreciation of Captain Sir John Ross's Character as an Officer and a Man of Science* (1835), by John Braithwaite, joint patentee of the boiler used on board the *Victory* and, in his view, unfairly blamed by Ross.[118] Rear-Admiral Ross, who had been elected to the club the previous year, then presented his *Explanation and Answer to Mr Braithwaite's Supplement* to the club on 12 May 1835, saying that he published it 'to refute the numerous misrepresentations contained in a work entitled "Voyages of discovery and research within the Arctic Regions &c" by Sir John Barrow', himself a highly influential original member of the Club.[119] Ross asked Magrath to 'lay the same before the Committee' and to move that it be placed 'on the table'.

Also in volume IV are papers on the ancient Irish by Sir William Betham (elected in 1828), Ulster King of Arms; on the Kolisurra silk-worm of the Deccan ('Communicated by the Bombay Branch of the Royal Asiatic Society'), by Lieutenant-Colonel William Henry Sykes (1837) of the East India Company; on hot springs and terrestrial magnetic intensity, by James Forbes (1833), physicist and glaciologist; on the tides, by the Revd William Whewell and Sir John William Lubbock, both original members; on Davy's paper on a volcano in the Mediterranean by Charles Daubeny (1824), who challenged Sir Humphry's conclusions; on Halley's comet by Captain (later Admiral) William Smyth (1835), hydrographer and astronomer; on a fabulous conquest of England by the Greeks and on the number of the lost books of Tacitus, by Lord Mahon (1827); on the genus *Chama*, on *Clavagella*, and on a new species of *Calyptræidæ*, by William John Broderip (1824), the lawyer and naturalist; and on the spikenard of the ancients, by Charles Hatchett (1824), who discovered niobium. Twenty of the twenty-seven pamphlets in volume IV are by members of the club, most of whom were also members of learned societies. It was at the Athenæum, however, with its well-stocked 'gentleman's' library, that experts in different disciplines met and interacted at their ease.

Most of these experts, amateur and professional, read outside their specialist fields, particularly in history, a subject of general interest. For Lieutenant-General Sir Henry Edward Bunbury, for example, an original member, 'English history, in all its branches, was the department to which he attached the greatest importance, and he sought particularly to make his collection as nearly complete, in all the important works on that subject, as circumstances would admit'.[120] Meanwhile his elder son, the naturalist Charles Bunbury, elected in 1852, recorded his response to Kinglake's *Invasion of the Crimea* and Froude's *History of England* in as much detail as his reading of Lyell, Darwin and Huxley.[121] The Bunburys' club library provided excellent research facilities. Among the pamphlet collection, for example, were nineteen 'Tracts relative to the Pretender and Scotland' (1726–50), bound in two volumes, and a set of eleven tracts on the Revolution of 1688.[122] When Carlyle wrote to the General Committee in 1859, suggesting that the collection of tracts formed by George Morton Pitt in the eighteenth century should be catalogued, they immediately conferred with Spencer Hall and employed an additional assistant to produce a handsome manuscript catalogue that was 'much approved of' by members when it was 'laid on the table'.[123] Printed books, such as John Rushworth's *Historical Collections* (8 vols, 1721), John Thurloe's *Collection of State Papers* (7 vols, 1742) and an extensive collection of historical public records in nineteenth-century editions, were important sources.[124] The library of a club which included Macaulay, Milman, Carlyle and Froude among its members benefited from donations such as Sharon Turner's 'History of the Anglo Saxons – 3 Volumes', 'His History of the Middle Ages – 5 Volumes', 'His History of Henry the 8th – 2 Volumes' and 'His History of Mary Edward & Elizabeth 2 Vols', in 1831.[125] The following year he added 'His Sacred History of the World, 1 vol.', and Henry Hallam, a more significant historian, joined the Library Committee.[126] The acquisitions approved by successive Library Committees reflected the needs of at least three varieties of historical investigator – the antiquarian (who was in the majority), the archaeologist and the historian.[127] The influence of clergy and Royal Academicians also ensured that ecclesiastical and art history were not forgotten.[128]

The mainstays of the collection in the early years were theology and the Classics, along with history, reflecting both the education and the professional profile of the membership. Literature, science and the fine arts were represented, in a club explicitly created to provide a home for their practitioners. Political economy was a prominent and highly contested emergent field in the 1820s and 1830s, and again both the library catalogue and the membership list include the names of some of the leading figures. Following an appeal in 1830 for titles relating to overseas travel, and with a regular turnover of foreign honorary members elected for short periods, the collection acquired a striking number of foreign-language books, especially in French, as well as strong holdings in Americana. The word 'voyage' occurs frequently in the library catalogues,[129] along with 'topography', 'exploration', 'travels', 'tours' and 'excursions': the Athenæum has a complete set of Hakluyt Society publications, for example, and a section of Spencer Hall's catalogue is devoted to 'Maps on rollers in the Morning Room'.

In May 1852, three months after his election to the club, Charles Bunbury (elder brother of Edward) wrote to Mrs Henry Lyell: 'Such a library! I spent my days studying and extracting from valuable foreign botanical works, known to me before only by name.'[130] This from a member of the Linnæan Society. Works in the collection by French men of science included Laplace's *Mécanique céleste* (5 vols, 1807) and *Exposition du système du monde* (2 vols, 1808), Lamarck's *Histoire naturelle des animaux sans vertèbre* (7 vols, 1815–22) and Baron Georges Cuvier's *Le Règne animal* (5 vols, 1829). In July 1859 Charles Bunbury met Hermann and Robert Schlagintweit in the clubhouse, describing them as 'those enterprising young men, Humboldt's protégés, who have penetrated further into Central Asia than anyone before them'.[131] Two months earlier they had published *Official Reports on the last Journeys and the Death of Adolphe Schlagintweit*, about their brother whose fate had recently come to light: having stayed on in 'High Asia' in 1857, when his brothers returned home, he was accused of being a Chinese spy and beheaded in Turkistan. *Official Reports* is in the Athenæum library, as is Adolphe's *Atlas zu den Neue Untersuchungen über die physicalische Geographie und der Geologie der Alpen* (1854). Narratives of scientific discovery and topographical exploration frequently merge in the nineteenth century, as in accounts of the long voyages of British biologists such as Charles Bunbury's friends, Darwin and Joseph Dalton Hooker, and the domestic journeys of those members engaged in the Geological Survey, all described in books in the club library which were mostly written by members. Meeting fellow members in the clubhouse and reading one another's work were elements of a continuing conversation.

Light relief was also available in books such as Richard Penn's *Maxims and Hints for an Angler, and Miseries of Fishing* (1833), illustrated by Chantrey, Abraham Hayward's *The Art of Dining* (1852) and the British novelists series, which included Walpole, Beckford, Sterne, Fielding, Richardson, Smollett, Barbauld, Ainsworth, Austen, Bulwer, Scott, Galt, Martineau, Radcliffe and Mary Shelley. Whereas English and Scottish poetry has always been taken seriously, however, fiction has never been collected systematically at the Athenæum, even when the 'literary' novel achieved a higher status for the form, later in the nineteenth century. It was assumed that members would buy and read novels at home, or borrow them from the circulating library. In Spencer Hall's 1845 catalogue, for example, only the *Pickwick Papers* (1837) is listed under 'Dickens (Charles)'.

Dickens's elaborate notes for his later fiction are creative memoranda rather than detailed observations of, say, London labour and the London poor. Most of his fellow Athenians also had a notebook in their pockets, but usually for recording data, as in the geological notebooks of Ruskin and Sir Astley Paston Cooper.[132] Whereas exceptional figures such as Lyell and Darwin developed ground-breaking theories on the basis of patient observation and recording, many natural philosophers were more like Davy's friend, George Bellas Greenough, the first president of the Geological Society of London, whose *Geological Map of England and Wales* was in the morning room in 1845, and who was known as an accumulator of facts, recorded in numerous notebooks, rather than as an original thinker. Emerson, an honorary member who had great respect for the club, noted in 1856 that, for the most part, the 'natural science in England' is 'as void of imagination and free play of thought as conveyancing'.[133]

Statistics, published in government blue books and scholarly journals, provided the basis for technological development, social reform and the new social sciences of the nineteenth century, to which generations of Athenians were to make major contributions. Thomas Henry Lister, who became the first Registrar General for England and Wales in 1836, was elected in 1830. It was as an economist that the Revd Richard Jones also succeeded in the elections that year. His *Essay on the Distribution of Wealth and on the Sources of Taxation*, published the following year, offered a critique of Ricardian economics, and in 1833 he was appointed professor of political economy at King's College London. Having co-founded the Statistical Society of London in 1834, together with two original members of the club, Malthus and Whewell, and two non-members, Charles Babbage and Adolphe Quetelet, he succeeded Malthus, with whom he respectfully disagreed, in the Chair of Political Economy and History at the East India College (Haileybury). Jones's inductive methods, based upon the accumulation of facts, were also embraced by other influential figures in the club, such as Colonel William Henry Sykes, elected in 1837. Sykes had held a commission from the East India Company, and had later been asked by Mountstuart Elphinstone to return to India as a statistical reporter to the Bombay government. Works such as *Statistical Illustrations of the British Empire* (1827), *Report on the Statistics of the Four Collectorates of Dukhun* (1832) and his *Description of the Wild Dog of the Western Ghāts* (1833) reflect a desire not only to name the species, like Adam, but also to number them. (He became president of the Royal Statistical Society in 1863.)

Among the club's other number crunchers was William O'Byrne, elected in 1857, who published his exhaustive *Naval Biographical Dictionary* (1849) in 1,400 closely printed royal octavo pages, and who applied his passion for statistics to his own club in his 'Analysis of Athenæum List corrected to 14 July 1884'.[134] When the 8th duke of Argyll became Postmaster General in 1855 he recorded that he could 'only stare and wonder at Rowland Hill's extraordinary powers of statistical analysis and of arithmetical calculations'.[135] The General Committee duly elected the 'able and ingenious' Hill, whose opinions were 'never arrived at hastily', under Rule II in 1860. In the clubhouse one day he met a friend, 'a man of superior education and varied knowledge, who had long held an important post in the Far East, almost on the shores of the Pacific':

'Why,' asked this friend, 'do you not establish an Australian mail by the Panama route?' 'Why should we?' was the counter-question. 'Because it is the shortest,' replied the friend. At once Rowland Hill proposed an adjournment to the drawing-room, where stood a large globe; the test of measurement was applied, and thereupon was demonstrated the fallacy of the wide-spread popular belief, founded on ignorance of the enormous width of the Pacific Ocean – a belief, as this anecdote shows, shared even by some of those who have dwelt within reach of its waters.[136]

It is tempting to speculate that Dickens, the scourge of Utilitarianism and of the blue book in *Hard Times* (1854), a novel dedicated to Carlyle, felt uneasy in the clubhouse partly because the 'inclination of the Members', as Hallam phrased it, was more towards fact than fiction, and more towards the objective than the subjective. The natural philosophers, however, the statisticians, politicians, clergy and literary gentlemen of the Athenæum, worked alongside each other in the south library, and became figures of legend in the nostalgic recollections of their successors. Here is an Edwardian example:

> Macaulay's corner, near the books on English history, is a well-known feature of this library, which the late Mark Pattison said he thought the most delightful place in the world, especially on a Sunday morning. At the table in the south-west corner Thackeray used constantly to work, whilst here also Theodore Hook dashed off much brilliant work. Lord Lytton, the novelist, Abraham Hayward, Samuel Wilberforce, and many other clever men were constant frequenters of this delightful room, the very atmosphere of which is replete with literary associations of the most distinguished kind.[137]

And here is Henry Tedder, secretary and librarian of the club, describing the room that for him was 'full of reminiscences', in a centenary essay for *The Times*:

> Many famous men of letters have worked here. Some portions of *Esmond* were dictated by Thackeray to Eyre Crowe at the central round table at which, in after years, Richard Burton doggedly sat through the day, snuff-box at his side, busy at his translation of *The Arabian Nights*; and after him, Andrew Lang, bending over the table, writing for long hours without notes or references. In a corner close to the English history section was the favourite chair of Macaulay, after him frequently used by Hallam, Sir Henry Maine, Matthew Arnold, Mark Pattison and Lord Acton. At the other corner, John Morley, when he edited the *Pall Mall Gazette*, came every day after he had 'put the paper to bed' and sought rest in a large armchair.[138]

Both accounts include Thackeray, with whom we began this chapter and with whom we should end, in a third description of his ardent sensibility: 'At the Athenæum Club he was often seen writing by the hour together in some quiet corner, evidently unconscious of his surroundings, at times enjoying a voiceless laugh, or again, perhaps when telling of Colonel Newcome's death, with "a moisture upon his cheek which was not dew".'[139]

# 6

*‿*

# LIBERAL HOSPITALITY

As club life was grounded in tolerance, open breaches between members of the Athenæum were deprecated. A row between Dickens and Thackeray, perhaps nineteenth-century Clubland's most famous quarrel, began at the Garrick and ended at the Athenæum. Thackeray believed that one of his rival's literary protégés, Edmund Yates, had attacked him in print at the behest of Dickens. So Thackeray asked the committee of the Garrick, where all three men were members, to expel Yates for conduct which was 'intolerable in a society of gentlemen'.[1] Dickens in turn resented Thackeray's having taken Catherine Dickens's side after the couple's widely publicised separation in 1858. Thackeray seems to have contributed, perhaps inadvertently, to the whispers about Dickens's mistress, Ellen Ternan, at the Garrick, where the membership voted for Thackeray and against Yates, leaving a furious Dickens with no choice but to resign from the committee.

For five years the rival novelists avoided each other in the clubs and other meeting places. Then, in 1863, Dickens recorded that he was just hanging up his hat in the hall of the Athenæum when he saw Thackeray looking old and ill: Dickens expressed concern, and the rift was healed. A neutral observer remembered the incident differently. Sir Theodore Martin was speaking to Thackeray when Dickens came into the clubhouse that day. Dickens passed close to his rival 'without making any sign of recognition', upon which Thackeray suddenly interrupted his conversation with Sir Theodore and reached Dickens just as the latter had his foot on the grand staircase: 'Dickens turned to him, and I saw Thackeray speak and presently hold out his hand to

Dickens. They shook hands, a few words were exchanged, and immediately Thackeray returned to me saying "I'm glad I have done this".' Peter Ackroyd finds this the more probable narrative, not least because Dickens was notoriously bad at reconciliation after a quarrel.[2]

Dickens was to be the last of a crowd of mourners to leave Thackeray's graveside in Kensal Green cemetery a few months later.[3] His own funeral, in 1870, was a strange affair, with Dean Stanley reading the burial service to a handful of mourners at Poet's Corner in Westminster Abbey, early in the morning. (Thousands visited the open grave on the days that followed.) Of the sixty-six other funerals for Athenians held in the Abbey between 1824 and 1897, one of the grandest was Lord Macaulay's, on 9 January 1860, when onlookers lined the streets to watch the cortège go by. All but one of the eleven pall-bearers (Evelyn Denison, Speaker of the Commons) were members of the club. Several were Liberal politicians and authors, like Macaulay himself: Sir George Cornewall Lewis, the duke of Argyll, Lord Campbell (the Lord Chancellor) and Lord John Russell. Whereas Russell wrote history on behalf of the Liberals, however, Lord Stanhope did the same for the Conservatives. Similarly, whereas Samuel Wilberforce, Bishop of Oxford, was a fierce critic of Darwin and Huxley in defence of orthodoxy, Henry Hart Milman, Dean of St Paul's, was a controversial liberal historian of Christianity.[4] At Macaulay's funeral, as at the Athenæum, differences could be accommodated.

Macaulay's death marked the end of an era, coming a year after the East India Company lost its administrative powers in India, and only a month after the 'earthquake shock' of Darwin's *On the Origin of Species by Means of Natural Selection; or, The Preservation of Favoured Races in the Struggle of Life*, published on 24 November 1859.[5] Of the other eminent habitués of the south library who were listed in the reminiscences quoted at the end of the last chapter, two had already died: Hook in 1841 and Hallam in January 1859.[6] Another pair born before Waterloo – Bulwer Lytton (1803–73) and Samuel Wilberforce (1805–73) – died after the publication of *The Descent of Man, and Selection in Relation to Sex* (1871), having contributed to the debates of the 1860s on the impact of Darwin's theories on the sciences and social sciences, and on theology and the arts. Abraham Hayward (1801–84) and Mark Pattison (1813–84), the other two older members, lived on to witness the full flowering of the arts and sciences in Victorian Britain, when the Athenæum was 'the focus of the intellectual life of the nation'.[7] Richard Burton (1821–90), Matthew Arnold (1822–83) and Andrew Lang (1844–1912) were contemporaries of other famous literary members, such as Browning, Trollope, Wilkie Collins, Henry James, Hardy, Robert Louis Stevenson and Kipling. Lord Acton (1834–1902), historian and politician, was said to have been the only man who could influence Gladstone, rather than be influenced by him. Gladstone's official biographer, John Morley (1838–1923), was one of several Athenians who edited highly influential reviews, while Henry Maine (1822–88) discussed with fellow members the application of Darwin's discoveries to the investigation of the role of law in the development of primitive societies.

In earlier chapters we have seen examples of the Athenæum's 'hospitality' towards a wide range of ideologies and social backgrounds among candidates and members. Lord Holland was described as being 'liberal' in valuing others 'more with reference to their general character, talents, and acquirements, than to their rank or station';[8] and the same could be said of the club. Non-partisan politically, it accommodated both sides in the Reform debates of the 1830s, with members engaging in pamphlet wars rather than calling for resignations, as happened at the political clubs. Similarly, the pattern of early Rule II elections indicates a willingness to introduce new members of outstanding ability in science, literature and the arts who were known to be the chief antagonists of equally prominent existing members. In the 1860s, the British intelligentsia debated the implications of new scientific discoveries and 'scientific' methods of biblical criticism with passion and a sense of urgency. Most of the influential figures in these debates were members of the Athenæum, where opposing factions now coalesced around liberal and conservative positions, and intellectual disagreements affected club life. (In contrast to the variegated group of pall-bearers at Macaulay's funeral in 1860, Darwin's were chosen as participants in a choreographed political act at the Abbey on 26 April 1882, devised and directed by Huxley and Dean Farrar at the Athenæum.)[9] This chapter examines some of the flashpoints in the club's history between 1860 and 1890, when liberal opinion in politics, religion and science assumed the ascendancy in Britain, and the Athenæum strove to maintain its tradition of tolerance and balance. It is at these flashpoints, and at times when conservative sexual mores influenced public life, that the relationship between national developments and the life of the club, conducted on the margins between the private and the public, is most revealing.

The formal alliance between the Athenæum and the learned societies that had been forged when the founding Committee first met in 1824 remained in place for over fifty years.[10] The link was weakened, however, after the death of Lord Stanhope in 1875, when it was decided that the presidents of the Royal Society, the Society of Antiquaries and the Royal Academy should only be *ex officio* members of the General Committee, rather than trustees for life.[11] There would now be three trustees, all elected by the membership at large in a more democratic age. Joseph Dalton Hooker, however, the distinguished explorer, director of the Royal Botanic Gardens at Kew and president of the Royal Society, regretted that 'the modified Rule overlooks the manifest intention of the Founders of the Club', which was to formalise the Athenæum's special interest in science, literature and the fine arts in its constitution.[12]

The notoriously irritable Hooker was wary of any move that might slow the march of science by disempowering its leading practitioners. Earlier in the 1870s he had defeated Richard Owen of the British Museum in a battle to defend the research collection at Kew. Whereas Owen had rejected Darwin's theory of natural selection, Hooker was Darwin's close friend and colleague, and the first to learn of and accept his theory of natural selection. During the 1860s the battles over the new biology and other developments in the sciences were fought out mainly in institutions and unofficial groups in London, such as the Royal Institution, the Government School of Mines and University College; the Royal Society, the Linnæan Society and the Geological Society; the X Club and the British Association for the Advancement of Science, which moved its annual meetings around the country. Darwin, Hooker and Owen were all active members of the Athenæum, where the main combatants met informally and discussed the scientific issues of the day in private.

Cambridge science and social science were also represented in the club in the nineteenth century, from the days of William Whewell, an original member, to those of the founders and first directors of the Cavendish laboratory.[13] A more clearly definable Cambridge grouping, however, were the Apostles, members of an elite secret society of undergraduates, most of them Trinity and Kings men, who held regular meetings at which a member would present a paper which was then discussed at some length. Of those who became Apostles between 1820 and 1887, a quarter later belonged to the Athenæum, which offered not only recognition and status but also wider opportunities for influence.[14] Apostles supported each other in elections, and fourteen of their number were elected under Rule II,[15] an honour so well known outside the club by the 1870s that it could be referred to by a biographer without explanation.[16] Canvassing for votes was a familiar feature of Clubland, epitomised in Browning's self-description as a 'great hungry spider', waiting at the head of the grand staircase at the Athenæum to entrap his prey on ballot days.[17] There was more to the Apostles' tactics, however, than the support of friends and colleagues: they were also part of a broader liberal campaign to which some leading members of the Athenæum also contributed.[18] Yet the club, founded by a high Tory of the old school, was regarded as the natural home of bishops and judges, the majority of whom held conservative views. Here was a potential source of conflict.

The most active pressure group in the liberal cause (lower-case 'l'), both inside and outside the clubhouse, were the nine members of the Athenæum who founded the X Club in 1864. Three of them – their leader Thomas Huxley, Sir John Lubbock and Herbert Spencer – were later to feature in *Ballot Day 1892* (see p. 6).[19] George Busk was a naval surgeon and naturalist,[20] Hooker an expert on the geographical distribution of plants and John Tyndall an outstanding physicist.[21] William Spottiswoode was a mathematician and physicist, Sir Edward Frankland a chemist, famous for his analysis of the public water supply,[22] and Thomas Hirst a mathematician, whose diaries provide unusually detailed accounts of attendance at the Athenæum.[23] All became FRSs apart from Spencer, who refused the offer in a sulk. That all but one of them (Spottiswoode) were elected to the club under Rule II also reflects their eminence; that all of them served on the General Committee, Lubbock as a trustee, indicates not only individual commitment but also a shared and overtly stated intent with regard to the shaping of the club.[24] Long before the formation of the X Club, its future members, the 'X network', were active in bringing liberal intellectuals into the Athenæum.

Their attention was first drawn to the candidature of Henry Thomas Buckle, whose *History of Civilization in England*, volume I, was published in 1857 to great acclaim. Buckle, a freethinker in religion and a radical in politics, was soon introduced to Darwin, Huxley and Spencer,[25] and the following year his name was due to come up for balloting at the Athenæum.[26] The clergy had 'not been lovingly treated' in Buckle's history, and his friends wanted to avoid a humiliating failure in the ballot by proposing him for election by the Committee under Rule II.[27] He insisted, however, on his name going forward for election by the club at large. Hooker was active in his support, encouraging the newly elected Huxley to pay his dues quickly and 'help to swamp the parsons & get Buckle in'.[28] Hooker need not have worried, as the membership was unwilling to be swayed by clerical opposition. Buckle's ballot card was so crammed with signatures that an extra sheet had to be pasted to it.[29] One member who was explicitly asked to vote against Buckle, 'because of his religious views', replied: 'If that is your reason, I shall certainly go and vote – for him.'[30] Indeed, the majority of the clergy voted for him and he was elected by 264 votes to 9 on 1 February.

Similar numbers of signatures were scrawled under the name of William Spottiswoode, elected in the ballot on 7 February 1859; and the campaign to bring in other liberal figures continued in 1860, when Tyndall seconded Henry Fawcett, duly elected on 30 March 1874 after a normal wait.[31] It was in March 1860 that another controversy led to a call to arms by the X network, when a group of Oxford-educated clergymen published *Essays and Reviews*. Instead of separating theology from science, the essayists argued, the concept of development should be applied to faith and to the documents of faith, applying new critical tools to old doctrines and ways of reading the Bible. The first essay in the collection, entitled 'The education of the world', was by Frederick Temple, headmaster of Rugby and an Oxford liberal. 'If geology proves to us that we must not interpret the first chapters of Genesis literally,' Temple wrote, 'if historical investigation shall show us that inspiration, however it may protect the doctrine, yet was not empowered to protect the narrative of the inspired writers from occasional inaccuracy; if careful criticism shall prove that there have been occasional interpolations and forgeries in that Book, as in many others; the results should still be welcome.'[32] Temple's appointment as Bishop of Exeter, nine years later, was greeted with howls of protest. The positive public responses to his subsequent translations were signs of more liberal times: in *Ballot Day 1892* he is shown as Bishop of London[33] and in 1897 he became Archbishop of Canterbury.

In 1860, however, the battle lines were soon drawn up, as *Essays and Reviews* became a *cause célèbre* throughout the Anglophone world, even outselling the *Origin of Species*. Most of the bishops were also Oxonians and disapproved of their liberal brethren's publication; and the most energetic among them, Bishop Samuel ('Soapy Sam') Wilberforce, was a prominent member of the club.[34] Wilberforce had already been vilified in the popular press over what appeared to be his High Church leanings.[35] The story of his demolition by Huxley, 'Darwin's bulldog', at the British Association meeting in Oxford in June 1860 requires no retelling. Recent research suggests, however, that the story has assumed legendary proportions, and that the defeat of the bishop was in fact largely the result of his unpopularity in Oxford.[36] Wilberforce's shocked response to *Essays and Reviews*, three months earlier, was based less upon what was said than upon who said it; and many clergy agreed.[37] He made this point in an anonymous review in the *Quarterly*, where he stated that there was in truth nothing in the book that was 'really new', and that Temple and Jowett were less culpable than others among the essayists.[38] (Ironically, Temple was the preacher at the British Association meeting in Oxford.)

It was Wilberforce's review that started a panic-stricken 'agitation' against the essayists by thousands of troubled English clergymen. Canon Arthur Stanley, then Regius Professor of Ecclesiastical History at Oxford, disapproved of *Essays and Reviews* and refused to contribute an essay himself.[39] Nevertheless, he was in favour of its liberal theology, and it fell to him to defend the essayists in the time-honoured manner, responding to the bishop's *Quarterly* piece in a long article in the *Edinburgh*. When the bishops' formal letter of censure against the essayists was published in *The Times*, in February 1861, their arguments were widely discussed in private correspondence between members of the Athenæum. Stanley expressed surprise that Tait, the Bishop of London, had subscribed to the letter, while Tait clearly believed that the essays of Temple, Pattison (a Rule II member from 1865) and Jowett (who was not a member) were not objectionable in themselves.[40] Others confided in their journals: the naturalist Sir Charles Bunbury, for example, found himself to be 'at a loss to find anything shocking or offensive, irreligious or unchristian' in either Temple's or Charles Wycliffe Goodwin's essays.[41]

It was characteristic of Athenians to clarify their thinking by writing. Among dozens of references in Wilberforce's journal to his writing sermons, reviews, speeches and letters in the clubhouse itself, one is particularly telling: 'To Athenæum, to finish part of sermon and write letter *undisturbed*' (emphasis added).[42] Yet in using the south library as a haven when staying in London for meetings, Wilberforce was also observed: we are told, for example, that he would pile 'huge folios' on his table.[43] Similarly, when he dined in the coffee room with the Bishop of Salisbury, Walter Hamilton, after Convocation in 1860, he would have been observed by members sitting nearby, including some who disagreed with him.[44] Contemporary assessments of a complex personality such as Wilberforce's were formed not only in public, when he preached in the Abbey or spoke in the House of Lords, or in private, when walking in St James's Park or riding at Cuddesdon, but also at the Athenæum, which offered a third, neutral space to its members.[45] If club life, public life and private life were represented by three circles, the first would overlap with the second more than with the third. Tensions associated with conflicting positions in the public realm could be resolved, or at least tempered, through mutual trust in shared club values, including confidentiality, making for freer exchanges of views than was possible outside. Wilberforce and Stanley disagreed in public about *Essays and Reviews*, and yet in private both thought that it was a mistake to publish. It was said by somebody who knew both of them well that 'they had agreed to love each other in private, and to do each other as much mischief as possible in public'.[46] Yet both the worldly Wilberforce, dining with his brother bishops, and the unworldly Stanley, who was soon to preside over liberal tea-parties at the Westminster Deanery (also observed and described in memoirs), played leading roles in Church politics, and in opposing camps.[47]

A crisis in the Church of England that was related to the controversy over *Essays and Reviews* led to the X network taking direct action at the Athenæum. Bishop John Colenso of Natal's liberal attitude towards polygamy, particularly with respect to the sacrament of baptism in a colonial context, brought him a degree of notoriety in Britain in January 1858.[48] Having been defended by F.D. Maurice, among others, Colenso lost his support later that year.[49] The publication of Colenso's essays on the Eucharist so disturbed his High Church metropolitan, Bishop Gray of Cape Town, that he consulted Wilberforce on the matter: the verdict was that Colenso was theologically vague but not heretical. In 1861, however, Colenso's commentary on the Epistle to the Romans, which represented a challenge to traditional teaching on sin and the Atonement, attracted accusations of heresy from one of his colonial colleagues and an official appeal to the English bishops. In March 1862, Hooker invited the Lubbocks to Kew to discuss how best to support Colenso. When Sir Charles Lyell then consulted Lubbock, Hooker, Huxley and Dr William Carpenter – biologist and registrar at University College, Unitarian and a Rule II member of the Athenæum since 1857 – the latter suggested getting Colenso into the club as a colonial bishop and Huxley urged Lubbock, who was on the Committee, to help.[50]

When the English bishops met in May 1862, Wilberforce, his friend Bishop Hamilton of Salisbury and Bishop Charles Sumner of Winchester seem to have led the attack on Colenso, who was soon to arrive in England. In July, Hirst, Tyndall and the Lubbocks gathered at the Busks to meet 'the renowned Bishop Colenso', who was hastily preparing the first part of yet another highly controversial book for publication.[51] Colenso had long been persuaded by Lyell's work that there had been no universal deluge; and he had recently absorbed *Essays and Reviews*. Now he applied 'scientific' principles to the hyperbolic arithmetic of the Old Testament in his *Pentateuch and the Book of Joshua, Critically Examined*. Setting aside the question of the book's crude methodology, the fact that a bishop wrote it was enough to cause a furore. This came to a head early in 1863 with the publication of the second part at about the same time as Lyell's *Antiquity of Man*, both books selling as fast as popular novels. Bishop Gray of Cape Town had been an honorary member of the Athenæum the previous year, and was re-elected for the usual period of a month on 13 January 1863, with renewal for a further month on 10 February.[52] A week later, Carpenter and Lyell proposed Colenso for honorary membership.[53] The General Committee was chaired that day by Lord Overstone, a trustee, phenomenally wealthy authority on currency and banking and friend and admirer of Wilberforce.[54] Members of the X network had canvassed support for each other and for like-minded friends in elections to the Committee: at least four of the twelve other members present – Carpenter, Lubbock, Tyndall and the diplomat Frederick Chatfield – could be relied upon to support the proposal. Unusually, a debate arose when the question was put and a vote was taken: Colenso was elected for a month by a majority of six (9:3). The Committee had maintained a balance between ecclesiastical authority, represented by Gray, and free enquiry and scientific principles, represented by Colenso. From the X network's point of view, however, this was a clear victory.

Later that month Colenso's name was 'passed over' in the list of vice-presidents of the Society for the Propagation of the Gospel,[55] and on 14 March 1863 the archbishops and bishops asked him to resign his vice-presidency: he refused. Three days later, with another trustee, Lord Stanhope, in the chair, the Committee of the Athenæum re-elected him for another month, continuing to provide access to a great library as he prepared his defence and to scientific allies whose lectures he attended in London.[56] One prominent member, Bishop Tait of London, was keen to resolve the clash between opposing forces in the Church, and had recently invited Colenso for a private talk: in his diary he recorded that the Bishop of Natal was 'very wild' and 'likely to go very far in discarding the old faith'.[57] A few weeks later Colenso commented in a letter to Lyell upon the attitude of the English bishops, led by Wilberforce, who 'cut [him] dead'.[58] Tait, whom he encountered near the Athenæum, was the sole exception:

I met him in Pall Mall a few days ago, where he was walking arm in arm with another Bishop, and I was going to pass him with a salutation. But he made a point of shaking me heartily by the hand, and stopping to ask me some friendly question, the other standing mute all the while. I could not see who it was: perhaps he did not know me.

Between April and November 1863, X Club members on the Committee managed to get Colenso's honorary membership of the Athenæum renewed, in spite of opposition from the classical and biblical scholar Dr (later Sir) William Smith among others.[59] The list of 'Colonists' was then full, however, and Colenso lost his membership.[60]

The year 1864 was to be an important one in the history of Victorian science, with the award to Darwin of the Royal Society's Copley Medal (although General Sabine PRS, a trustee of the Athenæum, insisted that no reference to the *Origin* should appear in the citation); the circulation of Lyell's *Geological Evidences of the Antiquity of Man* and Huxley's *Evidence as to Man's Place in Nature* (both 1863); and the formation of the X Club. It was also a momentous year for the Victorian Church. Two years earlier, H.B. Wilson and Rowland Williams, two of the contributors to *Essays and Reviews*, had been brought before the ecclesiastical courts. When the Dean of Arches rejected most of the charges against Williams and merely suspended both men from their benefices for a year, they and their supporters hailed the judgment as a victory: Anglican clergy could now teach in the light of modern knowledge.[61] Nevertheless, Wilson and Williams appealed to the Judicial Committee of the Privy Council in the hope of acquittal from all charges, which they duly received on 8 February 1864. Four of the five members of the committee who voted to clear them – Lord Chancellor Westbury, Lord Chelmsford, Lord Kingsdown and Bishop Tait – were members of the Athenæum, as were the two archbishops who dissented from the judgment.[62] What scandalised High Churchmen, some of whom left the Church of England for Rome, was that lords temporal had ruled on matters spiritual. Wilberforce, encouraged by the storm of protest that followed the judgment, brought the book before the Upper House of Convocation, which resulted in a 'synodical condemnation' in June, from which Tait dissented.

Meanwhile, at the Athenæum, Wilberforce had failed to sabotage the X Club's manoeuvrings in support of Bishop Colenso, whose honorary membership of the club was renewed.[63] In March 1865 the Judicial Committee of the Privy Council found for Colenso, thirteen months after they had found for Wilson of *Essays and Reviews*. In December 1865 Spottiswoode informed his fellow X Club members that 'the liberal party at Oxford were about to try to utilise the present movement for University Extension originated by the Theological party. The former would be glad to receive support from the friends of science out of the University.' The nine members of the X Club, most of whom were present or future FRSs and members of the Committee at the

Athenæum, were operating as a pressure group with liberal ambitions for both societies, as well as for the Church of England and Oxford University; and during the 1870s they held their monthly meetings at the Athenæum.

For the club, the historical significance of both the Colenso affair, which dragged on for several more years,[64] and the controversy surrounding *Essays and Reviews* lies in the Committee's measured response to a liberalising trend in the Church, society and Athenæum membership, which included not only the X Club agitators but also a number of influential commentators on political and cultural developments. Matthew Arnold, Herbert Spencer, Fitzjames and Leslie Stephen and Sir Henry Maine were all habitués and all published in periodicals with large circulations, in many cases edited by present or future members of the club. Among the Athenian editors of established titles in the 1860s were George Cornewall Lewis and Henry Reeve of the quarterly *Edinburgh Review*, William Macpherson and Dr (later Sir) William Smith of Murray's *Quarterly Review* (formerly Croker's house journal) and James Anthony Froude of the monthly *Fraser's Magazine*. Two new monthlies that appeared at around the same time as the *Origin of Species* heralded a new era in magazine publishing. *Macmillan's Magazine*, founded in November 1859, was edited by a succession of Athenians: the biographer and literary scholar David Masson was elected under Rule II in 1868, the year in which he was succeeded by George Grove, the music editor (elected in 1871), who in 1883 handed over to John Morley (1874, Rule II), later Gladstone's biographer. *Macmillan's* published serious articles on politics and religion, as well as some lighter material, and competed with its more popular and amusing rival, the *Cornhill Magazine*, which sold 100,000 copies when it was launched in January 1860. The *Cornhill* was edited first by Thackeray and in the 1870s by Leslie Stephen (1877, Rule II), whose 'Hours in a Library' complemented the essays, fiction and poetry contributed by some of the leading writers of the day. Between 1860 and 1877 the weekly *Economist* was edited by Walter Bagehot (1875), whose study on *The English Constitution* was first published serially in the *Fortnightly Review* (1865–67). Richard Holt Hutton (1871, Rule II) edited the *Spectator* from 1861 to 1897. The launch of the *Contemporary Review* in 1866, with Henry Alford, Dean of Canterbury (1856, Rule II), as editor, was in response to the secular *Fortnightly*, edited by Morley from 1867 to 1882. It was largely through these periodicals that the steps of the Athenæum gave access to the 'public square'.

Matthew Arnold, whose Hellenic addresses to the nation were delivered in this way, knew all the editors: he seconded Hutton's candidacy at the club,[65] he was a friend of Morley's and he mentioned Sir William Smith, Masson, Bagehot and Froude in a single letter to his brother Thomas, when helping him to place an article.[66] On his election in 1856, Arnold, like Darwin before him, gloried in a drawing room 'covered with books', which led on to other rooms full of books.[67] Whenever he returned to London from wearying journeys around the country as an inspector of schools, he used the south library as a refuge from professional and family commitments, commenting in one of his regular letters to his mother, 'I write from this delightful place, the only place where I can get any real work done', and in another, 'I work here at my French Eton from about 11 to 3; then I write my letters; then I walk home and look over Grammar papers till dinner; then dinner and a game of cards with the boys'.[68] Like Wilberforce, Arnold made frequent use of the club's letterhead: of his letters from the Athenæum in 1864, for example, no fewer than forty have survived. When Arnold donated a copy of his *Poems* (1885) to the Athenæum he inscribed it to the librarian, Henry Tedder, 'with very kind regards, and cordial acknowledgements of much help'.[69] Once, when feeling unwell at the club, he asked Browning not to write an elegy of more than ten lines.[70]

The introduction and opening chapter of Arnold's best-known essay began life as the last of his lectures as professor of poetry at Oxford in May 1867. This appeared in the *Cornhill* two months later and was followed by five other articles under the title of 'Anarchy and Authority'. The final article, 'Our Liberal practitioners', published in July and September 1868, has been described as 'almost an electioneering pamphlet', in advance of the general election that brought Gladstone the premiership.[71] *Culture and Anarchy*, published by Smith, Elder in January 1869, contrasts the Greek ideal of 'sweetness and light', embodied in the 'best that has been thought and said in the world', with the ugly reality of the Hyde Park riots of 1866, which Arnold relates to 'an Englishman's right to do what he likes; his right to march where he likes, meet where he likes, enter where he likes, hoot as he likes, threaten as he likes, smash as he likes'.[72]

Disraeli's Reform Bill was passed in 1867. Prussia defeated Austria in 1866 and France in 1870. Arnold's analysis of national and international politics in *Culture and Anarchy* is based upon observations made not only on his many journeys across Britain and the Continent, but also closer to home, in Belgravia and at the Athenæum. In a reprise of events in 1831,[73] panes in the morning room and writing room windows of the club were smashed by the mob on the evening of 24 July 1866, a month after the resignation of Lord Russell's Liberal government, which had failed to bring in a Reform Bill. Pasted into the minute book of the General Committee is a cutting from the *Pall Mall Gazette*, in which is described a hearing at the Bow Street police court next morning. Some of the 'lowest of the London "roughs"' were led from Trafalgar Square to Waterloo Place, via Gladstone's house in Carlton Gardens, by a seventeen-year-old cabinet maker named Thomas Ferris, whose missile – a stone he picked up in Waterloo Place – was retrieved by club staff and exhibited as evidence at the hearing.[74] Sir Richard Mayne, the indecisive police commissioner and an original member of the Athenæum, was hounded by the press during this period of rioting. Arnold observed his neighbour's plight from his balcony when Mayne's own windows in Chester Square were smashed. In a letter to his mother, Arnold concluded that, 'whereas in France, since the Revolution, a man feels that the power which represses him is the *State*, is *himself*, here a man feels that the power which represses him is the Tories, the upper class, the aristocracy, and so on'.[75]

Arnold does not look to the aristocratic 'Barbarians' for answers in *Culture and Anarchy*. 'What we want,' he argues, is 'a fuller harmonious development of our humanity, a free play of thought upon our routine notions, spontaneity of consciousness, sweetness and light; and these are just what culture generates and fosters.'[76] A 'man's life', he suggests, 'depends for its solidity and value on whether he reads during that day, and, far more still, on what he reads during it'.[77] Arnold's Athenian reflections crystallise in a comparison between France, with its Academy, and Britain, with its 'Philistine' Nonconformist shopkeepers. He fosters support for his views by implicitly including the reader among 'every one' and 'one':

> Every one who knows the characteristics of our national life . . . knows exactly what an English Academy would be like. One can see the happy family in

one's mind's eye as distinctly as if it were already constituted. Lord Stanhope, the Dean of St Paul's [Milman], the Bishop of Oxford [Wilberforce], Mr. Gladstone, the Dean of Westminster [Stanley], Mr. Froude, Mr. Henry Reeve, – everything which is influential, accomplished, and distinguished.[78]

It is as if he were casting his eye around the clubhouse: among Arnold's pantheon, only Gladstone, the club's *eminence grise*, was not a member; all the others served on the General Committee, Stanhope as a trustee. From the steps of his Athenæum, or Academy, Arnold could address the gentlemen and ladies who inhabited the public square. Harder to reach, however, was Thomas Ferris, a member of Arnold's 'Populace' and himself an orator, 'addressing the mob from the pedestal of the Nelson Monument'.[79]

In 1862, five years before Arnold's articles on 'Anarchy and Authority' appeared, the *Cornhill* had published an essay on liberalism by the Benthamite writer and future High Court judge, James Fitzjames Stephen, whose anti-democratic sentiments seem, from a twenty-first-century perspective, as illiberal as Arnold's comments on the 'Populace' and the dangers of Reform. Through the works of Dickens and other reformist novelists, Stephen argued, the 'working man' had been the subject of a 'sort of apotheosis'.[80] The danger of political liber-alism, he suggested, was in 'deifying . . . slight and ineffectual public sentiments', when in reality the 'highest function which the great mass of mankind could ever be fitted to perform' would be 'that of recognizing the moral and intellectual superiority of the few who, in virtue of a happy combination of personal gifts with accidental advantages, ought to be regarded as their natural leaders'.[81]

Two years later, in 1864, Stephen defended Dr Williams of *Essays and Reviews*, thereby enhancing his reputation as a barrister.[82] He also appeared for Colenso in his successful appeal and was unhappy about Matthew Arnold's critical essay on his client,[83] publishing a riposte in the *Saturday Review*. Arnold commented on this 'long elaborate' attack on him at the time, adding that Stephen 'meant to be as civil as he could, consistent with attacking me au fond; and yesterday he sent his wife to call, as a proof, I suppose, that he wished amity'.[84] While behaving as perfectly civil gentlemen, the 'unpolemical' Arnold and Stephen the contro-versialist kept up 'continual trench warfare' in subsequent years.[85] In 1868 Arnold encouraged his fellow club member William Thomson, the Archbishop of York, to be gentle with Colenso the man while correcting him on the line he had taken, and commented that 'the Liberal Party (as they call themselves)' were 'very angry' with him; that 'a certain section of Liberals were making capital out of Colenso'; and that this section was, in his opinion, 'able and disposed to damage the cause of true culture, which is the same as the cause of true religion'.[86] Fitzjames Stephen's liberalism, a revised version of Mill's, was closer in spirit to that of the bellicose X Club than to Arnold's.

In 1873 Fitzjames Stephen became a member under Rule II of the kind of elite that he described in 'Liberalism'. (In 1877 he was joined at the club by his brother Leslie, soon to be editor of that most Athenian and liberal of reference works, the *Dictionary of National Biography*.)[87] Fitzjames recorded that he and the jurist Sir Henry Maine, his Cambridge friend and fellow Apostle, had 'the queerest friendly battles on the subject of the proper method of theorizing about law'.[88] Maine, elected under Rule II in 1862, was devoted to the club, as was his friend Francis Galton (1855, Rule II), a cousin of Darwin's, who first publicised his theory of eugenics in *Macmillan's Magazine* (1865). In later life Galton spent many hours with Maine, discussing 'topics connected with primitive culture',[89] and with the polymath Herbert Spencer, whose books, including the ten volumes of his 'System of Synthetic Philosophy', made him the most famous British intellectual in Europe in the late nineteenth century. Spencer and Galton passed 'an hour or two of the afternoon, during many years, in the then smoking room of the Athenaeum Club, when quiet conversation was easy'.[90]

For Spencer, the club was 'more of a home than his own residence', providing him with a library, a billiard room in which he would beat all comers and a smoking room and drawing room in which he could talk.[91] In 'friendly battles' with his intellectual peers, Spencer was a notoriously bad loser, particularly when his grand theories came up against hard scientific evidence to the contrary. Galton recalled an occasion on which Spencer, Huxley and another member dined together at the club:

Spencer said: 'You would little think when I was young I wrote a tragedy.' Huxley instantly flashed out with 'I know its plot.' Spencer indignantly denied the possibility of his knowing it, he having never shown the tragedy nor even spoken of its existence to any one, before then. Huxley persisted, and being challenged to tell, said that the plot lay in a beautiful deduction being killed by an ugly little fact.[92]

Spencer served on several committees from 1874 onwards, wrote frequent letters of complaint to the secretary on housekeeping matters and introduced many new members, including the artists Lawrence Alma-Tadema and John Brett, and the Japanese statesman and diplomat Kentaro Kaneko (as an honorary member).[93] He was assisted by Henry Tedder, the club's librarian, in the preparation of his *Principles of Sociology* (1877–96).[94] The complete clubman, he rarely missed either a committee meeting at the Athenæum or an X Club dinner. He was selective in his commitments, however, and declined an invitation to join the Metaphysical Society,[95] a prestigious discussion group limited to forty members and initially convened at Stanley's Deanery in 1869 by the architect James Knowles, editor first of the *Contemporary Review* and then of the *Nineteenth Century*, who failed to be elected at the Athenæum.[96]

Browning also declined, as did John Stuart Mill and Alexander Bain (1875, Rule II), the inventor and engineer, and Matthew Arnold did not belong for some reason.[97] Forty-four of the sixty-two members in the short history of the Metaphysical Society (1869–80) were also members of the Athenæum, however; seven of the ten review editors in the Metaphysical Society were also Athenians, five of the seven were Rule II members and four of them members of the Committee. More than one-sixth of the Metaphysical Society's membership had come under the influence of the Apostles.[98] As in the clubhouse and the more highbrow reviews, discussion in the Metaphysical Society was among 'thinking men' rather than professional philosophers, to the extent that some younger members who joined later found it all rather amateurish.[99] A pattern of 'unity in diversity, of social homogeneity encouraging intellectual heterodoxy' in the meetings of the Metaphysical Society has been described as 'typical of the English mind'.[100]

Diversity and heterodoxy were certainly in evidence at the meeting in February 1873, when a number of prominent Athenians were present. The Bishop of Peterborough, Dr William Magee, who was famed for his oratory in the Lords, described the gathering in a letter to his wife:

I went to dinner at the Grosvenor Hotel. The dinner was certainly a strangely interesting one. Had the dishes been as various we should have had severe dyspepsia, all of us. Archbishop Manning [1870, Rule II] in the chair was flanked by two Protestant bishops right and left – Gloucester and Bristol [Ellicott, 1863] and myself [1869] – on my right was Hutton [1871, Rule II] . . . an Arian; then came Father Dalgairns, a very able Roman Catholic priest; opposite him, Lord A. Russell [1858], a Deist; then two Scotch metaphysical writers – Freethinkers; then Knowles . . . then, dressed as a layman and looking like a country squire, was Ward . . . earliest of the perverts to Rome; then Greg [1868, Rule II], author of *The Creed of Christendom*, a Deist; then Froude [1859, Rule II], the historian, once a deacon in our church, now a Deist; then Roden Noel, an actual Atheist and red republican, and looking very like one! Lastly Ruskin [1849, Rule II], who read after dinner a paper on miracles! which we discussed for an hour and a half! Nothing could be calmer, fairer, or even, on the whole, more reverent than the discussion. Nothing flippant or scoffing or bitter was said on either side, and very great ability, both of speech and thought, was shown by most speakers. In my opinion, we, the Christians, had much the best of it. . . . We only wanted a Jew and a Mahometan to make our Religious Museum complete.[101]

The gentlemanly conventions of the Metaphysical Society were similar to those of the Athenæum, where Jews and Muslims were among the membership in the 1870s and where discussion also reflected the 'continued struggle of the liberal mind with a seemingly inevitable pluralism of values'.[102] A particular stumbling block for the liberal mind was the taboo subject of sex, which proved to be divisive at the club. Abraham Hayward QC (1835, Rule II) made the Athenæum his headquarters in a long career as an essayist and translator, writing for both the *Quarterly* and the *Edinburgh Review*, and as an advisor to some of the political and literary celebrities of the day.[103] Back in the 1820s, when establishing himself in London, he had made his name by being one of the few moderate Tories who could 'hold his own' against John Stuart Mill (1830) at the London Debating Society, which was dominated by philosophic radicals.[104] Half a century later, Hayward, by now a moderate Liberal, published an obituary of Mill in *The Times* for Saturday 10 May 1873 in which he referred to Mill's 'recklessly offending the most respectable portion of [his] constituency' as a Member of Parliament.[105]

Next day the review was denounced from the pulpit of St James's, York Street, by the Revd Stopford Augustus Brooke, a liberal clergyman and fashionable preacher who was to secede to the Unitarian church in 1880, the year after his election to the Athenæum. In response, Hayward had the obituary privately printed, as well as an open letter to Brooke in which he referred to Mill's having fallen 'under the notice of the police by circulating copies of "Every Woman's Book, or What is Love?" and flinging down the areas of houses, for the edification of the maid-servants, printed papers or broadsheets containing practical directions for sexual intercourse without adding to the population'.[106] More recently, he added, Mill had fallen in love with 'the lady (a married woman) who afterwards became his wife' and had written 'a succession of papers in the *Examiner* against marriage as a lasting tie, and in favour of unlimited liberty of divorce'. To class Mill with Locke, Bentham, Adam Smith or Malthus was 'preposterous'.

These exchanges proved to be the opening shots in a long battle over Mill's reputation, not least in further obituaries.[107] Mill's relationship with Harriet Taylor had been the subject of speculation for years. At the Athenæum, his own club and also that of Harriet's husband, the matter was personal: when Mill had visited the Taylors' family home in Regent's Park, John Taylor had tactfully withdrawn to the clubhouse;[108] and Mill's visitors at the end of his life included fellow members Bain, Hare, Fawcett and Morley. Hayward sent a copy of his open letter to the diplomat and author William Dougal Christie, an admirer of Mill and a member of the club since 1846. Following a heated exchange of letters, Christie cut Hayward at the whist table, a 'convulsive' act.[109] Hayward circulated a further printed statement on this 'deliberate outrage on the proprieties of cultivated life', to which Christie replied in kind, saying that Hayward had not only denied Mill's 'intellectual greatness', unlike other obituarists, but had 'horribly' cast 'reflection on a deceased lady'.[110] Christie's reply was pointedly dedicated to 'the friend of [his] youth', Mill's deceased brother, James Bentham Mill, himself a former member of the club. When a memorial tribute to Mill was proposed, Hayward campaigned against it, persuading Gladstone to withdraw his support on the basis of Mill's views on birth control.[111] The duke of Argyll, Lord Salisbury and Lord Derby, however, pillars of the Establishment and members of the club, sent in their subscriptions.

We have seen that the Athenæum extended liberal hospitality to certain members whose private lives were irregular: in the early years Richard Heber, a homosexual, was a trustee and the membership included J.M.W. Turner, Theodore Hook and Thomas Barnes, all of whom lived with common law wives, as did Wilkie Collins, elected in 1861 under Rule II. Marital difficulties that became the subject of public scandal seem not to have affected the club lives of Ruskin, whose marriage was annulled in 1854, Dickens, who separated from his wife in 1858, and the equally successful Bulwer Lytton, who in the same year committed his wife Rosina to a private asylum, following her frequent public denunciations of him.[112] Although Mill was not alone among the club's literati in suffering public scrutiny of his private life, the internal dispute over his posthumous reputation and that of his wife was unusual. Nevertheless, members of liberal mind could hold conservative views on sex and marriage. Matthew Arnold's opposition to the Deceased Wife's Sister Bill, for example, discussed in *Culture and Anarchy*, was based upon his strong sense that 'the sacredness of marriage, and the customs that regulate it, were triumphs of culture which had been won, painfully and with effort, from the unbridled promiscuity of primitive life'; and the earl of Rosebery, Gladstone's successor as Liberal premier, referred to Morley as unsuitable for the foreign secretaryship because he had 'anticipated the ceremony of marriage'.[113]

The year of Lord Rosebery's election to the Athenæum, 1885, also marked the death of the popular Tory politician and poet, Richard Monckton Milnes. What Emerson probably did not know when he became an admirer at the club in 1848 was that Milnes owned the finest collection of erotic literature in England.[114] Writers and publishers became alert to the danger of prosecution after the passing of the Obscene Publications Act in 1857: in the case of Thomas Hardy, who was elected under Rule II in 1891 but preferred the Savile Club, censorship of his work drove him to abandon fiction after publishing *Jude the Obscure* (1894–95). Lord Campbell, the Lord Chief Justice and the main sponsor of the act, joined the Athenæum in 1853. He was a Liberal politician, lawyer and man of letters who believed that morality depended upon divine revelation, as in the story of the Ten Commandments (Exodus 20), and who considered pornography to be more poisonous than prussic acid. His successor, Sir Alexander Cockburn, modified the act in 1868, shifting its focus from intention to effect. A notorious womaniser and the father of two illegitimate children, Cockburn was refused a peerage by Queen Victoria, who commented upon the 'notoriously bad moral character of the Chief Justice'.[115]

Concealment was essential in such a society, as Richard Burton knew very well. To members of the general public Captain Burton of the Indian Army and the diplomatic corps was the manly adventurer of Frederic Leighton's portrait, with glittering eyes and a cheek deeply scarred by a javelin that had penetrated his mouth in Somaliland in 1855. To members of the Athenæum he was also the habitué of the south library described by Henry Tedder, doggedly working on his translation of *The Arabian Nights* in the 1880s, 'snuff-box at his side'.[116] (He petitioned, unsuccessfully, for smoking to be allowed in the hall.)[117] In 1861, the year of his marriage, election to the club and consular posting to Fernando Po, Burton had been embroiled in the famous dispute with his fellow traveller and explorer of the sources of the Nile, Captain John Speke, which fascinated the Victorian public and revived memories of Denham and Clapperton.[118] Burton's avid interest in sex was widely known in his own circle, which included both Leighton (elected in 1866) and Swinburne during his time as consul at Damascus (1869–71), and probably among fellow members of the Club. Later his wife Isabel lived in fear of his falling foul of the Obscene Publications Act, which he avoided by having his translations of *The Kama Sutra* (1883) and *The Perfumed Garden* (1886) published privately. It was in 1886 that this master of disguise, who had visited Mecca as a young man, was knighted.

Following his appointment to the consulship at Trieste, in 1872, Burton was frequently given leave and spent some of it in London. He endorsed the foreword to his unexpurgated translation of *The Book of the Thousand Nights and a Night* (15 August 1885), not from the Athenæum but the Wanderers' Club, based at 9 Pall Mall and providing 'a place of resort for men of travel and other gentlemen who have associated in distant parts of the world'.[119] Burton's was an 'unembarrassed mind', and his translation includes passages of exuberant and athletic sexual activity that earlier translations, such as Edward William Lane's, had omitted.[120] The British reading public, however, lived under what he described in the foreword as a 'despotism of the lower "middle-class" Philister, who can pardon anything but superiority'.[121] The ten privately printed volumes of the *Nights* sold much better than expected. Three years later, however, in the famous 'terminal essay' to the *Supplemental Nights*, he was still angry, bemoaning the fact that, in an age 'saturated with cant and hypocrisy, here and there a venal pen will mourn over the "Pornography" of The Nights, dwell upon the "Ethics of Dirt" and the "Garbage of the Brothel"'.[122] The bibliography in Lady's Burton's biography of her late husband includes no erotica.[123] On 5 January 1886 Robert Louis Stevenson published *Jekyll and Hyde*.[124]

Meanwhile the 'secret life' of the Victorian Establishment, the subject of 'Walter's' pornographic epic, had come under public scrutiny in July 1885 when W.T. Stead published his articles on 'The maiden tribute of modern Babylon' in the *Pall Mall Gazette*. Although Josephine Butler 'hated' the now sensationalist evening paper, she had agreed to join Stead's 'special commission' among the brothels of London, following parliament's failure to raise the age of consent from thirteen years to fifteen or sixteen, and thus help to curb the national and international trafficking of young girls.[125] On Tuesday 7 July 1885, the day after graphic details of the horrors witnessed by the special commission first appeared in the *Gazette*, the club's General Committee discussed a letter received from Sir Frederick Bramwell, a distinguished mechanical engineer, calling attention to the paper's treatment of 'Horrible Revelations of London Vice' and 'Virgin Victims Sold, Drugged, Outraged and Exported'. A proposal from the Queen's librarian at Windsor, Richard Rivington Holmes, and seconded by Sir Rowland Blennerhassett, a Roman Catholic journalist and Liberal MP, that the *Gazette* 'be removed from the List of Newspapers taken in by the Club till further directions', was followed by an amendment moved by John Bridge, a police magistrate, and seconded by Arthur Lucas, a civil engineer, that the *Gazette* 'be discontinued for to-morrow and Thursday all copies of Monday's & Tuesday's issue save the copy reserved for filing being destroyed'.[126] The amendment was carried on a show of hands (5:3) and Bramwell was thanked. Outside the clubhouse Messrs W.H. Smith and Son tried to suppress sales[127] and the prince of Wales stopped his paper. The Athenæum was not the only club to discontinue theirs, as Stead himself made clear in his final article, addressed 'To our censors', on Monday 13 July: 'When Bishop Temple and Mr. Spurgeon, Dean Vaughan and the

Salvation Army, the Bishop of Rochester and Mr. Stopford Brooke, the Bishop of Ripon and the Rev. Hugh Price Hughes, combine to lift up their voices in aid and support of our protest against the secret crimes of London, we need not concern ourselves very much about the censure of the clubs and the invectives of the vicious.'[128] Temple, Vaughan, Thorold (Rochester) and Carpenter (Ripon) were all members of the club, as were Josephine Butler's clerical supporters, Manning, Ellicott and her husband George, a residentiary Canon of Winchester. When the General Committee met the next day, 14 July, the lawyer Sir Frederick Pollock proposed that, inasmuch as the *Gazette* 'continues the publication of objectionable matter', it be 'dropped till further notice': this was narrowly defeated (6:7).[129]

The motives behind the rapid passing of the Criminal Law Amendment Act in August 1885 were thought to have been mixed: along with shocked concern and a desire to stop the associated demonstrations across the country, there may have been a desire to protect some of those sitting on the Treasury benches. Similarly, it is impossible to say whether the General Committee's decision on 7 July to cancel the paper for two days (8 and 9 July) was related to Stead's offer in his article of the 6th to report names and addresses in strict confidence to a select group of individuals, some of whom were members of the club.[130] Any sensitivity in the Athenæum concerning the source of Stead's title – the myth of Athenians sending a tribute of seven youths and seven maidens to the labyrinth of Dædalus in Crete every nine years – would have been heightened by the public exhibition on 25 July of an arresting painting executed in anger by one of their own number: George Frederick Watts's *Minotaur* shows the beast crushing a small bird in its fist while looking out for the next shipment of victims.[131] It was another member, Richard Webster (1883), the recently appointed Attorney-General, who successfully prosecuted Stead in October 1885 for 'buying' Eliza Armstrong. Stead, the self-appointed Theseus of London's labyrinth, gloried in his comfortable three months in Holloway Prison; but he was never proposed as a member of the club.

# Part III
# 'RESERVE AND DIGNITY'
## (1890–1939)

# 7

_⁓_

# STRANGERS AND BROTHERS

The period from 1830 to 1890 was one of rapid industrial development and urbanisation in Britain, from the age of the coach to that of the railway, from the days of the old East India Company to those of the mightiest empire in history. But it was also the period of _Pax Britannica_, in which there was only one change of monarch. The period from 1890 to 1939, to which we now turn, saw five monarchs on the throne and an abdication crisis, the advent of the motor car and the aeroplane, universal suffrage and a world war. In the early twentieth century the Athenæum was regarded as a bulwark against the forces of change and modernity. Indeed, one explanation for the club's becoming a byword for a traditionalist society lies in the contrast between its slow rate of change and that of the world outside. In the early years of the period, from 1890 to 1914, the subject of this chapter, the club did change its system of governance and made modifications to the clubhouse. Strenuous efforts were also made, however, to resist proposed changes to the Athenæum's policy on the most controversial subject in Clubland: the admission of 'strangers'. During a period of prosperity for the club, it focused instead upon reaffirming its identity as the leading literary club in London and celebrating the success of its most eminent members.

J. Walter Wilson's _Ballot Day 1892_, discussed in the Prologue, was published on 11 March 1893 as a large double-page pull-out supplement to an article on the club by the Revd Francis Waugh in the _Illustrated London News_. The drawing conveys a sense of Olympian calm and assured continuity, as a large group of eminent men gather to elect a handful of new members. The decorative scheme in their clubhouse was, however, undergoing such dramatic changes at the time that Henry Tedder, the club's vigilant secretary and librarian, called the artist back to amend his work.[1] The need for redecoration had become apparent in 1886, when the introduction of electric lighting made the walls of the hall in particular look cold and flat.[2] The desire to make a dramatic aesthetic statement in the process reflected a newfound confidence in the club's financial situation, which in turn resulted from changes in the way it governed itself.

In 1889 the recommendations of a special investigative committee were accepted by an Extraordinary General Meeting (EGM): a manager was to be appointed and the office of secretary, as then constituted, abolished, with 'such of the duties connected with the Secretary's office as are purely literary or clerical' being carried out by the 'Secretary and Librarian' (Tedder).[3] To the 'great regret' of the General Committee this involved the retirement of Claude Webster, whose services as secretary were 'long and valued', but also coincided with thirty-five years of 'chronic indebtedness'.[4] Alan Sandilands, formerly manager of the Thatched House Club in St James's Street, was duly appointed as manager in July 1889 with a salary of £260 per annum, and within a year was congratulated for his 'zeal and capacity' in reforming the 'system of domestic management'.[5] By December 1890, the club had achieved a cash balance of £1,072, having had 'no balance at all' since the mid-1850s.[6] The post of manager existed for less than seven years, however: Sandilands, later described by a member as 'a very smooth-tongued and plausible person, who did very well until he began dipping his fingers into the till', left in 1896, when he was found to be 'short in his cash'.[7]

A further constitutional change proved to be of lasting significance: the establishment of a 'Committee of Management', consisting of nine members, to deal with the domestic financial affairs of the club. The special investigative committee was reconstituted as the Executive Committee, a group which would soon be meeting weekly (on Tuesdays at 4 p.m.) and reporting to the General Committee, which would now meet monthly.[8] At their first meeting, on 21 May 1889, members of the Executive Committee put Sir Frederick Abel, an ordnance chemist and trustee, in the chair. Financial control would always remain their priority: they approved the budgets of other committees, for example, and were responsible for submitting accounts to the AGM. They also dealt with matters relating to the ballot, staffing, and everything from provisioning to boiler repairs, chimney sweeping, petty thefts and complaints. (It was not long before the first complaint against the Executive Committee itself arose.)[9] A new level of vigilance was now achieved: it was discovered, for example, that the number of ordinary members had crept up in error, necessitating a temporary reduction in the number of candidates who could be elected in order to reduce the main membership to the statutory 1,200.[10]

Sir Frederick had played a leading role in the electrification of the clubhouse. Now, as chairman of the Executive Committee, he created another sub-committee to make recommendations on the sensitive matter of redecoration.[11] Arthur Lucas, a civil engineer whose company was involved in developing London's underground railway system, had served on the electrification committee and now joined two other members of the new group, both of whom were distinguished artists. The 'inscrutably senatorial' Sir Edward Poynter was both president of the Royal Academy, and thus an *ex officio* member of the club's General Committee, and director of the National Gallery: he was the last practising artist to hold the post.[12] Like Poynter, his friend and colleague Lawrence Alma-Tadema, a genial and expansive Dutchman, was not only a painter, whose works included *Phidias Showing the Frieze of the Parthenon to his Friends* (1868), but also a decorative designer. Both men were prominent figures in the classical revival associated with late-Victorian Aestheticism, a movement led by Sir Frederic Leighton, one of the most influential members of the General Committee until his death in 1896.[13] Decimus Burton's restrained Greek Revival interior of 1830 had appealed to a generation of members who shared a background in the Classics and whose number included a few influential individuals who had visited Athens. Six decades later, Pompeii was as significant a source of inspiration as Athens for Poynter and Alma-Tadema as they prepared their Græco-Roman designs for a later and more widely travelled generation of members. Their archaeological approach was in tune with the times and their designs 'turned into reality' some of the paintings that had made them famous.[14]

Their most enduring innovation was the introduction of marble dadoes in the hall and on the grand staircase. According to William Gaunt, Alma-Tadema 'was wont to say that he first acquired his passion for marble in 1858 when he visited the handsome, marmoreal smoking-room of a club in Ghent, but this was only a faint, modern reflection of that ancient club – the public bath; and marble to be seen in its glory must be seen in Italy'.[15] There, Gaunt continues, as the artist 'looked on the tinted columns, framed in foliage and set against the wine-dark sea, he exclaimed, "And yet fools say that pale green and blue do not harmonize"'. In 1890 many of the sub-committee's bold proposals on paint colours were adopted, but the plan to replace scagliola columns with marble proved to be prohibitively expensive. The resulting scheme, though doomed to obsolescence within half a century, was a sea-change into something rich and strange.

The phasing of the work over three summer closures spread the costs and avoided disruption. First, in August 1891, the hall and grand staircase were redecorated in just four weeks, implementing designs by Alma-Tadema which took account of the Roman mosaic floor in the hall, the walls of which were described by Waugh as 'painted in primrose yellow of various tints' and dadoed with 'pavonazetto and other coloured marbles, the back with green cipolino'.[16] The art historian Bruce Boucher, who examines the whole decorative scheme in detail in *Armchair Athenians*, explains that part of the staircase was 'panelled with fine slabs of brecchia', but that Alma-Tadema's proposals for an entablature in beige and dark red, and columns to either side of the Apollo with green bases and shafts of brown and tawny yellow, were dropped.[17] The artist's floral stencilling in the wagon roof of the hall would be painted over at an unspecified date, but his pendant chandeliers, described by Waugh as 'very classical', are still admired today, as is his exotic lantern above the staircase, added in 1898 and described by Boucher as seeming 'closer in style to Venetian Renaissance than Burton's late neo-classical Hall' (Plate 17).[18]

In 1892 the principal rooms on the ground floor were 'adorned with beautiful and original designs after Mr. Poynter's sketches'.[19] Boucher argues that changes to the coffee room were, 'if anything, a more radical departure from Burton's original scheme' than Alma-Tadema's hall and staircase. Here the driving force was Poynter, 'who contrived to suggest a triclinium of a Pompeian villa'.[20] His elevations show 'a dado of black with decorative patterns in lilac, gold and off-white. Above this the walls were divided into panels framed in lilac with enrichments in red and white; the centres of the panels were in two tones of yellow with black beading'. In 1898 Alfred Baldry recorded that the dominant colours were 'golden yellow and black for the walls, and greyish white, pale purple, and green for the ceiling'.[21] Whereas Poynter's interventions in the coffee room later disappeared under numerous coats of paint, his morning room represents a late-Victorian survival in the clubhouse today, although originally the ceiling was coloured a 'deep but vivid blue' rather than green and was lavishly gilded (Plate 18).[22] Baldry described the room, 'with its gorgeous ceiling, its walls of gold Japanese leather, and its woodwork of broken brown', as 'wonderfully sumptuous and daring'. Here and throughout the ground floor the old windows were replaced with plate glass in polished mahogany frames.

By 23 August 1892 the Executive Committee could express its 'gratification with the work so ably & so satisfactorily accomplished' by the sub-committee and voted Tedder an honorarium of £20 for the extra work involved.[23] Similar sentiments were expressed a year later, when the 're-decoration (from designs kindly presented by Mr. Alma-Tadema) of all the rooms on the First Floor, as well as of the Smoking and Billiard Rooms in the Basement', was achieved in five weeks.[24] Tedder was particularly excited by the drawing room, which he described to Waugh as 'a brilliant surprise'.[25] The dominant red colouring (Plate 12) was replaced by green, and aluminium leaf was applied to the ornamentation of the central dome and the cornice and ceiling beams (Plate 19).[26] The room that had enchanted Charles Darwin and Matthew Arnold when they first joined was now beautifully embellished. External work in 1894, which included the construction of a new stone parapet designed by Alma-Tadema, was supervised by the sub-committee, who continued to make proposals for the maintenance programme for some years to come.[27]

All this decorative work, internal and external, was carefully documented by Tedder, whose archival habits in his dual capacity proved to be of lasting benefit to the Club: bound volumes of designs and correspondence, estimates and receipts, and the minutes of three different committees provide the historian with a wealth of material on which to work. Having researched this material, Boucher places his reconstruction of the new decorative scheme 'in the context of late Victorian historicism in art and architecture, with its preoccupation with period style'.[28] Whereas the hall, coffee room and drawing room 'aimed at conveying a Graeco-Roman tone, more in keeping with the representational functions of a society dedicated to the traditions embodied by the Athenæum's name', the morning and writing rooms were 'redecorated in the high aesthetic mode, in keeping with the best of current fashion'. Boucher considers this achievement to be all the more remarkable in light of the 'generally conservative tastes' of other London clubs.[29]

During the first six decades of its tenure at the southern end of Waterloo Place, the Athenæum had itself taken a conservative line with respect to its clubhouse, which was widely known and admired. The specific inclusion of artists in the club's foundation, combined with the fact that successive presidents of the Royal Academy had *ex officio* roles on the General Committee, meant that many leading painters and sculptors were members. By the 1890s a new generation of candidates who had been trained in the visual arts was being elected under Rule II, men who might be expected to understand Poynter's and Alma-Tadema's intentions: Marcus Stone (1889), Hubert von Herkomer (1889), Thomas Hardy (1891), who was an architect, George du Maurier (1891), Linley Sambourne (1895) and John Singer Sargent (1898).[30] How was it, then, that the clubhouse, imaginatively redecorated within, came to be spoiled without, later in the 1890s, by the addition of an unprepossessing attic storey?

Back in the 1850s the introduction of an extra gallery to the south library, reached by a precipitous spiral staircase, had been the cheapest solution to the problem of space for bookcases, in a club whose members refused to increase either the fees or the size of the membership, and whose General Committee found it impossible to change the situation as they had to achieve a two-thirds majority at a General Meeting. Little had changed four decades later, by which time a number of proposals for an extra storey had been turned down. Decimus Burton, who had been frustrated by the club's dilatoriness in the mid-1850s, finally resigned in 1864 after another proposal for an extra storey, this time with a 'Library Gallery, 75 feet long by 19 feet wide' and a billiard room, had come to nothing.[31] During Thomas Henry Wyatt's time as honorary architect (1865–80) the problem of space became more pressing: in 1874 a group of members even proposed that the club should buy the lease of number 9 Pall Mall, on the corner of Waterloo Place north, and dig a tunnel to reach it from the clubhouse.[32]

Wyatt's successor, Charles Barry (son of Sir Charles), prepared a complete set of plans and sections based on measurements in 1882, as 'no means of dealing with any question as to the Building' was available.[33] This enabled him to submit fully worked up recommendations for the enhancement of the building five years later, when his drawings supplemented the most comprehensive review to date of the club's past expenditure and current needs by a 'Building Special Committee'.[34] Each year six or seven hundred volumes were being added to the fifty thousand already shelved in numerous rooms around the clubhouse. Barry proposed to build an additional library on a 'Second Floor', '57 feet by 30 feet, occupying the whole frontage to Carlton Gardens', and connected to the present south library by a 'new Circular Staircase'. He would raise the outer walls to accommodate the new top floor, create a new entrance on Pall Mall, in line with those of the Travellers and Reform Clubs designed by his father, turn the hall through 90 degrees and extend the coffee room. In 1888, when Barry's remodelling of the ground floor was rejected on grounds of cost (an estimated £40,000), he produced further drawings. His efforts were in vain, however, and the elegant view of the clubhouse from Carlton Gardens that he presented as a frontispiece to his 'proposed alterations & additions to the Club House' is left as a reminder of what might have been (Plate 20).

By now, however, it was clear that something had to be done about the club's 'chronic indebtedness' and its urgent need for space for up to twenty thousand volumes. Whereas the establishment of the Executive Committee as a response to the first problem proved to be of lasting benefit, the conversion of two rooms on the top floor to create a 'Store Library' was only a stopgap. (It cost just £127. 15s. 0d.)[35] By 1898 the General Committee had decided to looked outside for a permanent solution. Sir Frederick Abel was both secretary and director of the Imperial Institute in Kensington. Now the institute's architect, Thomas Collcutt, was asked to address 'the Question of Enlarging the Club House'. Collcutt claimed that his attic storey, 'treated as a component part of the building, would really enhance the architectural value of the latter': set back 'some six feet from the face of the main walls', it would add dignity.[36] His scheme provided for a card room, smoking room, billiard room, staff accommodation and a small book store. The General Committee liked the 'comparatively small cost of the proposals, being £13,267, as against £20,000, or even £40,000, on former occasions'.[37] Miraculously, the membership agreed and by 12 May 1899 Abel and his Executive Committee could approve a tender from Messrs Mowlem, contractors to the Imperial Institute.

A week later Charles Barry, a member since 1872, resigned as honorary architect, stating that he had been treated with 'great injustice', and circulated a pamphlet to support his claim.[38] Tedder was instructed to reply, saying that no discourtesy had been intended and regretting Barry's resignation.[39] This was not enough for the architect's brother, Sir John Wolfe Barry, a prominent civil engineer and a member of the General Committee, who also resigned in protest.[40] As work began, superintended by Alma-Tadema, Arthur Lucas and other members of the Building Committee, the club leased the top floor of Messrs Gullick's premises at 24 Pall Mall for six months.[41] The temporary protective structure erected on the roof of the clubhouse quickly became the butt of jokes in the press: the *Star* likened it to a birdcage and the *Graphic* described it as a Swiss chalet.[42] An article on the scheme in the *Builder* was far from jocular in tone, however: its reviewer announced that it was 'impossible to approve, on architectural grounds, either in regard to the building itself or the general effect of Waterloo-place; and it may be added that in a structural sense also the scheme is very objectionable'.[43] 'We shall have the spectacle', the writer continued, 'of a large building, designed with classic regularity and dignity, carrying on its roof a structure of inferior character and which has no obvious means of support, being erected within the main walls'. The question of professional etiquette was then addressed, with lengthy quotations from Barry's pamphlet and from correspondence with both architects. Although the *Builder* was forced to withdraw its description of Collcutt as 'unprofessional', this was unwelcome publicity for the club. Perhaps the most painful aspect of the article, however, was the fact that its aesthetic judgments were unanswerable (Plate 21).

While the clubhouse may have looked different by the end of the nineteenth century, the reputation of the club as an elite institution was undimmed. The fact that 1,600 candidates were waiting for a decade and a half before coming up for election was regarded as a badge of honour. It was also a cause for concern, however: a generation of deserving middle-aged men had been 'blocked in their laudable desire of joining the Club by a mass of younger Candidates'.[44] Although the Candidates Books of the late-Victorian period are littered with the names of sons and nephews of existing members who sought entry to 'the family club', the requirements remained exceptionally high, and many of the new members had no family connections with the Athenæum. Outsiders regarded the club as conservative and intellectually grand. A reviewer of Waugh's short history declared that, for 'men of letters and science the Athenæum is the Mecca of club-land. The pilgrimage is long and arduous.'[45] In the 1880s and 1890s the number of professors rose as the number of peers went down, and in 1902 Alfred Kinnear placed the Athenæum 'at the head of the erudite clubs of London', a 'magnificent temple dedicated in a sense to literature, the church, and the arts'.[46] It was Burton's temple that appeared on the cover of Joseph Hatton's *Clubland, London and Provincial* in 1890, and at the end of the period under review, after Collcutt had done his worst, Stanley Ramsey could still write, 'The intelligent stranger cannot fail to recognise at a glance that this is an institution associated in some way with the liberal arts; and the premier position that the club holds in the literary world is effectively characterised in its architectural presentment'.[47]

The Athenæum's 'premier position' had been confirmed at the turn of the twentieth century when some of its most gifted members were garlanded with newly established prizes and honours. Today's visitors to the clubhouse are often guided to the Nobel Book, a large volume that is proudly displayed on the main landing. Of the 835 prizewinners between 1901 and 2012, no fewer than 50 were members of the Athenæum. When Sir Alcon Copisarow, chairman of the General Committee (1989–92), showed the book to the Swedish Ambassador he could not resist saying, 'Before we elect a candidate to the club we make sure he has won the Nobel Prize'; to which Leif Leifland replied, 'And before we select a Prize winner, we always check that he is a member of the Athenæum.'[48] The malariologist Sir Ronald Ross was the first Athenian to receive the prize, in his case for medicine, in 1902, only seven years after Sir Frederick Abel and James Dewar had been successful in defending a legal action brought against them by Alfred Nobel.[49] The long delay in Ross's election to the Athenæum under Rule II in 1922 may have been for personal reasons: he was a belligerent and vain man, 'easier to admire than to love'.[50] Of the first eight recipients, however, four were elected to the club *after* their Nobel prizes had been awarded,[51] and of the total number, twenty-six prizewinners – just over half – were elected later, almost all under Rule II. A club which prided itself on its elite status now ensured that it built up a fine collection of Nobelists.

Honours and awards were bestowed upon individual Athenians so frequently, by the monarch or by learned societies and universities at home and abroad, that the club did not celebrate their successes in any overt way. When Alma-Tadema was knighted in 1899, for example, a banquet was held, not at the Athenæum, but in the Whitehall Rooms of the Hotel Metropole.[52] In 1902, however, the club held the first banquet since its foundation, in order to mark a signal achievement by a number of members: nine of the twelve recipients of the Order of Merit, newly established by King Edward VII, were Athenians. The nine were Field-Marshal Earl Roberts of Kandahar, Field-Marshal Viscount Wolseley, Lord Rayleigh, Lord Kelvin, Lord Lister, the Right Honourable John Morley, the Right Honourable William Lecky, Sir William Huggins and George Frederick Watts.[53] All these men had been elected to the club between 1867 and 1881 under Rule II, which reflected well on the General Committee's record in choosing members 'of distinguished eminence in Science, Literature, or the Arts, or for Public Services'.[54] Having received representations from the membership, the General Committee, with Abel in the chair, decided to hold a dinner for 150 on 4 July.[55] The ballot for tickets available to club members at 35/-, to include wine, was heavily oversubscribed. Abel lent 'a number of screens, candelabra, knives & forks & other articles' for an occasion which was clearly beyond the Club's resources.[56] Financially, however, all was well: expenses were balanced by receipts.

With characteristic thoroughness, Tedder prepared a bound volume of papers to commemorate the event. This includes the announcement in the *London Gazette*, in which the Athenæum is mentioned, photographic portraits of the OMs, a table plan, a menu, transcripts of the speeches, based on shorthand notes taken by Thomas Hill, the assistant secretary, and miscellaneous notes. Inevitably there were diary clashes and other complications. Viscount Wolseley sent his regrets from the Admiralty yacht *Iolaire*, Skye. Watts, who had sorrowfully given up his membership in 1895 through ill health, could only manage the pre-dinner reception in the drawing room, as could Morley, who was due to be the chief guest at a political dinner for MPs at the Reform that night. Morley's absence was regretted by Lord Avebury (John Lubbock) when he toasted the guests as chairman of the General Committee: 'If we cannot all share his political views', he commented in the spirit of a non-partisan Club, 'we recognise his consistency, his courage and courtesy, and offer him our hearty congratulations.'[57]

Each OM who was present responded in turn. The diminutive Earl Roberts, a national hero and a trustee of the club, endeared himself to the company in his closing remarks:

Before he sat down he would like to refer to the fact that it was one of the proudest recollections of his life to remember that it was now 21 years ago since he was elected to membership of the Athenæum an honour which had been conferred by the Committee of the Club under the famous rule II and that in former times the same honour has also been conferred on Field-Marshals, Lord Clyde, Sir W. Gomm, Lord Napier of Magdala, Viscount Gough, Sir G. Pollock, Lord Strathnairn, and last but greatest of all the Duke of Wellington who was an original member of the Club.[58]

Lord Rayleigh and Lord Kelvin also registered their pride in the club, and the astronomer Sir William Huggins struck the keynote of the evening with a proverb from the Latin, 'that the highest praise was praise from the men who are praised', adding that 'when he looked round the room he felt that to be the guest of such a company was praise indeed and the honour of being a recipient of the Order of Merit was greatly enhanced by the compliment paid by the Athenæum'.[59] When Lord Lister concluded, however, 'that the King had been pleased to confer the Order of Merit upon him owing to his official connection with His Majesty's illness but he could assure them that he had very little to do with the actual treatment of the King', many of his medical colleagues in the coffee room would have agreed with him.[60]

The climax of the evening came when the prime minister rose to propose the vote of thanks. Arthur Balfour, a member since 1886 and a later recipient of the Order of Merit, had taken office less than two weeks earlier, following a Conservative victory in the general election. Having been greeted with 'hearty cheers' and made some self-deprecating remarks, he 'supposed that never in the history of the great metropolis, probably never in the history of this country had there been gathered in a room of that size such a body of undiluted distinction'.[61] Lord Avebury responded and read a 'gracious reply from His Majesty the King' to the loyal telegram that had been sent to the Royal Yacht at Cowes earlier in the evening. In the days that followed, press coverage of the dinner was extensive and exuberant. 'It is both natural and fitting', suggested the *Westminster Review*, 'that "the club of the literati" – as the polite Baedeker has called the Athenæum – should desire to do special honour, in the customary English fashion of a dinner, to the first twelve members of the newly established Order of Merit, seeing that most of them are already within its own exclusive circle.'[62]

Such dinners were not only customary in 1902: they were also gargantuan. 'Those meals!' exclaims Sebastian in Vita Sackville-West's novel, *The Edwardians*: 'Those endless, extravagant meals, in which they all indulged all the year round! . . . How strange that eating should play so important a part in social life!'[63] The king's dinners, private as well as official, normally consisted of twelve courses. 'House dinners' at the Athenæum were generally limited to ten. On these occasions the Owls of Pall Mall really were 'gorging', as an unattributed ditty had put it:

All ye who pass by, just stop and behold,
    And say – Don't you think it a sin
That Minerva herself is left out in the cold
    While her *owls* are all gorging within?

Held in the morning room, house dinners were restricted to the club's 'exclusive circle' and were occasionally hosted by a group of members in honour of one of their number. A striking example is the dinner in April 1903 for Randall Davidson, who had been nominated by Balfour as Temple's successor at Canterbury and enthroned there in February. The Revd Henry Scott Holland, a Canon of St Paul's, who used his position as editor of *The Commonwealth* to promulgate his Christian Socialist views, had offered some advice to Davidson on his translation from Winchester to Canterbury:

Bishop Davidson's point of danger is not the Court. He has survived its perils with a singular simplicity. Rather it is to be sought at the Athenæum.

There dwell the sirens who are apt to beguile and bewitch him. They have ceased to be mermaids with harps and have adopted the disguise of elderly and excellent gentlemen of reputation, who lead you aside into corners and, in impressive whispers, inform you what will not do and what the intelligent British public will not stand. The Bishop has a deep veneration for the judgement and the wisdom of important laity of this type. Yet the Athenæum is not the shrine of infallibility. Its elderly common sense has no prophetic *afflatus*.[64]

Scott Holland had been entered in the club's Candidates Book in 1875 but was not elected.[65] Davidson, proposed the previous year, had been delighted by his election in 1890, by which time he had been resident chaplain at Lambeth Palace to Archbishop Tait – a prominent member of the club since the time of the Colenso affair – and then Dean of Windsor, where he was in effect the main advisor on ecclesiastical matters to both the queen and Archbishop Benson, the central figure in *Ballot Day 1892* (see p. 3). Davidson soon became 'one of the best known and most esteemed members of the Club', where bishops were often to be seen (Plate 22),[66] and went on to serve as a member of the General Committee (1901–4) and as a trustee (1914–30).[67] His biographer, Bishop George Bell, records that some of his lay friends in the club took Scott Holland's comments as a challenge and 'determined to show by entertaining him at dinner how highly they appreciated his frequent presence among them'.[68] Bell's account of the dinner is worth quoting in full, as the hosts, most of whom attended the OM dinner the previous year, epitomised the club's 'undiluted distinction' in the Edwardian era:

As the available room in the Athenæum could only seat about a couple of dozen, there was a difficulty in selecting the hosts from among so many who would wish to do him honour. The guest, on being sounded, would not go further than to hint that perhaps, on such an occasion, his 'brethren' would hardly be in place. Accordingly there were no bishops present at the dinner on 24th April 1903; and the only two hosts in Holy Orders were men who held positions necessarily in close touch with lay opinion, the Dean of Westminster, Dr. Armitage Robinson, and the Master of the Temple, Canon Ainger.

The then Prime Minister, Mr. Balfour, was in the Chair, with the guest of the evening on his right. The American Ambassador, Mr. Choate, was there among the hosts; so were Lord Roberts, then Commander-in-Chief; the Speaker of the House of Commons, Mr. Gully; and the President of the Royal Academy, Sir Edward Poynter. Four statesmen, two Liberal, two Conservative, attended – Mr. Asquith, Lord Goschen, Lord Knutsford (Sir Henry Holland), and Mr. John Morley, the latter, with Mr. Birrell, representing literature as well. For the law came the Lord Chief Justice (Lord Alverstone), the Master of the Rolls (Sir Richard Henn Collins), and Lord Robertson (Lord of Appeal). Oxford and Cambridge were well represented by Sir William Anson and Sir Richard Jebb. Science had an exponent in Lord Avebury, the principal Trustee of the Club; and the party was completed by Lord Balfour of Burleigh, Sir Henry Craik, Sir Charles Dalrymple, and the then Editor of *The Times*, Mr. G.E. Buckle. One of the hosts, a man of caustic wit, after looking round the big circular dinner-table, said to his neighbour, 'I suppose we here are the kind of folk whom the historian of the future will describe as *alors célèbres*'. At least they were a brilliant representation of the Club at the time; and the Archbishop, in replying to the toast of his health proposed by Mr. Balfour, showed how deeply he felt the compliment, and how highly he valued his intimate association with the Athenæum.

Several of the *dramatis personae* listed by Bell reassembled a month later for a 'dinner to Mr. Chamberlain by personal friends in the Athenæum', when the prime minister again took the chair. Writing in 2001, Roy Jenkins considered that 'men of fairly quiet learning' had been the core of the club since the nineteenth century, and had 'provided the incentive for politicians, often off-shore members, none the less to feel that they were privileged to be admitted to an academy of letters'.[69] Jenkins might have taken Joseph Chamberlain as an example, judging by the friendships, including with political opponents, that he had made since his election to the club in 1882. The Chamberlain dynasty had a more turbulent time at the political clubs. Henry Lucy recorded that when Richard Chamberlain became a Liberal MP in 1885, Joseph put his younger brother up at the Reform Club.[70] Animosity against 'Joe', Lucy continued, 'which that strong personality has in all the varied circumstance of public life succeeded in evoking, found expression in more than sufficient black balls to keep the new M.P. out'. Chamberlain, 'incensed at this rebuff, forthwith resigned his membership, and has never since entered the stately hall of the Reform'. Lucy would see Chamberlain's son Austen at the Reform occasionally, but only during the annual cleaning of the Devonshire Club in St James's Street. Later, in 1911, Austen was to join the Carlton Club, along with other prominent Liberal Unionists, and in 1922 was to lose the Conservative leadership there, at the famous 'Carlton Club Meeting'.[71] On 29 May 1903, however, having been elected to the Athenæum eight months earlier and more recently become Balfour's Postmaster General, he attended the house dinner in honour of his father, no doubt monocled and looking remarkably like him.

Winston Churchill's description of Joseph Chamberlain as 'the man who made the weather' was never more pertinent than in the spring of 1903, when the Colonial Secretary's ideas on tariff reform dominated the political agenda. Only fourteen days before the dinner was held, and presumably after it had been arranged, Chamberlain had delivered his momentous speech in Birmingham, where he argued that a 'Federal Union' of Britain and the self-governing white settler colonies would 'make the British Empire powerful and influential for good beyond the dreams of any one now living'.[72] Seated on his left at the dinner was Balfour, 'Uncle Bob' Salisbury's successor as prime minister, who sought a middle way on tariff reform for his coalition of Conservatives and Liberal Unionists. In an act of precise social geometry, Herbert Henry Asquith the Liberal Imperialist was seated directly opposite Chamberlain the Liberal Unionist. Later that year, in September, when Chamberlain resigned in order to run a platform campaign, his message would be countered by Asquith in dogged pursuit around the country. Halfway between these political antagonists sat Sir Robert Herbert, for twenty-one years permanent secretary to the Colonial Office, who was to become chairman of the Tariff Commission at Chamberlain's invitation in December. Next to Herbert was Sir Rowland Blennerhassett, president of Queen's College Cork, and, next to Asquith, John Morley, another former Liberal colleague of Chamberlain's who had cultivated him in the 1870s and seconded his nomination at the club in 1882. Morley opposed Imperial Preference, not least in defence of India's interests. Rudyard Kipling, seated on Austen's right, was a great admirer of his father, with whom he had dined twice at the club during the Boer War.[73]

On Kipling's right was Sir George Goldie, who had clashed with Chamberlain in the 1890s when defending the interests of the Royal Niger Company, which he had founded. Yet here they all were, allies and opponents of the Right Honourable Joseph Chamberlain at Westminster, but 'personal friends' of Joe's at the Athenæum, celebrating the man who, like Gladstone, Viscount Goschen (on Asquith's right) and Churchill, changed parties in mid-career, but who, unlike them, also split both parties.

Several of the other hosts were pillars of the Establishment who also attended the archbishop's dinner and whose attendance on this occasion would have been expected: Viscount Alverstone, the Lord Chief Justice; William Gully, the Speaker; George Earle Buckle, editor of *The Times*, who had seconded Austen Chamberlain; Sir Henry Craik, Secretary at the Scottish Office; and Earl Roberts, seated next to Balfour.[74] Allied to this group was Henry White, first secretary at the American Embassy and a leading socialite, beloved of the Souls, who was elected in 1903. Other friends ranged from Mr Justice Bigham, formerly a Liberal Unionist MP, and his neighbour Major General Sterling, Commander of the Coldstream Guards, to Henry James, who had shaved off his beard to greet the twentieth century and, like the close-shaven Chamberlain, looked like a modern man. James's bearded friend Sidney Colvin, keeper of prints and drawings at the British Museum, looked venerable. It was in 1903 that Chamberlain was painted by Hubert von Herkomer, whose sitters included many members of the club, among them Sir George Goldie, John Morley and Lord Kelvin, all present that evening. The oldest member at the dinner was the genial Sir Frederick Bramwell, active as an engineer at the birth of the railway and of the motor car, and who, like Blennerhassett, had deplored W.S. Stead's exposés in the *Pall Mall Gazette*.[75] One of Stead's supporters was also present, however: Boyd Carpenter, the liberal Bishop of Ripon, whose brother was a Unitarian minister in America and would have been more acceptable to the Unitarian Chamberlain than some other bishops who frequented the club; he would also have said grace.

The banquet for the OMs and the two house dinners for the archbishop and the Colonial Secretary were inward-looking affairs at which members celebrated the achievements of their brethren. Strangers fared less well, and while the club was often saluted for the eminence of its membership, it was also criticised for its attitude towards outsiders. In 1888 the *Society Herald* reported that 'an inexpressible something filters through one's being in entering the Athenæum as if the champions of letters and science were holding a solemn conclave upon the destruction of an intruder'.[76] The tiny space off the hall that was allotted to strangers had been the subject of adverse comments since 1830, and around 1914 a writer could comment: 'I have always thought that the Athenæum is a little inclined to treat visitors as though they were pickpockets. If a great man asks you to see him there, and you are both hurriedly concealed in a sort of telephone-box, you will perhaps think the same.'[77]

The status quo did not go unchallenged, however. In 1892 an EGM considered a proposal that 'the Executive Committee be instructed to appoint forthwith a special Committee to consider the conditions on which Strangers may be admitted to the Clubhouse': the motion was lost.[78] A proposal to admit strangers to the coffee room was defeated (125:132) after a division at the 1901 AGM. The following year a similar proposal received from two non-members, Sir William Lee-Warner and Sir Henry Stewart Cunningham, was more heavily defeated (110:140) at the AGM, which also had before it a printed circular to which forty-five members had put their names, including Waugh, Abel, Poynter and Frederic Harrison.[79] First and foremost, the circular proclaimed, 'the Club is used for literary purposes in the evening by members, to whom quietude is of great value, and as all the rooms on the first floor, and also the upper Smoking Room contain books, the only apartment to which guests could, without inconvenience, be admitted before or after dinner is the Billiard Room, so that members themselves would be deprived of any chance of playing after dinner'.[80] This highly significant statement gives substance to what might otherwise be dismissed as a cliché – that the Athenæum was once a library with a club attached, for example – or as merely a *bon mot*, such as Kipling's remark that the drawing room in the afternoon was like a cathedral between services.[81] The furniture in the drawing room, which Decimus Burton labelled as the 'Library' in 1829, was in fact still arranged as in the library of a great house, for 'literary purposes', in the 1920s (Plate 23).[82]

The circular went on to assert that 'the reserve and dignity of the Athenæum cannot but be materially affected by the introduction of restaurant facilities quite foreign to the objects of the Club', and that 'our Club from the sense of quiet which pervades it, is, and always has been . . . valued by men in every walk of public life as a safe retreat'. The second point encapsulates one of the defining features of the Athenæum as an institution in the Victorian and Edwardian eras, when so many of its members served on public bodies and turned to the club's collection of books and pamphlets for information or refreshment, as in the cases of the duke of Newcastle, Samuel Wilberforce, Matthew Arnold and H.H. Asquith. Outside what Ralph Nevill called the 'foremost modern literary club',[83] however, its 'reserve and dignity' were often interpreted as frostiness and pomposity, as in Harry Graham's 'Club Cameo':

> Dignified, austere, infestive,
>     Stands the stately Athenæum,
> With an atmosphere suggestive
>     Of a mausoleum.
> Freezing silence reigns within
> (You can hear the falling pin!)
> And the punster points with pride
> To the *frieze* you get outside![84]

Indeed, so quiet was the Athenæum that *Punch* reported on the club's addiction to dancing, singing, boxing and late-night debauchery in the only full-page article on Clubland in the history of the magazine to that date (Plate 24).[85]

In 1907, the year after George Morrow's cartoon appeared in *Punch*, the Executive Committee received letters from Sir Edwin Durning Lawrence expressing his concerns about the future of the Athenæum and of London clubs in general. In an article on 'The Slump in Club-land', published in the *Observer* on 14 July, Sir Edwin lamented the length of waiting lists and the 'old-fashioned' views of committees.[86] 'It must not be forgotten', he argued, 'that whereas the fundamental idea of club life is rest and routine, the guiding principle of modern life is restlessness and constant change.' Although the article was 'received' by the Executive Committee, no discussion was minuted. Humphry Ward's comment that 'few periods in the history of the Athenæum have been so lacking in events, and perhaps for that very reason so happy, as the twelve years which intervened between the Banquet of 1902 and the Declaration of War' indicates that 'rest and routine' were highly valued in the club.[87] Far from being 'quietly progressive' in this period, as Ward goes on to suggest, the club was slow to respond to pressure for change in its policy on strangers. In 1908 the Executive Committee made the absurd suggestion that the west end of the coffee room, 'near the serving door shall be screened off and five tables set apart' for members entertaining guests, with limited access to the clubhouse after dinner.[88] When a motion to this effect was put to the vote at an EGM in November, it was defeated (148:155).[89] Six years passed before the General Committee decided that the matter had to be reopened, 'in view of the changing tendencies in Club life'.[90] Of the estimated 347 members who attended the AGM in May 1914 – a huge turnout – about 23 dissented on a show of hands.[91] Only the morning room and the billiard room were to be accessible to members with guests after dinner, which was to be served early, between 6.30 p.m. and 8.15 p.m., at five tables 'set apart' at the west end of the coffee room: the idea of screens seems to have been dropped.[92] Although hedged about with restrictions, the change in policy was significant enough to attract the attention of the press. One unidentified newspaper reported that strangers were now permitted to dine at the Club 'without being hidden in a private room', adding: 'The Athenæum has for many years represented all that is stiffest, most conservative, and most exclusive in club life, and it is only within recent times that members could smoke except in the basement'.[93]

The private room referred to here was the morning room, where small numbers of strangers had been admitted as guests at private 'members' dinners' since 1887, when a motion from the General Committee to allow this was passed at the AGM (111:62).[94] Although strangers were intended to be kept behind closed doors on these occasions, opinion remained divided among the membership. The regulations were therefore reviewed by the Executive Committee three years later and printed for the attention of members: 'I. House Dinners, for Members of the Club exclusively, may be served, as heretofore, in the Morning Room. II. Members' Dinner. – A Member or Members may invite Members of the Club and Strangers to a private Dinner in the Morning Room; provided always that when Strangers are entertained the proportion of Members dining shall never be less than one in four.'[95] Elsewhere in Clubland, regulations on the proportion of members to strangers at special dinners led to abuses, such as the loan of an absent member's name in order to accommodate more guests.[96] Henry Lucy, a non-member, recalled in his diary that, following a 'long agitation' by younger members of the Athenæum, a compromise had been reached whereby one member might invite to dinner a single guest.[97] 'On this concession', he added, 'an ingenious system was built up whereby four, six, or more members clubbed together, each inviting a stranger, and so making up a dinner party'. Lucy continued with an anecdote concerning Herbert Spencer, the club's most outspoken habitué, who 'regarded this innovation with horror':

> He fought against it tooth and nail while it was discussed, and absented himself from the club for a long time after the custom had been established. One evening he chanced to look in at a time when a well-known author was entertaining a small party of equally eminent men at dinner. Spencer, passing the ante-room, saw the strangers gathered, and furiously cross-examined a waiter as to what they did there. A few moments after the circumstances had been explained to him the strangers, their host, and the other members of the club who completed the party, were startled by the appearance of an irate elderly gentleman bursting into the room, trundling an arm-chair behind him. This he propelled in the middle of the ground surrounding the host, and producing a copy of the *Standard*, opened it to the widest extent of its sheet, and proceeded to read the news of the day.

Like many of the best stories about the club, this one was later 'contradicted'.[98] Nevertheless, the very sight of strangers does seem to have upset many members: hence the tiny strangers' room like a telephone box, the proposed screen in the coffee room and the use of the morning room as an 'ante-room'.

Members' dinners were generally of ten courses, with saddle of mutton virtually a fixture as the main meat course. Copies of the menus, printed in French on stiff card, are retained in the club's archive, and many of them have a handwritten list of those who attended on the reverse. Whereas the house dinners for Davidson and Chamberlain tell us something about those individuals' friendships in the club, the inscribed menus for members' dinners provide evidence of external as well as internal relationships and of a wide range of motives for holding a dinner. Factors, however, such as the convention of reciprocity in an age of 'endless, extravagant meals', and the inevitable mixing of business (in a general sense) with pleasure at such events, make those motives difficult to determine, as a glance at a selection of members' dinners held in the early 1900s will demonstrate.

First, however, a dinner hosted on 17 April 1893 by Sir Reginald Welby, permanent secretary to the Treasury since 1885 and a member of the club since 1866.[99] His principal guest was Gladstone, a non-member, who was accompanied by his principal private secretary, Sir Algernon West, also a non-member. The eighty-three-year-old premier, now halfway through his fourth and final ministry, noted in his diary that he had seen both West and Welby during the day and then 'dined with Sir R. Welby' and 'sat till 11.30'.[100] Also present was Gladstone's Home Secretary, Asquith, a recently elected member of the club, who on the previous Friday had led for the government with a long speech, on the seventh night of the second reading of Gladstone's Home Rule Bill. He was later to describe his host as one of the 'past masters in all the arcana of Gladstonian finance'.[101] Welby had contributed to Gladstone's current difficulties, however, by making some uncharacteristic errors when working on the troublesome subject of the financial settlement for Ireland.[102] Another of Welby's guests was Lord Acton, a member of the club since 1860, who considered himself, rather than Morley, to be the main author of Gladstone's home rule policy, and who was considered by Gladstone to be the best-read man in Europe.[103] So this gathering in the morning room of the Athenæum, held on the eighth day of the debate, when both Gladstone and Asquith had briefly intervened during an opposition speech by George Goschen, would appear to have been a political dinner. Yet Gladstone himself regarded dining out as a source of refreshment in the midst of political struggles,[104] and the table talk was probably as wide-ranging as his many interests and affiliations. The presence, for example, of Sir Henry Acland, Regius Professor of Medicine at Oxford since 1858 and a member of the club since 1844, who had spent time with Gladstone when the latter stayed at All Souls in 1890, would surely have brought the arcana of Oxford into the discussion.[105]

Of the sixteen Athenians depicted in *Ballot Day 1892* who had served as Liberal parliamentarians, seven broke with Gladstone over home rule.[106]

John Morley, then Gladstone's Chief Secretary for Ireland, made over 360 interventions during the 80 sittings of the Home Rule Bill in 1893.[107] Whereas Gladstone was a politician who also wrote books, drawing upon his huge library at Hawarden Castle, Morley was a 'man of two trades', politics and literature.[108] Well known as the author of books such as *On Compromise* (1874), his monographs on Voltaire (1872) and Rousseau (1873), and his two studies on Burke (1867, 1879), Morley was also a reader for Macmillan and an influential editor, first of the *Fortnightly Review* and then of *Macmillan's Magazine*. As general editor of Macmillan's highly successful English Men of Letters series between 1878 and 1892, he chose Athenians to write thirty of its thirty-nine volumes. In the early 1900s, when working on his monumental *Life of Gladstone*, Morley hosted a number of members' dinners at the Athenæum which reflect the interweaving of official duties with 'literary purposes' that characterised his own life, as both a political and a literary patron, and the life of the club.

Among his ten guests on 11 December 1901, for example, was Viscount Goschen, seated in front of him in *Ballot Day 1892*.[109] Goschen, author of works on the theory of foreign exchange and on local taxation, was 'one of the very *cleverest* men' Morley knew, as well as one of his most able political opponents.[110] Four other members on the guest list illustrate a characteristic form of continuity in the club with respect to high office: Sir John Scott Burdon-Sanderson succeeded Acland as Regius Professor of Medicine at Oxford; Sir Francis Mowatt was one of Welby's successors as permanent secretary to the Treasury; George Buckle was the fourth editor of *The Times* in an unbroken line since 1830; and Sir Richard Henn Collins was the most recent Athenian to become Master of the Rolls, who on his death in 1911 was replaced as a trustee by his successor as Master of the Rolls, Sir Herbert Cozens-Hardy. Among the non-members was the twenty-seven-year-old Winston Churchill, who had given his maiden speech as a Unionist MP earlier in the year and had already published four books. When Churchill the politician and author was subsequently elected under Rule XII in 1908, as President of the Board of Trade in Asquith's Liberal government, he was proposed by Lord Morley of Blackburn and approved by the General Committee, whose chairman was Sir Richard Henn Collins, by then also a trustee.[111]

Like the Murray and Longman families, the directors of Morley's publisher, Macmillan, were active members of the club, where the boundaries between literary conversation and business could be blurred with gentlemanly aplomb.[112] George Augustin Macmillan, Alexander's second son, was elected in 1894 and later served on the General Committee (1912–15). Specialising in Greek literature, archaeology and music in the firm, he entertained his cousin Maurice and a selection of their authors at a members' dinner in February 1901.[113] George liked to 'hobnob with bishops' at the Club, where he spent most of his time,[114] and on this occasion he included two bishops who were Macmillan authors – Exeter (Herbert Edward Ryle) and Winchester (Randall Davidson) – as well as the Bishop of Wakefield (George Eden) and William Cecil Spring Rice, diplomat and author of 'I vow to thee my country', who were not. The writer and historian George Walter Prothero, also a member, was editor of Murray's *Quarterly Review* and published with Macmillan, whereas Sir Charles Bruce, governor of Mauritius and a Macmillan author, was a non-member. Frederick Macmillan, Daniel's eldest son, who worked harder than George and only read the evening papers at the club, hosted a similar members' dinner only three weeks later, which suggests that these events were not only 'paternalistic' in spirit but also part of the firm's business strategy.[115] An impressive group of present and future members who attended as Macmillan authors indicates that Murray's dominance in the club was over: John Morley, Henry James, Sidney Lee, James Bryce, Professor Ray Lankester, Sir Norman Lockyer, Orby Shipley, Gilbert Parker and Alfred William Pollard.[116]

Members' dinners also provided opportunities to bring together fellow professionals from inside and outside the club. Chemists dined together, as did engineers (always a significant presence in the club), Royal Academicians and fellows of the Royal Society; judges met at the beginning of each legal year, on or near 24 October; and looser affiliations, such as professional connections with Ireland or India, shaped other guest lists.[117] Individual members such as Buckle, so often a guest, reciprocated by holding large dinners to which colleagues and friends were invited.[118] Arthur Conan Doyle celebrated his arrival in the club by hosting a members' dinner in April 1901, soon after his election under Rule II.[119] Among the strangers were Edmund Gosse and J.M. Barrie, who was to be elected the following year. Most of the guests were members, however, including Buckle, who was Doyle's proposer, and two writers – Anthony Hope and Major Arthur Griffiths, inspector of prisons and the author of sixty books, who had been providing Doyle with information on crime in London for some years.[120] Other literary dinners included one hosted by the poet Lord de Tabley in June 1894, to which he invited five strangers, including Edmund Gosse and George Saintsbury, and only two fellow members, Austin Dobson and Thomas Hardy. Hardy was better suited to the Savile Club than to the Athenæum: although he was happy to accept this dinner invitation he seldom visited the clubhouse and referred in a letter of 1906 to the 'regulation Athenæum fogies', by which he probably meant the kind of habitués who disapproved of members' dinners.[121]

The grandest of the dinners under review was held on 11 May 1904, when several of the nation's leading scientists gathered in the presence of HRH the prince of Wales, one of only two strangers that evening.[122] Arthur Balfour, prime minister and philosopher, was present, together with three scientific peers, Lords Avebury, Kelvin and Rayleigh (John William Strutt); eight knights, Crookes, Evans, Foster, Geikie, Huggins, Lockyer, Roscoe and Rücker; two professors, Darwin and Dewar; and Dr Lockyer (probably William James Stewart Lockyer). Prince George was taking on public and representative duties at this time, and would have been encouraged to support British science by his father, King Edward VII, who had attended Faraday's lectures at the Royal Institution as a boy and presided at Strutt's lectures during the centenary celebrations for Faraday in 1891 and for the Royal Institution itself in 1899. This lecture focused upon Thomas Young, perhaps the most brilliant of the club's original members.[123]

The year 1904 was an *annus mirabilis* in the history of British science, concluding with the award of the Nobel prize to Lord Rayleigh and Sir William Ramsay (elected to the club under Rule II in 1905). It was also the year in which Professor James Dewar was knighted. Dewar had been elected to the club under Rule II in 1884, having liquefied oxygen in bulk for the first time in Britain. He was also known at the Royal Institution as a man of 'quarrelsome disposition and ungovernable temper'.[124] His lecture there on 25 March 1904, less than two months before the royal members' dinner, was immortalised in a painting by Henry Jamyn Brooks (Plate 25), although in fact, like

*Ballot Day 1892*, it presents to the viewer a combination of individuals who had never been simultaneously in the same place together: the picture was a 'speculative enterprise' of the artist's, based upon photographic *cartes de visite* solicited from prominent members of the Royal Institution.[125] Nevertheless, the painting and its key confirm not only the continuing strong ties between the Athenæum and the Royal Institution, but also the number of Athenians who contributed to or took an interest in the flowering of British science in the early twentieth century. Half the male figures in Brooks's painting are present or future Athenians, and eight of those figures, including the prime minister in the front row on the left, were later present at the members' dinner in the morning room on 11 May 1904.[126]

# 8

*જ઼*

# CULTURE WARS

Three of the largest group portraits in British art history were commissioned after the Allied victory of November 1918 and donated to the nation. Sir Abe Bailey, a financier and politician in South Africa, wished to honour the senior British and colonial admirals, generals and statesmen who had served during the war, but left the choice of names to Viscount Milner, Secretary of State for the Colonies, and Viscount Dillon, chairman of trustees at the National Portrait Gallery. Both peers were members of the Athenæum, as were the three selected artists, but only one of the twenty-two naval officers portrayed by Sir Arthur Cope – Admiral Wemyss, elected in 1918 – and three of John Singer Sargent's twenty-two army officers – Generals French (1904), Haig (1917) and Byng (1918) – were Athenians.[1] The third, more sensitive commission was declined by both Cope and Sargent but eventually accepted by Sir James Guthrie, who had to raise the height of his studio to accommodate the enormous canvas. The six statesmen most prominently displayed in his group portrait were all Athenians: Arthur Balfour (elected in 1886), H.H. Asquith (1892), Alfred Milner himself (1897), Edward Grey (1903), Winston Churchill (1908) and David Lloyd George (1908).[2]

The years 1914–18 proved to be a watershed in the political and social history of Britain. Although the same could not be said of the country's more conservative institutions, including the West End clubs, these were nevertheless extremely difficult times in Clubland. For the historian, the defining values and characteristics of the Athenæum are thrown into sharper relief during the First World War than in the previous ninety years. As Lord Macmillan recorded, the club 'proved of inestimable value to its many members whose duties kept them in London in these trying times',[3] as a bolthole for those who carried the heaviest responsibilities and as a place where members could hear the latest news from the Front or exchange views and develop ideas with their colleagues. Like other clubs and institutions, the Athenæum suffered losses and contributed to the war effort as best it could, through corporate donations and by adhering to wartime regulations. More unusually, and possibly uniquely, its long-established tradition of attracting members who combined creative ability with a readiness to engage in some kind of administration or public service now bore fruit at a time of rapid development in many fields, not only through the work of its leaders and officials of Church and state, senior military men, armaments directors, engineers and scientists, but also its intelligence officers and those writers and artists who worked in the penumbra of propaganda. Members of Britain's leading literary club not only helped to run the war, they also wrote it, often drawing upon a tradition of Hellenism and Arnoldian 'culture' in their opposition to German *Kultur*. In this chapter we consider how the history of the Athenæum relates to that of the nation over a short period of four tumultuous years.

In the summer of 1914, following months of tension and anxiety, the outbreak of hostilities came suddenly and unexpectedly. Years later Josiah Wedgwood DSO, MP, a member of the club, recalled the Saturday before war was declared:

Four children and I were to bicycle home from Bedales School to Moddershall. It was a two days' trip, and we were off by 5 a.m. on the lovely morning of 1 August 1914. As we rode through Farnborough, on those old dusty roads we found a khaki battery in full kit on the move – then another, and another. I had not believed war possible – international finance would not allow it! Still this was something beyond the ordinary; we got a morning paper. So at Sonning by the Thames I left them to pedal on alone, and took train to Town. At the Athenæum Club I sought to cash a cheque for five pounds. 'Very sorry, sir,' said the porter, 'the bishops have cleared me out.' The Athenæum Club was famous for its silence and its ecclesiastical dignities. But this looked more serious still; and the first business in the House on Black Monday, 3rd, was to suspend payments of obligations, and to extend by three days the bank holiday. All questions were postponed. Grey's famous speech followed.[4]

Like cash, information was now at a premium.[5] The architect Edwin Lutyens frequented the clubhouse in the early days of August 'to get the news'.[6] 'So war was declared last night', he wrote to his wife on the 5th: 'I heard it at the Athenæum, too late to telegraph you. Crowds singing outside – an offshoot from the Buckingham Palace crowd. Walked home.'

The Executive Committee postponed its Tuesday meeting to the Wednesday, when the first reference to the war in the club records appears in the minutes: 'Members of the staff embodied: (a) A.H. Brown. Junior Clerk. Territorial (b) G. Weeks. Sculleryman. Army reservist.'[7] Five years earlier the General Committee had approved a donation of £10 to the West End Club Servants Rifle Association.[8] In the first month of the war the Executive Committee assumed that the membership at large would be pleased to know that members of staff were volunteering. The notice that appeared in the public rooms on 8 September, however, also betrays a wariness of the notorious grumblers among the habitués:

> The Committee are assured that the Members of the Club will be glad to be informed that all the unmarried Male Servants of the enlisting age have offered to serve in the Army.
>
> Ten of these have passed the medical examination and have joined His Majesty's forces.
>
> The waiters who have enlisted are now being replaced by older men. The Committee do not anticipate that any inconvenience will be caused to Members but should any slight inconvenience arise, they trust that Members generally will realise the special circumstances.[9]

(Six months later the Athenæum was to be the first West End club to introduce waitresses.[10]) The names of thirteen members of staff were inscribed in gilt letters on a framed wooden board under the heading 'Athenæum Roll of Honour of those who have joined His Majesty's Army, 1914'.[11] An announcement by

Sir Henry Trueman Wood, chairman of the Executive Committee and long-serving secretary of the Royal Society of Arts, was also displayed in the servants' hall: 'Any Servant of the Athenæum who enlists now and is accepted for service in the BRITISH ARMY will receive two months' wages in advance from the Committee. The interests of such Servant will not be forgotten by the Committee after the War.'[12] These pledges were duly honoured.[13]

Over the ensuing four years the club struggled with shortages and rising prices while complying with increasingly onerous wartime regulations. When the secretary, Henry Tedder, was nominated as the official 'enumerator', he helped some of the resident servants to complete the registration forms.[14] A club that was notorious for its frostiness became chillier in the autumn of 1917, when coal restrictions led to the fires being 'regulated' in the public rooms during quieter periods.[15] Other economies were voluntary, as in the case of the Library Committee's self-imposed reduction of its annual expenditure by a quarter: they saved on books, binding and even the eagerly sought-after newspapers.[16] Restrictions on lighting in London, imposed in December 1914, became matters of security after the first air raids.[17] In June 1915 Tedder reported to the Executive Committee on 'precautions in case of fire & alarm at night', which included a reference to the long-established escape route to the Travellers Club from the roof.[18] By the following March new lighting orders required 'all buff blinds to be obscured';[19] in November 1917 the club insured the contents of the building, valued at £18,300, against air attack;[20] and an air-raid shelter was provided in the basement. Stoic resistance to the inconveniences associated with enemy action was epitomised in one of the 'old Peers' with whom the American ambassador dined at the Athenæum in March 1918, described by Walter Page in a letter to President Wilson:

'Here, steward, what's that noise?'

'A hair raid, milord.'

'How long has it been going on?'

'Forty minutes, milord.'

'I must be deaf,' said the old fellow, with an inquiring look at the company . . .

'Well, there's nothing we can do to protect His Excellency. Damn the air raid. Pass the port.'[21]

Port was in short supply by the end of the war, the most unwelcome restrictions having been those relating to food and drink. The regulations on the consumption of alcohol that were issued to Clubland from New Scotland Yard limited the hours at which liquor could be served: in November 1915 these were 12.00–14.30 and 18.30–21.30 on weekdays, 13.00–15.00 and 18.00–21.00 on Sundays.[22] Spirits were to be diluted. In April 1915, when Lloyd George was concerned that drunkenness was adversely affecting the war effort, he persuaded King George V to set an example by eschewing alcohol in the royal household. Thomas Buxton suggested that the Executive Committee should follow suit and 'suspend sale of intoxicating liquors in the club during the war'.[23] Their reply was the familiar one: the Committee had 'no power to take this action'.[24] Six months later the *Daily Sketch* printed a photograph of a brewer's dray outside the clubhouse, unloading 'barrel after barrel of *beer*!': 'Beer in the Athenæum – the place where Bishops go to before they die!'[25] In November 1917 the government's Food Controller issued a 'strong appeal' to the members of clubs to drink 'light wine, and to refrain from drinking Beer in order that there may be more Beer for the working classes'.[26] The club's response is not recorded.

Among the members with a sweet tooth was Major Stephen Norris, author of *The South African War*. In February 1917, when the steward reported that 'on more than one occasion' the major had 'asked for additional sugar which might have been allotted to a particular member not using sugar', the Executive Committee ruled that it could not sanction his behaviour.[27] They also had to remind him that the servants' quarters were 'not open to the visits of members', when they heard that he had gone into the still room in the basement in search of sugar. The steward's life was made easier when the Food Controller imposed further restrictions a year later and a notice went up in the coffee room stating that no sugar could be served.[28] While gently reprimanding miscreants, the Executive Committee also encouraged exemplary behaviour: in February 1917, for example, it announced that, for the convenience of members who wished to 'adopt the practice of one or more meatless days each week, there will be provided both at luncheon & dinner a large choice of special dishes of fish or vegetables every Tuesday and Friday'.[29] The Revd Carew Hervey St John Mildmay, however, perhaps the most troublesome member in his day, behaved as badly during the war as he did in peacetime. Inserted in the minutes of the long-suffering Executive Committee is a précis of the forty-two letters exchanged between him and the club in 1916/17, in which he complains about everything and has recourse to law over a disputed bill for two shillings, and of further letters between 1917 and 1920 in which his fellow members complain about him, especially his habit of lying full length on the sofas and snoring loudly.[30] Marmaduke Tudsbery was to tell the story at the 1965 AGM, on retiring as chairman of the General Committee, adding that Mildmay (whom he did not name) remained a member for sixteen years before inheriting a public house, drinking the entire stock and dying of his intemperance.[31]

'The War' ran like a dark thread through the fabric of club life. The rise, for example, in the total number of meals served in the clubhouse, from 27,320 in 1915 to 35,761 in 1919,[32] is only partly attributable to the fact that guests could now dine in the coffee room: it also reflects wartime conditions, including food shortages and the closure of some private houses, and a desire for camaraderie and news at the club. Ever ready to review the rules, the committee turned its attention to the definition of a 'cabinet minister' in Rule XII, when governments with war cabinets were in office.[33] Long before the outbreak, arguments for and against war with Germany had been ventilated in the club, as they had been throughout the country. Once war was declared, however, an appeal to support medical services at the Front was uncontentious. On 20 October 1914 Humphry Ward's proposal that members subscribe for a 'Motor Ambulance to be presented to the British Red Cross Society at a cost of £400' was taken up with alacrity: donations were to be limited to £1 and sent to Tedder.[34] Two weeks later George Darroch offered his own car as a motor ambulance and himself as chauffeur.[35] By 23 November, Tedder could announce that £583. 19s. 6d. had been subscribed by 583 members, and that Darroch, 'who had been driving his own motor in France during the early months of the war, in connexion with the Intelligence Department', had been informed that the Red Cross had enough ambulances, but that his offer was gratefully accepted for another purpose and he and his car were now 'doing good work in France for the Society'.[36] In March 1915, further funds were raised for an ambulance for the French Red Cross.[37] The suppliers of this powerful vehicle, designed for 'rough usage over French roads', had an elegant local address: Bianchi Motors Ltd, 26 St James's Street.

Meanwhile the club had received news of several casualties. The first members of staff to join up – Lance Corporal Alfred Holdsworth Brown, junior clerk, and Private George Weeks, sculleryman – were also the first to be killed in action, at Messines on 1 November 1914, a 'fateful day' that was later described in detail by Conan Doyle in *The British Campaign in France and Flanders*.[38] Whereas little is known about the lowly Weeks, whose age is unrecorded, the club's archive contains a cache of correspondence relating to the thirty-year-old Brown, who had accepted a new post at the University of London on 5 August, just as the war began.

Brown's first letter to T.W. Hill, the deputy secretary of the Athenæum, is dated 7 September, when the 14th Battalion, London Scottish (the 'London Regiment'), was still in England. It reveals a friendly relationship between an aspiring clerk and his former superiors: 'The cards Mr Tedder sent are awfully appreciated and Colours told me he had written formally to Mr Tedder to acknowledge them. My Mater was here yesterday & said how very much she hoped to meet you and Mrs Hill again shortly. We are about 3 miles from Watford, I wonder if you would care to come over say next Saturday.'[39] By 2 October Brown was writing from an undisclosed location in France, using small perforated sheets from a notebook. It was cold, but both he and his brother were well and had 'nothing to grumble at', as there was 'plenty of grub' and tobacco, and they were sleeping on straw and under blankets in a railway shed. A form had arrived from the university relating to army pay, which he hoped to receive soon, and he closed with kind regards to Mrs Hill and a request to be remembered to 'all at the Athenæum'. On 25 October he sent Hill a postcard, thanking him for a letter and saying that their chance was coming: he hoped to 'see something of the fighting soon'. 'Don't pass this news home', he added and, in the margin, 'Bless you'. Tedder took up Brown's case in a letter to Sir Henry Miers, principal of the University of London and a member of the club, on 8 November, a week after Brown was killed and three weeks before he was listed among the wounded and missing in the press.[40] In December, Mrs Brown sent news that her son had been wounded in the leg and was thought to have been taken prisoner. In February 1915 she wrote again with a cutting from the *Morning Post*, announcing that he was still listed among the wounded and missing, and in April she wrote to Hill saying that there was no news of Alfred: 'It is very despairing.' Brown's name is inscribed on the Menin Gate in Ypres and on the war memorial at Richmond, Surrey.

At the other extreme of social, military and club hierarchies, the first of twelve members of the club who were casualties of war was buried in St Paul's Cathedral on 19 November 1914. Earl Roberts had died of pneumonia while visiting Indian troops in France at the age of eighty-two, less than a fortnight after Brown and Weeks were killed. Among the troops escorting the gun carriage through the London streets on a dark, wet morning were members of Brown's 14th Battalion of the London Scottish.[41] Among the congregation were King George V, Prime Minister Asquith, and representatives of the Athenæum, who had lost a trustee.[42] Countess Roberts and her daughters sent a printed mourning card in response to a letter of condolence from the club, followed by a private letter of thanks two months later.[43] *Punch* published an obituary of Lord Roberts VC, KG, KP, GCB, OM, GCIE, KStJ, VD, PC by its editor, Owen Seaman, a Rule II member of the club, and a 'big cut' entitled 'A Pattern of Chivalry' by its principal cartoonist, Bernard Partridge, who was to be elected under Rule II five months later.[44]

Lord Roberts's gun carriage was the one that his son had tried to save at Colenso, Natal, when he was killed in 1899 and awarded a posthumous Victoria Cross. During the First World War, Lord Curzon spent many hours writing letters of condolence to friends whose sons had died in action: as early as November 1914 it seemed to him like 'the obliteration of a whole generation'.[45] Most members of the Athenæum were too old to fight, but many lost sons. Among the Davids lamenting over their Absaloms were Asquith, Conan Doyle, Kipling and Lutyens; George du Maurier, illustrator, cartoonist and novelist; Sir William Flower, the first director of the Natural History Museum; Sir Alfred Gould, vice-chancellor of London University; Sir Oliver Lodge, physicist and principal of Birmingham University; John Horner, barrister; Sir Charles Parsons, inventor of the steam turbine; Rowland Prothero, author and politician; Lord (Hallam) Tennyson; Sir Aston Webb PRIBA; Lord Shuttleworth, Liberal politician, who lost two sons; and Lord William Cecil, Bishop of Exeter, who lost three. (Another son was wounded twice, but survived.) Forty-seven of the men, mostly younger men, whose names were in the Candidates Book during the war are listed as 'killed in action': many of them had been proposed by their fathers. Kipling had asked his friend Lord Roberts for a commission for his son John, and 'Bobs' had obliged.[46] Much later, Kipling and his wife discovered that John was using his revolver when he was shot with the Irish Guards during action associated with the Battle of Loos. At the time it was believed that his body was not found, as in the case of Alfred Brown and tens of thousands of other casualties.[47] After the war, Rudyard Kipling was among the originators of the plan to inter the Unknown Warrior in Westminster Abbey.

For some, spiritualism provided more immediate comfort. William Butler Yeats, later a Nobelist and Rule II member of the club, wrote in memory of Lady Gregory's son Robert, 'What made us dream that he could comb grey hair?'[48] In 1911 the poet's interest in 'faery' and the occult had taken him into the Ghost Club, members of which were convinced believers in the paranormal. Among a number of Athenians in the club were Conan Doyle, who published a clutch of books on spiritualism after his son Kingsley died of influenza aggravated by war wounds in 1918, and Sir Oliver Lodge, a past president of the Society for Psychical Research. Lodge's son Raymond, killed in action on 14 September 1915, inspired a book that went through numerous reprints and helped thousands of mourners. *Raymond* offers as evidence several descriptions of séances, a number of messages from the dear departed and a group photograph of officers in which a hand rests on Raymond Lodge's shoulder. The book concludes with a passage that echoes Tennyson's *In Memoriam*: 'Let us learn . . . that those who have been, still are; that they care for us and help us; that they, too, are progressing and learning and working and hoping; that there are grades of existence, stretching upward and upward to all eternity.'[49]

When another Raymond, Asquith's son, was killed on 15 September 1916 at the age of thirty-seven he was mourned by many outside the family, for he represented the best of his generation. John Buchan recorded that he had never met anyone 'so endowed with diverse talents', Churchill described him as 'my brilliant hero-friend' in a letter to his widow, and a private soldier described him as 'one of the finest men who ever wore the King's uniform' in a letter home.[50] Proposed by his father and seconded by Augustine Birrell, Raymond Asquith had been elected in May 1915 and was the youngest of the Athenian casualties, whose average age (setting aside Lord Roberts) was forty-five. The range of talents lost is striking. Asquith was a barrister, whose letters from the Front are brilliantly crafted and unnervingly incisive;[51] Lieutenant Rowan Hamilton, elected in 1913 and killed in October 1915 at the age of thirty-eight, was a composer; and Colonel Victor Flower, elected the same year and killed in August 1917 at forty-one, an architect.

Others died in khaki while serving abroad in their peacetime professional capacities. Dr George Almond joined the Royal Army Medical Corps at the outbreak and became a pathologist at a base hospital in France. In 1918 he was sent to serve at the Front with the 4th Dragoon Guards and was killed on 9 August aged forty-one, four months after his election to the club. The eminent physiologist and surgeon Colonel Sir Victor Horsley FRS had been a member since 1895, was already commissioned in the Territorial Army when war broke out, and served with the Royal Army Medical Corps in France, Egypt and Mesopotamia, where he died from heatstroke in July 1916.[52]

Medicine was one of several fields in which current and future members of the Athenæum made significant contributions to technical developments that were expedited by the war. When Sir Arbuthnot Lane was the chief consultant at the hospital in Aldershot, the wards overflowed with facial injuries after the Battle of the Somme. He subsequently opened Queen Mary's Hospital in Sidcup, where reconstructive surgery was pioneered.[53] Sir George Makins served in France as a consulting surgeon from September 1914. Having supervised the newly established hospital centres at Camiers and Étaples, and made frequent trips up the line to the Front, he established a research centre where new methods of wound treatment were developed.[54] Makins shared a cottage on the River Test with his old friend, Sir George Savage, who served as a consultant psychiatrist at Knutsford and addressed the Medico-Psychological Association on wartime mental disabilities.[55] Lane and Makins were in their sixties during the war, and Savage in his seventies. In contrast, Charles Myers, who had established the first laboratory in England especially designed for psychological experiments at Cambridge, was only in his early forties when he used the soldiers' own term, 'shell shock', in a 1915 *Lancet* article. Appointed consultant psychologist to the British armies in France in 1916, he was elected to the Club in 1919. Several of the younger doctors who treated the victims of shell shock – William Brown (who treated Wilfred Owen), Gordon Holmes, Arthur Hurst and William Rivers ('perhaps the most famous of the Great War psychologists')[56] – were to be elected to the club in the 1920s.

After fourteen months of conflict a leading electrical engineer had no doubt that this was 'a war of engineers and chemists quite as much as of soldiers'.[57] Judging by the contribution of Athenians, he might have added the physicists. On 12 November 1914 the president of the Royal Society, Sir William Crookes, chaired a meeting of selected fellows at which they decided to establish a War Committee.[58] Crookes was a chemist and a science journalist who had been a member of the club since 1882, when the Royal Society was rejecting his papers on the authenticity of mediums. Also present were the physicist Lord Rayleigh, by now chancellor of Cambridge University, who focused upon aeronautics during the war and who shared Crookes's interest in the paranormal; Sir Ernest Rutherford, who worked on submarine warfare and underwater acoustics and was elected to the club in 1917; and the brilliant young physicist and crystallographer Lawrence Bragg, joint winner with his father of the 1915 Nobel prize in physics, who developed new techniques for locating enemy guns from the sounds of their firing and was to be elected to the club in 1932.[59]

Bragg's father William, also a future member, was among the leading scientists recruited by the Admiralty to form the Board of Invention and Research in June 1915, when H.G. Wells caused a furore by arguing that Britain was falling behind Germany in technical achievements.[60] Other Athenians on the board included Rutherford, the legendary Sir J.J. Thomson – Rutherford's predecessor and Lord Rayleigh's successor as Cavendish Professor at Cambridge – Sir Charles Parsons and Sir Oliver Lodge. Again, when Lloyd George responded to a further crisis in August 1915 by establishing a Munitions Inventions Department, Thomson was drawn in and was joined by Horace Darwin (the ninth child of Charles Darwin), a civil engineer and manufacturer of aircraft instruments, who was knighted in 1918; Richard (later Sir Richard) Glazebrook, director of the National Physical Laboratory, where fundamental research was undertaken on the production of optical glass, on aeronautical problems and on radio communications; and Sir Alexander Kennedy, professor of mechanical engineering at Imperial College London.

In June 1916 Lloyd George was succeeded at the Ministry of Munitions by a fellow Athenian, Edwin Montagu of the Treasury, who secured an agreement with J.P. Morgan & Co. which saved the Allies millions of pounds in their American purchases.[61] (John Pierpont Morgan was elected to the club under Rule II in 1920.[62]) By the end of the war, with Churchill in charge of 12,000 officials at Munitions, 2.5 million British workers were engaged in the production of guns and shells, and of 1,000 tons of high explosives per day. Since the outbreak another Athenian, the judge and politician Lord Moulton, had headed the explosives supply department: he controlled the nation's gasworks, coke ovens and suppliers of fat and oil, and took responsibility for the production of poison gas, to be used only if the enemy released it first.

That this was indeed 'a war of engineers' is illustrated by the development of armaments, an area in which a remarkable Athenian dynasty, both familial and professional, played a leading role. In 1859, the year of his election to the club, Sir William Armstrong had separated his Elswick Ordnance Company (EOC) from the rest of his engineering operation on Tyneside, reuniting the companies five years later when he left government service. Sir Andrew Noble, a gunnery expert who was elected in 1873, rose from being Armstrong's assistant to the chairmanship of Armstrong Whitworth in 1900, the year of his son Saxton's election to the club: Sir Saxton became the company's managing director. Through his father James Meadows Rendel, a successful hydraulics engineer and a friend of Armstrong's, Stuart, later Lord Rendel, became London manager of Armstrong Whitworth and by 1913 was vice-chairman of the company. Father and son were both members, as was Sir Joseph Whitworth (elected in 1862), whose company was to merge with Armstrong's in 1897, ten years after Sir Joseph's death. The inventor and designer of armaments Josiah Vavasseur CB merged his business with Armstrong's, whose board he joined in 1883, and was elected to the club in 1903 with Sir Andrew Noble as his proposer.[63] John Meade Falkner, elected five years later, had been tutor to Sir Andrew Noble's sons in Newcastle before becoming secretary to the board at Elswick, a role that he combined with his writing: among other publications were two of Murray's handbooks and three successful romances.[64] He became a director in 1901 and chairman in 1915, at the height of the munitions crisis. Future Athenians who worked for Armstrong Whitworth during the war included the ballistics engineer Sir George Hadcock, formerly Sir Andrew Noble's personal assistant and later managing director of the company, and Falkner's son-in-law Alfred Cochrane, cricketer and company secretary.[65] Much of the ordnance and ammunition commissioned by the British government in huge quantities during the First World War was stamped 'EOC'.

In 1913 Armstrong Whitworth also became involved in aeronautics, the most eye-catching aspect of engineering at the time. It had been Richard Haldane at the War Office who not only saw the need to develop a Territorial Army and to plan an expeditionary force, but also to test the potential of aircraft in warfare scientifically. The joint advisory committee on aeronautics, chaired by Lord Rayleigh, a fellow member of the club, was created in May 1909. Haldane, himself an intellectual polymath, recognised in Mervyn O'Gorman an electrical and aircraft engineer whose blend of scientific and administrative skills would enable him to develop a research and manufacturing centre at Farnborough, where most of the aircraft that were flown to Amiens in August 1914 were designed. Lieutenant-Colonel O'Gorman was elected to the club in 1917, as increasing numbers of aircraft played a crucial role in reconnoitring and bombing enemy trenches, and in defending Britain during the dreaded Zeppelin raids. Meanwhile Colonel Bertram Hopkinson, formerly a youthful professor of applied mechanics at Cambridge, had established an experimental station for the Royal Flying Corps at Orford Ness, where he supervised the testing of aircraft. Elected to the club in February 1916, he was killed on one of many solo flights in August 1918 at the age of forty-four, a 'knight-errant of the air'.[66]

When Churchill announced that Britain was leading the race to develop the seaplane, in March 1914, *Punch* celebrated with a cartoon that set the standard for Bernard Partridge's famous wartime work.[67] In October 1916 *Punch* carried an piece of doggerel by Charles Larcom Graves of the kind that was popular on the Home Front: it celebrates British tanks and ends:

> They deserve a metric tribute from the LAUREATE at least,
> Though perhaps his classic Muse would shy at such a comic beast,
> But I'm sure that RUDYARD KIPLING would appreciate the pranks
>     Of the Tanks.

Then here's to their inventor, though I know not if he's Manx,
Or Cambrian or Scotsman, or hails from Yorks or Lancs,
But anyhow he's earned the admiration of all ranks
      With his Tanks.[68]

The joke about Robert Bridges, who was not a member, and Kipling, who was, would have been appreciated at the Athenæum, where both the originator of the tank and his political master were also members. It was in February 1915, the year in which many of the official scientific advisory committees were established, that Churchill formed a Landship Committee at the Admiralty, under the chairmanship of Eustace Tennyson d'Eyncourt, the naval architect who was to design the battle cruiser *Hood*.[69] Initially surprised to be involved, Tennyson d'Eyncourt set to work and kept the project alive, in spite of opposition from the army, when Churchill was forced out of the Admiralty in May 1915. Nine months later, when a prototype was demonstrated to Balfour, First Lord of the Admiralty, Lloyd George, Minister of Munitions, and Kitchener, Secretary of State for War, only Kitchener remained unconvinced.

With an abrupt end to the import of specialist glass from Germany and France at the outbreak of war, British industrialists needed home-grown chemists to fill the gap. In October 1914, the year of his election to the club, Herbert Jackson headed an advisory committee to define formulae for these glasses, and, working with his team at King's College London and in his private laboratory, produced over fifty formulae himself.[70] He was knighted in 1917 and was active in club affairs after the war, as were Makins and O'Gorman. Another urgent need arose in April 1915, when the Germans first used large quantities of chlorine gas on the Ypres salient. Kitchener summoned Richard Haldane's brother, the Oxford physiologist John Haldane, to the War Office.[71] As an expert on gas poisoning in mines, Haldane was able to design a simple respirator as a temporary measure and later, after a more effective gas hood had been introduced, to advise on the use of oxygen in the treatment of victims of poison gases, exposure to which damaged his own health. John Haldane was elected to the club in 1917, a year before Arthur Smithells, professor of chemistry at the University of Leeds. Smithells served as chief chemical advisor on anti-gas training between 1916 and 1919, devoting much of his time to alerting the public to its dangers.[72]

The shock felt by the British public when Germany first used poison gas intensified the demonisation of all things German and the witch-hunt for pro-German sympathisers. Lieutenant-Colonel Smithells, when vice-president of the Royal Society, strongly resisted efforts to remove from office the German-born British physicist, Arthur Schuster, secretary of the Royal Society and a member of the club. (Schuster was knighted in 1920.) Richard Haldane, who had studied in Göttingen and spoke fluent German, was subjected to sustained xenophobic attack. Asquith twice refused to accept his offers of resignation, but did not include him in the coalition government in May 1915, a month after the first gas attack, thus jettisoning the man who had done much to prepare the country for war.[73]

Objectors to the war also came under increasing pressure, as in the case of Bertrand Russell in 1916. Russell was a Cambridge Apostle and one of the most highly respected fellows of Trinity College when he was elected to the club under Rule II in 1909. Five years later he argued that wars were justifiable under certain circumstances, but that this war resulted from a misguided foreign policy, as Germany was a highly civilised country. (Viscount Morley resigned from the cabinet on similar grounds in August 1914.) In May 1916, when Russell was an active member of the No-Conscription Fellowship, he was found guilty of breaking the Defence of the Realm Act and was sacked from his Trinity fellowship. On 10 June Major General John Sterling, retired, wrote to the Executive Committee of the Athenæum saying that 'the conduct of Mr B. Russell as certified by a Court of Justice does not justify his remaining a member of this club', and adding that he had 'personal evidence' that Kipling, Chisholm and Stanford agreed with his views.[74] Sir Steuart Bayley, an old India hand in his eightieth year, was in the chair when the Committee discussed the letter on 4 July and passed the responsibility to the General Committee, adding that they were 'by no means unanimous as to the desirability of taking action or not'. When the General Committee discussed the matter at a specially convened meeting, Bayley moved and Bishop Ryle, Dean of Westminster, seconded the question, which was put to the vote and declared to be carried by the chairman, Lord Cozens-Hardy, Master of the Rolls.[75]

Herbert Ryle was a Cambridge man himself, formerly a fellow of King's College and president of Queens', a respected liberal Broad Churchman and a member of the club since 1901, who led the midday intercessions in the Abbey personally and was responsible for many special services during the war.[76] At crucial points in Ryle's career he discussed appointments that he had been offered by the prime minister with Randall Davidson, his predecessor as Bishop of Winchester, at the clubhouse.[77] Whereas Ryle played a leading role in applying German critical methods to his biblical criticism, Davidson had been untouched by the theological controversies that raged in Oxford when he was an undergraduate, and had risen in the Church through his mastery of Anglican affairs and as a courtier. Archbishop Davidson, however, valued his contact with Germans such as Adolf von Harnack, a liberal Lutheran theologian and director of the Royal Library at Berlin. Having always considered war between two great Protestant powers to be 'unthinkable', Davidson resisted the narrow chauvinism of many of the clergy and was criticised for omitting a direct prayer for victory from intercessions prepared for the first Sunday of the war.[78] But he was soon caught up in the spy mania that swept the country and in 1915, following the publication of Lord Bryce's report on German atrocities, declared that Britain was 'fighting against what is veritably the work of the devil'.[79] Two years later, when frost delayed ploughing and the need to sow was urgent, Rowland Prothero, president of the Board of Agriculture and Fisheries, wrote to Davidson for his opinion on Sunday labour on the farms. 'We make a temporary departure from our rule', the archbishop replied, while taking care not to force those who could not work in all conscience.[80]

Randall Davidson, the pragmatist, emphasised the steadying influence of the Church in wartime and considered it his duty to avoid embarrassing the government of the day. As Primate he was frequently in touch with ministers of state – men such as Prothero – both in the Houses of Parliament and at the Athenæum, where Lord Bryce, Liberal MP, historian of the Holy Roman Empire and ambassador to Washington (1907–13), was also a member. What George Bell described as Davidson's 'intimate association' with the club was closest during his long trusteeship, from 1913 until his death in 1930. He regularly attended and sometimes chaired meetings of the General Committee during the war, when other members of the Committee included Sir Edward

Poynter, Sir William Crookes, Arthur Balfour, George Buckle, John Murray IV, Sir Henry Trueman Wood, Sir Owen Seaman, Sir Archibald Geikie, Humphry Ward and Sir J.J. Thomson.

In a club where bishops went before they died, according to the *Daily Sketch*, clerical controversy was heightened during the war when liberals clashed with High Churchmen over ethical questions, as well as the usual liturgical and doctrinal matters. When Lloyd George, the first nonconformist to be prime minister, was determined to nominate Dean Hensley Henson, a liberal friend of nonconformity, to the see of Hereford in 1917, against Davidson's advice, Bishop Charles Gore led an agitation against the consecration and Lord Halifax wrote to the press deploring the proposed appointment. All five protagonists were members of the Athenæum, where Henson encountered 'friends and enemies alike'.[81] Sir Henry Newbolt visited his table in the coffee room to assure him of his goodwill, but there were 'divers Bishops who looked away, or cast down their eyes' when they saw him coming. In the coalition government he was warmly supported by Prothero, son of a clergyman, who said that the bishops had behaved abominably, and another Tory member of the club, Walter Long. Henson was duly consecrated as Bishop of Exeter in 1917 and translated to Durham in 1920, again on Lloyd George's recommendation.

Henson recorded that Asquith was 'quite kind' when they met at the club during the Hereford furore. Before the war, *Punch* had been amused by the Liberal leader's being 'hunted' by suffragettes from Downing Street to 'sanctuary at Athenæum Club', and his old friend Augustine Birrell being assaulted by them on his way there from the Commons.[82] According to Margot Asquith, nine days before the Chief Secretary for Ireland resigned over his handling of the Easter Rising of 1916, she asked her husband what Birrell was doing: 'Reading the memoirs of Boufflers in the Athenæum!'[83] Asquith too used the clubhouse as a bolthole, particularly in the early years of the war when he was under enormous pressure as prime minister.[84] On 10 October 1914 he was pleased to learn that his beloved confidante, Venetia Stanley, had received the previous day's letter 'before the day was out': he had posted it with his own hand 'at the Athenæum *before* 6 p.m. (for I looked at the clock)'.[85] In subsequent letters written in 1914–15 he told her that he had left a long meeting on the War Loan for a 'short respite to the Athenæum', where he read ' "The

Double Mr. Burton", not at all a bad novel',[86] that he had read a 'not bad Russian Nihilist novel by Leroux' in the clubhouse[87] and had tried to read a new book by Maurice Hewlett, a member, entitled *A Lover's Tale*, but had made little progress with it, as his thoughts were with her.[88] Emotional support and mental rest were to be found in his friendship with Venetia and his membership of the club, described in these letters as a place of 'respite', 'refuge', 'the only place where I am free' and 'one of the few places where one is secure from interruption'. No Athenian would dream of interrupting a fellow member when reading, even if the member in question was the wartime premier and the book was a work of fiction chosen from the circulating library.[89] The shock that Asquith received in May 1915, when Venetia announced her engagement to his colleague Edwin Montagu, Financial Secretary to the Treasury, was compounded by the fact that Montagu was elected to the club that year.

Asquith's cabinet included eight Athenians.[90] When America entered the war on 6 April 1917, two of the four ministers in Lloyd George's war cabinet were members of the club: Lords Curzon and Milner. The Century Association in New York expressed its commitment to the war in a cable to its sister club in London. The president of the Century was Joseph Choate, a former American ambassador and honorary member of the Athenæum. He and Henry Osborn Taylor, the Century's secretary, wrote:

> The Century Association assembled in monthly meeting after pledging to President Wilson its heartiest support in the present war for humanity sends fraternal greetings to the Athenæum Club and through it to the great nation whose refusal to compromise the interests of honor and freedom oppose the malign objects of the Hohenzollern dynasty. We regard it as a national honor to fight beside England and France and their Allies for the security of representative government and the liberty of mankind.[91]

Choate regarded a message to the club as a message to the British nation.

While a handful of Athenian politicians helped to run the war from Whitehall, other members of Britain's leading literary club took up the challenge of writing it. Thirteen of the forty authors who signed a declaration in defence of a 'righteous war', published in *The Times* on 18 September 1914, were members and four others were future members.[92] The declaration, entitled 'Britain's destiny and duty', originated in meetings held at Wellington House in Buckingham Gate, London, where the writer and Liberal cabinet minister Charles Masterman had established the secret War Propaganda Bureau.[93] The authors met in circumstances similar to those surrounding the formation of the scientific advisory groups described earlier, in response to a national crisis. Thomas Hardy recalled that 'the yellow September sun shone in from the dusty street with a tragic cast upon them as they sat round the large blue table, full of misgivings, yet unforeseeing in all their completeness the tremendous events that were to follow'.[94] Several of them agreed to write books and pamphlets, of which over a thousand were to be published, in support of the government, which early on was particularly concerned about losing the propaganda war with Germany in America.

'Many of us regard German culture with the highest respect and gratitude', the authors stated in their declaration, 'but we cannot admit that any nation has the right by brute force to impose its culture upon other nations'. Definitions of 'culture' were already the subject of anti-German satire in *Punch*, edited by Seaman. A cartoon published on 26 August and entitled 'The Triumph of "Culture"', in which the Kaiser stands over the corpses of a Belgian family, holding a smoking gun, was by Partridge.[95] British propaganda focused upon a secondary meaning of the German word *Kultur*: 'culture emphasizing practical efficiency and individual subordination to the state'.[96] In a *Punch* cartoon by Leonard Raven Hill, published soon after the Germans first used poison gas in April 1915, the Kaiser is represented as a demonic alchemist producing 'The Elixir of Hate': *Kultur* is represented as a snake at his feet.[97]

*Punch* sold well at home during the war, as Seaman, who came from a humble background, was careful to reflect public opinion in the magazine and understood the cathartic value of laughter for an increasingly despondent civilian population. Two national characteristics, the stiff upper lip and the recourse to humour in the face of adversity, were exploited and gently mocked in *Punch*, as they were in a popular book on the vermin that tormented soldiers in the trenches by the Master of Christ's College Cambridge and Reader in Zoology in the university. Dr Arthur Shipley, a member of the club, playfully entitled his book *The Minor Horrors of War* (1915), and confessed in the preface that the articles in the *British Medical Journal* upon which the book was based were 'written in a certain spirit of gaiety', the 'reflex of the spirit of those who have gone to the Front and of my fellow countrymen in general', and that British civilians could also be a torment in wartime:

> The contents of this little book hardly justify its title. There are whole ranges of 'Minor Horrors of War' left untouched in the following chapters. The minor poets, the pamphlets of the professors, the people who write to the papers about 'Kultur' and think that this is the German for Matthew Arnold's over-worked word 'Culture,' the half-hysterical ladies who offer white feathers to youths whose hearts are breaking because medical officer after medical officer has refused them the desire of their young lives to serve their country. Surely, as Carlyle taught us, '*There is no animal so strange as man!*'[98]

*Punch*'s reviewer commented that Shipley's 'unexpected quips' had kept him 'in chuckles'.[99] The propaganda war over 'culture' arrived at the Athenæum's door at the end of 1915, in a *Punch* cartoon depicting the Kaiser mounting the steps from which Matthew Arnold had, in symbolic terms, addressed his Victorian readers in the 'public square' on the subject of culture and anarchy (Plate 26).[100] The artist Frederick Henry Townsend, was not a member, but the nuanced references to the club in the accompanying anonymous verses suggest that Seaman, by now a member of the Executive Committee, was the author:

> When William comes with all his might
> And sets the river Thames alight,
> I shouldn't be at all surprised
> If London Town were Teutonised.
>
> Bidding his bands to play *Te Deum*
> He'll occupy the Athenæum,
> And Pallas' Owl become a vulture
> Under the new *régime* of culture.[101]

Some of the Owls who were lunching, but not gorging within the club-house in 1915 were writing two kinds of material that were more widely read than the work of what we now call the 'war poets': documentary accounts of the war itself and prose fiction. Conan Doyle produced examples of both. As an historian of the war from a Wellington House perspective he published six volumes of *The British Campaign in France and Flanders* (1916–20). As a writer of fiction he published an admonitory story near the end of the war entitled 'Danger!', on the threat of German submarines, which he had drafted before the outbreak. 'It is a matter of history', he boasted in the preface, 'how fully this warning has been justified and how, even down to the smallest details, the prediction has been fulfilled.'[102]

A year earlier Conan Doyle had brought the famous private investigator of Baker Street into direct contact with the enemy in 'His last Bow: the war service of Sherlock Holmes', published in the *Strand Magazine* in September 1917. Having chronicled much carnage by this date, Conan Doyle invested the story's setting in the week before the outbreak with a sense of foreboding that is reminiscent of descriptions of the end of the world and the Last Judgment in Victorian verse: 'It was nine o'clock at night upon the second of August – the most terrible August in the history of the world. One might have thought already that God's curse hung heavy over a degenerate earth, for there was an awesome hush and a feeling of vague expectancy in the sultry and stagnant air. The sun had long set, but one blood-red gash, like an open wound, lay low in the distant west.'[103] As the *Strand* announces on the cover, 'Sherlock Holmes Outwits a German Spy'. Von Bork, who is about to return to Germany with stolen secrets, is visited by his associate Baron Von Herling in an English country house. A later visitor is Von Bork's Irish-American agent, Altamont, in fact the disguised Holmes who has been working in counter-espionage for two years and who now arrests the German spy, ably assisted by Watson and the housekeeper Martha, who has been in the pay of Holmes all along. What separates the antagonists is obvious: our British heroes are gentlemen, whereas the Germans are not.

When Von Bork mocks the docile Englanders' 'good form' and 'playing the game' and 'that sort of thing',[104] Conan Doyle echoes an influential book by Sir Charles Waldstein (later Walston), a fellow Athenian, published just two months earlier. Waldstein, an eminent classical archaeologist at Cambridge, had been educated in New York and Heidelberg, and was suspected of pro-German sympathies. *What Germany Is Fighting For* offers a critique of the ideology of *Kultur*, whereby the people are 'persuaded that, in establishing and furthering their own Kultur, they are directly benefiting humanity at large and all other nations'.[105] Waldstein believed that, in contrast to the cult of the Superman and 'the apparently complete absence of any impulse which makes for fair-play or manifests the possession of altruistic imagination, sympathy, the sense of proportion and of humour', the English ideal of the gentleman is 'really the Hellenic ideal of life, in which all faculties of man, physical, mental, social, were to be harmoniously blended and to produce as well the most efficient patriot as the most perfect social being'.[106]

The Hellenic ideal of the Athenæum, expressed as Arnoldian sweetness and light, was embodied in that urbane Edwardian gentlemen, Sir Henry Newbolt, one of the signatories to the declaration on 'Britain's destiny and duty', and described by John Buchan, a fellow member, as one of the most interesting people he had ever met.[107] The poem for which Newbolt was best known, 'Vitaï Lampada' ('The Torch of Life', 1896) – 'Play up! play up! and play the game!' – influenced later critics of *Kultur* and became the poet's 'Frankenstein's Monster' of his own creation.[108] Earl Roberts was in the chair when the General Committee elected the author of *Admirals All* (1897) and other works under Rule II in 1912.[109] During the war Newbolt divided his time between writing and service at the Admiralty and the Foreign Office, culminating in his becoming controller of wireless and cables. *Punch* printed favourable reviews of *The Book of the Blue Sea* (1914), *The Thin Red Line* (1915), *Tales of the Great War* (1916) and *Submarine and Anti-submarine* (1918), emphasising the timeliness of his books for boys, books which 'stir the pulses';[110] and *Punch* celebrated Newbolt's knighthood in 1915 in verse, 'Because he bids us play the game / And not the super-egotist'.[111]

Newbolt not only epitomised the Athenian combination of creativity with public service, but also moved easily between the writers and the statesmen in the clubhouse, as an habitué.[112] One of his closest friends was the poet and art historian Laurence Binyon, an assistant keeper at the British Museum, who was elected to the club under Rule II in 1914. (His proposer was Archbishop Davidson.)[113] Binyon felt little of the euphoria experienced by other writers at the outbreak of war and did not attend the secret meeting at Wellington House described by Hardy.[114] He signed the declaration, however, and his 'requiem-verses', 'For the Fallen', were printed in *The Times* less than seven weeks after the outbreak:

> They shall grow not old, as we that are left grow old:
> Age shall not weary them, nor the years condemn.
> At the going down of the sun, and in the morning
> We will remember them.

Sidney Colvin suggested to Elgar, a fellow member of the club, that he might set 'For the Fallen' and two other poems from Binyon's *The Winnowing Fan* (1914) to music. The London première of Elgar's *The Spirit of England* at the Queen's Hall in May 1916, described as 'one of the most extraordinary musical events of the war', featured the soprano Clara Butt, who sang in five further performances in aid of the Red Cross, one of which was attended by King George V.[115]

Binyon served as a Red Cross ambulancier and orderly in a French military hospital for periods in 1915–16 and was then sent to report on the British volunteers who supported French victims of the war. *For Dauntless France* (1918) combines detailed documentary reports on that work with vivid accounts of conditions at the Front:

> The two vast tides clash in a conflict that never ends, that never sleeps; that dies down to intervals of seeming quiet, but wakes again to double and triple fury. And all along that line the earth is blotched, pounded, pitted, scorched. The trees are splintered stumps. It is a landscape that is to the natural green and brown like the face of an idiot among the healthy and bright-eyed. An insane landscape, smelling of evil. It resounds with all the noises of chaos. By night it alternates thick gloom with sudden and sinister illumination. Yet the larks go up in the dawns and sing above the cannonade.[116]

*For Dauntless France* opens with a reference to *The Dynasts* (1904–8), which Thomas Hardy himself described as an 'epic-drama of the war with Napoleon'.

1. The founder of the Athenæum, John Wilson Croker, was a true blue Tory who ensured that a majority of Whigs served on the inaugural committee, and that members of this new kind of non-partisan club were elected on the basis of achievements rather than birth.

2. 12 Waterloo Place, shown here on the left, facing the viewer, was the temporary home of the Athenæum between 31 May 1824 and 8 February 1830. When the building was demolished in 1912 the club rescued a shattered volute (Roman cement painted black) as a keepsake.

3. Athena/Minerva's association with owls, like the one at the Temple of Minerva, is honoured in some of the club's silverware and in stuffed specimens on display in the clubhouse. It also explains the sobriquet attached to the club's members: bookish 'Owls'.

DESIGN FOR THE CLUB SEAL
Original drawing by Sir Thomas Lawrence, Bart., P.R.A.

4. William Wyon's seal for the Athenæum was based upon this design for Athena's helmeted head by Sir Thomas Lawrence, the fourth president of the Royal Academy, a portraitist and an original member. Athena was the goddess of wisdom in ancient Greece. Her Roman counterpart was Minerva.

5. Having been lavishly refurbished by the prince regent, Carlton House was demolished in 1826, thus creating the space for the southern continuation of Waterloo Place on which the new Athenæum clubhouse was to be built. Among the sumptuous rooms that Croker knew was the crimson drawing room.

6. This may be Decimus Burton's design elevation for the Athenæum's clubhouse at its first proposed site, the newly developed Pall Mall East, in 1824. Presented in a domestic idiom, it is simple, appropriate to its scale, self-assured and elegant.

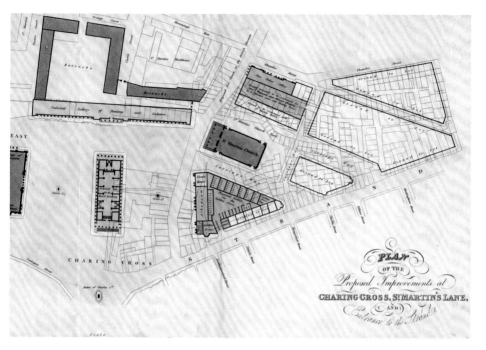

7. The second site proposed for the Athenæum is shown on the eastern side of Union Square (later Trafalgar Square), where South Africa House now stands. The building is shown with a portico of five pillars, between the Royal Academy of Literature and the 'Vicar's House' for St Martin-in-the-Fields.

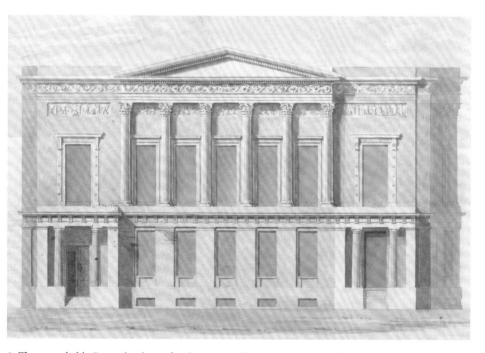

8. This is probably Burton's scheme for the proposed Union Square site. Written at the bottom of the sheet are the words 'N.B. The panels are proposed to receive the Elgin Frieze'. A Panathenaic frieze, based on the Elgin Marbles, is the most famous external feature of the built clubhouse in Pall Mall.

9. The built clubhouse was painted for Decimus Burton by an unknown artist, from across Waterloo Place. Like the balcony, the entrance portico and the large spearless statue by Edward Hodges Baily (based on the Pallas Athena of Velletri in the Louvre), the Panathenaic frieze was a beautiful addition to a building that would have been very plain without it. Next door is the Travellers Club.

10. In 1841 the spectator was 'immediately struck by the classic taste, the refined feeling of the design' of the hall. The introduction of statues and the absence of pictures intensified the aura of academic classicism in the Grecian style.

WEST SIDE OF LIBRARY.

EAST SIDE OF LIBRARY.

11. The drawing room is identified as the 'Library' in Burton's original designs. Had all his proposed classical motifs been adopted, the room would have continued the antiquarian theme of the hall and landing even more clearly.

12. In 1833 Burton was asked to design these larger classical bookcases, reflecting the fact that the club's collection of books and pamphlets was growing rapidly. The bookcases were topped with plaster busts of famous literary, scientific and artistic figures – a fitting pantheon for a British 'Athenæum'. The open door on the right reveals what is now known as the north library.

13. We are looking north in 1842. To the west of Waterloo Place are the clubhouses of the Athenæum (Decimus Burton, 1830), the Travellers Club (Charles Barry, 1832) and the Reform Club (Charles Barry, 1841). John Nash's United Service Club (1828) is on the eastern side of Waterloo Place.

14. Eleven of Lord Aberdeen's cabinet in 1854 were members of the Athenæum: Aberdeen, Charles Wood, Sir William Molesworth, the duke of Argyll, Lord Clarendon, Lord Lansdowne, Lord John Russell, Lord Granville, Lord Palmerston, Sir George Grey and the duke of Newcastle.

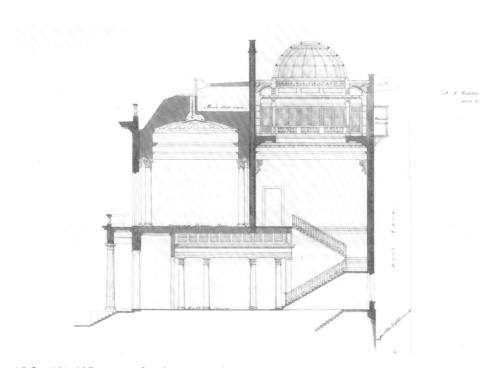

15. In 1853–54 Burton produced numerous alternative plans and elevations in response to the General Committee's request for 'greater accommodation' for the library and morning room. Most of these involved 'an Upper Story or Attic being placed in the external walls, so as to provide additional accommodation for the Library and Servants' Sleeping Rooms'.

16. In order to expand capacity at minimum cost, this impressive three-tiered arrangement of galleried bookcases was completed in 1856. Visitors are enchanted by the view from the drawing room through the glazed doors, whereas members who suffer from vertigo rely upon the intrepid library staff to fetch books from the galleries for them.

17. Two members, Sir Lawrence Alma-Tadema and Sir Edward Poynter, designed schemes for the redecoration of the clubhouse in the 1890s. Among the elements of their designs that have survived is this exotic lantern above the staircase, more Venetian Renaissance in style than anything approaching Burton's Greek revival.

18. The morning room. In 1898 Sir Edward Poynter's 'gorgeous' ceiling was coloured a 'deep but vivid blue' rather than green and was lavishly gilded; the room's walls were of 'gold Japanese leather, and its woodwork of broken brown'. It was all 'wonderfully sumptuous and daring'. Poynter's redecorated morning room is a late Victorian survival in the clubhouse.

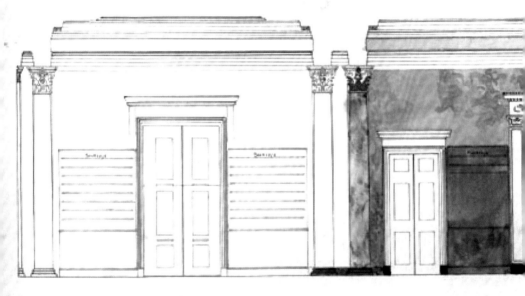

ATHENÆVM CLVB

Elevation of

19. In Sir Lawrence Alma-Tadema's elevation of the drawing room (1893), the dominant red colouring (Plate 12) has been replaced by green, and aluminium leaf applied to the ornamentation of the central dome and the cornice and ceiling beams. The room that had enchanted Charles Darwin and Matthew Arnold when they first joined was now beautifully embellished.

Drawing - room

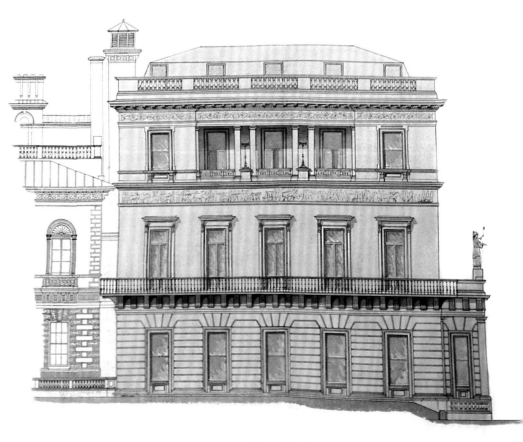

ATHENÆUM - CLUB

PROPOSED ALTERATIONS 1888

ELEVATION - TOWARDS - CARLTON - GARDENS

20. This is the frontispiece to the 'proposed alterations & additions to the Club House' which Charles Barry (son of Sir Charles) was asked to present as the club's honorary architect. Rejected on cost grounds, his scheme is a reminder of what might have been. Barry resigned, along with his brother.

THE ATHENÆUM PREVIOUS TO 1899.

THE ATHENÆUM AT THE PRESENT TIME, 1925.

21. When Collcutt's scheme was approved in 1899, *The Builder* announced that 'We shall have the spectacle of a large building, designed with classic regularity and dignity, carrying on its roof a structure of inferior character and which has no obvious means of support, being erected within the main walls'. The article's aesthetic judgments were unanswerable.

22. In his letter addressed to 'Ruddy, my dear', Sir Edward Burne-Jones promised that the newly elected Rudyard Kipling would soon 'know more of the inner life of bishops than in a hundred biographies of them'. Bishops' distinctive dress led to their number being exaggerated.

23. This image from a complimentary postcard marking the club's centenary shows that the furniture in the drawing room, which Decimus Burton labelled as the 'Library' in 1829, was still arranged as in the private library of a great house, for 'literary purposes', in the 1920s. The dome disappeared in 1927–28 when the clubhouse was remodelled.

24. George Morrow's ink drawing was for a *Punch* cartoon entitled 'Raid on the Athenæum Club' (1906) in the series called *Our Untrustworthy Artist in London*. So quiet was the Athenæum that *Punch* reported on the club's addiction to dancing, singing, boxing and late-night debauchery in the only full-page article on Clubland in the magazine's history to that date.

25. James Dewar, seen here lecturing on liquid hydrogen, was elected to the Athenæum under Rule II in 1884 and was knighted in 1904. The club had close ties with the Royal Institution: half the male figures in Brooks's idealised group portrait were present or future Athenians.

26. The propaganda war over 'culture' arrived at the Athenæum's door in a *Punch* cartoon of 1915 depicting the Kaiser mounting the club's steps. The artist Frederick Henry Townsend was not a member, but nuanced references to the club in the accompanying anonymous verses, 'When William Comes to Town', suggest that Sir Owen Seaman, editor of *Punch* and a member of the Executive Committee, was the author.

27. George Morrow's 'Bringing in the Boiled Owl' was the festive contribution to a series of *Entertainments at Which We Have Never Assisted* in *Punch*. It was first used as the club's Christmas card in 1956.

28. Among the many writers and artists who were proposed by Sir William Rothenstein, the most popular proved to be his close friend Max Beerbohm, whose cartoons of 'Club Types' (1892) had included a bespectacled intellectual from the Athenæum.

ATHENÆUM.

THE NEW MEMBER OF THE ATHENAEUM CLUB WHO ASKED THE WAY
TO THE COCKTAIL BAR

29. H.M. Bateman achieved international fame through *The Man Who* series of cartoons which focused upon social gaffes, such as 'The Man Who Lit His Cigar before the Royal Toast'. The 'New Member' cartoon (1930) reflects the popular image of the Athenæum as a retreat for the elderly, who were served drinks on silver salvers.

30. In 1936 no. 6 Carlton Gardens, formerly owned by Gladstone, became the ladies' annexe to the nearby Athenæum. The house provided five reception rooms, four bedrooms for members and ten maidservants' bedrooms for twenty maids. Faded photographs and negatives in the club's archives reveal soft furnishings and modern furniture.

31. Although 'mercifully spared damage by Flying Bombs, beyond the breaking of windows', the clubhouse was pockmarked by the end of the Second World War. Athena, camouflaged in bronze green, grasps her spear and looks down at an aboveground splinter shelter that was built by Westminster City Council in the spring of 1940 to accommodate 1,050 people.

32. ''Pon my Word, Barnstaple' (1962). The Athenæum gratefully accepted the originals of several *Express* cartoons by Sir Osbert Lancaster featuring senior clerics. Today they are displayed in the lobby next to the lift and adjacent to the gents.

33. In 1967 Sir John Betjeman resigned from the Athenæum in protest against 'the ugly new lighting in the entrance hall and the trivial wallpapering of the Great Room on the first floor'. Having been readmitted twice he finally left in the early 1980s. He would not have liked another 'Trust House' style of intervention when the hall floor was covered with PVC 'chessboard' tiling in 1969.

34. In 1979 the General Committee felt the need to promote 'friendly relations among Members', encouraging those who used the 'communal tables' in the coffee room to 'sit next or opposite to places already occupied'. John Nevinson, a retired civil servant, donated a dedicated long table for the purpose in 1986, since when 'Club Table' has become one of the most cherished aspects of life at the Athenæum.

35. In 1974 the chairman of the General Committee met 'a group of Members opposed to Lady Guests being allowed the use of the Drawing Room after dinner'. This group, known as 'The Misogynists', later wisely changed their name to 'The Traditionalists'. Meanwhile Osbert Lancaster's Maudie Littlehampton says, 'Tell me Bishop, is it true that even the Athenæum's thinking of going bi-sexual?'

36. Most of the original smoking room was hidden from view in 1958 when plaster walls and false ceilings were introduced to create extra bedrooms for staff, later converted to members' bedrooms. These additions were removed in 2009, revealing elegant plasterwork in a second drawing room that could be used for meetings and private events in an increasingly busy clubhouse.

When the next major European war broke out, Hardy felt that 'as the leading older poet he ought to set an example', and his popular poem 'Song of the Soldiers' appeared in *The Times* on 5 September 1914.[117] Angry anti-German poems followed, including 'England to Germany in 1914', 'On the Belgian Expatriation', and 'An Appeal to America on behalf of the Belgian Destitute'.[118] Deeply affected by the death of a cousin at Gallipoli in August 1915, he wrote an elegy entitled 'Before Marching and After' which explores the workings of memory and association when bad news from the battlefield enters the domestic space:

> When the heath wore the robe of late summer,
> And the fuchsia-bells, hot in the sun,
> Hung red by the door, a quick comer
> Brought tidings that marching was done . . .[119]

Arthur Benson, who used the Athenæum as his London base, recalled an occasion there around 1912 when he 'felt like Alice between the two Queens', acting as an interpreter between Hardy and Henry James, neither of whom could hear a word that the other was saying.[120] As a fellow and later Master of Magdalene College Cambridge, that most gentlemanly of institutions, Benson supported the principle of electing leading literary figures to honorary fellowships, the first of whom was Thomas Hardy in 1913. Yet Benson recorded in his diary that Hardy had the face 'not of a farmer or peasant, like old Carlyle, but of a village tradesman'. The American Henry James, on the other hand, looked and acted like an English gentleman, and responded to the war by being naturalised as a British subject in July 1915 because of his 'attachment to the country and his sympathy with it and its people'. Among his sponsors in that process were two members of the club: Asquith and Rowland Prothero's brother, George, editor of the *Quarterly Review*.[121] James volunteered to help Belgian refugees, visited wounded soldiers in hospital and became president of the American Volunteer Motor Ambulance Corps. *Within the Rim and other Essays 1914–15* (1919) was a posthumous collection of pieces that he had contributed to the war effort, including an essay entitled 'The long wards' which ends, 'I believe in Culture – speaking strictly now of the honest and of our own congruous kind.'[122]

When Kipling read the announcement of James's naturalisation in *The Times*, he wrote to him, 'You don't know what it means or what it will go on to mean not to the Empire alone but to all the world of civilization that you've thrown in your lot with them.'[123] Kipling, the empire's unofficial laureate before and during the war, lunched regularly in what he called the 'solemn halls of the Athenæum', where he met many of the political leaders.[124] While not agreeing to write sponsored propaganda, he devoted his time to projects related to the war, including writing the history of the Irish Guards, his son's regiment, and joining the Imperial War Graves Commission, for which he provided most of the words, including those inscribed on the Stone of Sacrific in the cemeteries – 'Their name liveth for evermore' – and becoming a Rhodes trustee.[125] Like Henry James, he published collections of essays and reviews in aid of the war effort, with titles such as *The New Army in Training*, *France at War on the Frontier of Civilization* and *Fringes of the Fleet*, all published in 1915. His most effective study of hatred of the Germans, in which he came to share, was 'Mary Postgate', published in *A Diversity of Creatures* in 1917, a story of revenge with powerful psychological and sexual undercurrents.

Kipling had helped his friend Sir Rider Haggard with some of his plots. Famous for his exotic African romances of exploration and derring-do, Haggard had been elected under Rule II in 1895. He was knighted in 1912 and appointed KBE in 1919 for public service, and was a member of the Empire Settlement Committee for the relocation of war veterans to parts of the Empire. Escapist romances were popular during the war, and Haggard's *Finished* (1917), which featured an image of a Zulu on the dust-jacket, took the reviewer in *Punch* back to his schooldays. The title was worrying, however – was this the end of Allan Quatermain? – and 'whether the old careless rapture is altogether recovered is another matter'.[126] Millions viewed the propaganda film *The Battle of the Somme*, released in August 1916, and were shocked by sequences which are now known to have been reconstructions. Haggard was moved to write, 'There is something appalling about the instantaneous change from fierce activity to supine death. . . . War has always been dreadful, but never, I suppose, more dreadful than today.'[127]

Visual representations of life and death at the Front were available through the *Illustrated London News*, which carried maps, photographs and dramatic graphic reconstructions of hand-to-hand fighting, together with a page or two of small studio photographs of fallen officers, week after week. Among the war artists recruited by Wellington House to work in France were three future members of the club: William Orpen (elected in 1920), William Rothenstein (1925) and Francis Dodd (1935). Older artists, such as the three members who produced the commemorative paintings discussed at the beginning of this chapter, worked mainly or exclusively in their studios in Britain. Solomon Solomon was an exception. Elected under Rule II in 1907, he had been taught in the Royal Academy Schools by Leighton, Millais and Alma-Tadema, all former members, in the late 1870s. Having explained the significance of camouflage to the War Office at the outbreak, Lieutenant-Colonel Solomon of the Royal Engineers was sent to help the French in 1916 and to establish a camouflage section in Flanders. He opened a camouflage school in Kensington Gardens, focusing upon the concealment from the air of large areas of terrain, and published a book on camouflage in 1920.[128] A *Punch* cartoon of June 1917 entitled 'The Arts in War-time' was the first of several to make fun of a subject which for Solomon became something of an obsession: at one point he believed that the Germans had huge armies under netting.[129]

Strongly held views among members on matters relating to the war became problematic when the club's name was invoked in their dissemination. No subject was more controversial in the years leading up to the war than naval expansion, and the Library Committee took care to build up a significant holding in naval history.[130] Admirals Fisher and Beresford were both members. Fisher, who was to be reinstated as First Sea Lord in October 1914 at the age of seventy-three, pursued policies that were supported by the British Navy League, whereas between 1908 and 1913 Beresford's support came from the Imperial Maritime League (or 'Navier League'), of which Lionel Horton Smith, a fellow member, was co-founder and secretary. In 1913 the Executive Committee warned Horton Smith against using the club's address in published statements, but then changed its mind. On that basis Horton Smith repeated the practice in 1915, in three letters to the press that were later reprinted in pamphlet form – *The Issue; or, Why We Are at War* (August 1914), *Never to Rise Again: 'Deutschland unter alles'* (June 1915) and *The Perils of Ignorance* (July 1915) – all endorsed with the club's address. Although the Executive

Committee were clearly anxious to suppress the practice in wartime, they were tired of corresponding with him and declined to discuss the matter further in October 1916.[131]

As a literary club with an unwritten rule of confidentiality and a membership which included cabinet ministers and senior civil servants, the Athenæum was better suited to those writers who worked secretly for Wellington House. In September 1914 Masterman established a subdivision of his organisation with the express purpose of distributing propaganda in America. Gilbert Parker was highly successful in the role, for which he was unpaid, accumulating over 13,000 American contacts, including academics, scientists, doctors and politicians, and distributing the works of authors such as Kipling and John Galsworthy, a future member of the Athenæum.[132] Having published novels and a study of the war entitled *The World in a Crucible* (1915), Parker was given a baronetcy for his service in 1915, became a Privy Counsellor in 1916 and was elected to the club in 1917.

Wellington House also produced its own newspapers, including one based on the *Illustrated London News* and printed on its rollers, and recruited lecturers, the most popular of whom was Gilbert Murray.[133] Murray, elected to the club in 1917, had won all the prizes when he was up at Oxford with his friend Laurens Fisher, himself an excellent classicist. After Fisher was made Secretary of the Board of Education by Lloyd George in December 1916, Murray worked part time in the department and used his position to help those imprisoned as conscientious objectors, most notably Bertrand Russell.[134]

Fisher, who had been elected to the club in 1908, was the vice-chancellor of Sheffield University. He served on the Bryce committee that investigated alleged German outrages in 1914–15 and that received over 1,200 depositions made by witnesses.[135] Only one of the committee was not a present or future member of the Athenæum. When the academic lawyer Frederick Pollock was elected in 1879 he had become the third generation of Pollocks in the club; Sir Kenelm Digby, a member since 1889, was a retired lawyer and civil servant who was appointed as an additional member of the committee in January 1915; Harold Cox MP, an economist and journalist, would be elected in 1919; and Alfred Hopkinson, who had retired as vice-chancellor of Victoria University of Manchester, in 1931. Their report, published in May 1915, was later found to be unreliable, as it was based on evidence that had not been corroborated.

Like George Darroch, Captain Bertrand Stewart worked in intelligence. Appointed to General Allenby's staff, he left for France with the Cavalry Division and on 12 September 1914 became the first member of the club to be killed in action, aged forty-two. The fact that his death was not announced until the Annual Report was circulated in May 1916 perhaps reflects the sensitive nature of his work. Buchan's intelligence work provided material for his novels, which 'stirred the pulses' with their improbable accounts of German spies and heroic British counter-espionage. *The Thirty-nine Steps*, published in *Blackwood's Magazine* (August–September 1915) ends with Hannay commenting, 'I had done my best work, I think, before I put on khaki.' The previous year Buchan had suggested to his partners at Nelson's that they should publish a history of the war. After Conan Doyle and Hilaire Belloc had declined the commission, Buchan took on the task himself, eventually producing a work of over a million words in twenty-four volumes and donating the royalties to war charities.[136] Masterman quietly subsidised some of Nelson's output, thus keeping the business afloat. When the War Office finally agreed that journalists could visit the Front, as the war was clearly going to be protracted and the civilian population needed to be supplied with better news coverage, one of the first five to go there was Buchan. His reliance on General Headquarters for casualty figures meant that British losses were played down and the Germans' exaggerated, although by 1916 Buchan had access to much better information.[137] Late in 1917 Lloyd George made Buchan Director of Intelligence in a Ministry of Information under Lord Beaverbrook.[138]

At the beginning of the war, Lutyens went to the club 'to get the news', and the thirst for first-hand information became even greater towards the end. Buchan was in a powerful position in this regard. Newbolt later told Buchan's wife, Lady Tweedsmuir, of his 'steadiness through every crisis' and of his impact in the coffee room:

During the dark days of the German break-through in 1918, when Haig's despatch containing the words 'Our backs are against the wall' had sent a shudder through the nation, Henry described to me the lunch hour at the

Athenæum Club, where busy men were rapidly eating a war-time meal. When John came in all heads turned in his direction and whispers were rife. 'How does he look to-day? Does he look more cheerful than yesterday?' Henry always said that John's imperturbable calm did not vary, and that this did a great deal to steady people.[139]

In the years 1914–18 the club provided those members whose contributions to the war effort kept them in London with a haven where information could be exchanged in confidence. Afterwards, a few leading members also helped to shape the nation's memorialisation of its dead. Kipling provided the words that were inscribed on war graves designed by Lutyens, who also designed the Cenotaph in London. Words from Binyon's 'For the Fallen' were read at war memorials throughout the country at Remembrance Sunday services. Curzon, who introduced the two-minute silence and the sounding of the last post at the Cenotaph, also organised the project that culminated in the burial of the Unknown Warrior in Westminster Abbey on 11 November 1920. Kipling's Recessional ('God of our Fathers') was sung at the service, and the Dean, Herbert Ryle, wrote the inscription for the tombstone, which ends with words from the second book of Chronicles: 'They buried him among the kings because he had done good toward God and toward his house.'

# 9

*ᴊᴄ*

# A ROOMFUL OF OWLS

In December 1918 General Julian Byng was welcomed home at Charing Cross station by an official party which included members of the cabinet.[1] He was then driven down Pall Mall in an open carriage with General Plumer, on their way to lunch at Buckingham Palace. As they passed the Athenæum, where Byng had recently been elected under Rule II, the generals waved enthusiastically. When various members waved back – surely an unprecedented moment of spontaneity – they were unaware that the conquering heroes were in fact responding to the club's chambermaids dancing on the upper balcony. The generals were convulsed in laughter and further waving ensued. Byng clearly enlivened the club later, too. In the lavatory there one day he asked Archbishop Davidson whether he had noticed that three pairs of nail scissors had disappeared since the election of the last three bishops; and in January 1921 Sir Henry Newbolt, Sir Owen Seaman, the architect Sir Reginald Blomfield and the classicist Dr W.H.D. Rowse chose Viscount Byng of Vimy to be their chairman when they planned a dinner for André Maurois, author of *The Silence of Colonel Bramble*.[2] One day in October 1926 Newbolt described how he was lunching at the Athenæum when Byng came in and was 'quite embarrassingly affectionate before the whole roomful of Owls'.[3]

George Morrow's cartoon, 'Bringing in the Boiled Owl (Athene's Sacred Bird) at the Christmas Dinner at the Athenæum Club', had appeared in *Punch* the previous year (Plate 27).[4] This was one of a series of cartoons entitled 'Entertainments at which we have Never Assisted', in which famous clubs and learned societies are gently teased and fictitious clubs invented. In the case of

the Athenæum, the fact that both the editor and chief cartoonist of the magazine were 'Owls' would have been relished around the famous *Punch* table and
in the club's smoking room.[5] The Owls of Pall Mall did not go in for exuberant
celebrations or public expressions of affection, and their reputation for 'reserve
and dignity' was sustained throughout the 1920s and 1930s – the subject of
this chapter – when a particular breed of highly educated and deeply serious
members played leading roles in club life. Political decisions on national reconstruction were often based upon reports from advisory groups of the kind that
had been needed during the war, and again many members of the club served
as expert advisors in a wide range of fields. The influential civil servants and
economists, bankers and industrialists, scientists and engineers who exchanged
ideas over lunch or checked their references in the library would have acknowledged the force of Sir William Beveridge's comment in his autobiography:
'Influence, as the word is used here, means changing the actions of others by
persuasion, means appeal to reason or to emotions other than fear or greed; the
instruments of influence are words, spoken or written; if the influence is to be
for good, it must rest on knowledge.'[6]

Athenians had always valued the opportunity to meet fellow members with
different interests and from a wide variety of professions, and the freer spirits
among them now enjoyed engaging with a generation of writers and artists
who specialised in satire and caricature. Although the traditions of the club
were still fiercely defended in the inter-war years, this was a period of innovation, with the ending of the ballot and the introduction of bedrooms for
members, monthly Talk Dinners and an annexe where ladies could be entertained. Change, or rather adaptation was under way, both inside and outside
the Athenæum.

At first the club struggled to balance its books. In June 1919, soon after the
appearance of the Annual Report, the *Daily Mail* singled out the Athenæum
(the 'premier institution') among the leading clubs that had financial difficulties and planned to increase their subscriptions.[7] Following losses in 1917 and
1918, a 'serious crisis in the financial affairs of the Club' was announced in the
report.[8] As a result annual subscriptions, which had been held at 8 guineas
since 1885, increased to 10 guineas in 1920 and then, after further increases
in prices, to 12 guineas the following year, a rise of 50 per cent in just over

12 months. During the tortuous process of consultation on the finances, via a specially appointed Joint Committee of Enquiry (half General Committee members, half others) and subsequent EGMs and AGMs, administrative changes were also made. Guided by the Joint Committee, an EGM held in November 1919 'further resolved that an Executive Secretary, who would also act as Manager and be responsible to the Executive Committee, should be appointed, in order to relieve Mr. Tedder of a portion of the onerous duties which he has discharged since his promotion in 1889 (after 15 years' service as Librarian) to the combined office of Secretary and Librarian. Mr. Tedder will in future be styled General Secretary and Librarian. Captain C.T.A. Hankey was chosen to fill the post of Executive Secretary, and commenced his duties on February 1st, 1920.'[9] The Joint Committee believed that Henry Tedder was 'the embodiment of Athenæum spirit and tradition; and his loss from this point of view would be irreparable'.[10] On his retirement in 1922, Tedder the quintessential librarian was replaced as secretary by Clement Hankey, an army officer who had 'acted for some years as Camp Commandant, and Permanent Mess Secretary to the Political Mission attached to the Palestine Expeditionary Force'.[11] Educated at Rugby and Balliol, he was the elder brother of the Cabinet Secretary, Sir Maurice Hankey, and of Donald Hankey, author of *A Student in Arms*, who was killed in action on the Somme in 1916.

In July 1922 the Executive Committee suggested that a suitable way of marking the centenary of the club in 1924 would be the election of fifty new members, thus boosting not only the membership but also the income of the club.[12] The resolution that was approved by an overwhelming majority at an EGM the following November was proposed by Hugh Chisholm, whose 12th edition of the *Encyclopædia Britannica* was published in 1922, and seconded by Sir Herbert Jackson. It specified that the General Committee should be empowered to elect not more than fifty members from a special 'Centenary List' of candidates, the names to be 'of mature age on the Candidates' Book, as being men of such fully established reputation in Science, Literature, the Arts, Finance and Economics, Law, Professional life, or Public service in Church or State, as to add distinction to the membership of the Athenæum by their immediate election'.[13] The Executive Committee set to work, furnished with a printed list of candidates and typed notes on how things were done in 1838, when the 'Forty Thieves' were elected; and by April 1923 they could send a shortlist of sixty-five men to the General Committee, most of them nominated by either Chisholm or Jackson, from whom the final fifty were selected.[14]

Whereas many of the Forty Thieves had been young men of great promise,[15] the Centenary List were of mature age and established reputation. While they included distinguished individuals such as Sir Johnston Forbes-Robertson, the finest Hamlet of his generation, their election, together with that of the middle-aged men included in the 'advanced ballot',[16] did nothing to lower the club's age profile, already high and the subject of adverse comment from members and non-members alike. A.C. Benson, elected in 1901, noted in his diary that the Edwardian Athenæum was 'a rather terrible place, so much infirmity, such limping & coughing'.[17] (Cab drivers called the club 'The Cough and Spit'.[18]) Meade Falkner's jocular description of everyone at the club being 'old and bald and blind' in 1918 was written to amuse a godchild;[19] but even after the Second World War an historian of White's commented that no club in London could count so many 'white-haired and bald men' among its members as the Athenæum.[20]

After a fruitless search for furnished rooms to be at the disposal of members, the General Committee acknowledged in 1923 that there was a 'growing demand among Members for bedroom accommodation'.[21] Here was an opportunity to improve the club's facilities and further increase its income. Sir Aston Webb, architect and president of the Royal Academy, was asked to prepare a scheme for an additional storey to the clubhouse.[22] Although approved by a group of distinguished Athenian architects, the scheme was rejected by the membership in time-honoured fashion and the search for rooms continued, much to the amusement of the *Evening News*, which reported in 1925 that 'even the old-fashioned Athenæum is feeling the pressure of this modern movement'.[23] Again the search failed and again some of the in-house architects – Sir Edwin Lutyens, Burke Downing, Detmar Blow and Professor Frederick Simpson – were asked to develop a scheme to provide members' bedrooms in the clubhouse. This time the members were persuaded by their arguments, in May 1927,[24] and plans were made to close the clubhouse between 29 August and 6 February 1928, temporary facilities having been arranged at neighbouring clubs.

A circular to members described the remodelling of the clubhouse to something that members would recognise today. On the second floor there were '7 bedrooms, well lighted, fitted with lavatory [i.e. wash] basins (hot and cold water), warmed by central heating and furnished by Heal, with two bathrooms and two W.C.'s', at a charge of 8s. 6d. per night; on the third floor a suite of similar rooms 'at present occupied by part of the Staff, will be available in the future if required'.[25] 'A new lift with a larger car than before and fresh machinery, gives access from the ground floor to the Upper Smoking Room and to both suites of bedrooms.' Alterations had to be made to the ceiling of the drawing room, which now lost its dome, and the opportunity was taken to redecorate the room. (Strangely, no record of the new décor is to be found in the club's archives.)

The guest room on the ground floor, formerly the writing room, was equipped with a service bar and lift from the kitchen, enabling members to 'entertain guests at all meals'. A lavatory was available on the ground floor, but the main lavatory was now situated in the basement adjoining the corridor to the billiard room. The great hall and staircase were redecorated under the directions of a sub-committee chaired by Sir Frank Dicksee PRA. The perennial problem of the 'rapidly increasing needs of the Library' was addressed by installing bookcases in the billiard room corridor and storing heavy folios and books not in frequent demand in a space under the drawing room floor and above the ceiling of the hall, 'access to which can now be had by means of a ladder through a small door cut in the wall on the back stairs'.

It was the provision of bedrooms rather than the athleticism of the library staff that attracted attention outside. In August 1928 the *Graphic* printed an article entitled 'Bed and breakfast at the Athenæum! – The idiosyncrasies of intellect: true stories of the brainiest club in the world'.[26] Readers were assured that, in spite of innovations relating to bedrooms and guests, the club was still a 'tremendously intelligent place' which made longevity a speciality. This last point will have touched a nerve. More pressing in 1927/28 was the need to finance works which cost about £27,000 to complete.[27] Like architectural expertise, financial advice was readily available in-house. In December 1927 the Executive Committee received proposals from Mervyn O'Gorman and Alan (later Sir Alan) Barlow, then a senior civil servant at the Ministry of

Labour. In their report Barlow was understandably pessimistic about potential contributions from members, as they had 'never shown themselves at all ready to provide funds for the needs of the Club'.[28] Three months later the financial sub-committee consulted Frederick Goodenough, the founding company secretary of Barclay & Co. and a member since 1925. The club then offered members redeemable notes without interest at £25, each note purchased leading to a deduction of a guinea from subscriptions, which were now set at 15 guineas per annum (almost double the rate in 1920). In May 1928 Hankey could report that he had received applications amounting to £16,700 and by 19 June £11,050 had been received in cash.[29] Combined with income from bedroom rentals and an increase in the number of meals served, partly as a result of providing bedrooms and a guest room,[30] these measures set the club's finances on a secure footing, with a membership that remained steady at around 1,370 ordinary members.

The clearest index of the 'Athenæum spirit and tradition' that Henry Tedder was said to epitomise is the manner in which the club planned and executed the celebration of its centenary. In 1921, a year before the idea of electing fifty new members was mooted, an official history was proposed. Tedder was the obvious choice as the author of the book, which would be illustrated and would be published by the club at its own expense.[31] The first change of hand in the club minutes since 1889 occurred on 11 April 1922, following Tedder's retirement, when he became an honorary member for life with no fees.[32] In March 1924 it was reported that the history was expected to be ready for publication before the end of the centenary year.[33] Anxious enquiries were made in May,[34] but Tedder's labour of love was left unfinished at his death on 1 August 1924. Having first lamented the loss of Tedder and made provision for his widow, the club turned to the author and journalist Humphry Ward, a member since 1885 and now serving on the Library Committee, to undertake the work, which duly went forward once the legality of paying a fee to a member had been confirmed.[35]

At least two-thirds of the time needed to complete such a project is taken up with research, and Tedder had done the research. So Ward 'recast, rearranged and rewrote' Tedder's 'mass of material', following his arrangement 'pretty closely', and produced a narrative of 111 printed pages in twelve months.[36] (The remaining 242 pages are biographical sketches of the Rule II members elected since 1831, many of which duplicate information available from the *Dictionary of National Biography*.) The handsome *History of the Athenæum, 1824–1925* was published in the spring of 1926 at 1 guinea to members and 25/- to booksellers. The cost of printing, binding and distributing the history was £582 and receipts from sales up to December were £423.[37] A suggestion, made as late as September 1925, that more portraits of deceased members of distinction would 'add much to the attractions of the book',[38] had been accepted by the Library Committee, who were responsible for the production. The work involved in reproducing these portraits, which account for twenty-five of the thirty-three black-and-white illustrations in the history, and an appeal for donations of originals to mark the centenary combined to enrich the Athenæum Collection, more than half of which is portraiture.[39] Portraits were now exhibited around the clubhouse, although bookcases still had priority for wall space and the mainly bare walls of the hall and coffee room still honoured the classicist intentions of the founders and their architect.

In June 1923, having already set in train both the club history and the Centenary List of new members, the General Committee received a report from its Centenary sub-committee in which further suggestions were made. The most significant of these was a dinner in the coffee room along the lines of that for the Order of Merit (1902), to be held on or about 28 May 1924, 'being the date of the occupation of the original Club House . . . and the adoption of the name of *The Athenæum* in place of *The Society* as that of the Club'.[40] Eight months later, on 16 February 1924, the raising of the flag (presumably the Union Flag) 'to the top of the mast' was drawn to members' attention, this being 'Foundation Day' on which the inaugural committee had met in Somerset House in 1824.[41] Thirty-three places at the dinner were reserved and a ballot was held for the remaining 136, with tickets at 2 guineas, including wine and cigars.

As in 1902, a complete record of the centenary dinner was later placed in the archive. This reveals that dinner was duly served on Wednesday 28 May, with the inevitable *selle de mouton* as the main meat course.[42] In 1902 Arthur Balfour MP had proposed the vote of thanks at the OM dinner as the newly elected prime minister. In 1924 the earl of Balfour, by now a trustee of the club, rose after dinner to propose the toast of 'The Athenæum', in a voice that was once described as being like a 'silvery bell'.[43] He seized the opportunity to review the club's early days, arguing that Croker was the true founder of the Athenæum and that he 'did not deserve the full extent' of the attacks upon him by three of the most powerful writers of his time who were all members of his club – Macaulay, Disraeli and Sir George Trevelyan – 'considering the literary service he had done to his time and country': the 'unamiable strain of their criticism' was, he said, 'an unnecessary vengeance on his portrait and memory'.[44] Balfour struck the keynote of the evening when he pointed out that the Athenæum was unlike other clubs that had been formed under what he called a 'Separatist System', whereby men of letters consorted with men of letters, scientific men with scientific men, and so on. The idea of the Athenæum as a place where 'different worlds met and associated in the common life of the common Club' we owe entirely to the 'originality and genius of John Wilson Croker', he said. The strength of feeling in this statement reflects the magnitude of the injustice done to Croker and his memory both inside and outside the club since 1824. Balfour's reassessment of Croker is echoed in Ward's history of the club, written the following year, and in Cowell's history of 1975, but is more strongly supported in the early chapters of this book.

The Centenary List of 1923 had included 'men of such fully established reputation in Science, Literature, the Arts, Finance and Economics, Law, Professional life, or Public service in Church or State', as we have seen. The categories of finance and economics, law and 'professional life' reflect the fact that the ordinary membership had always been drawn from a wide range of backgrounds.[45] When choosing speakers to respond to Balfour's centenary toast, however, the Committee naturally turned to senior figures from the worlds of science, literature and the arts – the categories specified in the club's foundational documents – and of 'public service', which had been added as a criterion for election under Rule II in 1848.[46] First came the president of the Royal Society, the physiologist Sir Charles Sherrington, who was admitted to the Order of Merit in 1924, published a slim volume of verse in 1925 and was a trustee of the British Museum.[47] Scientific men, he said, 'had enjoyed many dinners and consumed much tobacco in the Club House, in the card room they had held both good hands and bad, they were even reported occasionally to have slept in the chairs; they had indeed behaved very much as other members; they had in short felt at home'.[48] Like Balfour he celebrated the drawing together of men from science, letters, arts and public service, who 'learned one from another'.

Rudyard Kipling had declined an invitation to speak at the centenary dinner,[49] as was usual with him; so it was Sir Henry Newbolt who replied on behalf of literature. Newbolt elaborated Sherrington's theme, saying that 'We were here for giving and taking, for mutual pleasure, help, information and contradiction which we got from one another – in short, for the sake of common life. Such a Society, as well as Literature, had the same problem to solve – they both had to unite freedom with consideration, independence with interdependence, commonness with refinement.'[50] He then linked this need for balance with the definition of a gentleman, a subject that had preoccupied the late Victorians and the Edwardians, and that had always been an unspoken criterion for election to the Athenæum:

> There was a phrase in Tacitus which might be taken as a motto both for life and for Literature – *Dignitatis suæ, Libertatis alienæ, memor* – 'never forgetful of his own dignity or of the rights of others'. It was said of a particular Roman, but it might serve as the definition of a gentleman. At any rate, it described exactly the likeness which existed between our life here and the great human Society of Literature – the perpetual effort to keep a perfect balance between familiarity and dignity. The aim that was set before us by our Founders was this combination of common life and personal distinction, and so long as we kept it in view, so long we should be on the way to realising the type of the ideal Club.

Newbolt was speaking two years after the *annus mirabilis* of English literary Modernism, with the publication of T.S. Eliot's *Waste Land* and James Joyce's *Ulysses*, a novel that gleefully upsets the 'balance between familiarity and dignity': his conservative views are those of an urbane and deeply patriotic 'Georgian'.[51]

Newbolt was to have been followed by the president of the Royal Academy. Sir Aston Webb was unable to attend, however, having been badly injured in a traffic accident on his way home from an Academy dinner, and so his fellow architect, Sir Reginald Blomfield, stood in as the speaker on behalf of the arts. Part of his speech was devoted to an attack upon Impressionism, Cubism, Futurism, Vorticism 'and the reduction ad absurdum of the whole thing, non-representative art'.[52] What would the club's many distinguished artists – Turner, Chantrey, Lawrence, Leighton, Millais, Burne-Jones and others – have thought of these works which 'the enthusiasm of dealers and the ingenuity of journalists sought to impose on the public as masterpieces'? Blomfield argued that the real remedy was a 'wider culture, knowledge and understanding of the past, the knowledge of the heart as well as of the head, and that Humanism which had been too often over-ridden by science and sometimes forgotten by Literature'. As the chairman had pointed out, he continued, the Athenæum was 'founded as the home and headquarters of Humanism and in its hundred years of existence it had never failed of that high and honourable tradition'.

When Archbishop Davidson, the senior trustee, rose to offer the fourth and final response to Balfour's toast 'on behalf of Public Service' he referred to W.E. Gladstone who, 'for all his eminence, declined the honour of election to the Athenæum'.[53] Rather than bemoaning the club's loss, Davidson, tongue in cheek, invited his fellow members to 'think of the difference it would have made to him if he had been a member of this Club and think what he lost by his refusal to join the Athenæum'. Membership, he believed, 'helped to break down the grooviness and narrowness' of prosaic everyday life, and he felt 'supreme thankfulness for what he at least found to be a gain – recreation – uplift – which was afforded by the Club of which they were so proud – a Club which is both the seedplot and cementing of friendships precious to them all'. All that remained after such a heartfelt tribute was for the toast to the chairman by Sir Edward Henry, retired chief commissioner of the Metropolitan Police and chairman of the Executive Committee, to be 'carried with acclamation and musical honours', and for Lord Balfour to make a brief reply, before proceedings ended.

Two months later the club continued its celebrations with a conversazione to which the king and queen had been invited. A significant number of Athenians – statesmen, presidents of learned societies, royal chaplains and medical advisors – moved in court circles, and the issuing of this invitation, which was graciously declined, reflects the General Committee's view of the club's place within the British Establishment. On 3 June 1924 members and their guests, 'together with Honorary Members and their guests, and representatives invited from about 25 West-End Clubs, making a total of about 1100 persons, were received under the clock on the Grand Staircase by Lord Justice and Lady Warrington and Sir Edward and Lady Henry'.[54] Some of the treasures of the library, together with an old Candidates Book, the first minute book of the club and an old candidate's certificate, were displayed on the tables in the drawing room, together with specimens of the first service of china and plate, normally kept in the strong room. Photographic souvenir postcards of the drawing room (Plate 23) and the library were 'distributed about the House and were much appreciated, – about 400 of each having been taken by the guests'. Refreshments, provided by Messrs J. Lyons, were served at a buffet in the coffee room. No members of the press were admitted and no photographs taken, but a communication was sent to *The Times*, which duly covered the story.

The conversazione presented an opportunity to honour the club's musicians.[55] Sir Hugh Allen, director of the Royal College of Music, was asked to select a musical programme of compositions by past and present members, which was performed by the London Chamber Orchestra. Three musical knights – Sir Frederick Bridge, Sir Walter Parratt and Sir Charles Villiers Stanford – had died within eleven days of each other only three months earlier, in March 1924.[56] Bridge and Parratt were organists whose compositions were mainly of church music. Stanford's work was represented at the conversazione, however, together with that of Sir Arthur Sullivan, Sir William Sterndale Bennett and Sir Hubert Parry, all deceased, and two living composers, Edward Elgar and Sir Alexander Mackenzie.[57] Mackenzie, regarded in his day as Scotland's greatest composer, was cosmopolitan in his tastes but conservative in his compositions. This was also true of many of the club's writers and artists, as well as musicians, in the inter-war period, and at a time when the 'Englishness' of English music was being reasserted, Allen's other choices would have been generally welcomed by those who attended on 3 June.

The final celebratory event took place four days later – the staff ball, to which each member of staff could bring two guests.[58] All were received in the drawing room by Captain Hankey and Sir Edward Henry, who gave a short speech of welcome. The various forms of entertainment that were offered to those who were still regarded as members of the servant class contrast markedly with earlier centennial solemnities:

> The Coffee Room which was specially laid with parquet flooring, was used as a dancing hall, the music being provided by a small orchestra under Mr Percy Clark of Clapham. One end of the Drawing Room was fitted up for Progressive Whist; the North Library was furnished with a number of parlour games including 'Ping-pong', 'Draughts', 'Halma' etc, and the Morning Room was fitted up as a Buffet at which was served refreshments provided by Holys Supply Agency (the firm who had organised the service of the Dinner on May 28th). During an interval a short Concert was improvised in the Coffee Room and at the close of the evening, Mr Veale, one of the guests, asked for a vote of thanks to the Committee for generously providing the Ball, to Sir Edward Henry and Capt Hankey for being present, and to Mr Hill for undertaking the responsibility of the arrangements. This was received with great acclamation and the singing of 'For They are Jolly Good Fellows'. The proceedings terminated at 11.30 with the National Anthem.

Once the parquet flooring and the 'ping-pong' had been taken away, normal services were resumed for a club which still included substantial numbers of members who excelled in the four areas represented by the speakers at the centenary dinner. Senior scientists of the post-war era included Sir Ernest (later Lord) Rutherford OM, Sir George Beilby, Sir David Prain, Sir Herbert Jackson, Sir Arthur Eddington OM and Sir James Jeans OM, all of whom were elected before they were knighted. Another scientific knight, the Nobelist Sir Frederick Hopkins OM, made a characteristically Athenian proposal in his presidential address to the British Association for the Advancement of Science in 1933, when he 'urged the formation of a "Solomon's House" of the wisest (men) in the land who would assemble to synthesise knowledge, appraise its progress and assess its impact on society'.[59]

Ten of the club's best-known writers of the inter-war period – Thomas Hardy OM, Sir Rider Haggard, Joseph Conrad, Sir J.M. Barrie OM, Sir Henry

Newbolt, Rudyard Kipling, W.B. Yeats OM, Sir John Galsworthy OM, G.K. Chesterton and Sir John Buchan (Baron Tweedsmuir from 1935) – were born in the years between 1840 and 1875 and died between 1924 and 1940. Four of them were admitted to the Order of Merit, still virtually an Athenian preserve, two were Companions of Honour (Newbolt and Buchan) and three were Nobelists – Kipling, Galsworthy and Yeats, who was elected under Rule II in 1937. 'It is, I fear, too expensive for me', he confessed to Lady Dorothy Wellesley, 'but as election under that rule is looked on as a great honour I join for a year at any rate.'[60] Yeats added that he had 'always had a childish desire to walk up those steps & under that classic façade – it seems to belong to folk lore like "London Bridge" & that is my subject'. He was enchanted by the library.

Among a younger generation of writers, born in the 1880s, were Alfred Noyes, A.A. Milne, Sir Hugh Walpole, Michael Sadleir, Aldous Huxley and T.S. Eliot. Honours came late to Eliot: his OM and Nobel prize were awarded in 1948 and membership of the Athenæum the following year, when he was sixty. By contrast, Huxley was elected in January 1922 at the age of twenty-seven, by which time he had published four volumes of poetry and his first novel, *Chrome Yellow*.[61] Huxley used the clubhouse during the day in the summer of 1927, when staying with an aunt in Hampstead, and returned frequently when in London.[62] A member of a distinguished club dynasty, he revisited controversies that had engaged his forebears and that were now relevant in new and alarming ways. In his 'note on eugenics' (1927) he addressed a theme that had often been discussed in Galton's clubhouse[63] and that was soon to become a hideous reality in Nazi Germany. The 'socially efficient and the intellectually gifted', he argued, 'are precisely those who are not content to be ruled, but are ambitious either to rule or to live in an anti-social solitude. A state with a population consisting of nothing but these superior people could not hope to last for a year.'[64] In *Brave New World* (1932), as much a critique of Utilitarianism as it is of eugenics, one of the club's original members is recalled in the 'Malthusian belts' that are used for carrying contraceptives and the Athenæum in the erotic 'Aphroditeum' club, the latest in a long line of plays on the club's name, such as the 'Palladium', the 'Dinatherium' club, the 'Pathénaeum' and the 'Asineum'.[65] Indeed, Charles Larcom Graves's description of the 'Megatherium' club during refurbishment, in 'Changes in Club-land'

(*Punch*, 1920), anticipates Huxley: it is being decorated a pale pink outside and a sumptuous dormitory is being built on the top floor, where 'slow music will be discoursed every afternoon'.[66]

Sir Reginald Blomfield, a 'genial figure in the billiard-room of the Athenæum up to the last',[67] published his trenchant views on Modernism ten years after his centenary speech in a book entitled *Modernismus* (1934). Here he attacked R.H. Wilenski's 'devastating assertions' in *The Meaning of Modern Sculpture* 'on the validity of Greek sculpture as we know it'. 'For myself', Blomfield wrote, 'I hold to the Platonic Idea of beauty as the best working hypothesis, both for the practice and the criticism of art: that is to say, that beauty is absolute, in the sense that what is once beautiful is always beautiful, given the necessary intelligence to see it'.[68] It is now assumed, he argues:

> that man can suddenly divest himself of his inherited instincts, and shift his emotions from one point of view to its exact opposite, so that, at the word of command, the man who has hitherto delighted in the Hermes of Praxiteles, or the Venus of Cyrene, will find himself enraptured by the Genesis of Mr. Epstein or the "Compositions" of Mr. Henry Moore; and the admirers of Turner or Constable will transfer their admiration to M. Picasso or M. Braque or M. Matisse.[69]

Both Henry Moore and Jacob Epstein, whose *Night and Day* had been the subject of an hysterical rant by Blomfield in 1928, were to be elected to the Athenæum, but only much later in their careers, when Moore was in his sixties (1963) and Epstein in his seventies (1955).[70] Blomfield's views were echoed years later by Sir Alfred Munnings, who was knighted and brought into the club on his election to the presidency of the Royal Academy in 1944, and who scandalised the art world in 1949 with his hour-long diatribe at an Academy dinner on those 'foolish daubers', Cézanne, Matisse and Picasso, whose influence had defiled British tradition.[71] The artist and art administrator Sir William Rothenstein, who served as chairman of the club's Art Committee in 1935–36, was himself unmoved by post-Impressionism. By this time the club's policy of displaying portraits and other works of art on the walls of the clubhouse had encouraged the artists among the membership to donate original works, thus introducing what has been described as 'an entirely new dimension' to the Athenæum Collection, which contains original works by Mervyn O'Gorman, D.S. MacColl, formerly keeper of the Tate Gallery, and by his friends, Philip Wilson Steer and Henry Tonks (both non-members), Rothenstein himself, Max Beerbohm, A.M. Hind, Charles March Gere, Randolph Schwabe and Francis Dodd.[72]

Rothenstein was one of the most active Academicians in the clubhouse. Six years after his election in 1925 he recorded that, having been a member of the Savile Club for some years, he had never thought of joining the Athenæum, believing it to be a club for the 'solemnly eminent'.[73] When he was elected under Rule II, however, he 'could not but accept membership' and was 'soon disabused of the idea of the solemnity of the Athenæum': 'it became a second home for me, where I enjoy converse with men of varying pursuits'. Among the many writers and artists who were proposed by Rothenstein, the most popular proved to be his close friend Max Beerbohm, another member of the Savile (since 1899), whose cartoons of 'Club Types' in *The Strand Magazine* (1892) had included a bespectacled intellectual from the Athenæum (Plate 28). Beerbohm was presented to the General Committee in 1929 as the author of *A Christmas Garland* (in which eight of the parodies are of Athenian writers), *Seven Men, Caricature of Twenty-five Gentlemen, Book of Caricatures, Rossetti and his Circle* and other works, and was duly elected under Rule II.[74] Beerbohm was seconded by Newbolt. The Athenæum had previously admitted comic writers and cartoonists, but in honouring Beerbohm in this way they recognised 'the greatest caricaturist of the kind – that is, portrayer of personalities – in the history of art', as Edmund Wilson was to describe him.[75] Beerbohm himself regarded Oscar Wilde and W.M. Thackeray as the main influences upon his writing, and said that Thackeray, the archetypal literary clubman and an Athenian, had given him 'an ideal of well-bred writing'.[76] A further clue to Beerbohm's acceptance in the club, and to his enjoyment of his membership, lies in T.S. Eliot's observation that he was 'the defence and illustration of the benefits to a writer of the discipline of the classics'.[77]

Many of the writers and artists who crossed the Athenæum's 'classic façade' still shared a classical background with those in 'the Public service in Church or State'. On certain matters, however, the latter group were more conservative than the former, as Beerbohm knew when he proposed Lytton Strachey for membership under Rule II. Only a man who was universally liked would have risked saying, in a letter to members of the General Committee, that unless Strachey was admitted he would resign 'as a protest against the doltishness of a Committee that prefers essentially unimportant big-wigs to a man of genuine distinction'.[78] 'I should greatly miss the Athenæum, which I love', he added, 'but my love for the art of English prose is even deeper; and I should delight in my self-sacrifice in its cause!' Strachey, presented as the author of *Landmarks in French Literature, Eminent Victorians, Queen Victoria, Elizabeth and Essex* and other works, and seconded by his fellow Cambridge Apostle 'Goldie' Lowes Dickinson, succeeded at the third election in 1931.[79] Sir John Reith, who was present at all three meetings, would have regarded himself as far too important a big-wig to take offence, although he may well have been uneasy about honouring a man of the 'Oscar Wilde type'. Beerbohm had made his case for Strachey, however, on the basis of classical literary standards laid down by earlier generations. In campaigning for Strachey he also sought to preserve the prestige of Rule II membership, when each of the 'stodgers' on the Committee had 'some stodgy old friend whom he wants to get in under Rule II, some Major General or Minor Canon or Chemist (and possibly Druggist)'.[80] Beerbohm assured Strachey that he would like the Athenæum, as it had 'a real charm of its own': 'Though solid and staid and tranquil, as a club should be, it is also a very genial place.' (Maurice Bowra, the Oxford classicist who described himself as a member of 'the Immoral Front',[81] was also elected in 1931, and the decidedly unstaid Dadie Rylands of King's College Cambridge, a close friend of Strachey's, in 1932.)

Like two of the previous speakers at the centenary dinner, Archbishop Davidson had been a substitute: the prime minister, Ramsay MacDonald, was invited to speak on behalf of public service, but had to decline.[82] Four months earlier MacDonald had figured in a political fantasy in *Punch* by its editor, Seaman, in which Asquith and Baldwin meet secretly in the billiard room of the Athenæum to discuss the general election of 6 December 1923 and the resulting hung parliament, in the absence of MacDonald, who is 'not a member of the Club – at present'.[83] More recently he had been elected under Rule XII on 4 March 1924, as a cabinet minister,[84] and had made an ill-fated first visit to the clubhouse which provided material for a gossip column. Unfortunately he had not been briefed on the rules governing guests, rules that were now so complicated that a sheet of 'Tabulated particulars of public rooms' was produced internally, indicating times and days of the week, room by room.[85] On 16 March the *Sunday Express* announced that:

> The Prime Minister's first venture into the Athenæum Club after his unanimous election as an honorary member produced quite a nice little comedy.
>
> Mr. MacDonald, naturally enough, took a guest with him to lunch. But it was Tuesday.
>
> If it had been Saturday or Sunday, and twenty-four hours' notice had been given, the Premier would not have had to fly incontinently from the club elsewhere.[86]

The first Labour prime minister was the illegitimate son of a farm servant and a ploughman, and was quick to take offence, even from an over-zealous waiter. The club's embarrassment was compounded by the *Express* reporter's statement that a friend of his had told him that Sir Richard Gregory, 'when he heard of the awkward incident, announced his intention of going to the House of Commons and inviting Mr. MacDonald to dine at the Athenæum – the tacit suggestion being that the prime minister might feel some diffidence about re-entering the sacred portals'.

Consternation at the club and a flurry of letters. Gregory, himself the son of a cobbler and a friend and colleague of MacDonald's, had been elected to the Athenæum in 1919, the year in which he was knighted and became the editor of *Nature*. In an anguished letter to the secretary he explained that on the evening of the incident he had related it to the poet and educationalist Alfred Graves, a member, and to Graves's son, whom he thought was also a member.[87] Gregory therefore assumed that the conversation in the smoking room was private. In fact Charles Graves worked for the *Express* and was not a member. Graves senior wrote to the chairman the same day, giving his son's name and address in case they wished to express their 'strong resentment' at the action he had taken; and the managing editor of the newspaper wrote a gracious letter of apology to Graves, sharing 'the breach, if any, of good faith'.

Although the matter was upsetting for all concerned, the General Committee was grateful for the 'frank exposure of the indiscretion' and Ramsay MacDonald was soon to be seen regularly in the clubhouse, lunching quietly with non-political friends and having a 'touching respect for writers and painters'.[88]

To outsiders the Athenæum still seemed a place of 'reserve and dignity', of 'solemnity' and 'austerity'; and for many observers, particularly those living overseas, its aloof distinction epitomised the British governing classes. Take, for example, Herbert W. Horwill's account of Ramsay MacDonald's election to the club in the *Baltimore Sun* of 12 April 1924, headed 'MacDonald makes his bow to clubland':

> The Athenæum, most respectable of British institutions, has invited the Labor premier to share its exclusiveness. There is no more piquant indication of the silent revolution that has just been accomplished in England than the unanimous election of a Labor Premier as member of the Athenæum Club. It remains only for Oxford to give Mr. MacDonald the hallmark of its honorary D.C.L., and the acceptance of the new régime as part of the established order will be complete.
>
> . . . For sheer respectability there is nothing in England to beat the Athenæum Club.[89]

If Horwill knew about MacDonald's first visit, he chose not to mention it.

An aura of respectability was created not only by the presence of the bishops and the permanent officials who ran the country from Whitehall, but also of those in public service who played significant advisory role on the basis of their specialist knowledge. Consider, for example, what Beveridge described as the 'Bloomsbury battle' on behalf of London University.[90] Once Rockefeller money had been promised in 1927, pressure was applied to the duke of Bedford to sell enough land to accommodate an ambitious building programme on the site. Among the academics and administrators who supported the project were several current and future members of the Athenæum. Eustace Percy, president of the Board of Education and later elected to the club and raised to the peerage, was asked to persuade Stanley Baldwin, the prime minister and himself a member, to write to the duke; William McCormick, chairman of the University Grants

Committee and a member, was petitioned to recruit Lord Balfour to the cause; Frederic Kenyon, director of the British Museum and a member since 1908, was asked for his support; and both Gregory Foster, provost of University College, and Sir Holburt Waring, chairman of London University's Finance Committee, both members, contributed to the effort. Beveridge, the main networker in the project, described how the securing of the site and the closing of roads that ran across it became a practical issue, and that he found himself working with 'well-tried allies' in the London County Council, including the chief education officer, Sir George Gater, a future member. He later also praised the contributions of Edwin Deller, a future member and founding principal of London University, John Hatton, principal of East London College and a member, and Charles Holden, who was appointed as architect to the project and would be elected to the club in 1946.

John Maynard Keynes used to speak of 'the ins', the 'politicians, officials, administrators and educated readers of the weekly journals who ran or partici-pated in public life'.[91] The BBC had been led since its inception by one of the leading 'ins' of the period, John Reith, whose formidable energies as a committee man were expended in the public domain and at the Athenæum. Having managed the British Broadcasting Company, he became the first director-general when the organisation became a corporation with a royal charter in 1926. The following year he was knighted – recording in his diary that an 'ordinary knight-hood' was 'almost an insult', considering what he had achieved[92] – and was elected to the club under Rule II. Some of his colleagues at the BBC subsequently felt that his views on programmes 'sometimes owed less to what he had heard over the air than to what he had over the lunch table'.[93] Soon he was making his presence felt on the General Committee and the Executive Committee, of which he was deputy chairman in the 1930s. The man who startled one interviewee at the BBC by first asking whether he accepted the 'fundamental teachings of Jesus Christ' succeeded in persuading the club that the Moderator of the Church of Scotland could be elected as an honorary member during his year of office.[94] It is questionable whether an offer from William Holman Hunt's widow to lend the club the strangest of his large religious paintings, *The Miracle of the Sacred Fire in the Holy Sepulchre at Jerusalem*, would have been accepted had Reith not been in the chair when the Executive Committee met in July 1931.[95] Although Reith attended most of the meetings that year, even he had to confess that his official duties would not permit him to succeed Major General Sir Frederick Maurice as chairman of the Executive Committee in 1933.[96] Nevertheless, three years later he was still active in the Committee, arranging for one of his staff to work for a week at the clubhouse in order to establish an efficient office filing system, and taking the chair in March 1936 when Herr von Ribbentrop, the German ambassador, was invited to be an honorary member, together with other foreign representatives attending a conference at St James's Palace.[97]

Another leading committee man, Lord Macmillan (Hugh Pattison), seemed unable to resist an invitation to chair yet another commission or advisory body, and as a law lord he was considered to be a man with 'too many irons in the fire'.[98] He served, for example, as chairman of the Court of London University (1929–43), the Great Ormond Street Hospital for Sick Children (1928–34), the King George V Memorial Fund and the Advisory Council of the BBC (1936–40), as well as the General Committee of the Athenæum (1935–45). Macmillan and four other members of the club played leading roles in the creation of the Pilgrim Trust, funded by the American philanthropist Edward Harkness. In his reminiscences Macmillan explains that Sir James Irvine, principal of the University of St Andrews, was a friend of Mr Harkness's. One day in 1930 Irvine spoke to Macmillan at the Athenæum and, 'without giving more than a hint of what was afoot', asked him to meet Harkness on his arrival in London.[99] Harkness duly hosted a dinner at Claridge's on 5 May at which Irvine, John Buchan (also a member of the club) and Macmillan were present. Two other members, Stanley Baldwin and Sir Josiah Stamp, the statistician and company director, were subsequently brought in to complete the inaugural board, and Buchan drafted the preamble to the Trust Deed, in which it was stated that Harkness's donation of £2 million (the same figure as Carnegie's Trust for the Universities of Scotland in 1901) was prompted by his 'admiration for what Great Britain had done in the 1914–18 war and, by his ties of affection for the land from which he drew his descent'. In 1936 Harkness dined with the trustees of the Athenæum, of which he was made an honorary member under the chairmanship of Lord Macmillan.[100]

During the inter-war period it was men such as Reith and Macmillan, serious men who applied their gifts to public service at a time of national reconstruction, high unemployment and economic turmoil, who set the tone in Kipling's 'solemn halls' of the Athenæum, where there was no bar, let alone a cocktail bar (Plate 29).[101] When monthly 'Talk Dinners', as they came to be known, were first proposed in November 1926, the choice of subjects reflected the members' engagement with the pressing social and political issues of the day. The miners' strike that had led to the General Strike of May 1926 continued for a few further months. (In June, 'coal economy' allowed hot soup and fish to be available at the club but not hot joints.)[102] By the end of November most miners were back at work, having achieved little or nothing, and many remained unemployed. Rollo Appleyard, a consulting engineer, wrote to the General Committee on behalf of a group of members that included Mervyn O'Gorman, the wartime aeronautical engineer who was also known for his art works, and Joseph Pease, a barrister and writer on law, 'asking sanction from the Committee to arrange a monthly dinner for members and their guests on Mondays under conditions in contravention of existing regulations'.[103] These meetings would provide the opportunity to 'hold afterwards an informal discussion on some topic of general interest, the subject for discussion and the choice of a chairman for each evening to be arranged beforehand'. Sir Henry Newbolt would take the chair at the first dinner and no more than one or two guests were expected to be present. The Committee allowed two such dinners to be held and would 'decide thereafter to what extent the regulations should be amended'.

Knowing that they were breaking new ground, the steering group gathered the signatures of the twenty-three members and five guests who attended the first dinner in the morning room on 22 November 1926.[104] Sharing the top table with the chairman, Newbolt, and the principal speaker, Sir Austin Hopkinson, were those mentioned in the letter to the committee, together with Sir Martin Conway, director-general of the Imperial War Museum, and A.A.C. Swinton, one of five engineers attending the dinner, whose many letters to *The Times* on scientific subjects were generally written from the Athenæum.[105] Sir Austin's subject was 'Coal'.[106] In 1908 he had invented a revolutionary coal-cutting machine which was manufactured by his own engineering firm, where he was respected as a humane employer who lived frugally.[107] After war service as a trooper he had represented constituencies in present-day Greater Manchester as an Independent MP who disliked trade unionism and socialism, was forthright in his speeches in the Commons and was in demand as a speaker outside the House. Following his talk there was a discussion to which seven members and guests contributed.

At the second dinner, held a month later, O'Gorman chaired Sir Herbert Stephen, clerk of assize for the Northern Circuit and the author of several books on the law, who opened a discussion on 'Crime' that was attended by thirty-eight members and five guests. The experiment had been a success, and monthly Talk Dinners continued the following year when Charles Larcom Graves of *Punch* (Alfred's brother and a member of the General Committee) introduced a discussion on 'The Old and the New Journalism', the parliamentarian Sir Arthur Griffith-Boscawen on 'Party Government', Sir Richard Gregory on 'The Influence of Science' and Professor Arthur Eddington on 'The Philosophical Tendencies of Modern Science'. The informality of the discussions extended to the dress code. When the secretary, Colonel Hankey, wrote to ask G.M. Trevelyan to open a discussion entitled 'Is History a Science?', in October 1929, he added: 'As you have not, I think, attended any of these dinners previously, I should mention that the proceedings are quite informal; most members wear morning dress; the time is 7 for 7.15 p.m. and the proceedings are usually over at 10 o'clock. The price of the dinner is 7/6d exclusive of wine.'[108] The popularity of the dinners, due largely to the 'unremitting care and thought' of Appleyard, was duly noted at the AGM in 1930 and by November that year the demand for places had become so great that the coffee room was made available, with a ceiling of 130 in attendance, setting a pattern that is still followed today.[109]

Inevitably a sub-committee was established, which Appleyard chaired for five years. Cards were printed listing the dinners for the coming season. In 1932–33 most of the speakers were knights or peers. Although one or two lighter topics featured in the programme, such as 'Music as Literature', subjects such as 'The Fruits of Sea-power' and 'Idle Men and Underworked Acres' were more typical.[110] Sober subjects for sober times, from the Wall Street Crash of 1929 to Hitler's rise to power in 1933, and at home the formation of a coalition government in order to deal with a failing economy and the challenges of slum clearance and unemployment, running at over 2.6 million by the end of 1931. At the Athenæum, the General Committee's choices when appointing two new trustees in 1929/30 were further signs of these testing times. The earl of Balfour resigned his membership on health grounds in November 1929.[111] First his brother Gerald was approached to replace him, which would have pleased the earl and secured a safe appointment, if not a brilliant one: as a politician Gerald Balfour was respected for his integrity, serenity and sound judgment, and was often consulted in private by Arthur. When the invitation was declined, the chairman wrote to Stanley Baldwin, the steady pipe-smoking ironmaster whose second premiership had ended in April 1929. Baldwin accepted, and between 1930 and 1947 the club had as a trustee the only prime minister in history to serve under three monarchs, and perhaps the most underestimated statesman of the modern era.

Archbishop Davidson's death in June 1930 precipitated a second search for a trustee that year. Lord Crawford and Balcarres was too busy with his personal affairs to serve, so in October three candidates were presented to the General Committee by its chairman, Lord Warrington: William Temple, who had been enthroned as Archbishop of York and elected to the club under Rule II only a year earlier, the painter Sir William Llewellyn, president of the Royal Academy and also elected in 1929, and the eminent physicist Sir Ernest Rutherford OM, president of the Royal Society and a member since 1917.[112] The Committee chose Temple, who accepted the honour but suggested that, as he could not spend long in London, they might wish to reconsider their decision. The fact that they did not indicates the strength of his support, for which there are several possible explanations, including his father's former prominence in the club, Archbishop Davidson's excellent record as a trustee and Temple's own attributes, not only a brilliant mind and strong social conscience but also great personal charm and a famous booming laugh. Above all, however, he was Archbishop of York, which meant that the club now had a primate and a premier, two bright stars in the Establishment firmament, as trustees.

Temple, who was to be translated to Canterbury in 1942, served as a trustee until his death in 1944, when he was succeeded by Geoffrey Fisher and subsequently Donald Coggan.[113] One of his most significant contributions in the social field was the commissioning of a report on unemployment entitled *Men without Work* (1938), produced with the help of a special committee and the Pilgrim Trust, that most Athenian of charitable foundations.[114] Other episcopal members of the club who engaged with social issues included Dr Cyril Garbett, Bishop of Southwark from 1919, the first chairman of the religious advisory committee of the BBC in 1923, elected to the club in 1938 and Temple's successor as Archbishop of York in 1942. It was while at Southwark that Garbett published a pamphlet entitled *The Challenge of the Slums* (1933), urging the government to deal with overcrowding south of the river. Clearly some bishops had their uses, but the presence of so many in the club was felt to be oppressive in certain quarters. The literary scholar and historian Sir Walter Raleigh, for example, whose father was a Congregational minister, described the Edwardian club as a 'pool of Bethesda for Bishops' and commented in 1920 that 'we have plenty of bishops at the Athenæum', adding that he was in favour of exchanging them, 'at a low valuation, for junior Naval Officers'.[115]

By the mid-1930s there was to be an annexe to the 'Bishops' Mortuary', as Raleigh called the clubhouse. In 1935, seven years after the provision of bedrooms for members in the main building, Sir Frederic Kenyon chaired an EGM which rejected the proposed acquisition of a lease on 7 Carlton House Terrace and alterations made for its use as 'an annexe to the Club including a Drawing Room and a Dining Room in which member may entertain lady guests'.[116] The General Committee tried again the following March, when, in spite of Blomfield's protests, a fresh scheme for 6 Carlton Gardens was accepted by an EGM attended by about 220 members (Plate 30).[117] This large house, formerly owned by Gladstone ironically enough, provided five reception rooms, four bedrooms for members and ten maid-servants' bedrooms for twenty maids (thus releasing eight more bedrooms for members in the clubhouse).[118] Faded photographs and negatives in the club's archives reveal soft furnishings and modern furniture of a lightness that contrasts with Decimus Burton's classical (and masculine) furniture in the clubhouse. Yeats was pleased that, as a member of the club, he would now have somewhere to entertain Lady Dorothy Wellesley, and for twenty-five years some members and their wives found it most conven-ient.[119] In 1939, however, only three years after it opened, Sir Alan Barlow reported to an AGM that fewer than a fifth of the membership had used the annexe, in spite of good reports on the food and service provided there, and that the receipts from bedrooms were also disappointing.[120]

Meanwhile a steep decline in the number of candidates awaiting their turn for the ballot prompted further changes at the club. From a high point of over 1,500 candidates in the 1880s and 1890s the number had decreased to fewer than 250 by 1935, and half the members were now over sixty years of age.[121] In view of these statistics, and of poor attendance on ballot days, it was decided that elections should in future be the responsibility of the General Committee. A loose-leaf Supporters' Book was ordered and the Committee prepared to consider the next sixty candidates on the list for election.[122] A wide range of backgrounds among the Committee members was now essential. Lord Macmillan was in the chair for the first election on 7 January 1936.[123] Among the eighteen other members present were Alan Barlow, civil servant; Sir William Bragg, physicist; Sir Frederic Kenyon, Greek scholar and museum director; Sir Edwin Lutyens, architect; Sir Henry Lyons, geologist and museum director; John Mackail, classical scholar, literary critic and poet; Sir John Reith, director-general of the BBC; Sir William Rothenstein, artist and art administrator; and Marmaduke Tudsbery, consulting engineer. Once the chairman had explained the procedure, 'each Candidate was submitted separately with a statement of qualification by the Election Secretary together with a précis of the confidential correspondence', a convention that is still followed today. Being the first election of its kind, care was taken over the minuting of decisions that set precedents for later meetings. Of the eighteen men elected on a show of hands, two were 'advanced candidates', older men whose waiting period had been shortened. The process of rejecting a candidate is described in some detail. When the name of Sir James Purves-Stewart was reached, the chairman received a motion, which was duly seconded, 'that this candidate be not elected'. The motion was carried unanimously and the secretary was directed 'not to make any communication to the candidate in accordance with the usual practice that only in the case of satisfactory election is any notice sent to a candidate'. Sir James, an advanced candidate, born in 1869, was a distinguished neurologist whose publications included a medical book that ran through ten editions. Discussions in the General Committee were confidential and unminuted, but it is reasonable to suppose that his reputation for volubility and 'gesticulations that seemed hardly native' on ward rounds weighed heavily with the Committee.[124] He also held controversial views on voluntary euthanasia and on the administration of euthanasia by physicians.[125]

Far more controversial were the views of the anthropologist George Pitt-Rivers, yet he was duly elected at this first meeting. A respected scientist and agriculturist, educated at Eton and Oxford, Pitt-Rivers had strong associations with the club. In *The Clash of Culture and the Contact of Races* (1927), where he argued that the mixing of races leads to group or national destruction, he had referred to the work of a number of Athenians, including his grandfather, General Augustus Pitt-Rivers, Francis Galton, Sir James Frazer and Lord Balfour.[126] He had been proposed by Professor Reginald Gates, the botanist and geneticist, and seconded by Sir Arthur Keith, museum curator and palæo-anthropologist.[127] Both eminent supporters were to be criticised for their published work on race and heredity at a time when these were highly sensitive subjects. Whereas Gates became convinced, however, that the 'simplistic hereditary theories of the Fascists and Nazis were political rhetoric rather than rigorous science',[128] Pitt-Rivers's racial theories and right-wing politics were intertwined and were reinforced as he became infatuated with Hitler and Nazism in the mid-1930s.[129] In 1936 questions were raised in the club regarding his 'unconventional attire', but whether this included the gold swastika badge that he later affected in Clubland is unclear.[130] In *The Czech Conspiracy: A phase in the World-War plot* (1938) Pitt-Rivers described Hitler as a simple soldier, a great statesman, the leader of his people, a man of destiny, 'yes, and a friend of England'.[131] In his Prologue he referred to Gilbert Murray, classicist, internationalist and Athenian, who had written to him in a 'somewhat jocular tone': 'It is sad that the Jews have so much influence over the Conservatives, the Bishops and the Cecil family, but I am still more disturbed at the rumour I hear of the control exercised by the devil-worshipping Yezidis over the Wessex farmers and the Pitt-Rivers family. How little we suspected these things when we had that pleasant dinner together.'[132] And at the end of *The Czech Conspiracy* Pitt-Rivers reprinted a letter to *The Times* which deprecated 'the attempt which is being made to sabotage an Anglo-German rapprochement by distorting the facts of the Czecho-Slovak settlement'. Four other members of the club – Douglas Jerrold, Professor Arthur Pillans Laurie, the marquess of Londonderry and Arthur Rogers – were co-signatories.[133]

Lord Londonderry was entertained by Nazi leaders during his private visits to Germany in 1936–38 and reciprocated by inviting the German ambassador,

Joachim von Ribbentrop, to his family estates in Durham and Northern Ireland. While Ribbentrop, known as the Londonderry Herr by society wags and 'Brickendrop' by his British counterparts, was converting his gracious embassy at numbers 8 and 9 Carlton House Terrace into a Nazi stronghold full of bored SS men,[134] he was also enjoying his honorary membership of the Athenæum, just a few steps away, to which he had been elected as a matter of course.[135] There he had access to a wide range of views on Hitler's Germany, from Londonderry's on the right to Bishop George Bell's on the left. Many of those on the right, including Londonderry and Bishop Arthur Headlam, were motivated by a strong antipathy to socialism in general and Bolshevism in particular, against which fascism seemed to offer a powerful defence. With the outbreak of war the German ambassador was withdrawn and Pitt-Rivers was one of around 750 British fascists and fellow-travellers to be interned under defence regulation 18B, which may explain why he was late paying his annual subscription to the club.[136] Meanwhile another member had obeyed his masters in Moscow, penetrating this citadel of the English governing class by feigning extreme right-wing views and working his way upwards in the Secret Intelligence Service. His name was Kim Philby.

Part IV

# 'MORE THAN JUST ANOTHER LONDON CLUB'

## (1939–)

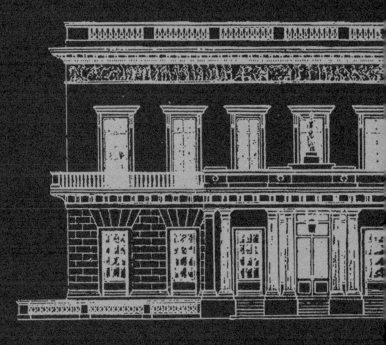

# 10

*ᴊᴄ*

# 'THE SECRET POWER OF ENGLAND'

In 1947, five years after his election to the Athenæum, the patriotic historian Arthur Bryant published a florid piece in the *Illustrated London News* on the 'historic clubs of London', the 'sheltered abodes of men of polished dignity and assurance'.[1] 'I know of nowhere', he wrote, 'not even the officers' mess of a great regiment, where the secret power of England is so clearly revealed. Hitler, who never entered one of these ancient temples, had already – though he knew it not – met his doom in them before he crossed his Polish Rubicon.' Bryant rehearses the point made by Sir Charles Waldstein (later Walston) thirty years earlier when he contrasted the Kaiser's ideology of *Kultur* with the 'Hellenic ideal of life' embodied in the cultured English gentleman.[2]

In the final section of this book we test Sir Percy Faulkner's claim in 1974, when he was chairman of the General Committee, that the Athenæum is 'more than just another London club'.[3] The current chapter, which considers the Second World War and its aftermath, reveals that the clubhouse provided a meeting place for those members whose contribution to the war effort kept them in London in 1939, as it had in 1914, and for those engaged in new debates on economic and moral reconstruction which arose before war broke out, continued throughout hostilities and shaped the national agenda in 1945. In the case of Bryant's and Waldstein's own club, the 'secret power of England' was to be found in the lives and work not only of its leading politicians and serving officers who ran the war and became household names, but also its moralists, theologians and economists who applied their minds to the demands of a future peace. Crucial to the war effort were those less well-known civil servants and intelligence officers, scientists and engineers who used the club-house to which Andrew Cowan referred in a post-war broadcast for the Canadian Broadcasting Corporation. 'I hate to think', he said, 'what would have happened if a bomb had landed on the building at lunch time when it was filled with most of the "back room boys" of the British Empire.'[4]

One particular night raid was recalled during the club's AGM in 1947, when Sir Edmund Brocklebank, one of the many Conservative MPs who had lost their seats in the Labour landslide of 1945, spoke in support of proposed improvements to staff facilities in the clubhouse. The minutes report Sir Edmund's description of

> an ugly night during the war when the Carlton Club was bombed, the Union Club and the German Embassy were in flames, and Athene rocked. The Travellers too was on fire and this was put out by hoses from the Athenæum. Bombed out people came to the Club and were given food and shelter during the night. In spite of this, breakfast was served to the members punctually at 8.30 a.m. next morning. Sir Edmund said that he felt the Members all owed the Staff a deep debt of gratitude and he welcomed the proposed improvement in the Staff amenities and arrangements, which had not been altered since the time of Decimus Burton.[5]

The motion was carried unanimously.

The Carlton's clubhouse, then to the west of the Reform's on Pall Mall, suffered a direct hit, possibly from two almost simultaneous bombs, at about 8.30 p.m. on 14 October 1940.[6] Harold Macmillan, Douglas Hogg (Lord Hailsham) and his son, Quintin Hogg, were among those who emerged from the ruins. Sir William Beveridge was at the Reform that night and was first under the table.[7] Refugees from the Travellers were later offered hospitality at White's, at the top of St James's Street. From 7 September 1940 London was bombed on fifty-seven consecutive days and, like other Londoners, the clubmen of St James's helped each other through these critical times. On the afternoon of 14 October the Executive Committee of the Athenæum directed that no more than sixteen members should sleep in the members' air-raid shelter in the basement, and that 'no-one should sleep in the Lavatory'.[8] Most of the windows were broken that night, but fortunately the glass did no damage owing to the 'cellophane and protective solution' that had been applied.[9]

Defensive measures had first been introduced during the invasion scare of September 1938, when a gas refuge was prepared in the basement for members and staff, two of whom were given the full decontamination course while seventeen others were trained as air-raid wardens.[10] In the summer of 1939 uncertainty about the nature of the threat if war were to be declared resulted in rapid changes of policy on possible closure in the Executive Committee, chaired by Sir Alan Barlow.[11] During the 'phoney war' that autumn, male members of staff who were engaged in fire-fighting duties used the smoking room as a dormitory and female staff slept at the annexe.[12] Early in 1940, having recommended that the club's mirrors be treated with rubber solution, the Executive Committee estimated the cost of emergency arrangements in case of the need to close.[13]

In fact the clubhouse remained open throughout the war years. So great were the dangers associated with this policy, and so frequent were enforced adaptations to wartime conditions, that Annual Reports were supplemented with interim reports in October or November from 1940 to 1944. These reports informed members of the latest changes to regulations relating to rationing, meal times, the black-out and the closure of rooms in the evenings, as well as news of further defensive measures, such as the bricking up of the two large windows in the front hall, and of the number of incendiary bombs on the roofs of the clubhouse and the annexe that had been extinguished by the club fire-fighting squads, made up of members and staff.[14] Serious bomb damage recurred in the vicinity of the clubhouse. In February 1944, for example, four high explosive bombs damaged an area of 6 acres between Jermyn Street and Pall Mall. Alongside news of the casualties (nine dead, forty-eight injured) was one of the bizarre twists that characterised many such accounts: one bomb fell on Pall Mall itself, opposite a taxidermist's establishment, 'scattering a disquieting heterogeny of stuffed beasts into the street'.[15] Later that year the interim report recorded that the clubhouse and the annexe had 'mercifully been spared damage by Flying Bombs, beyond the breaking of windows'.[16] A photograph taken at the end of the war (Plate 31) shows a pockmarked clubhouse and a corner of the aboveground splinter shelter that had been built in Waterloo Place by Westminster City Council in the spring of 1940 to accommodate 1,050 people.[17]

245

Concern for the safety of the Athenæum Collection was first expressed in June 1940, when the club's valuable bust of Pope by Rysbrack was removed to the basement.[18] In November 1941 it was reported that All Souls College, Oxford, was 'generously storing some of the Club port', and that several thousand of the most valuable library books, the 'principal Art Treasures' and the most important records, such as early ballot books, had been dispersed to the country houses of members who offered to accommodate them for the duration of the war.[19] Sir Follett Holt, chairman of the Entre Ríos Railways and the first chairman of the Tower Hill Improvement Trust, assured Robin Udal, the club secretary, that he could house a few cases in his squash court at Riffhams, Danbury in Essex, but could not guarantee that his barns were free from rats.[20] Some non-members also helped: two wooden cases of art treasures returned safely from Highclere Castle, Newbury, for example, owned by Lord Carnarvon, in July 1945.[21] By the spring of 1946 the librarian, Miss Eileen Stiff, could report that of the 16,600 books that had returned to the clubhouse, about 400, chiefly from the pamphlet collection, had been damaged by water, a few irreparably; the remainder had been rebound or repaired.[22]

Within the partly denuded clubhouse it was the familiar wartime story of keeping calm and carrying on. In May 1940 the General Committee, chaired by Lord Macmillan, noted that 'the usual Derby Sweep list' had been put up in the hall.[23] Four years later they thanked those members who had 'so generously lent pictures for the two loan exhibitions in the Guests' Luncheon Room', which had been 'much appreciated'.[24] Strange misjudgments of taste among the membership surfaced occasionally, however, as they did in peacetime. An Executive Committee minute of February 1940 reads: 'Offer by Sir Harold Wilberforce-Bell recently retired from the Punjab where he had served as Resident to present bison heads, not accepted'.[25] More often the minute books record timeworn concerns such as the shortage of shelf space. In July 1944 a special sub-committee on 'Library Accommodation' made some radical suggestions for additional shelving in the upper smoking room. The architect William Curtis Green, best known for his extensive work in Piccadilly in the 1920s, suggested that some 4,500 books could be accommodated 'by erecting on each side of the room two projecting spurs, each about six feet long and eighteen inches wide, with books on each side, dividing the room into three bays, with a clear view down the middle'.[26] While this proposal, which would have made the smoking room more like a further library or reading room, was rejected, the report's more predictable recommendation was accepted: that the Library Committee should aim at 'disposing of not less than 3,500 books and as many more as is reasonable'. In 1945 the Library Committee, prompted by the General Committee, agreed to present 'certain sets of periodicals (many of them incomplete) to Libraries, some of which have been seriously damaged by enemy action'.[27] By donating periodicals that were said to have been more useful to the recipients than to themselves, the club was also releasing 'shelf space urgently needed'.

While valiant efforts were made to maintain the usual services during the war, many aspects of club life were adversely affected. Talk Dinners were suspended, for example, in both the clubhouse and the annexe, in October 1939.[28] In February 1940, one was held in the light luncheon room (now the picture room) as an experiment.[29] No more were held, however, until 1949.[30] In May 1940 only the General Committee and about fifty other members attended the AGM and it was decided that, during the war, the committee could select candidates for advanced election in excess of the number of twenty laid down in Rule III.[31] By October 1941 many names had been withdrawn from the Candidates Book, presumably for a variety of reasons associated with the war, and the number remaining had dropped to about 150, one-third of whom had asked to be considered for membership after the war.[32] With enough candidates for only one year's elections, members were encouraged to take 'immediate steps' to increase their number: election was likely to follow in only a year's time, and for advanced candidates after a few months.[33] In spite of 'war casualties, high taxation and the uncertainties of the time', the number of members rose. By the autumn of 1943 demand for the club's services had increased to the extent that the clubhouse was overcrowded; so the General Committee announced that they would elect fewer Rule III members the following year.[34] Their other concern was the 'apparent preponderance of candidates belonging to the medical profession' among the new members, an observation which was repeated in 1947 and from time to time up to the present day.[35] Medical professionals seem to be as gregarious as engineers and lawyers.

In its domestic economy the Athenæum's responses to the exigencies of war were often reminiscent of those recorded in 1914–18. Shortages led to all kinds of restrictions, such as limiting the minutes of Executive Committee meetings to one sheet of paper and replacing tablecloths with table mats in the coffee room.[36] From November 1941 the drawing room and upper smoking room were closed after 7 p.m. in order to economise on light and fuel.[37] (The north and south libraries remained open.) Rationing affected the menu, as it did elsewhere. In one anecdote, however, Percy Colson, the historian of White's, managed to link two half-truths relating to the Athenæum's food and its bishops:

> The food there has never been particularly good – perhaps owing to epis-
> copal influence on the committee, and during the late war it was unspeak-
> able. I lunched there in 1940 and after a revolting meal, my host said: 'Let's
> have a liqueur with our coffee to take away the taste of the food'. (The
> coffee, incidentally, had no recognizable taste.) We asked for Grand Marnier,
> Kümmel, Cointreau, Benedictine – they had all disappeared, probably
> down the throats of the Bishops. Finally we managed to obtain a very infe-
> rior cooking brandy.[38]

Coffee, which had always been the subject of complaints, was now available on a self-service basis in urns to which spoons were attached by wires.[39] 'Wineless days' were reinstated in 1943 and the rules on alcohol became more complicated thereafter. In 1944 it was announced in the Annual Report that, 'owing to shortage of Wine stocks: - (a) Port may be served only in the Coffee Room. (b) Sherry may be served only the Sitting Rooms. (c) Whisky may be served only the Coffee Room, except after dinner. (d) Tuesdays, Wednesdays and Thursdays will continue to be wineless days, except for Port, Sherry and (while stocks last) Algerian Burgundy. (e) Spirits, beers, etc., can be served every day as hitherto.'[40] Meanwhile the club made donations of between 1 and 5 guineas to hospitals, and the members opened a Spitfire fund in September 1940, a more belligerent response than the ambulance fund in the First World War.[41]

As in 1914–18, members of staff who joined the services were given special treatment. In May 1940 it was decided that married members of staff with more than five years' service would have their pay and allowances made up to their current income when they were called up; that other cases would be considered on their merits (in some cases *ex gratia* payments were made); and that places would be kept open for them as far as possible at the end of the war.[42] Staff shortages led to some mechanisation: a 'dish-washing machine' was acquired in April 1941 and 'towel machines and soap containers' were installed in the members' lavatories.[43] The loyalty and service of the staff were gratefully acknowledged throughout the war, by the end of which there was a new sense of mutual respect and comparative informality.[44] At an AGM held six days after the Germans' unconditional surrender, the secretary, Robin Udal, 'thanked Members most sincerely for the unfailing kindness and consideration shown to them [the staff] during the years of war, and said that this was the main reason for their being able to keep staff in face of the competition from hotels. He also thanked the Members for their great generosity in giving up the West Library as a Recreation Room for the Staff, and said that this was highly appreciated.'[45]

Udal occasionally gave his son lunch at the 'Secretary's window table' in the coffee room, and there was usually a brief tour during which the boy was introduced to members of staff before returning to boarding school.[46] John Oliver Udal, in adult life an assistant commissioner in the Sudan and a member of the club, offers a unique glimpse of wartime staff members in his reminiscences, naming figures such as Mr L.W. Middleton, who had been the hall porter for forty-seven years, and Mr H.G. Hendy the club chef, who wrestled below stairs with the problems of wartime rationing. Miss Sue Shipton, who was later to work for Lord Reith, was the first secretary to marry a member, Mr Philip Nicholls of the Treasury.

Udal adds that the staff were 'a happy team and, augmented by a few from the Orleans Club, were able to field a team under the leadership of Mr Harry Pfeiffer, Receiving Clerk, to win the Clubs' knock-out football competition', the final of which he witnessed with delight in Hyde Park.

The homes of 'more than twenty' members of staff were seriously damaged by bombing during the war.[47] In October 1944 it was reported that some 'American friends', who wished to remain anonymous, had provided funds to enable gifts of £5 each to be made to those who had suffered in this way. Records in the archives of the Athenæum chronicle one leading establishment's response to a new kind of warfare. 'Hitler's War' saw fewer casualties among British servicemen and women than in the 'Great War', but many more among civilians on the Home Front. It involved the whole population, marking a much more significant change in the course of history, and its battle cry was one of effort rather than of sacrifice.[48] Whereas thirteen members of staff had been killed in action in 1914–18, only one died on active service in the Second World War. Frederick Caveswell, who had been a drawing room waiter since 1929, was killed in November 1943 when serving overseas with the Rifle Brigade: the whole amount of the club contributions to his pension was paid to his widow.[49]

The membership, most of whom were again too old to be called up, suffered more as a result of bombing than on active service. The first announcement of casualties, in the interim report of November 1940, conforms to this pattern: 'The Committee very much regret to report that Lt.-Col. Sir Arnold Wilson is missing, believed killed, and that Mr. W. Lionel Hichens and Dr. C.H. Merz have been killed by enemy action.'[50] Hichens, an industrialist and public servant, died when a bomb hit Church House on 14 October, the day that 'Athene rocked'.[51] Charles Merz, the best electrical supply engineer of his generation, was killed the same night at his home in Kensington, along with his two children and two servants; his wife was injured but survived. Similarly Lord Stamp, the statistician and businessman, was killed with his wife and eldest son in his shelter at Shortlands in April 1941, and William Sclater, a curator at the Natural History Museum, died from his wounds after a V-1 flying bomb 'fell over his home' in Chelsea in July 1944. Stress also took its toll: Hugh Walpole's biographer suggests that the writer, a diabetic, had been worn out by the blitz when he died in June 1941.[52]

Sir Arnold Wilson had become a pilot officer in October 1939 and then a rear-gunner with a bomber squadron: he died on 31 May 1940 at the age of fifty-five when his plane was shot down over France.[53] In the 1920s he had served as a colonial administrator in Mesopotamia and later published several books on the region. A devout Anglican, he had supported General Franco and met both Mussolini and Hitler in the 1930s, but his admiration for Hitler was tempered by a distaste for Nazi extremism. Colonel Jack Macnamara's association with the Nazis was more intimate. Elected to the club in 1938, Macnamara was a homosexual Conservative MP with an espionage background and connections in the Hitler Youth; he had organised sex trips to Germany in the mid-1930s with Guy Burgess, his parliamentary secretary and fellow member of the Anglo-German Fellowship.[54] Macnamara was killed in Italy while serving with the 'Black Cats' in December 1944: his commemorative shield hangs in the chamber of the House of Commons.

A third member to be killed in action was Richard Latham, a flying officer whose plane went down on a reconnaissance mission over the coast of Norway in August 1943; no trace of the missing aircraft or crew was found. A personal tribute in *The Times* referred to the war's 'merciless wastage of young men of the highest promise' and recorded that Latham would be 'missed at the Athenæum, and his gallant behaviour one night in trying to put out a fire in the middle of a blitz will never be forgotten'.[55] It is difficult to tell how many candidates died on active service, as in this war the phrase 'Killed in action' was no longer used in the Candidates Book, being replaced by the more anodyne 'Died' or 'Deceased'. A similar change in sensibility is noticeable in the commemoration of members' sons who had been killed in action. Sir Oliver Lodge's frequently reprinted book about his son Raymond, who was killed in 1915, is grounded in spiritualism's consolation of a life 'on the other side'.[56] In contrast, Michael Sadleir's *Tommy, 1916–1942*, printed in a limited edition of 105 copies in 1943, offers a this-worldly quotation from Pericles as an epitaph to his naval officer son, killed by a splinter from a German shell in the North Sea: 'He gave his body to the Commonwealth and received for his own memory the grandest of all sepulchres, not that in which his mortal bones are laid but a home in the hearts of men: and his story is not graven only on stone over his native earth, but lives on far away without visible symbol, woven into the stuff of other men's lives.'[57] In April 1946 the General Committee decided against putting up a roll of honour in the clubhouse. Their response to Victory Day had been equally muted: there were flambeaux, but no decorations, no dinner and no war service brooches for the female staff.[58]

Whereas the casualty list contrasted with that of 1914–18, when twelve members, thirteen servants and forty-seven candidates had been killed in action, the pattern of war work on the Home Front was similar, as was the clubhouse's function as a place of respite. The writer Hector Bolitho, who believed himself to be of partly Maori descent, later described life working and sleeping in the Air Ministry building in King Charles Street in 1940/41. After a night spent in squalid conditions he would walk through St James's Park to the Athenæum, where he shaved, bathed, ate his breakfast and read the morning newspapers. 'I liked to sit in one corner of the drawing-room', he recorded:

> near a revolving case of etchings by Charles Meryon [who] went to New Zealand in a French sloop, in 1842; he made many sketches of the colony, and . . . used some of them as subjects for his etchings. The print-case was by a window in the club, overlooking Waterloo Place. I could peer at the engraved outlines of the coast of my native land, with its graceful trees and ferns, and then suddenly glance beyond the window at Florence Nightingale, in bronze, and at the canyon of Pall Mall, coming to life after a night of fear.[59]

During the AGM in May 1940 Lord Macmillan commented from the chair that the club was 'serving a very useful public purpose as a meeting place for the large number of Members doing important National Work, where they could also find rest and relaxation from their arduous duties', a point that he reiterated in 1942.[60] As in 1914–18, several ministers in the war cabinet were members, including Neville Chamberlain (1938), Woolton (1939), Anderson (1942) and Attlee (1943).[61] (Bevin, Ismay and Halifax joined in the early 1950s.) There was also the usual tally of foreign diplomats who became honorary members during their time in London, the most significant of whom was Ivan Mikhailovich Maisky, the Russian ambassador and an important ally at a time when the Red Flag flew over Selfridges and *Soviet War News* was published from offices in Trafalgar Square.[62] Fifteen months after Maisky's election in September 1941 the BBC intercepted a message from the German broadcasting station purportedly based in Britain that featured a clichéd misrepresentation of the club. Entitled 'Aid to Russia: A Club conversation' and addressed to the workers, it reported the findings of 'our snoop' who 'went poking around the snooty clubs of the West End, suitably shaved and dolled up to look like one of the upper ten'.[63] The 'best bit of Capitalist conversation' was one that took place in 'that haunt of high hats, the Athenæum Club in Pall Mall'. It was between 'a trio of pot-bellied, purple-faced old aristocrats, and they were gossiping over the brandy and cigars': the third says, 'Hitler will soon make the world safe for gentlemen. And the old sod gaffawed into his brandy. When they've finished cutting each other's throats and all Bolshies and Nazis and the rest of them have been slaughtered, there'll be peace again and prosperity, declared one of the trio.' The workers were reminded that, when sending aid to Russia, the government preferred to send too little rather than too much.

Some of the 'high hats' at the Athenæum applied their own literary skills to morale-boosting projects during the war. Sir Richard Gregory, for example, a former editor of *Nature*, published *British Scientists* (1941) in praise of famous men. Noël Coward, a member since 1937 and for a time engaged in intelligence work, was best known for the films that he made in collaboration with David Lean – *In Which We Serve* (1942), *This Happy Breed* (1943) and *Brief Encounter* (1945) – and 'Play Parade' which toured the country in 1942–43, featuring *Blithe Spirit*, *This Happy Breed* and *Present Laughter*.[64] In the first act of *Present Laughter*, Henry Lyppiatt complains about Garry Essendine's sherry, to which Garry, the Coward figure in the play, replies, 'You ought never to have joined the Athenæum Club, it was disastrous.' Henry: 'I really don't see why.' Garry: 'It's made you pompous.' Henry: 'It can't have. I've always been too frightened to go into it.'[65] In act III, however, he returns from the clubhouse with Morris Dixon to berate Garry for his night with Joanna Lyppiatt. 'False, friend! False, friend!', Morris exclaims ('*just a trifle intoxicated*'), to which Garry replies, 'Come come Morris, you're not in the Athenæum now.'[66]

A new phenomenon at the club was the election of exiled foreign leaders and their ministers, creating a veritable League of Nations there. The sequence of their election reflects the progress of the war. First there were the Poles, Sikorski and Zaleski, prime minister and president in exile, elected after the signing of a Polish-British Military Agreement in August 1940.[67] Dr Knežević, the minister of the royal court of Yugoslavia, accompanied the government into exile in London and was elected in October 1941.[68] Two months later Emmanouil Tsouderos, the Greek prime minister, was elected, together with General de Gaulle, leader of the Free French and often regarded as a tiresome presence in British military and government circles.[69] The fact that overcrowding in the clubhouse was given as a reason for limiting the number of honorary memberships in 1947, and that this problem had also arisen in 1943, suggests that honoraries made good use of their membership.[70]

The resignation of Lord Simonds as post-war chairman of the General Committee in 1951, when he became Lord Chancellor, ended a period of thirty years during which judges had been in the chair. His successor, Sir Alan Barlow, who had been involved in the governance of the club since the 1920s, was the most active among a remarkable group of senior civil servants whose presence, together with that of the judges and the bishops, did much to set the tone in the clubhouse during and after the war. If anyone could be described as the consummate Athenian it is Barlow, elected in 1915 and the son of Sir Thomas Barlow, physician to three monarchs, first baronet and a member of the club. Having taken a first in *Literae humaniores* or 'Greats' at Oxford, Alan Barlow entered the civil service, where he had a distinguished career as something of a reformer and retired as second secretary at the Treasury in 1948. Meanwhile his interest in the arts and science developed with that of his wife Nora, Darwin's granddaughter and editor, and was later reflected in his chairmanship of the trustees of the National Gallery and presidency of the Oriental Ceramic Society. Precious pieces from Sir Alan's Islamic pottery, a collection of national importance, are on permanent display in the clubhouse today.[71] The title of 'consummate civil servant', however, has been applied to another member who was actively engaged in the club's committee work, particularly in the immediate post-war years: Sir Findlater Stewart, elected to the club in 1931, chairman of the national home defence executive in 1940, chief civil staff officer (designate) to the Commander-in-Chief, Home Forces, and later charged with the logistics of the American forces stationed in Britain.[72] Sir Percy Grigg, described as 'one of the quickest and ablest brains' of his generation and elected in 1939, became chairman of the standing committee on army administration the following year, and, most unusually, was appointed Secretary of State for War by Churchill in February 1942.[73]

Several of the most senior officers from all three services became members during the war. General Sir Robert Haining was elected in 1940 and was a member of the Committee at the end of the war.[74] General Sir Archibald Wavell was elected under Rule II in January 1942, six months after the failure of his operation Battleaxe against Rommel.[75] Wavell's literary work included his 1939 Lees Knowles Lectures at Cambridge, later published as *Generals and Generalship* (1941), a copy of which Rommel carried with him during the north African campaign. After the election under Rule II of General Eisenhower in 1944, the Supreme Allied Commander Europe flouted convention by going upstairs to see his election card.[76] Three field marshals were elected under Rule II after the war: Earl Alexander of Tunis (1946); Viscount Montgomery of Alamein (1946), who failed to get his subscription reduced; and Sir William (later Viscount) Slim (1951).[77]

The club's association with the navy had been strong ever since it was founded by John Wilson Croker of the Admiralty. In 1918 Sir Alexander Gibb had been the civil engineer-in-chief at the Admiralty, where he developed the 'mystery towers' in the Channel, designed to counter the submarine threat but never used: he had chosen Major John Reith as his assistant.[78] Elected in 1927, Sir Alexander served on the General Committee during the Second World War and in 1950 covered the full cost of re-gilding the statue of Athene / Minerva.[79] Among other wartime habitués was Rear-Admiral Henry Thursfield, elected in 1919. Following his retirement in 1932 he served as editor of Thomas Brassey's *Naval Annual* (1936–63) and, like his father before him, as a naval correspondent of *The Times* (1936–52).[80] Admiral Thursfield proposed the beleaguered First Sea Lord, Admiral of the Fleet Sir Dudley Pound, for membership in October 1941. Elected under Rule II in January 1942, Pound was dying of cancer the following year when he was succeeded by Admiral of the Fleet Andrew Cunningham, himself elected under Rule II in January 1943.[81]

One of the academics attached to the Admiralty during the war was the Cambridge marine geophysicist Dr (later Sir) Edward Crisp Bullard, who had been a member since 1935. Having worked successfully with Patrick (later Lord) Blackett, his former research supervisor, on mine-sweeping and the demagnetising of ships, he joined Blackett's naval operational research group at the Admiralty ('Blackett's Circus') in 1941, working on strategies for conducting marine warfare and for attacking firing sites in northern France.[82] The close connection between aerial and sea-borne operations was exemplified in the work of Bullard and Blackett (who was elected in 1942), and of the mathematical physicist Dr (later Sir) Ralph Fowler, elected to the club in 1937 and soon afterwards serving on the Admiralty committee on the potential influence of air power on the navy.[83] It was in the development of Allied air power that the contribution of the 'back room boys' of the Athenæum proved to be most decisive.

In the mid-1930s a number of scientists and politicians had recognised that Britain's defences were inadequate and that the RAF would play a crucial role in any future war against Nazi Germany. Four of these men – all academics and all members of the club – recruited many of the younger scientists who developed radar and the atomic bomb. The most influential of the four, the physical chemist and scientific administrator Sir Henry Tizard, later wrote in a memorandum to Sir Alan Barlow at the Treasury that the majority of these scientists had worked in 'fields far removed from their pre-war activities'.[84] Scientific research and development in what Isaiah Berlin described as a 'don's war' was interdisciplinary and depended upon collaboration with engineers and military men.[85] Where better, then, to bring them together than at the Athenæum, always the natural home of FRSs, engineers and civil servants, and now also of senior officers?

The oldest of the four was the government scientist Harry Wimperis, whose work on the design and testing of aircraft during the First World War had entailed flying himself: he was born in 1876 and elected to the club in 1918. He was later surprised to become director of scientific research at the Air Ministry in 1925, when Tizard declined the post. The deputy director, David Pye, who had met Tizard at Cambridge, was to be elected to the club in 1934, when Wimperis served on the Executive Committee.[86] It was in that year that Wimperis recognised the need to fill an alarming vacuum in Britain's defences. Being responsible at the Air Ministry for assessing inventions of various kinds of 'death ray', Wimperis invited Archibald Hill, professor of physiology at University College London and another of our four pioneers, to discuss the matter over lunch at the Athenæum on 15 October 1934.[87] Following their meeting Wimperis prepared what proved to be a momentous note for Lord Londonderry, Secretary of State for Air and himself a member. He proposed that a committee of scientists be established to work on air defence, broadly defined. 'An excellent chairman', he wrote, 'might be found in Mr. Tizard, the present Chairman of Aeronautical Research Committee and a former R.F.C. pilot. The other members should, I suggest, be Professor A.V. Hill, F.R.S., and Professor Blackett, F.R.S., who was a Naval Officer before and during the War, and has since proved himself by his work at Cambridge as one of the best of the younger scientific leaders of the day.' In accepting this proposal, Londonderry

initiated the process whereby the 'boffins', as they came to be known, partici-
pated in the planning and execution of highly technical forms of warfare,
alongside the 'top brass' of the Second World War.

Henry Tizard was a fellow of Oriel College Oxford before the First World
War, during which he developed new flying techniques and methods of accurately measuring aircraft performance. He then returned to Oxford and was
made a Reader in chemical thermodynamics. In 1919 he helped Frederick
Lindemann, the last of our quartet, to secure an Oxford chair. Tizard's genius
was not in original research but in identifying and supporting projects and
scientists of great promise: he hated the term 'boffin' and the phrase 'back-
room boy', as he believed that scientists should be in the front room.[88] In 1929
he became Rector of Imperial College London, to which he recruited some of
the nation's future leaders in science and technology, while maintaining his
own interest in defence. A year later he was elected to the Athenæum under
Rule II. In January 1935, only three months after Wimperis's lunch with Hill,
Tizard chaired the first meeting of his committee at the Air Ministry. Blackett
and Hill added scientific weight and understood how the armed services operated; Wimperis and his former personal assistant, Albert Rowe (elected to the
club in 1948), provided a channel of communication with the Air Ministry.[89]
A month later Tizard, Wimperis and Sir Christopher Bullock, formerly permanent secretary at the Air Ministry and a non-member, lunched at the Athenæum,
where they discussed a paper on 'Detection and location of aircraft by radio
methods' by Robert Watson-Watt, the inventor of radar. Next day Wimperis
suggested to Sir Hugh Dowding of the Air Council that £10,000 should be
spent on investigating Watson-Watt's ideas, and the process to develop this
secret technology was under way.[90]

In June 1935 Frederick Lindemann (later Lord Cherwell), Churchill's friend
and advisor, was placed on the Tizard Committee at Churchill's insistence.
During the First World War Lindemann had worked at Farnborough on the
problem of 'spin' in aircraft, testing his theories empirically in the cockpit.
Dubbed 'The Prof' by his tennis partner Lord Birkenhead in the post-war
period, when he was Dr Lee's Professor of Experimental Philosophy (meaning
physics) and a fellow of Wadham College, he lived at Christ Church from
1922 until the end of his life, visiting the great houses of England whenever

time allowed.[91] Like Tizard, Lindemann was an effective recruiter of talent, being responsible for bringing to Oxford Jewish refugee scientists from Hitler's Germany. Like Tizard, he recognised the need to strengthen Britain's air defences. But unlike Tizard, who was determined to concentrate on the development of radar, Lindemann insisted upon broadening the scope of the committee's advice, including support for R.V. Jones's research on infra-red technology.[92] The inevitable rows that ensued need not detain us here.[93] Matters came to a head in July 1936, when both Hill and Blackett decided to resign over Lindemann's threat to write a minority note on the committee. Hill set off for the Athenæum to write his letter to Lord Swinton, the Air Minister, whose committee employed the time-honoured device of dissolving Tizard's committee and then re-establishing it without the troublesome member, in this case Lindemann.

Tizard's biographer records that the decisions on new defence enterprises which led to the birth of radar were now taken 'between the Athenæum and Tizard's flat in St James's Court'.[94] Tizard proposed forty-three candidates and seconded forty-seven between 1935 and 1951. His record reflects his commitment not only to the club but also to the institutions that he led: having brought in colleagues from Imperial College he transferred his allegiance to Magdalen College Oxford on becoming president in 1942.[95] In the 1930s and 1940s, however, his support for seventeen of the leading scientists and administrators who worked in air defence or nuclear energy was more strategic. Between the establishment of his committee and the outbreak of war, Tizard seconded Robert Watson-Watt and proposed Ralph Fowler and Air Marshal Sir Philip Joubert de la Ferté, who was to have special responsibility for the practical application of radar in the RAF in 1939, by which time all three were members. During the war he seconded Herbert Gough, director of scientific research at the War Office; Stanley Livingstone Smith, superintendent of the Engineering Department at the National Physical Laboratory; and Patrick Blackett. He proposed John (later Sir John) Cockcroft, whose contributions to the development of radar and of nuclear power were to make him one of Britain's most famous Nobelists; Wing Commander William Helmore, inventor of the nose cone searchlight in fighters fitted with radar; and Air Chief Marshal Sir Wilfrid Freeman, who was responsible for aircraft production as well as research and development. In his professional capacity Freeman recruited Arthur (later Lord) Tedder as his deputy in 1938 and Solly Zuckerman, a biologist who became an expert on the effects of bombing, as his chief scientific advisor in 1943. At the club, Wimperis proposed Tedder, who was duly elected under Rule II in 1944, and Tizard proposed Zuckerman, seconded by Blackett and elected in 1948.

So Tizard's famed ability to recruit innovative research scientists was displayed in both Whitehall and the Athenæum, where an unwritten code of confidentiality enabled him to hold discussions on highly sensitive matters. Free to focus on radar once more from the autumn of 1936, Tizard devoted most of his time to committees, conferences and receptions, and to meetings with 'those quiet effective men with whom one could, after dinner at the Athenæum, settle down in the library to discover just what could really be done about the latest worrying problem'.[96] Within eighteen months it was clear that the development of a chain of radar stations would require a large team of scientists to become involved in the event of war. Professor Cockcroft of the Cavendish Laboratory, Cambridge, later recorded that he was invited to lunch at the Athenæum by Tizard in the spring of 1938 to discuss 'new and secret devices we were building to help to shoot enemy planes out of the sky' and the possibility of the Cavendish supplying the scientists to 'nurse' them.[97] Cockcroft duly obliged by recruiting about eighty physicists. Several of the leading figures in the development of radar, apart from those already mentioned, were elected to membership of the Athenæum after the war: Sir John Turton Randall (1950) and Henry Boot (1966), inventors of the cavity magnetron; Albert Rowe (1948), Watson-Watt's successor as superintendent at Bawdsey Research Station; Robert Hanbury Brown (1986), the physicist and astronomer; Bernard (later Sir Bernard) Lovell (1963), whose subsequent work in radio astronomy was informed by his collaboration with Blackett during the war, and Edward Bowen (1962), head of the Airborne Radar Group at Bawdsey. Bowen and Cockcroft joined senior service personnel as members of the famous Tizard Mission to Canada and the USA from August to October 1940, the culmination of Tizard's efforts to persuade the government that the production of defence technology could be expedited by sharing Britain's most carefully guarded secrets with the Americans, whose own military efficiency would also be enhanced.[98]

The months leading up to the departure of the Tizard Commission witnessed Dunkirk, the surrender of France and the beginning of the Battle of Britain. In London anxiety in government circles that walls had ears became particularly acute. Hugh Dalton, newly commissioned by Churchill to 'set Europe ablaze' with anti-German partisan and terrorist activity in July 1940, told Lord Cherwell that he was 'appalled at the amount of quack quack which goes on in West End Clubs and other public places over matters relating to the war': 'Some tell me, I say, that the Athenaeum is a little safer than some other Clubs, but I doubt even this. It is always observed, I say, who is with whom, and intelligent guesses are then made as to why they are together.'[99] Cherwell told Dalton, a non-member, that there was an old proverb that 'At the Athenaeum you can't hear yourself speak for the noise of the grinding of axes.' Hardly surprisingly, Tizard and Lindemann, both powerful grinders of axes, held opposing views on the proper use of bomber command.[100] The ethical debate, however, on the question of retaliation was the province of the bishops, and particularly Bishop George Bell of Chichester, whose honoured place in the Anglican pantheon has only recently been contested. As well as speaking in the House of Lords and writing letters to *The Times*, Bell mobilised opinion through meetings with key individuals and often chose the clubhouse as a meeting place. Here is a characteristic letter, dated 4 March 1940 and addressed to the military advisor and historian Sir Basil Liddell Hart:

> The Rev R.A. Edwards, vicar of Dartington, has just written suggesting that we should meet. I should particularly appreciate the opportunity. I am almost certain to be lunching at the Athenæum 1.30 on Wednesday, instead of the debate in the Lords that afternoon. Could we meet then? I hear you are a member of the Club. (I am not sure whether I can do any good by speaking on this particular occasion.) If you would like first hand knowledge about Sweden & Finland, I strongly recommend your seeing the Bishop of Lund (Dr. Rodhe) staying at the Grosvenor Hotel S.W.1. He has things to say. Ring him up, and say I advised you.
>
> Yours sincerely George Cicestr:[101]

A rapport between the two men was soon established on the subject of the 'bombing match' between Germany and England, and a voluminous further correspondence included references to leaving messages at the club-house and arrangements to meet there.[102] When William Temple died in 1944, Churchill passed over Bell and recommended Geoffrey Fisher as Archbishop of Canterbury.[103]

Meanwhile the possibility of developing an atomic bomb was opening up a new front in the technological battle, and again a number of current and future members of the Athenæum were in the vanguard. C.P. Snow's role as director of personnel at the Ministry of Labour from 1942 was to mobilise scientists for work on both radar and nuclear weapons. Having been elected to the club in 1946, he returned to his 'Strangers and Brothers' series of novels and the saga of Lewis Eliot's career as an academic and administrator. In the fifth novel of the series, *The New Men* (1954), Snow used Clubland as a significant point of reference in his depiction of Eliot's relationship with his younger brother Martin, a brilliant member of the team working on the 'uranium project' during the war. Fictional 'lunches at the Athenæum' in the novel mirror life. Like several of his fellow Athenians, including Sir Alan Barlow, Snow was also a member of the Savile Club in Mayfair, where he could enjoy a more relaxed atmosphere among the writers, journalists and artists who gathered in the bar. In *The New Men* Eliot walks through the 'deserted fringes of Mayfair' towards his own club, where he is questioned on the bomb.[104] At the end of the novel Snow uses the topography of Clubland in his depiction of Lewis's argument with his brother, as they emerge from Pratt's, where they have been drinking with Bevill, and walk up St James's Street: 'We looked across the road, where the lights of Boodle's shone on the moist pavement . . . We had gone past Brooks's before I said: "I can't help it" . . . As we walked past the club windows I could think of nothing else . . . We were standing still, facing each other, at the corner where the street ran into Piccadilly'.[105]

The potential of nuclear fission was discussed in defence circles in the spring and summer of 1939, and Tizard was naturally involved. Having first been approached by Professor Tyndall of Bristol University and then officially asked by the Committee of Imperial Defence to investigate the possibility of constructing a uranium bomb, Tizard once again drew upon his wide network of scientific contacts, the most significant of whom was the physicist Professor (later Sir) George Thomson, Tizard's colleague at Imperial College since 1930 and a member of the Athenæum since 1935.[106] When Rudolf Peierls and Otto Frisch showed their famous memorandum on the possibility of a nuclear weapon to the head of physics at Birmingham University, Professor (later Sir) Marcus Oliphant, in March 1940, Oliphant sent it on to Tizard.[107] All but one member of the MAUD (Military Application of Uranium Detonation) Committee who were charged with addressing the question were current or future members of the club: George Thomson, the chairman (elected 1935, awarded the Nobel prize 1937); John Cockcroft (February 1941, Nobel 1951); Patrick Blackett, the sole dissenter from the committee's report of July 1941 (1942, Nobel 1942); James Chadwick, who largely wrote it (1938, Nobel 1947); and Marcus Oliphant (1946). Philip Moon was not a member.

Chadwick, who had discovered neutrons in 1932 and was Rutherford's successor at the Cavendish, developed a cyclotron at Liverpool in 1939 and by the spring of 1941 had concluded that a nuclear bomb was not only possible, it was inevitable. As a result he began to lose sleep and resorted to sleeping pills for most of the rest of his life.[108] Later in 1941 he travelled to the United States with Oliphant and Peierls, and by 1943 the secret British project, masquerading as 'Tube Alloys', was collaborating fully with the huge Manhattan project. William (later Lord) Penney, who was to be elected to the club in 1951, joined the Manhattan Project in 1944 and visited Nagasaki and Hiroshima in 1945 to gather material such as bent poles and crushed cans from which he could measure the yield of the two weapons back in England, where C.P. Snow suggested that he should become chief superintendent of armament research.[109] Joseph (later Sir Joseph) Rotblat, one of Chadwick's most gifted protégés, also worked on the Manhattan Project, but later played a leading role in the international campaign against the nuclear arms race. He was elected to the club in 1964 and was joint winner of the Nobel prize for peace in 1995.

After the war, opposition to the development of nuclear weapons eventually led to the founding of the Campaign for Nuclear Disarmament in 1958 and the (brief) imprisonment of Earl Russell in 1960 at the age of eighty-nine. (Having been excluded from the club in 1916, having been fined for impeding recruitment and discipline, Russell was re-elected under Rule II in 1952, by which time he had received the Order of Merit and the Nobel prize for literature.)[110]

More immediately, ethical questions were raised by Allied war crime trials. In a letter to Liddell Hart dated 8 June 1946, Bishop Bell recalled Philip Kerr, marquess of Lothian, a non-member, saying to him 'in the Athenæum one day, before he went to the U.S.A. [1939], when he had just had a private talk with Ribbentrop, that the British people would never make friends with Germany while the Germans behaved as they did with regard to the Jews and other victims of concentration camps'.[111] By 1946, however, Bell's focus had changed as he became the most prominent Anglican bishop among a group of anti-trial activists who used their West End clubhouses as ad hoc committee rooms where they could coordinate their campaign.[112] Among the group were other Athenians, including Liddell Hart, Montgomery Belgion, author of *Epitaph on Nuremberg* (1947), Lord Pakenham, Lord Maugham and (from 1952) Lord Hankey, author of *Politics, Trials and Errors* (1950).[113]

Most leading members of the 'Moot' were also present or future Athenians. This group had met from time to time since 1938 to discuss moral and spiritual aspects of social and political reconstruction, and the role of elites in modern Britain from a Christian perspective. Its founder was Joseph Oldham, a missionary and campaigner who had considerable influence on William Temple and who, like George Bell, often sounded out writers, thinkers and broadcasters over lunch at the Athenæum.[114] At the Moot, Oldham brought together nineteen men and three women from different confessional and political backgrounds (not unlike Croker in 1824) to form what he thought of as a cell or order whose reflections would influence society via its influential members. Whereas the proceedings of such groups are often documented only sketchily, records of each meeting of the Moot, usually held over a weekend in a retreat house or conference centre, were made and circulated before the next: complete transcripts of nineteen of these gatherings are available in print.

Four Athenians who were recruited by Oldham in 1938 are representative in the range of their professional backgrounds. One of its leading lights and most regular attenders was Sir Walter Moberly, the first full-time chairman of the University Grants Committee, who had been seconded by Lord Macmillan for election to the Athenæum in 1935.[115] His friend William Temple put him on the committee that supervised the Pilgrim Trust report on long-term unemployment, *Men without Work* (1938), much of which was written by Walter

Oakeshott of Winchester College, who joined the Moot in 1938 and was elected to the club in 1941.[116] Christopher Dawson, elected in 1936, was a cultural historian of independent means and a convert to Roman Catholicism who became vice-president of the proto-ecumenical movement, 'Sword of the spirit'. Finally, Gilbert Shaw's independent work as an Anglican priest in Poplar, East London, and his campaigns on behalf of those most in need, were much admired by Oldham: Shaw had been elected to the club in 1919.

Fred (later Sir Fred) Clarke, director of the Institute of Education in London, was elected to the Athenæum in 1940, the year in which he became a central figure in the Moot and published *Education and Social Change*, where he developed Karl Mannheim's idea of 'planning for freedom', a resonant phrase for the group. Mannheim, a Hungarian by birth, was appointed to a lectureship in sociology at the London School of Economics after being dismissed from his professorial chair in Frankfurt by the Nazis. He joined the Moot in 1938, became a British citizen in 1940 (the year in which his *Man and Society in an Age of Reconstruction* was published in English), was proposed as a candidate at the Athenæum by William Temple in 1942 and elected two years later.

The *Times* obituary describes Mannheim as 'more English than the English themselves'.[117] The same description was equally applicable to the Moot's most famous member, T.S. Eliot, author of *The Idea of a Christian Society* (1939) and *Four Quartets* (1936–42), who frequently attended meetings of the Moot from the beginning. Papers by members were circulated before meetings, and in January 1941 Eliot offered 'Notes on Mannheim's paper'. This concluded with commentary on why he found the Moot itself so profitable personally:

> What is valuable is the formulation of differences within a certain field of identity – though the identity may be very difficult, if not impossible, wholly to formulate; what is valuable is association with people who may hold very different views from one's own, but in general at the same stage of development and detachment – these are the people *worth* disagreeing with, so to speak. This I think we have in the Moot, and this we ought to keep.[118]

He would have found something similar at the Athenæum on his election under Rule II in 1949.[119]

During the meeting of the Moot in January 1941, Sir Walter Moberly commented on the need for 'practical political reconstruction and religious integration'.[120] 'Reconstruction' was not only a formalised branch of government in wartime. A broad movement of progressive thought that contributed to the Labour victory of 1945 originated in the thinking of policy-makers before 1939; and during the war the Labour team could 'applaud and encourage the work of Butler, Beveridge, Reith, Keynes and others'.[121] Keynes, elected to the club and raised to the peerage in 1942, wrote in that year: 'In 1918 most people's only idea was to get back to pre-1914. *No-one* today feels like that about 1939. This will make an enormous difference when we get down to it.'[122] Keynes helped William Temple, a trustee of the Athenæum, to write *Christianity and Social Order*, published in 1942, the year of Temple's translation to Canterbury: this has been described as 'one of the foundation piers of the welfare state and perhaps the most-read Keynesian tract of all'.[123] R.A. Butler, who was to be elected in 1954, wrote on becoming president of the Board of Education in 1941, 'The crisis of modern war is a crucial test of national values and way of life. Amid the suffering and the sacrifice the weaknesses of society are revealed and there begins a period of self-examination, self-criticism and movement for reform.'[124] His Education Act passed into law in 1944. Early in the war J.B. Priestley, a member since 1937, commented in one of his popular 'Postscripts' on the wireless that the 'New World' was the second topic after the war itself, and David Astor, elected in 1943, took an anti-Establishment stance that reflected a generalised longing for a 'New Jerusalem'.[125]

One of the most widely read *critics* of post-war 'progressivism', the political theorist Sir Ernest Barker, came from the opposite end of the social scale to Astor's, having made his way from humble beginnings to a classical education at Manchester Grammar School and Oxford, and never lost his broad Manchester accent. Elected to the club in 1922, when he was principal of King's College London, Barker wrote patriotic pamphlets for the Ministry of Education and the British Council during the war, and was knighted in 1944 for his efforts as chairman of the Books Council, which distributed books to allied countries whose libraries had suffered bomb damage. Oxford University Press then approached him to edit a volume that was designed to be 'a monument to the England of these days' and accordingly to be 'inspired by a general sympathy for its achievement', but without 'self-laudation'.[126] In the preface to *The Character of England*, which was published in 1947, he thanked both Sir Alan Barlow, who helped in the planning of some of the chapters, and Clement Attlee, also a member of the club, who would have contributed had he not been called to other duties after the general election of 1945. Of the twenty-seven contributors, ten were current and two future members of the Athenæum, including G.M. Young on government, Lord Simonds on the law, James Sutherland on literature and Basil Willey on thought.

*The Character of England* celebrates Englishness as the nation faces an uncertain future. Lord Simonds explains the context of his chapter, written in the summer of 1945: 'In this hour, from the hearts of men all over the world, the cry goes up for law and order, for peace and security, for justice and liberty.'[127] Professor Sutherland echoes Arnold and quotes Shelley in his discussion of the future of literature in the context of 'a new social and political order': 'If the world's great age is indeed to begin anew, no one class can contribute more to a spiritual regeneration . . . than those "unacknowledged legislators of the world", the poets and the creative writers of all kinds.'[128] Professor Willey also draws upon nineteenth-century models, arguing that 'we need the Victorian seriousness more than ever, to counteract the present-day dissolution of moral standards'.[129] Most characteristically Athenian, however, is Barker's closing chapter entitled 'An attempt at perspective', where he argues that 'there is, after all, some inner affinity between the spirit of England and the spirit of Athens', and that Aristotle 'has been domiciled among us since the Middle Ages'.[130] Many of Barker's literary predecessors in the club, including Matthew Arnold, Sir Charles Waldstein and Sir Henry Newbolt, could have made one of his concluding remarks: 'It is impossible to think of the character of England without thinking also of the character of the gentleman.'[131]

Ten years before the publication of *The Character of England*, Captain Liddell Hart had received a printed card from the lawyer Sir Cecil Carr, honorary election secretary at the Athenæum, canvassing his views on a young candidate who was unable to meet members of the Committee as he was away in Spain. 'We all realise', Carr wrote in a covering letter, 'that candidates necessarily come up for election more quickly than they did'; on the other hand the Committee had 'not been afraid to elect young men if of the right sort': 'can we say the candidate is a good fellow, likely to be clubbable, showing promise and ability in the profession he has chosen?'[132] The Committee would scarcely reject him, as he was the son of a distinguished member, but they might suggest that he be withdrawn and re-entered when he was older. Liddell Hart replied that he had formed a 'very good impression' of Mr H.A.R. Philby, who was certainly on the young side for election but seemed to 'have a promise of making a good member of the Club'. Having passed the first test in the form of an exchange of views between gentlemen, and then having received support in the new Candidates Book from, among others, the librarian and scholar Sir Stephen Gaselee and the classical scholars Maurice Bowra and E.V. Rieu, Kim Philby was elected by the Committee on 19 April 1937 at only the second such election meeting after the abolition of the ballot.[133] He was twenty-five. His proposer was his father, St John Philby, a brilliant Arabist and explorer, who has been described as having an 'old-fashioned tory's addiction to *The Times*, the cricket score, the honours list, the Athenæum'.[134] Educated at Westminster and Trinity College, Cambridge, Kim Philby had impeccable credentials as an English gentleman in the making. Yet by 1947 the 'greatest spy in history' was copying large amounts of classified material to his Russian paymasters on a daily basis.[135] He was not of the right sort.

When recruited by the Russians in 1934, Philby was instructed to sever links with his communist past and adopt a far-right-wing stance. He joined the Anglo-German Fellowship, of which Jack Macnamara and Guy Burgess were also members,[136] and covered the Spanish Civil War for *The Times*. (He was decorated by Franco.) On his return to England he sent a note to Liddell Hart, thanking him for his 'very kind help and support' in his election to the club.[137] Membership served as a badge of probity and offered an entrée to the ranks of the English governing class from which a career in the Foreign Office and M16 could unfold. Following Philby's escape to Moscow in 1963 and the publication of his apologia, *My Silent War*, in 1968, Hugh Trevor-Roper published a rebuttal entitled 'The Philby affair' in *Encounter*. Drawing upon his own experience as an intelligence officer, Trevor-Roper commented on the Secret Intelligence Service (SIS) of the 1930s: 'Novels of clubland heroes may have given it a factitious lustre, but essentially it remained an amateur organisation with a slender budget, dependent often on voluntary assistance.'[138] Nevertheless,

Clubland played a significant role in the careers of the Cambridge spies, and it is surely no coincidence that while Philby achieved an early election to the Athenæum, Donald Maclean joined the Travellers next door and Guy Burgess the Reform Club next door but one, thus spreading their intelligence-gathering net, a miniature version of the chain of radar stations that was strung across southern and eastern England. Russia was Britain's ally, however, and it was not until the post-war years that Philby inflicted serious damage as a double agent, most notably in his leaking of the planned liberation of communist Albania in the early 1950s, a project that began life at White's in St James's Street and ended with the deaths of about three hundred infiltrators.[139]

Philby had a low opinion of Sir Percy Sillitoe, MI5's director-general in the post-war years, who was elected to membershp of the Athenæum in 1950. As we will see in the next chapter, both Sir Maurice Oldfield, head of MI6, and Sir Alec Guinness, 'Smiley' to millions, were members in the 1970s.[140] In closing this chapter, however, let us briefly consider two members whose special treatment by the club reflected the high esteem in which they were held during and after the war. First the politician and secularist Lord Snell, whose father's name had never been registered on his birth certificate and who had become a bird scarer at the age of eight, like Thomas Hardy's Jude. He served as a Labour minister in the 1930s, was elevated to the Lords where the party was under-represented, served on the committee of Chatham House and was elected to the club in 1939. Two years later the Executive Committee, with Sir Alan Barlow in the chair, recorded 'Lord Snell's generous gift of sixteen volumes of L.C.C. Survey of London'.[141] Snell's fondness for the club was clearly reciprocated, as the following year, when the Executive Committee decided that no bedrooms should be let in the clubhouse on monthly tenancies, but only in the annexe, they made an exception in the case of Lord Snell, who was unmarried and in his seventy-seventh year.[142] In May 1944 his death was described as a 'great loss' in the General Committee's minutes: he had 'made his home in the Club for the past few years and was regarded with deep affection by all'.[143]

Second, after the war the significance of Sir Henry Tizard's new government responsibilities as chairman of both the Defence Research Policy Committee and the Advisory Council on Scientific Policy was recognised by the General Committee, who ordered building work to be carried out at the annexe in order to provide him with a bedroom.[144] In December 1946, as the bells of Magdalen rang a peal of 5,000 changes to mark Tizard's departure from Oxford, the Athenæum became his second home.[145] At the clubhouse he could still conduct discussions with scientists in private, whereas at Storey's Gate he lacked the freedom that he had enjoyed as a government advisor in the early days of radar, and felt increasingly confined by civil servants. Bizarrely, his defence committee did not directly concern itself with nuclear weapons, which Attlee, now prime minister, kept under his own control.[146] While radar had contributed to victory in Europe and the atomic bomb had ended the war in the East, attention now turned to reconstruction at home.

# 11

$\backsim$

# CULTURAL REVOLUTION

On 23 May 1974 a dinner was held to mark the 150th anniversary of the founding of the Athenæum.[1] HRH the Duke of Edinburgh, an honorary life member, proposed 'The Club', drawing heavily on the speeches made at the centenary dinner of 1924. In his reply, Lord Morris of Borth-y-Gest, an appeal judge and a trustee, reviewed the club's early history, extolled its library and celebrated its luminaries past and present with a light touch. As is appropriate on such occasions, both speeches glorified the past and celebrated the present. Apart from a quip from the duke about 'pop-idols', neither speech referred to the rapidly changing contemporary scene which was to figure prominently in a new commemorative history of the club.

As Richard Cowell stated in *The Athenæum: Club and social life in London, 1824–1974* (1975), 'inevitably the history of a Club, in common with all history, bears the stamp of the period in which it was written'.[2] Like earlier historians – Waugh in his slim volume of the 1890s and Ward in his centenary volume – Cowell was celebratory. Unlike Waugh and Ward, however, he was also nostalgic, as he regarded the mid-1970s as a low point in British social history and questioned whether the club would survive to celebrate its bicentenary.[3] In this chapter we consider the period from the mid-1950s to the mid-1980s. Although some aspects of the 'cultural revolution' that so disturbed Cowell at the time created divisions among the membership, others suited the club in the long term, allowing it not only to survive but also to position itself for the process of reinvention that was to take place in later decades (the subject of the final chapter).[4]

270

During the 1960s and 1970s life at the club carried on much as before, in spite of recurrent financial difficulties. As Lord Morris said in his speech, the members continued to be 'fairly reserved, rather modest and quite self-controlled'.[5] The decorous tradition of 'lunch at the Athenæum' had become proverbial in public discourse, as published novels, memoirs and diaries recorded conversations there in which bonds of friendship were strengthened, or matters of state and church quietly arranged in private. In Anthony Powell's *Books Do Furnish a Room* (1971) the narrator returns to Oxford after the war and meets Leonard Short, once an undergraduate a year ahead of him and now a civil servant, in Sillery's familiar rooms. 'You must lunch with me one day at the Athenæum, Nicholas', says Short on their departure.[6] Richard Crossman recorded a busy day at the Ministry of Housing in 1965 when, in spite of a hangover, he gave Charles Pannell lunch at the club in order to 'sort out a whole number of minor items', including why an appointment had been announced without his guest being consulted in advance.[7] Later that year Crossman gave Alan Bullock, a fellow member and Master of St Catherine's College, Oxford, a 'snappy lunch at the Athenæum': 'He had refused the job of chairman of the Parliamentary Boundary Commission. I wanted him to be the chairman of my new Commission on Local Government. Now after only an hour he said he was interested. That was a triumph. He is the one man in England in whom I would have complete confidence.'[8] The following year Crossman records, 'I took the two Parliamentary Secretaries to lunch at the Athenæum, where we began to divide up our jobs. Bob Mellish will remain in charge of London housing and have all responsibility for New Towns.'[9]

The Right Revd John Bickersteth claims to have been the last bishop appointed by the 'lunch at the Athenæum' method, even though his meeting with Stuart Blanch in 1970 was actually held at another club, the Commonwealth.[10] The presence of bishops in the clubhouse had long been proverbial, as T.S. Eliot knew in 1948, the year before his election, when he wrote, 'To ask whether the people have not a religion already, in which Derby Day and the dog track play their parts, is embarrassing; so is the suggestion that part of the religion of the higher ecclesiastic is gaiters and the Athenæum'.[11] 'We have respect for our Bishops', Lord Morris said in 1974.[12] An unbroken line of archbishops of Canterbury served as trustees between 1942 and 2000. Among the diocesan bishops, the majority of whom were members, the most active was Henry Montgomery-Campbell, famed for his trenchant views and biting wit: on the appointment of Mervyn Stockwood, a fellow member, to the diocese of Southwark, he announced that he had taken steps to have the Thames widened.[13] Elected to the General Committee in 1953 when Bishop of Guildford, then to the Executive Committee in 1956 as Bishop of London and finally to the chairmanship of the General Committee in 1959, Montgomery-Campbell must have enlivened many meetings in the clubhouse. Geoffrey Fisher, described by Montgomery-Campbell as 'a hard man – he boils his eggs in widows' tears',[14] proposed to the General Committee that certain archbishops and presiding bishops attending the Lambeth Conference in 1958 be offered temporary honorary membership during their stay. The Bishop of London happened to be in the chair that day, and the archbishop's proposal was swiftly approved.[15]

Bishops at the Athenæum presented the *Express* newspaper group with opportunities for light relief.[16] In January 1957 the *Sunday Express* claimed that Fisher had 'looked like a startled boy' when the club let it be known that his criticism of government policy on Cyprus was not welcome there: it was regarded as 'not quite good form' and 'at the Athenæum that is enough to quell any man'.[17] Bishop Montgomery-Campbell attended the meeting of the Executive Committee at which the article, headed 'The Athenæum rebukes Dr. Fisher', was discussed in the light of a letter from the archbishop himself.[18] Marmaduke Tudsbery, the pioneering civil engineer to the BBC, gave his views from the chair, and a letter to Fisher was drafted saying that 'everybody in the Club' knew the story to be untrue. This must have been regarded as consolation enough, as no further action was taken. Fisher's visits to the clubhouse were rare, however.[19] Relations with the *Express* group seem to have improved since the publication of the embarrassing story about Ramsay Macdonald's first visit to the clubhouse as a member in 1924.[20] The club gratefully accepted the originals of several *Express* cartoons by Sir Osbert Lancaster featuring senior clerics at the Athenæum, including 'Have a care, Fontwater – we're not in White's!' (1951) and ''Pon my word, Barnstaple, it must have been worse than the Athenæum on boat race night' (1962; Plate 32), in which two Anglican bishops read a *Daily Express* headline, '3000 Bishops in Rome'.[21] Today four of

Lancaster's clerical cartoons are displayed in the lobby next to the lift and adjacent to the gents.

While enjoying affectionate teasing by cartoonists, the club tended to stand upon its dignity in the 1950s. Conducting business in the clubhouse, for example, was regarded as inappropriate behaviour by the guardians of a tradition of high-mindedness. Stiff notes were posted by the committee in 1955 requesting that the practice of some Athenians 'dictating letters to their Secretaries in the Front Hall or elsewhere in the Club' should cease, as many members had protested against it as 'unsuitable'.[22] Annoyance had also been caused by members meeting in the clubhouse, often with guests, 'in order to discuss business matters'.

Indeed, the dignity of the club was to be preserved at all costs. In 1951 the Executive Committee, which had and still has budgetary responsibilities, recommended that a cinema company be allowed to use the front entrance for a scene from a film, but only on condition that the club's name was not used.[23] It also stipulated that no inconvenience should be caused to members, which was the reason given for the General Committee's turning the proposal down. Two decades later the committee decided not to accede to a request from a French television company to film a sequence in the clubhouse on a Saturday in connection with a programme about science in Britain.[24] In 1981, however, the secretary, Captain Wyatt RN, was authorised to negotiate with Southern Film Ltd, who paid £750 to film a scene from *Winston Churchill: The wilderness years* in the clubhouse when it was closed on a Sunday, 'at no inconvenience to members'.[25] In the chair that day was the structural engineer Alfred Goldstein, who as chairman of the Executive Committee did much to strengthen the club's financial position.[26] Two years later, in January 1983, he reminded members of the General Committee that filming at weekends brought in income, but cautioned against advertisements being made, as the club's anonymity could not be guaranteed.[27] The Annual Report that year encouraged members who had 'any connection with the media industries' to bring this facility, 'for use if appropriate', to the notice of their professional contacts.[28]

A section on trading operations in the same report recorded that the experiment of introducing outside catering management, which came into effect in November 1981, had been successful financially and had led to an 'improvement in the quality and standards of food offered to Members'.[29] The experiment had been partly in response to staffing problems: in June 1981 Captain Wyatt informed the General Committee that he had had to reprimand staff for making members feel unwelcome if they arrived for dinner after 8 p.m., half an hour before last orders could be placed, a sad reflection of the poor state of industrial relations in Britain at the time.[30] A more entrepreneurial approach to the management of the club was also reflected in the Committee's gratification that many members were taking advantage of the facilities offered for private functions and were reporting that a high standard was being achieved.[31]

These developments in the early 1980s followed decades of financial instability that had originated in the general decline of Clubland after the war, when money was short and the energies of candidates and many members of clubs were directed towards the rebuilding of civilian careers and domestic lives. At the 1948 AGM of the Athenæum, the chairman, Lord Simonds, said, 'some of our Members are rich and are willing to pay more for their meals, but most are not rich and have to be careful in their expenditure'.[32] Sir Findlater Stewart underlined the point at a subsequent meeting of the Executive Committee, when the club's financial situation was to be reviewed with the auditor present: this is 'a poor man's Club', he declared.[33] Subscriptions were kept low and the Athenæum survived, whereas several clubs closed or were amalgamated in the 1960s and 1970s.[34] The possibility of amalgamation was seriously addressed by the Athenæum in 1952 when the chairman of the General Committee, Sir Alan Barlow, met his opposite number at the Travellers, next door, to discuss the idea. Could they keep their individual identities as clubs while making savings by sharing staff and kitchen facilities? The Committee decided that the disadvantages, such as high engineering costs, outweighed the advantages of the scheme, which was not pursued.[35]

The very idea of the Athenæum amalgamating with the neighbouring 'Foreign Office canteen' would have astounded members of both societies before the war. In the 1950s it reflected the gravity of the situation. Another significant indicator of financial embarrassment was the sudden increase in donations to the club by individual members. Colonel Mervyn O'Gorman's gift of £500 in July 1955, 'to be expended or invested in any way the Committee may direct for the good of the Club', was soon followed by Thomas Cannon

Brookes's donation of £200 'from sale of a piece of land', and Richard Lewis's 'anonymous gift of shares to celebrate 30 years of his membership, worth £400'.[36] A handsome leather-bound Benefactors Book was promptly ordered, to be placed on a table in the drawing room.[37] Later gifts, some of them touchingly trivial, focused upon specific shortcomings in the clubhouse. In 1968, for example, Desmond Cannon Brookes tackled a perennial problem when he donated approximately £70 'for the purchase of coffee containers and thermos flagons for milk to replace the coffee urns at present in use in the Drawing Room and Morning Room'.[38] The pattern of donations recorded in the Benefactors Book provides a rough guide to the changing state of the club's finances: three gifts in the 1930s, five in the 1940s, twenty-two in the 1950s, sixty-seven in the 1960s, fifty in the 1970s, thirty-six in the 1980s, thirty-two in the 1990s and ten in the 2000s.

Price inflation and steep wage increases lay at the heart of the problem in the mid-1950s, when staff recruitment and retention became a matter of concern. In May 1956 the Executive Committee reported that by Whitsun a majority of the present waitresses would have left to take up the 'very lucrative employment offered them at seaside establishments during the summer months', and the AGM agreed to the General Committee's proposal that they increase the number of candidates to be elected that year, bringing the membership to 1,750.[39] (The ceiling was raised to 2,000 ordinary members in 1980.)[40] Bedroom charges increased and in 1959 subscriptions rose from 21 to 25 guineas.[41] (By 1985 they were £330.)

In 1953 *The Times* printed a paragraph reporting 'A letter from Broadmoor': 'From here (Block 6, where reside the "disturbed class", of whom a few are incorrigibly violent and a threat to all who approach them) there is a continuous gradation to the more stately and formal surroundings of Block 2, the atmosphere of which has been described by someone familiar with both as identical with that of the Athenaeum Club.'[42] Institutional standards of catering and bedroom provision in the clubhouse would have provided supporting evidence for the comparison. Major Frederic Newhouse, author of *Irrigation in Egypt and the Sudan*, complained at the 1962 AGM that the 'amenities of the Club had been reduced considerably in the last few years' and called upon the Committee to 'face facts and realise that to attain the same amenities as the

Club enjoyed in 1939 the subscription ought to be raised to 35 or 40 guineas'.[43] Two years later, when Malcolm Muggeridge speculated on which particular clubs C.P. Snow had in mind as centres of gossip in the 'Strangers and Brothers' series, he described the Athenæum as the place where 'seedy clerics and atrocious dons desperately wash down bad food with bad wine', a characteristically acerbic assessment which is inaccurate in respect of the wine.[44]

The clerics who frequented the clubhouse may or may not have been seedy, but their surroundings were certainly shabby. Sir David Wilson, formerly director of the British Museum, recalls that the furniture was 'in a mess' when he joined the club in 1969: 'the dining-room chairs routinely collapsed and were taken away to be repaired'.[45] Whenever redecoration became unavoidable in the post-war era the most economical solution was adopted. In 1954 the Committee accepted the art sub-committee's recommendation that Poynter's beautiful decorative scheme in the coffee room should be 'abolished' and that a 'simple ceiling and wall treatment be adopted', thus saving £1,000.[46] After long delays the work was completed in 1956 according to a scheme prepared by the architect Professor Sir Albert Richardson, president of the Royal Academy, who had been responsible for restoration work on several significant bomb-damaged buildings in London, including St James's, Piccadilly. Difficult though it is to believe, the opportunity was taken, 'with the cordial support of Sir Albert, to treat the ceiling with acoustic tiles, thereby saving expense, and reducing considerably the reverberance of the room'.[47]

When the ladies' annexe in Carlton Gardens was due to close in 1961,[48] and the basement of the clubhouse was remodelled to provide facilities for lady guests, the proposed modern decorative and furnishing scheme for the new space followed the precedent of 1936 in providing a contrast to the main public rooms of the clubhouse.[49] The furnishing sub-committee approved most of the proposals of a Mrs Spong for the scheme, which included bucket chairs in red corduroy by Sanderson, a 'Banquette' to be covered in material of a 'peacock colour', and a mural, 'to be placed at the West end of the bar-lounge, above the settee', which, it was believed, would be 'most attractive'.[50] (The sub-committee called for a sample of the banquette material and the Executive Committee hoped that a benefactor might be found to pay for the mural.) Changes were made to the lyre-backed dining chairs when the Art Committee pointed out that the lyre was 'of one period and wrong in detail, while the rest of the chair was of another period'.[51]

Three years later, in 1965, another sub-committee was formed to tackle the thorny question of a decorative scheme for the drawing room. Marmaduke Tudsbery and his colleagues inspected 'two samples of washable material resembling silk obtained by Mr. Darcy Braddell from Sandersons' and called for a sample from Coles of Mortimer Street.[52] They also thought it best to consult a specialist before Ajax was used to clean the scagliola columns! In 1966 the hall decoration and repaving sub-committee recommended that the 'Key' pattern border to the floor should be repaired where necessary and the remainder repaved with 'Roman Stone' marble.[53] Although the repaving work was deferred while the financial implications were examined, approval was given for the redecoration of the hall and staircase, estimated at £4,000, and 'electrical re-wiring and improvements', costing £1,450, in August 1966.[54]

One member found these incompetent interventions too much to bear. John (later Sir John) Betjeman already had many friends and acquaintances in the club when he was elected in January 1948: fifty-seven members signed his page in the Supporters Book on the basis of 'personal acquaintance' and thirty-three of knowing his work.[55] Frequently combative on architectural matters – 'We'll do in that bloody fool Blomfield yet', he once wrote to James Lees-Milne[56] – and the declared enemy of 'ghastly good taste', Betjeman made his views clear to his fellow members in 1954 when he introduced a Talk Dinner on the perils of modern architecture and helped to organise a celebratory dinner in the clubhouse for the Anglo-Catholic architect and church furnisher, Sir Ninian Comper.[57] In December 1966 he announced in a letter to the Revd Harry Jarvis, who was not a member, that he was 'going to leave this place, they've done it up like a Trust House and though it is in its way a super-sophisticated joke to do such a thing, I find myself getting too simple for such jokes. I shall try and join the RAC instead.'[58] This he did.

Betjeman's resignation letter of February 1967 is a model of the genre:

Dear Mr Secretary,

Your letter to me of last year following my protest about the ugly new lighting in the entrance hall and the trivial wallpapering of the Great Room on the first floor put me in a dichotomy. You will remember that you said that the lighting couldn't be altered as it had just been put in and that my letter would be 'borne in mind'. Alas, that phrase – a Committee-like civil servant's – means nothing will be done and my letter is now in the waste-paper basket. I must tell you, and I hope you will tell the Committee, that I have had to weigh up in my mind my regard for the splendid club servants and my many friends among the members against the deep disquiet at the affront to Decimus Burton and T.E. Collcutt which the present lighting and decoration are. I fear I must resign. I am sending a copy of this letter to my friend Sir John Summerson. The Athenæum is indeed a club for intellectuals, but not for aesthetes like

Yours faithfully, John Betjeman.[59]

Betjeman could not make up his mind about the Athenæum, however, perhaps because he missed his friends. Twice he applied successfully for read-mission, in 1970 and 1974, before finally disappearing from the list of members in the early 1980s.[60] He would not have liked another 'Trust House' style of intervention, when the hall floor was covered with PVC 'chessboard' tiling in 1969 (Plate 33).[61] Other members, however, who were as much aesthetes as they were intellectuals, still celebrated the appearance of the clubhouse in the 1960s and 1970s. When Sir Eric de Normann, chairman of the Ancient Monuments Board for England, spoke on the occasion of Claude Parry's retire-ment as secretary in 1962, he thanked him for helping to make the Athenæum 'a fulfilled beatitude': 'One never came into it without being struck by the dignity of it all, and the peace of mind it engendered.'[62] And when Lord Pearce, chairman of the Press Council and an exhibited landscape painter, retired as chairman of the General Committee in 1971, the artist John Ward RA testified that he had 'devoted much of his time to this Club which was a place of immense beauty; the atmosphere of the Drawing Room was one of peace and serenity, and it was an achievement to have retained the original architectural grandeur of this Club in these difficult times'.[63] Caring for the Schedule I listed building continued to be a struggle in the later 1970s, when the club explored various avenues for external funding and found its way blocked by the need to open the clubhouse to the public, as in National Trust properties.[64]

Caring for the library was also a struggle. As the journalist and art historian Iolo Williams pointed out in 1952, when he chaired the Library Committee, 'weedings out' had always been necessary in order to make space for new books.[65] Later in the 1950s it was calculated that about two hundred books were usually eliminated each year and about three hundred new acquisitions made.[66] The ladies' annexe contained about eight hundred volumes and, with the prospect of its closure, a sub-committee of the Library Committee, chaired by the historian Sir Charles Webster, reviewed the whole question and selected many more titles for disposal.[67] Runs of periodicals were sold or donated to other libraries and, with 'great regret' on the part of the Library Committee, a microfilm was substituted for the Club's run of *The Times*.[68] Between 1960 and 1962 about six thousand books were disposed of, including first editions of significant works by former members: over £7,000 was raised.[69] Order was brought out of chaos on the shelves, surprisingly late in the history of the library, after income from these sales provided the salary of a professional cataloguer for five years from 1964. The library staff gradually shelved books on any one subject 'together in one room': history in the south library, art in the north library, religion in the west library, and so on, as today.[70]

With funds in such short supply, however, the club was tempted to sell some of the books of 'historic, artistic, or bibliophilic interest' that Williams had vowed to retain. In 1953 the General Committee, with Sir Alan Barlow in the chair, sought the advice of the Executive Committee on the desirability of selling Gould's *Birds of Great Britain* in forty-eight volumes, valued at £2,000.[71] When the Library Committee were consulted they were unanimous in opposing the suggestion, and treasures that are still exhibited on special occasions in the clubhouse were saved. Williams set out the reasons for retention in a memorandum: first, selling such treasures was bad for the club's standing; second, valuable gifts of books would soon dry up; third, owning some rare and beautiful books represented one of the club's general amenities; and finally, the club had a very large number of ornithological members for whom the Goulds were of special interest. Similar arguments were put forward in 1959, when William Dawson & Son Ltd offered first £800 and then £1,500 for the club's set of Hakluyt Society publications, which were unarguably of great scholarly significance and were retained.[72] Five years later, the decision to sell the club's copy of Goya's *Los Desastres de la guerra* (1863), valued by Sotheby's at £1,000, was rescinded when it was pointed out that the book had been presented to the club by the royal Academia de San Fernando, Madrid, in the year of its publication.[73] A first edition of Newton's *Principia* remained in the sale, however, and raised £1,500, £500 below the reserve. (Under the headline 'Unprincipled', the *Evening Standard* announced that the Athenæum, 'that famous ecclesiastical and academic redoubt', seemed to be 'in need of ready cash'.)[74] In 1970 the General Committee accepted the recommendation that the set of Royal Society Proceedings (1830–1965) should be sold: the proceeds were to be devoted to the binding of books.[75]

In November 1982 Alfred Goldstein reported to the General Committee that the cost of 'essential works' had led to negotiations between Captain Wyatt and both the Library Committee and the Art Panel 'on the basis that some contributions might be forthcoming from the Club's assets'.[76] Five months later, Goldstein informed the General Committee that the club's Meryon prints would be auctioned at Sotheby's on 16 June.[77] This valuable collection of etchings by Charles Meryon was part of a generous bequest to the club by the company director and Conservative MP Colonel Francis Lucas, who died in 1918. A specially designed 'swing-frame' had been made, allowing fifty-two prints in twenty-four frames to be viewed by members and their guests in the drawing room, and providing particular solace to Hector Bolitho early in the Second World War.[78] Having then been moved to a place of safety, this 'revolving case of etchings' was subsequently reinstated. Years later the mechanism of the stand broke down and the etchings were again withdrawn from exhibition. Fifteen of the etchings raised £11,840 and the remaining nine were re-auctioned.[79] A statement was prepared in case their ownership was spotted, but the membership was not informed of the sale.

The sale of Newton's *Principia* in the 1960s and of Meryon's etchings in the 1980s did nothing to improve either the club's standing or its self-esteem. The occasional defensiveness that can be detected in the General Committees from the 1950s to the 1980s can, however, be traced back to the post-war years, when not only were the finances of 'a poor man's Club' precarious, but some members were complaining that the Committee were not requiring a 'sufficiently high standard for election under Rule III'.⁸⁰ In response, the election secretaries were asked to interpret the club's founding principles for a new generation. Sir Cecil Carr, an eminent lawyer, and Sir Alan Barlow, who retired from the Treasury that year, reminded the Committee in 1948 that a candidate should be expected to have 'some positive qualifications for membership', rather than simply having nothing against him, and argued that, 'generally speaking, if the Committee is doubtful, it should harden its heart'.

Sir Findlater Stewart, chairman of the Executive Committee, presented his own report in 1948 on the choice of 'new Committeemen'. 'For the General Committee', he wrote, 'we want to cover a wide and varied field of experience and connections for the purpose of elections under Rules II, III and IV. We also want to "dress the window".'⁸¹ Sir Cecil Carr rephrased this last point the following year, when he argued for the choice of 'impressive names' to be on the Committee, 'exemplifying the eminence and learning of our member-ship', before coming to the need for 'names representing experience and knowl-edge of the various fields from which we draw our candidates'.⁸² For the Executive Committee, however, it was 'common-sense, way-wise chaps' that were wanted, not necessarily 'super-eminent', but preferably regular attendants at the club.

The eminence of its more illustrious members had always been a source of pride in the club. When Clubland was at its zenith in the 1890s, the Athenæum had controlled the way in which it was presented to readers of the *Illustrated London News* by arranging for a member, the Revd Gledstanes Waugh, to write the article on the club in a series entitled 'In Clubland'.⁸³ Eminence was clearly the first criterion in choosing those members who were to figure in the accom-panying drawing entitled *Ballot Day 1892* (see p. xviii): eighteen of the fifty-nine individuals portrayed there were Rule II members, fifty had titles of some kind, and of the other nine only three went to their graves as plain 'Mr'. Comparing these fifty-nine Victorian Athenians to the sixty-five members mentioned by name in the previous chapter, on the Second World War and its aftermath, we find that only five of the latter group remained 'Mr' (there were twenty-six knights, fifteen life peers, one hereditary peer, two honourables, three senior clergy, eight academic doctors, five professors and one colonel) and that eleven of them could be described as 'super-eminent': four were Nobel laureates, seven were members of the Order of Merit and six were Companions of Honour (Lord Blackett received all three accolades).[84]

Forty of these sixty-five members had been educated at independent schools. The sixteen educated at grammar schools, many of them ancient foundations and/or future 'direct grant' grammar schools (1945–76), and the nine from other, mostly lowlier establishments, were simply the latest in a long line of members elected on the basis of ability rather than background, one of the club's founding principles.[85] When Harold Macmillan formed a new administration in 1957 he recorded in his diary that 'many considerations had to be borne in mind', not least 'U and non-U (to use the jargon that Nancy Mitford has popularised) that is, Eton, Winchester etc on the one hand; Board School and grammar school on the other'.[86] When choosing its own Committee men three years later, the Athenæum drew upon both U and non-U members, while also 'dressing the window' and representing the range of interests in the club, as Sir Findlater Stewart had recommended. The three *ex officio* members (as serving presidents of learned societies) were Sir Maurice Bowra PBA (educated at Cheltenham), Professor Sir Howard Florey PRS (St Peter's Collegiate, Adelaide) and Sir Charles Wheeler PRA (St Luke's Higher Grade School, Wolverhampton).[87] The elected chairman was the brilliant and shy physician and medical administrator Sir Russell (later Lord) Brain (Mill Hill). Among the elected members were Sir Ralph Richardson (Xaverian College, Brighton), Lord Pakenham, who retired from the Committee in 1962 as Lord Longford (Eton), Lord Denning (Andover Grammar School) and Lord Robbins (Southall County). The products of grammar schools who were elected by successive Committees during the 1960s and 1970s included Alan (later Lord) Bullock, George (later Lord) Porter, Denis (later Sir Denis) Rooke, Lord Kearton and Lord Beeching.

The upward social mobility associated with an expanded middle class (25 per cent of the population in 1911 and 43 per cent in 1971)[88] was the theme of two commentators whose key terms – 'meritocracy' and 'cultural revolution' – soon became common currency. Published a year after Macmillan declared that Britons had 'never had it so good', Michael Young's satirical essay of 1958 entitled *The Rise of the Meritocracy* offered a left-leaning critique of a society in which a minority of grammar school children was destined to flourish at the expense of the majority through the 11-plus system.[89] (The fact that 'meritocracy', a positive counter in British politics today, was a pejorative term in Young's lexicon is often overlooked.)[90] Writing at the other end of the political spectrum, Peter Hitchens introduced his retrospective analysis of the 'cultural revolution' that had taken place between the *Lady Chatterley* trial of 1960 and the election of Tony Blair in 1997 with the observation that 'a series of important coincidences' had combined with 'the spirit of the age and the growth of a new type of middle class, mainly state educated and state employed, to bring about an entirely new culture'.[91]

Members of the Athenæum were particularly influential in two areas that shaped this new culture: education and science. The committee that produced the Robbins Report on higher education in 1963, for example, was chaired by a product of Southall County School and University College, London, who had been a member of the club since 1955: Lord Robbins CH became the first chancellor of Stirling University in 1968. Three of the founding vice-chancellors of the new 'plate-glass' universities were members of the club – John (later Lord) Fulton at Sussex (appointed in 1959), Lord James of Rusholme at York (1962) and Sir Charles Carter at Lancaster (1963) – and Jack (later Lord) Butterworth joined three years after his appointment at Warwick (1963). James and Butterworth were both educated at grammar schools. Randolph (later Lord) Quirk, who was educated at Cronk y Voddy School on the Isle of Man and University College, London, joined the club in 1962 and became vice-chancellor of the University of London in 1981. He enjoyed other clubs, but the Athenæum was '*the* club, remaining comfortingly academic': he also found it 'handy to have informal contact with virtually all the UK's other vice-chancellors'.[92]

On 1 October 1963, three weeks before the Conservative government accepted the conclusions of the Robbins Report, Harold Wilson addressed the Labour Party Conference at Scarborough on the subject of 'Labour and the scientific revolution', arguing that a 'new Britain' would need to be forged in the 'white heat' of this revolution.[93] Having warned against the danger of applying the 'old-boy network approach to life' internationally and relying upon 'special relationships' with those who can 'bail us out', Wilson emphasised the impor-tance of the universities, including a proposed 'university of the air', for the delivery of a new, self-supporting technological Britain. A specialist in technical education, Sir Peter Venables, who was to chair the planning committee of the Open University and serve as its first pro-chancellor, was elected to the club in 1963. The following year Wilson himself joined under Rule IV, two months after becoming prime minister.[94] Whereas Earl Attlee was proud of his close connections with Haileybury and the Athenæum, Wilson preferred not to mention his membership of the club, his house in Hampstead, his children's private education and his predilection for cigars. 'Attlee was a member – a humble member if you like – of the Establishment', wrote one journalist at the time, whereas Harold Wilson, the first product of a grammar school to get to the top, 'is not'.[95] The leading scientists among Wilson's fellow members included Sir John Cockcroft (Todmorden Secondary School), Sir James Chadwick (Manchester Secondary School), Sir William Penney (Sheerness Technical School), Sir John Kendrew (Dragon School, Oxford), Sir Lawrence Bragg (St Peter's College, Adelaide), Ted Allibone (Central School, Sheffield) and Patrick Blackett (Royal Naval College). Blackett, a 'key influence' upon Wilson in the 1950s,[96] and Penney were both to accept peerages from the Labour premier a few years later.

C.P. Snow described the world inhabited by several of these scientists in his novel *The New Men* (1954), where the longing of those outside the top-secret uranium project to be 'in the know' is illustrated in an episode set at the Athenæum: 'a bald bland head' whispers '*March 22nd*' to the narrator from the adjacent stall of the lavatory and raises a finger to his lips.[97] Five years later Snow, long a member of the club famed for the interaction of the sciences and the arts, delivered the controversial lecture in Cambridge that was subsequently published as *The Two Cultures and the Scientific Revolution*, in which he lamented the scientific illiteracy of a generation which still privileged Classics and the humanities in its education system and cultural hierarchy. Following a spirited response from F.R. Leavis, Snow reconsidered his position in a book published in 1963, where he wrote more optimistically about the potential of a mediating third culture.

The 'two cultures' debate was characteristic of a decade defined by a series of polarities and divisions, ranging from the Cold War to the tension between a new 'youth culture' in Britain and an older generation scarred by the Second

World War. Richard Crossman wrote of the 1960s: 'How separate we keep ourselves in Britain. There is the legal world, the doctors' world, the artistic world, the dramatic world, the political world. We are tremendously separate.'[98] In this period of rapid sociological change, it has been argued, professionalism 'contrived to restructure society on a different principle from class as traditionally understood, in a new vertical structure of rival career hierarchies, a fragmented society of competing elites in which a single dominant elite or ruling class was hard to find'.[99] Here is a clue to the survival and later reinvention of the Athenæum, which could claim to be an informally constructed elite that was tied to no single profession or indeed either of the two 'warring factions' of professions (public and private sectors), and that fostered social and intellectual exchange between them. The Athenæum had always provided a meeting place for professionals from all of Crossman's 'worlds', and continued to do so in the 1960s and 1970s, when the club was said to be 'populated with the meritocracy or, as the secretary [Allan Peebles] puts it, "people who have established themselves in whatever professions they have pursued" '.[100]

In order to maintain its status as a loosely knit elite based upon ability rather than class, the Committee had to maintain high standards in its choice of candidates for election. And here the definition of a 'gentleman', always fundamental and yet frequently contested in British society, came into sharp focus. The selection policy of the General Committee in the 1970s was unacceptable to Monsignor Alfred Gilbey, a colourful old-school habitué since 1927. Having been virtually a resident in the years preceding his permanent move to the Travellers Club in 1970, he subsequently resigned from the Athenæum with great reluctance, after fifty years of membership, when one of his candidates was turned down 'because he had not yet reached a sufficiently high grade in the civil service'.[101] According to the architectural historian David Watkin, himself a member at the time, Gilbey was 'appalled at the consequent implication that the club had ceased to be a gentleman's club but was now some sort of professional association'. Although the Athenæum had always been populated with professional gentlemen, for Gilbey it was the latter term that counted. Lord Quirk knew the club for over a decade before he joined in 1962, and was aware that, in 'hobnobbing with such eminent folk as Henry Tizard, David Pye, R.V. Jones, Leslie Farrer-Brown, Ifor Evans, Solly

Zuckerman, John Wolfenden and C.K. Ogden', he was privy to 'weighty and confidential power-broking matters'. He also recognised that it was 'an institution of enormous importance for careers, not only in academia but the other major professions'.

In the 1970s, however, when other clubs were closing due to inflation, Monsignor Gilbey used to say that the Athenæum would always survive as 'the canteen of the establishment'; and Lord Morris joked in his speech of 1974 about the possibility of changing the name of the Athenæum (briefly 'The Society' in 1824) to 'The Establishment'.[102] Anthony Sampson, writing in 1962, regarded the idea of 'the Establishment' as a post-war myth based upon the pre-war reality of circles such as the Cliveden set and its influential arguments for appeasing Hitler.[103] The Athenæum was not the natural home of the 'Establishment' that enjoyed country house weekends, but of a professionalised 'establishment' that had been shaped by two world wars, an irreversible shift of power away from the landed aristocracy and the expansion of the middle class. In 1939 the Athenæum was listed far below the Turf Club or the Marlborough, 'so far as social importance goes'.[104] A few years later it was described as 'at once the most exclusive club in England and the most inclusive' in terms of eminence, largely professional eminence: 'Nothing quite like it ever happened before; even in London men stand in awe of it.'[105]

In his 1975 history of the club, Richard Cowell, educated at Roan Grammar School and King's College, London and a member since 1944, devoted much space to its most eminent members and its civilised traditions. In a chapter entitled 'Spirit of place', however, he also recorded his shocked response to the undermining of traditional values in society at large, a trend that was often associated with the 'cultural revolution'. Having retired from the Foreign Office in 1946, Cowell wrote a number of successful books on Cicero and everyday life in ancient Rome, and studies on modern 'cultural values' and the work of the sociologist Pitirim Alexandrovich Sorokin, whom he greatly admired. All these interests are reflected in *The Athenæum: Club and social life in London, 1824–1974*, which was published with the club's imprimatur.[106] Here Cowell's celebration of the club's Ciceronian urbanity follows in a classical tradition extending from Matthew Arnold to Ernest Barker.[107] His lament over modern Britain was written amidst the general gloom surrounding the miners' strike and 'three-day week' of 1974, a year of continued IRA bombing in London and of student unrest.[108] Cowell believed that the club's values could arise 'only in a society in which cultural life is honoured':

> Elsewhere the author has written about the nature of 'culture' as being all that which, transmitted orally by tradition and objectively through writing and other means of expression, enhances the quality of life with meaning and value. It is this inheritance that alone makes possible a development of the human mind towards, first of all, the mere discovery or formulation; next the realisation, appreciation and possession; and finally the personal achievement by constant practice and striving after qualities summarised by those traditional abstract nouns, 'truth', 'beauty' and 'moral worth'. By such means alone is it possible to ensure the perpetuation and the progress of the sciences, of the arts and of worthy behaviour. All who seek relief from the humdrum round of everyday, workaday existence, not to mention the dismal downward vortex of mere sensuality, sexuality and animality, can find it by activities that qualify as 'cultural' in the sense here defined.[109]

If the cultural revolution heralded the end of culture as Cowell understood the term,[110] what role remained for the club? Indeed, did it have a future? At the end of his history Cowell acknowledged that the pessimists did not 'lack reasons for fearing there there may be no celebration of the first two hundred years of the Athenæum in A.D. 2024'.[111] The one reply available to optimists, he believed, was Nelson's motto, 'Engage the enemy more closely'. Perhaps the struggle against poverty, ignorance, envy, greed, hatred and violence which the best spirits can mount 'in the environment of the Welfare State' will so raise all standards that the values of the Athenæum and other clubs will once again be appreciated, 'because the need for them will be seen to be ever greater'. This seemed a faint hope, however, in the context of Cowell's negative views on a rapidly changing society outside the clubhouse.

Traditionalists were particularly concerned about the new 'youth culture' of the 1960s and 1970s. When commenting on student unrest, Cowell cited his fellow club historian Sir Almeric FitzRoy, who had tried to locate and describe the aura of the Travellers Club in the 1920s.[112] 'Recent events in the student world', Cowell wrote, 'have demonstrated that some new universities and colleges have by no means yet succeeded in realising "urbanity, the flower and flavour of intercourse", neither could they be credited with "imparting a delicate note to the social graces of courtesy, accessibility, and tact".'[113] The contrast between the dignified classicism of these clubmen and the undignified behaviour of the young rebels of 1974, caught up in what Cowell describes as the 'dismal downward vortex of mere sensuality, sexuality and animality', could hardly be starker. The 'permissive society' had come to prominence a decade earlier, with the *Lady Chatterley* trial (1960), the arrival of the Pill (1961) and of Mary Quant's miniskirts (1963), the year of the Robbins Report and of Wilson's 'white heat' of technology speech. And it was the strivers of the state-educated middle class who registered the greatest shock, not least because of revelations concerning the upper echelons of society.

The 'year of sensations', 1963, witnessed the resignation of the Harrovian Secretary of State for War John Profumo, and the trial of the society osteopath Dr Stephen Ward, eliciting from Malcolm Muggeridge the observation in the *Sunday Mirror* that 'last week the Upper Classes passed unquietly away'.[114] In retrospect the real scandal was not the minister's affairs or even his lying to the Commons, but the framing of Ward, a process in which certain members of the Athenæum were involved, directly or indirectly. In the second week of June, some days after Ward's arrest, there was a meeting at the clubhouse, described here by Phillip Knightley and Caroline Kennedy:

> Those present were mostly patients of Ward and some of them had known him socially as well. All of them held important positions in public life. All of them had been asked by Ward's solicitors if they would be prepared to appear at the Old Bailey to give character evidence for their client. Each wanted to know what the others had decided.
>
> We have spoken with a man who was present at this meeting, a former high-ranking Foreign Office official. He does not want to be identified because, to this day, he remains ashamed of what happened and his part in it. 'We discussed the problem. On the one hand we liked and respected Ward and we wanted to help him. On the other, if we were seen to be involved in such a sordid case in no matter what role, then we would be

ruined. We decided that if Bill Astor, Ward's oldest friend and patient, was not going to give evidence on Ward's behalf, then we could also decline.

'Of course, we risked being subpoenaed, but we felt that, on balance, Ward's counsel would not risk this course of action in case, in order to save our own skins, we turned hostile. We've all had to live with our decision. For my part I can't tell you of the moral awfulness of abandoning a friend when he most needs you, and a friend, moreover, who was completely innocent of the charges against him.'[115]

As no numbers or club affiliations are provided here, we can only be certain that at least one of these unnamed but shamed figures – the individual who hosted the meeting – was a member of the Athenæum.

Two senior Athenian lawyers with official roles relating to the Profumo Affair were motivated, not by a desire for self-preservation, but by a determination to limit what Anthony Wedgwood Benn described as 'the decay of the old British Establishment' in June 1963.[116] Sitting with two other appeal judges, Lord Chief Justice Parker of Waddington, a member since 1954 and fond of his old school, Rugby, set aside the recent conviction of 'Lucky' Gordon and concealed Christine Keeler's extensive perjury at his trial, thus undermining Ward's defence at his.[117] (Once Ward was convicted, Keeler was tried for perjury and sentenced to nine months' imprisonment.) Lord Denning, educated at Andover Grammar School and a member since 1944, produced a report in September 1963 which sold over 100,000 copies in a few days.[118]

Equally sensational in 1963 was the revelation that Kim Philby's 'old-boy network approach to life', to coin Harold Wilson's phrase, had served him well in betraying his country.[119] On 1 July it fell to the Lord Privy Seal, educated at Chatham House Grammar School, Ramsgate, and soon to be nicknamed 'Grocer Heath', to announce in the House of Commons that the Wykehamist Philby was the Third Man in the Cambridge spy ring.[120] When Sir Alec Guinness was about to play Smiley in the BBC adaptation of *Tinker, Tailor, Soldier, Spy* (1979) he wanted to 'savour the company of a real old spy', according to John le Carré (David Cornwell).[121] So Cornwell invited Guinness to lunch with Sir Maurice Oldfield, who was head of the SIS, commonly known as 'MI6', until 1978. Oldfield, educated at Lady Manners School, Bakewell (now a comprehensive) and Manchester University, had not met Guinness, who was educated at Roborough School, Eastbourne (a minor independent school), even though both were members of the Athenæum, where occasional complaints were made about the presence of heavily built protection officers when Oldfield was in the clubhouse.[122] In his account of the lunch, Cornwell, educated at Sherborne and Oxford, refers to Oldfield's 'homey north-country voice' and records part of the conversation: '"You should join the Athenæum, David," Oldfield says kindly, implying that the Athenæum will somehow make a better person of me. "I'll sponsor you myself. There. You'd like that, wouldn't you?"' (Cornwell did not take up the offer, but joined the club for a few years in the late 1990s at the suggestion of his agent, Bruce Hunter.)[123]

In 1973 Oldfield was said to spend much of his spare time 'at his old haunt, the Athenæum, where he's often to be seen at table, a small, paunchy, convivial figure. He talks quietly, listens intently and has a wry, donnish sense of humour and a gift for merging into the background; one person who met him was reminded of George Smiley.'[124] Oldfield's humble background was unusual for a head of SIS,[125] but not for a member of the club, where origins are less relevant than ability and clubbability, and where the most affirmative term applied to an individual is 'interesting'. Like several other civil servants, Oldfield contributed to the governance of the club, serving as a member of the Executive Committee and briefly as a membership secretary in the 1970s, while he was in office. A table published in 1969 indicates that the Athenæum, with eight senior civil servants, came second only to the Reform Club which had fifteen.[126] R.A. Butler recalled his first act as Chancellor of the Exchequer in 1954, the year of his election to the club:

> I started my Treasury life by responding to an invitation to meet Edward Bridges and William Armstrong at the Athenæum Club. The first was head of the Treasury and, in those days, of the Civil Service; the second, destined to head the Civil Service himself in later years, was to be my Private Secretary. We sat at a table in the window and ate what remained of the Club food after the bishops had had their run; for we were somewhat late, and the bishops attack the sideboards early.[127]

Butler was 'comforted' by the personalities with whom he was to work. Bridges had been elected to the club in 1946 and Armstrong was to join in 1970.[128]

In 1963 Frank Lawton, Assistant Solicitor to the Ministry of Labour, provided the Executive Committee with the latest 'classification by occupation of the members of the Athenæum', together with 1955 figures for comparison. Of the 1,971 ordinary members, 121 came from the Home Civil Service, about the same number as before, and 90 from the Colonial Civil Service, a decrease.[129] There were only 11 farmers and landowners, another decrease. Several categories remained about the same, including the 149 FRSs and 144 from banking, industry and commerce. Others showed an increase: there were now 65 engineers, 82 other scientists, 147 lawyers, 21 from the BBC and national corporations, 60 from learned and other societies and 187 practising members of the medical profession. Twenty years earlier the Executive Committee had been concerned about the 'apparent preponderance of candidates belonging to the medical profession' among the new members, an observation which was repeated in 1947.[130] Now they were reviewing the proportion of medical members on an annual basis – 13.8 per cent in 1963, 14.0 per cent in 1964 – in order to avoid an imbalance in the membership.[131]

The number of painters and architects (69) in Lawton's figures for 1963 remained about the same as in 1955. The election under Rule II of some of Britain's leading artists over the next couple of decades came when they were in their sixties or seventies, and had already been garlanded with other honours. Sir Jacob Epstein was elected in 1955, the year after receiving his knighthood; Henry Moore in 1963 (CH 1955, OM 1963); John Piper in 1974 (CH 1972); and Graham Sutherland (OM 1960) in 1974. Charles (later Sir Charles) Wheeler was elected in 1957 as the president of the Royal Academy. Sidney Nolan, the Australian painter, was elected under Rule II in 1978 at the age of sixty, having been proposed by the historian the Hon. Sir Steven Runciman and seconded by Henry Moore.[132] Nolan's close friend and collaborator Patrick White, the Australian writer, was infuriated by his remarriage in January 1978, following the suicide of his first wife in London. In 1981, the year of Nolan's knighthood, White lashed out at 'the chase after recognition by one who did not need it, the cameras, the public birthdays, the political hanky-panky . . . all of which, and the Athenæum Club, would contribute to the death of any painter'.[133]

Music was again strongly represented in this period, with elections including those of Sir Arthur Bliss in 1960 (CH 1971), Yehudi Menuhin in 1968/69 (OM 1987), Sir William Walton in 1973 (OM 1967), Sir Benjamin Britten in 1974 (OM 1965, CH 1972) and Sir Frederick Ashton in 1980 (CH 1970, OM 1977). Athenian knights of stage and screen included Sir Noël Coward, elected in 1937, Sir Ralph Richardson (1950) and Sir Terence Rattigan (1962). Among those involved in broadcasting were groundbreaking writers and presenters such as Alistair Cooke ('Letter from America', BBC Home Service and Radio 4, 1946–2004), Kenneth Clark (*Civilisation*, BBC 2, 1969), Jacob Bronowski (*The Ascent of Man*, BBC 2, 1973) and Robin Day (*Question Time*, BBC 1, 1979–89). Sir Robert Fraser, elected in 1967, was the first director-general of ITA under its first chairman, 'K' Clark, who recalled being 'very quietly, but unmistakeably booed' at the Athenæum, when the Television Act was passed in 1954.[134] 'There was a good reason for this demonstration', Clark commented: 'On a given evening fifty thousand people can read fifty thousand different books. But they can look at only one or two television programmes.' Habitués of the finest club library in the world were not yet ready to embrace the expansion of television.

The number of members categorised under 'literature and history' in 1963 (47) had decreased since 1955. Among the creative writers were T.S. Eliot (1949), John Betjeman (1948) and C.S. Lewis (1957);[135] Angus Wilson was elected in 1966 and Gore Vidal in 1983. But there was a marked rise in the number of academic literary critics and biographers, probably categorised by Lawton under universities, schools and museums (350, a large increase). The club had always been the natural home for the literary Oxbridge don and the gentlemen scholar: among the surviving Georgian literati, for example, were 'Dadie' Rylands of King's College, Cambridge (1932) and Lord David Cecil of New College, Oxford (1947, 1975).[136] Now began the march of the professors, including Norman Jeffares of Leeds University (1960) and Brian Morris of Lampeter (1977). American biographers whose work on eminent literary Athenians often brought them to Britain included Gordon Ray (1960), the Thackeray specialist, who was sponsored by Professors James Sutherland and Ifor (later Lord) Evans;

Leon Edel (1965), the leading expert on Henry James; and Richard Ellmann (1980), biographer of Yeats (as well as of Wilde and Joyce). Sutherland and Evans also sponsored Lionel Trilling (1958), whose work on the liberal imagination addressed a familiar Athenian theme and aspects of the 'two cultures' debate of the early 1960s. Other American literary scholars included Cleanth Brooks (1965), author of *The Well-wrought Urn*, who also served as a cultural attaché at the American Embassy, and Donald John Green (1979). Some professors, such as Joseph W. Reed (1962) and René Wellek (1971), were offered temporary honorary membership while they worked in London.

In 1975 the 'well-tried practice' of offering such temporary memberships was presented as a reason for turning down a proposal from the Cosmos Club in Washington to establish reciprocal arrangements for members.[137] A year later, however, informal approaches were made to both the Cosmos and the Athenæum's sister club in New York, the Century.[138] In 1981, following successful negotiations with both clubs, the General Committee 'endorsed in principle the desirability of increasing the number of suitable Clubs overseas, with which reciprocal arrangements might be negotiated'.[139] A rather warmer atmosphere could also be discerned domestically, in comparison with the notorious coolness and formality of earlier generations. In October 1969 a sub-committee had been formed to consider the suggestion from Sir Alan Burns, chairman of the General Committee, that a cocktail party or musical evening might be held the following summer, when members could invite lady guests.[140] By 1976 what came to be known as the Summer Party had become a popular fixture in the club's calendar, and Talk Dinners continued to be well attended.[141] Three years later the General Committee overturned the Library Committee's decision not to subscribe to *Private Eye*, and, in a rather laboured minute, spelled out the merits of promoting 'friendly relations among Members' by encouraging those who used the 'communal tables' in the coffee room to 'sit next or opposite to places already occupied'.[142] This last point was taken up at the AGM, and by 1986, when John Nevinson, a retired civil servant, donated a dedicated long table for the purpose, 'Club Table' had become one of the most cherished aspects of life at the Athenæum (Plate 34).[143]

The convention that members should join those already seated at Club Table brought individuals into immediate contact with others from a variety of professional backgrounds and widened social contacts within the club.[144] All clubs have coteries, however, and the Athenæum's most famous post-war coterie was named after another piece of furniture in the clubhouse. 'The Sofa', formed by retired civil servants, together with 'the odd technical authority', would commandeer a particular sofa in the drawing room after lunch, which was usually taken in the light luncheon room (now the picture room).[145] Active from the 1950s to the 1970s, this group of habitués defended its territory fiercely, forming an inner citadel within the clubhouse. Instigated by Sir Eric de Normann of the Office of Works, the Sofa's regulars were Sir Alan Burns, Marmaduke Tudsbery and the former governor of Sind, Sir Hugh Dow, who lived in the same block of flats in Pall Mall as Sir Alan. All four were born between 1886 and 1893, and none was educated at Oxford or Cambridge. John Udal adds two other names of the same vintage: General Sir William Platt, formerly Commander-in-Chief, East Africa, and Bishop Montgomery-Campbell.[146] John Charlton, an archaeologist and inspector of ancient monuments and historic buildings, was a younger member and the group's later chronicler. The Sofa became such a familiar feature of club life that De Normann's role as its founder was mentioned in his *Times* obituary.[147]

Another coterie began life as a pressure group. The context was a dispute about lady guests that came to a head at the 1974 AGM and to which Lord Morris referred obliquely in his 150th anniversary speech.[148] Two months earlier Sir Percy Faulkner, retired civil servant and chairman, informed the General Committee that a meeting had been held with Dr (later Professor Sir) Roger Scruton and representatives of 'a group of Members opposed to Lady Guests being allowed the use of the Drawing Room after dinner'.[149] This group, who were known as 'The Misogynists', but later wisely changed their name to 'The Traditionalists', was opposed to the experimental scheme and had suggested instead that members and lady guests should only be allowed into the morning room after dinner. The committee members present at the meeting had disagreed, but a compromise solution was sent forward to the AGM, namely that the experimental period be extended for one further year and that 'the south end of the Drawing Room be reserved for the use of Members only'.[150] A 'full and lengthy discussion' ensued, during which Guthrie Moir, the former controller of education and religious programmes at Thames

Television, argued that the proposal to cordon off part of the drawing room and then use the morning room to entertain ladies was 'contemptuous and illiberal'. He was supported by the Harley Street physician, Sir Edward Muir, and 'other members'. Dr John Casey, however, said that he was a comparatively new member who had joined the Athenæum for its 'unique masculine atmosphere' and felt that the introduction of ladies was out of place in the drawing room, a position supported by Dr David Watkin and 'a small number of members'. Once the offending final clause had been removed, the resolution was passed by a clear majority.

Dr Casey had only been elected in 1973 and Dr Scruton in 1972, the year after his appointment to a lectureship in philosophy at Birkbeck College, London, at the age of twenty-seven. Like Dr Watkin, who was to resign in the 1980s,[151] Scruton was a friend and admirer of Monsignor Gilbey, whom he had known as the Roman Catholic chaplain to Cambridge University.[152] Whereas Gilbey could be criticised for being out of touch, like others of his generation who took a conservative stance on such issues, Scruton, a very young leader of the opposition, was in a position to argue that this was not the club that he had recently joined. As in several other areas explored in this chapter, the argument over lady guests reflected wider social changes and clashes between new and old manners, between innovation and traditionalism. Arguments for the extension of the rights and freedoms of women in British society formed an important strand of the cultural revolution, a revolution with which some members of the club were more comfortable than others. The subsequent and much more difficult debate about the admission of lady members to the club will be discussed in the next and final chapter. For the moment, however, a last word from the *Express* newspaper group, in the form of Osbert Lancaster's cartoon of 18 February 1975, in which Maudie Littlehampton disconcerts an episcopal member by asking whether it is true that 'even the Athenæum's thinking of going bi-sexual' (Plate 35).[153]

# 12

*少*

# *PLUS ÇA CHANGE*

Today, many of the young guides who lead walking tours from Trafalgar Square to Buckingham Palace pause at Decimus Burton's clubhouse, where they stand in front of the club's famous portico, under the aegis of Athena, and explain the workings of 'the British Establishment' to tourists. To join the Athenæum, some declare, your grandfather had to have been a member, and your name had to be put down before birth. Journalists can also be wide of the mark, as when the club was described in the *Daily Mail* as 'a favourite watering hole for cabinet ministers and other members of high society'.[1] In both cases the target is actually Clubland, often regarded with a sense of astonishment that such a cluster of grand private societies should still exist in a country whose economic power and global influence have declined since the Second World War. The historian Robert Tombs ends his study on the English with a critique of what he calls 'declinism', a widespread alarm about decline which has been 'increasingly fixed on economic performance' since the 1950s.[2] In contrast, this specialist in French history applies to England the epigram, '*plus ça change, plus c'est la même chose*'. The 'Establishment', he argues, 'after faltering, proved remarkably resilient and adaptive. It would have been hard to imagine during the 1960s that, half a century on, the monarchy would be revered, the public schools booming, gentlemen's clubs expanding, the armed forces almost above criticism, the Prime Minister [David Cameron] an Etonian, and Cambridge and Oxford hailed as Europe's leading universities. Like much in England, they changed and remained the same.' Nowhere was this more true than at the Athenæum.

296

This final chapter considers the paradox that greater changes in the Athenæum's constitution, tone and activities have taken place since the mid-1980s than in any previous period, changes that reflect an accommodation to consumerism; and yet the club has remained the same, retaining a strong sense of tradition, claiming a unique identity for itself as 'more than just another London club', and maintaining principles embodied in its foundation through its members' professional contribution to the national life. In the 1960s the Athenæum was still famed for its high thinking and plain living, whereas in the 1990s it began to invest heavily in the refurbishment of its facilities and in creating comfortable amenities for its members and guests. These changes were part of a process of reinvention that included the introduction of women members, from 2002, and an increase in private entertaining and diaried events. Whereas ballots used to be held in order to elect new members from a long list of candidates, they are now needed to determine which members can secure a place at one of the many and varied events in the club's calendar which are oversubscribed.

First, then, the changes, beginning with the improvement of the estate. The enhancement of the clubhouse became possible only after the club's finances had been stabilised and some of its treasures sacrificed. Two years after Alfred Goldstein and his Executive Committee had organised the sale of the club's prized Meryon prints in 1983,[3] a further raid on the club's assets was contemplated. Patrick Gilbert, general secretary of the Society for Promoting Christian Knowledge, announced from the chair at a General Committee meeting in October 1985 that he, together with Keith Davey, formerly legal advisor to the Department of the Environment, and Richard Smith, the probationary secretary, had met the club's solicitors to discuss amendments to the new lease agreement. After discussion it was agreed that, following the decision of the Executive Committee, Rysbrack's bust of Alexander Pope would be sent to auction 'in order to cover much of the cost of the new lease'. No fewer than thirteen members of the General Committee had sent their apologies to the meeting, including the chairman, Sir Basil Hall, legal advisor to the Broadcasting Complaints Commission, Donald Coggan, formerly Archbishop of Canterbury, and Sir David Wilson, director of the British Museum.[4] When Sir Basil returned to the chair a month later it was agreed that the club would have 'lost its Pope but gained eternal life'.[5] By Christmas the National Portrait Gallery had acquired the bust for £250,000 and in January an 'excellent marble dust copy' was displayed on the central mantelpiece of the drawing room.[6] A private sale overseas would have raised more funds, but the playful suggestion that a special entry should be made in the Benefactors' Book concerning the club's 'gift' of the bust to the nation was not taken up. (The official history of the Athenæum Collection reports that the bust was sold after a spate of burglaries, as it was too vulnerable to be kept in the clubhouse.[7] It was also too valuable to insure.) In the light of experience, the club now reserves funds annually in anticipation of lease renewal from the Crown Estate Commissioners in 2084.

Senior current members recall the later 1980s as a period during which there was no budget, the lavatories tended to block, the roof leaked, the wrong paint was applied to the pillars of the portico, the archive was scattered among numerous cubby-holes around the clubhouse and some committee chairmen refused to communicate with their fellow chairmen. Sir Basil Hall, however, and his even more 'quiet and unostentatious' successor as chairman, Judge Paul Baker,[8] began the process of improving conditions in the clubhouse; and this process continued between 1989, when Sir Alcon Copisarow, a government scientist turned management consultant, became chairman, and 1998, when Lord Cuckney took the chair and began a series of investigations into current practice.[9]

The most significant building works in those years were initiated in 1996, when Ian Hay Davison, chairman of the Executive Committee, and the secretary, Richard Smith, masterminded the removal of most of the staff who slept in the upper floors to external accommodation, in order to provide more bedrooms and en suite facilities for members. The number of bedrooms increased to twenty-three and they could 'accommodate wives'.[10] At the 1998 AGM the chairman, David Thomson, announced that these works, costing £700,000 in all, had not only been beneficial to members but would also have 'a positive effect on the economic health of the Club'. From that day to this the Athenæum has prioritised the maintenance of its economic health, closely linked in the minds of successive Executive Committees with the enhancement of its facilities for members and their guests. By 1998 many of those guests, whether dormitory wives or lady visitors in the coffee room, were female, and Britain had been transformed into a consumer society under Margaret Thatcher, with John Major and Tony Blair in her wake.

It was after the decision to admit women members had been announced, in March 2001, when more members from the worlds of finance and commerce were represented on the Executive Committee than formerly, that the process of upgrading the clubhouse's facilities accelerated. First, almost £1 million was expended on rebuilding and re-equipping the kitchens in 2002, thus making it possible to employ a leading chef, Ross Hayden, to head the catering team.[11] At Hayden's funeral in October 2015 the secretary, Jonathan Ford, paid tribute to his exemplary service, speaking of 'the Club's reputation for having the worst food in Clubland before Ross joined and the transformation in quality that he delivered'.[12] Second, the refurbishment of the garden room, formerly the ladies' annexe in the basement, was completed in September 2007, thus improving the setting for many of the club's most popular Talk Dinners and for the meetings and casual dining that took place there when other rooms were occupied. Third, in 2009, the Executive Committee, chaired by Lesley Knox, recommended that the sum of £650,000 be drawn from the club's savings and applied to the refurbishment of the bedrooms, raising them to the standard of a smart hotel, and the restoration of the original smoking room, most of which had been hidden from view by the plaster walls and false ceilings of some extra bedrooms that had been created in 1958 (Plate 36).[13] This charming space on the second floor, with its elegant plasterwork and bookshelves, was furnished with comfortable modern armchairs and sofas, to create a second drawing room in which members and their guests could be served a sandwich lunch and drinks, and which could be used for further club meetings and private events taking place in an increasingly busy clubhouse. By the second decade of the twenty-first century the clubhouse had been transformed into a gleaming palace, the result of a rolling programme of refurbishment and redecoration, overseen by the club's highly effective secretary.

Much of the drive for change came from the Executive Committee, to whom most of the credit also goes for absorbing the financial shocks associated with the enhancement of the clubhouse, particularly after 2009, when insufficient funds were paid back into savings, thus causing an unintended major loss and a financial situation from which Peter Chapman, a senior advisor to the Bank of England, rescued the club. The Executive Committee, chaired by women since 2008,[14] reports to the General Committee, which is responsible for the club's direction of travel. So it was the General Committee that asked the membership to consider a more fundamental change by addressing the vexed question of female membership three times between 1984 and 2001. In 1983, the year in which Mrs Thatcher was returned to power with a majority of 144, the General Committee established a working party, led by its previous chairman, Sir David Hunt, to consider the question of 'lady members'. Halfway through the working party's deliberations, the committee was mortified to learn that a female candidate had been entered in the Candidates Book, truly a Bateman moment (see Plate 29). On 7 December 1983 the late Mary Warnock, philosopher and senior research fellow of St Hugh's College, Oxford, was proposed by Lord Nathan, her contemporary as an undergraduate in the 1940s, and seconded by Sir Richard Southwood FRS, professor of zoology at the university.[15] In response, the General Committee sought agreement from her supporters that the nomination should be held over until 1985, by which time the question of lady members might have been resolved, and then fretted about the problem of confidentiality associated with a Candidates Book which needed to be readily accessible to members.[16] The report of the working party was circulated to members before the 1984 AGM. Its main conclusion was that, 'in the present age, when Parliament, the ancient Universities and learned societies, to mention three institutions with which our links are close, have abolished distinctions of sex it is desirable that the Athenæum should conform to the best modern practice. By not admitting Ladies eligible under our criteria the Club is depriving itself of potential Members of quality.'[17] The stage was thus set for a series of discussions in which those who supported the working party's position were to emphasise the last point concerning potential members of quality, while those who opposed it emphasised that the Athenæum was not an institution but a private gentleman's club.

As is usual in Clubland, much heat was generated by procedural wrangles during these discussions. Sir Basil Hall presented the 1984 AGM with a resolution to alter Rule XXVII, so that the two-thirds majority rule for constitutional changes would be applied to the number of those who voted in a referendum rather than the total ordinary membership.[18] Here was an easy target for the combative Patrick (later Lord) Cormack MP, whose list of recreations in a remarkably long entry in *Who's Who* includes 'avoiding sitting on fences'. The minutes record that he 'thought it was quite wrong, and indeed indefensible, that the Rules should be changed in order to obtain a result which the Committee obviously wanted. It seemed to him that this was in line with the worst of modern practice and if Lady Members were to be admitted on the basis proposed by the Committee he would certainly resign'. The rules were changed but Cormack did not resign.

One hundred and sixty members attended the EGM held the following January to debate the question of 'lady membership'. The minutes of the meeting summarise a renewed attack from Cormack in which he argued that the proposal would be divisive and 'might lead to resignations'.[19] Thanks to Alfred Goldstein's having assembled all the papers associated with these discussions, we also have access to the notes of the secretary's secretary, Anne Hegarty, which add, in truncated form, that Cormack said, 'Executive Committee wanted to bounce the Members', at which point the chairman interrupted.[20] Cormack continued, 'It left a nasty taste in many people's mouths.' According to the official minutes, Colonel Fleming Burns said that 'the motion to introduce lady membership would indicate a fundamental change in the Club; in his view most changes are changes for the worse, and he felt that time should be given to reflect upon this decision. He said that the voices of women in gossip in the public areas of the Club, however acceptable in general conversation elsewhere, would inhibit serious reading and research.' Hegarty's notes on Burns's speech offer a more colourful version: 'He knows there are many sorts of women eg. an ancient people such as the Amazons; whose women boast only one breast, but we are sensible to know that these cultures are only mythological! It is advisable to know if one is addressing a man or a woman. However were not given the ability to speak in baritone voices. I like the voices of women but I do note that any serious reading is impossible while these voices are taking place [sic].'

Goldstein's speech against the 'notion of lady membership' was more measured. 'If the Athenæum were an Institution', he said, 'the argument would follow, but it is a Gentleman's Club, a second home.' Supporters of the notion included Professor Ghita Ionescu of the University of Manchester, who invoked Pallas Athene and said that 'the Club was losing now the benefit of having half of the British intelligentsia as members', and London University's Professor

Eric Hobsbawm, the darling of the left, who was 'honoured to be elected to an assembly of persons of distinction' and who did not agree that 'females of distinction would change the character of the Club'.[21] Following the circulation of referendum papers which included a list of the arguments against, 806 members voted for the admission of women and 608 against.[22] Mary Warnock, who had been elected Mistress of Girton College, Cambridge, and made a life peer in 1984, never joined the Athenæum.

Having set the matter aside for a decade, on the basis that attitudes were not likely to change rapidly, the General Committee decided to test the waters at the 1994 AGM, when Colin Leach, formerly bursar of Pembroke College Oxford and now chairman of the Executive Committee, proposed that the General Committee 'be encouraged to hold a postal ballot' on membership for women.[23] He was seconded by Sir David Hunt, who had chaired the original working party on the subject. Many of the minuted thirty-one 'main points' in the ensuing discussion were perfectly sensible. In a written ballot, sixty-three members voted in favour of the proposal and sixty-seven against. At a subsequent meeting of the General Committee its chairman, Sir Paul Osmond, formerly Attlee's private secretary, decided not to proceed with a postal ballot.[24]

Osmond's successor, David Thomson, in turn handed on the chairmanship in 1998 to Lord Cuckney, whose varied experience as an intelligence officer in MI6 – always useful at the Athenæum – and as one the most astute industrial 'fixers' of his generation equipped him to bring a more managerial approach to the club's governance.[25] In February 1999 he proposed that a 'strategic review of the future of the club' be initiated in the autumn, in the light of the strong feelings among the membership on the question of women members which had led to some resignations, and of the fact that some had not joined because the club did not admit women.[26] The weighting of the first question put to members in a survey of April 2000 reflected the General Committee's position: 'Candidates for membership must be "persons of attainment in any field where their work is of an intellectual nature and of substantial value to the community". This criterion for membership does not specify gender. Should the Club continue the convention of only considering male candidates who meet the criterion?'[27] In the resultant vote, 345 members said Yes and 818 No. At the subsequent AGM, which proved to be Cuckney's last in the chair, bad feeling was expressed concerning the committee's tactics over the previous year.[28]

Cuckney's successor, Brian Gilmore, a retired senior civil servant, came to be regarded as the club's master strategist. He believed that the divisive plotting and whispering campaigns fomented by opposing cliques in the late 1990s could threaten the very existence of the club if allowed to continue. He therefore pressed for the ten-year moratorium from 1994 to be set aside and for the matter to be settled quickly, one way or another. In pursuit of this goal he read every letter that Cuckney had received on the subject, spent much time in the clubhouse hearing the views of members informally, arranged open meetings at which strong opinions could be aired rather than whispered, and wrote to all members at all stages. As a result, a much calmer mood prevailed in the clubhouse by the time that the 'Great Debate' was held at 6 p.m. on 14 December 2000, the very day of the annual Christmas lunch, one of the most bibulous events in the club's calendar. One hundred and eighty-three members attended the meeting.[29] David Thomson opened the case for change by arguing that the founding of the Athenæum in 1824 had itself been an 'act of change' in response to the needs of the rising professional classes after the Napoleonic wars, and that the club's original aim of representing 'people with intellectual interests' had always marked it out from other, purely social clubs such as Boodle's or Brooks's. Thomson asserted that the admission of women would lead to greater use of the clubhouse, and that there would also be a 'much better flow of potential male candidates coming forward for membership'. Patrick Cormack, the natural choice as spokesman for the status quo, had withdrawn in light of his public role. He was replaced at short notice by the convivial Malcolm Bishop, whose high-minded argument was more reminiscent of Lord Chesterfield than of Croker. The Athenæum, he suggested, being a 'Club of Gentlemen', enriched the whole of English society as a 'School for Gentlemen'. The journalist and historian Philipp Blom seconded Thomson with a speech warning against discrimination and a dwindling membership, to which Bernard Brook-Partridge, a barrister and businessman, responded by arguing against the 'tyranny' of political correctness. (Among Brook-Partridge's recreations listed in *Who's Who* is 'being difficult'.)

A large number of speeches from the floor followed, including a notable defence of the cultivation of diversity from the international museum consultant, Dr Peter Cannon-Brookes, who pleaded for a No vote; an admission from the late Professor David Kerr, formerly Dean of the Royal Postgraduate Medical School, that he had changed his mind on the question after meeting 'distinguished lady professors, lady deans, lady directors of public health', and so on; and an intervention from a 'relatively new boy', the diplomat and international funding advisor, Desmond Cecil, later a chairman and trustee, who was not 'in favour' of any kind of membership, including male, but who had joined 'an association of individuals of attainment; an association of creativity, of distinction, of fellowship'. In the subsequent postal ballot, conducted by the Electoral Reform Society, 1,160 members voted Yes to the inclusion of women, 489 No, and 49 returned invalid papers. This clear majority came as a relief to all, as it put an end to the cliques and conspiracies. By June 2002 the master strategist could report to the AGM that there was 'no blood on the carpet, no publicity in the newspapers and a total of 10 resignations before and after the vote', and that there were already '44 excellent new members and a further 22 in the Candidates Book'.[30]

The so-called First Ladies were both eminent and 'interesting', in an Athenian sense. Unsurprisingly, their profiles were similar to those of the men who had supported their candidacy, and the range of their professional backgrounds matched that of the membership at large, with an emphasis upon science and medicine, scholarship in the humanities, and public service. The first twenty-five women members to be elected by the General Committee in November 2001, with effect from 1 January 2002, included three baronesses, one Honourable, one Dame, two Ladies, one Right Honourable Lady Justice, eight professors and four doctors (of philosophy).[31] As pioneers and members of an initially tiny minority they exhibited the kind of independence of mind and spirit that had always been regarded as an asset at the Athenæum. (Significantly, they have never met as a body or created a group or coterie.) Their reminiscences, privately published by the club in 2013, make frequent reference to the civilised way in which they had been first received by members and staff, with one notable exception.[32] A number of contributors reveal their sensitivity to the manner of their reception by interpreting the rudeness of one notoriously moody former member of staff as misogynistic behaviour, when in fact he could be equally difficult with male members of the club.

Although only a small minority of male Athenians remain in the club in spite of the presence of women members, there exists one area of more general sensitivity. A month before the first admission of women, the General Committee asserted its firmly held view that 'the special nature and atmosphere of the Club, and the part the dress code plays in maintaining this, are principal factors of many members' enjoyment'.[33] In 2003 the committee elected Sir John Tavener as a 'super-eminent' Rule II member. He 'preferred not to wear a tie', however, and when his request to substitute a cravat was turned down he did not take up his membership.[34] Five years later a survey of members revealed that 64.3 per cent were not in favour of a change to the dress code and 35.7 per cent were in favour.[35] Meanwhile a sense of mild resentment had been expressed privately by many formally dressed men that some of the women were not meeting the club's agreed standards. Only a woman member could raise the issue at a meeting, however, and it was the biologist Professor Catherine Rice-Evans who addressed the 2010 AGM on the subject, noting that 'all the men present were very elegant because their dress code was clear' and asking to have the same standard for women, as the present guidelines were 'currently not very clear and widely interpreted by some Members'.[36] Although subsequent attempts were made to formalise matters, the disparity remained.

On a happier note, another landmark was reached in 2018 when Jane Barker, formerly the CEO of Equitas Limited and finance director of the London Stock Exchange, became the first woman to chair the General Committee. Ironically, it was during her watch that the question of the dress code exercised some members once again. Following an open meeting in February 2019, a ballot was administered by Electoral Reform Services, who reported that two-thirds of the 2,293 ordinary members had voted and 76 per cent of those who voted wanted ties as well as jackets to be removable in exceptionally hot conditions. More significantly, the majority for there being no further change in the dress code was much smaller than in 2008, the result being 783:715. The strength of feeling on the subject that was subsequently expressed at the 2019 AGM indicated that the question would remain in the club's pending tray. Meanwhile the vexed question of the dress code for women continued to be quietly avoided.

David Thomson's prediction in 2000 that the admission of women would lead to a better flow of potential male candidates proved to be incorrect: numbers of male candidates remained steady, while the total number of candidates rose appreciably. His belief that the admission of women would lead to a greater use of the clubhouse is more difficult to assess, not least because the club's enhanced programme of events has had at least as great an impact in this respect. Indeed, the expansion of the programme has been the most significant factor in a process of change and reinvention at the Athenæum. An awareness of the need for a more proactive approach to diaried events can be dated from the mid-1980s, when Club Table was also formalised.[37] In 1986 three events – a sherry party for new members, a Grouse Dinner and a members' Christmas Luncheon – were incorporated in the calendar. (It was noted at the subsequent AGM that the use of the clubhouse had increased.)[38] That was also the year in which the General Committee agreed to a request from the technical director of British Nuclear Fuels plc, Dr William Wilkinson, who had recently been elected, that his membership be delayed for one year due to 'pressure of work'.[39] The increase in the number of official serviced events was a response to modern patterns of residence and 'pressure of work'. In Croker's day, most members lived and / or worked near the clubhouse and could drop in frequently, in order to read the papers, pick up the latest gossip and perhaps have lunch or dinner in the coffee room. Today's programme of talks, concerts, films, discussion groups, dining groups and wine tastings, which is designed to attract increasingly busy working members to the clubhouse, to entertain its retired habitués and to bring members together, would have astounded the original members, although not quite as much as the popular outside visits to libraries, historic houses, theatres, motor rallies and ski slopes.

Even the first Talk Dinners were regarded as an experiment in 1926.[40] Once they moved to the coffee room, however, with an initial ceiling of 130 in attendance, they became a club institution, offering an opportunity to hear first from an authority on a subject of general interest (formerly an Athenian but later possibly a non-member) and then from members and guests in the audience during a chaired discussion on the subject. Much depends upon the quality of the speakers and the ability of the Talk Dinner Committee to identify and recruit them. At the 1993 AGM, chaired by Sir Paul Osmond, the 'brilliance' of the sub-committee was credited with 'having been responsible to some extent for the increased use of the clubhouse during 1992'.[41] In 1994 the ophthalmologist Professor Robert Weale, chairman of the sub-committee, 'alluded to the difficulty which had been created by having more Club Talk Dinners than members who were willing to speak'.[42] Moreover, during a subsequent trial period, when members could invite a male or female guest, a complicated arrangement was made whereby both the dress code and the gender of guests would be varied over a season.[43] Today these dinners are open to members and one guest, dressed in lounge suit or equivalent, with a charge of £68 for members and £78 for guests. The Athenæum is no longer 'the poor man's club', if it ever was.[44]

Dr Yolande Hodson, the map historian and former chairman of the Talk Dinner Committee, has categorised the talks given between 1988 and 2010 as follows: science and technology 61; art, drama and literature 39; religion 27; international perspectives (especially ambassadorial) 25; architecture/heritage 24; politics / government 22; public service 15; music 13; and history 10. The supremacy of science and technology (which here includes medicine) reflects the professional profile of the membership, whereas the low number of talks on music and history is surprising, given that these are the main private passions of many of today's members, judging by the conversation at Club Table and at other gatherings in the clubhouse. Something of the range and quality of club Talk Dinners can be gauged by considering those held in any one year. In 1988, a year chosen at random, the art historian Andrew Wilton introduced a discussion on 'Is Turner our national painter?'; Sir Harry Hookway, the former and first chief executive of the British Library, spoke on 'What is the information explosion?'; the place-names expert Dr John Dodgson asked, 'Can this age appreciate classical literature?'; Martyn Goff, administrator of the Booker Prize, considered 'Books today & tomorrow: universal communication or a minority hobby?'; the physician Dr Alex Sakula examined 'The bridge on the River Kwai: facts & fiction'; and Dr (later Sir) Roger Scruton looked at 'The pursuit of truth'. Only Dodgson was a non-member.

As with other diaried events, demand for the flagship Talk Dinners is greater than the supply of places available, with the result that the ballot has become controversial, particularly as some members apply for a large number of events in the hope of succeeding with some of them, leaving others with nothing. (Members are sometimes encouraged to apply by their spouses or partners, who are potential guests.) For a brief period it was decided to publish the number of applications for places at Talk Dinners, which inevitably meant that members could see which speakers and subjects were most popular. In 2014 the two most sought-after speakers were both non-members: the Conservative politician Sir Malcolm Rifkind spoke on 'Punching above our weight?' (470 applications for 150 places); and the conductor Sir Mark Elder on 'Two giants from 1813 – Verdi and Wagner' (469 applications).[45] Patrick Derham, headmaster of Westminster School and also a non-member, topped the poll in 2015 with a talk on 'Educating: a liberating force' (488 applications).

Talk Lunches, smaller spin-off events that are held in the refurbished garden room, have proved to be as popular as Talk Dinners. In 2014, for example, 442 applications were made for the 85 places at 'Murder and mystery: P.D. James and Ruth Rendell in conversation'.[46] Demand is usually also high for the annual Athenæum Lecture (in 2014 Sir Richard Sykes on 'The interaction and future of universities and commerce' attracted 309 applications) and for lectures organised to mark special occasions, as when the military historian Sir Max Hastings commemorated the centenary of the beginning of the First World World (548 applications). The popularity of Library Dinners and Lunches and Archive Dinners and Lunches, held in the garden room, reflects not only the membership's sustained interest in their outstanding library and archive, but also the events' more relaxed structure: a talk and brief questions are *followed* by convivial eating. Whereas formal talks and communal eating have largely become separate activities outside Clubland, the number of combined events has actually increased at the Athenæum: Forum Dinners aim to bring different generations together by taking topical subjects, announced only a month before each dinner; Wine Dinners and Lunches tackle a favourite club theme; Works of Art Committee Dinners are just that; and the Poetry Series, masterminded by poet and government official David Morphet, and now numbering over fifty meetings, combine discussions and readings of poetry with dinner. Other diaried events include the Athenæum Concert and, most recently, semi-staged operas in the drawing room (necessitating its closure for three days), as well as Interclub Duplicate Bridge, Social Golf and the Film Society, and hardy annuals such as the Summer Party, the Chess Dinner, the Christmas Lunch and the St Cecilia Concert, this last accompanied by printed booklets of verse and prose edited by Paul Tempest, formerly of the Bank of England. There are even Quiz Nights.

In 2016 the chairman of the General Committee, Graham Nicholson, formerly chief legal advisor to the Governor of the Bank of England, began his report at the end of his first year in office with these words:

> The sections of this Report detailing the events held in the Clubhouse and elsewhere over the year bear testimony to the vibrancy of the Club; not only Talk Dinners and Library, Works of Art and Wine Committee events but also music, film and poetry. I doubt that there has been a time in the Club's history when such variety and quality has been on offer; with the popularity of the events evidenced by the high level of applications for the ballot, and of course, corresponding disappointment on the part of unsuccessful applicants. Although it is perhaps invidious to pick out a particular event, the three nights of *The Marriage of Figaro* in March of this year were especially memorable.[47]

Nicholson is certainly correct in his historical assessment, and much the same could have been said by the chairmen of those other leading London clubs that have also expanded their programmes of events, and for similar reasons. In the case of the Athenæum, however, with its long and distinctive tradition of quiet scholarship and private conversation, his celebration of the club's 'vibrancy' strikes a new note.

The various forms of Talk Dinner that are in greatest demand at the Athenæum would, however, be regarded as rather cerebral in some clubs. The same is true of some of the unofficial and unserviced groups of members that meet regularly in the clubhouse, and whose activities are not organised by sub-committees or mentioned in Annual Reports. The oldest of these is the Discussion Group, which began life in a small way in 1964. The group meets monthly to dine in the coffee room before retiring to one of the smaller rooms in the clubhouse for a short presentation by one of its members, followed by discussion. The historian and broadcaster Christopher Lee, a current member of the group, outlined its history at a dinner to mark the half-century in June 2014. In the early years, between five and seven members of the group would meet with no announced agenda and no nominated speaker, and it was twenty-five years before the first presentation was made on a topical event. The heterogeneity of the topics presented reflects the varied currents of individuals' intellectual pursuits rather than current affairs. At the moment of the Falklands War, Lee pointed out, nine gathered in the north library to contemplate dreams and dismissed Freud as one who interpreted them too narrowly. Membership is by invitation of the group as a whole, which numbers between twenty-five and thirty. For many years the minutes of these evenings ended with the observation, 'an animated discussion ensued'. 'Isn't that the delight of the whole affair?' mused Lee: 'Fifty years of lively and animated discussion in a good company.'

Rabbi Professor Dan Cohn-Sherbok, long a member of the Discussion Group, was one of the moving spirits behind the more recently formed lunch-time group for literary members entitled the Algæ, which he chairs. Here the winning formula of communal eating combined with informed discussion on a topic presented by a member has been adapted to the professional interests of those who write and publish on a regular basis. So whereas a presentation to the Discussion Group might celebrate the novels of Tolstoy, an Algæ paper would probably include consideration of the problems associated with researching and writing about the novels of Tolstoy. Both these informal groups of members consider themselves to represent an essential strand of this 'literary' club's historic identity and ethos, gathering for discussion without guests being present. The chairmen of some of the better discussions held at these unofficial meetings will often close by commenting that those present have participated in a 'truly Athenian' event, and the same is said at some of the diaried Talk Dinners and lunches. As David Thomson commented at the Great Debate, unlike 'purely social clubs', the Athenæum is for 'people with intellectual interests'.

Like all major London clubs, the Athenæum has a long tradition of allowing and even encouraging external groups whose membership includes as least one of its own to hold occasional meetings, usually associated with lunch or dinner, in the clubhouse.[48] The Essay Club arrived in 2001, having started life at the Holborn Restaurant in 1907, tried various restaurants, settled at Bertorelli's and then moved to the Savile, where they lost the room in which they met to refurbishment.[49] The Study of Parliament Group held its first annual dinner at the Athenæum in 1965, when dinner cost £2 including sherry and wine, or £1 for teetotallers; later they tried other clubs.[50] Other visiting groups include the OWLS (Old Whitley Lags), the Romney Street group founded in 1917, the London Society for the Study of Religion and numerous others, including groups associated with schools, universities, livery companies and regiments.

These external groups tend to migrate, depending on the health of their Athenian member or members, or on changes of habitat at the clubhouse. In May 1998 the late Patrick Rivett, a member of the club and the first professor of operational research outside the USA, wrote to David Thomson, then chairman of the General Committee, as follows: 'I run a luncheon club named in honour of Patrick Blackett which meets three times a year in the Picture room. I also run three other groups, each of which meets once a year in the club. The latter groups will now no longer meet in the club simply because it is far too expensive and I am under pressure also to move the Blackett group elsewhere. It costs us an extra £20.00 per person to eat in a private room compared with the same meal in public.'[51] (The pressure to which Rivett refers includes the fact that the club did not then admit women members.)

As we have seen, the year 1998 marked the beginning of an era of change, in which successive Executive Committees took active steps to improve the economic health of the club by improving its facilities, thereby justifying commercial rates for room charges and encouraging an increase in what the retail sector calls 'footfall'. That increase has been achieved partly through the development of a full calendar of events and group activities, and partly through other changes that are mentioned in Graham Nicholson's report of 2016. 'High utilisation of the Coffee Room and bedrooms', he wrote, 'together with the use made by Members of Club rooms for private events has contributed to another financially successful year.'[52] Private dining has been a feature of club life since the late nineteenth century, when objections were made to the presence in the clubhouse of 'strangers' attending 'Members' Dinners' behind the closed doors of the morning room. When Lord Morley, for example, the Liberal statesman and author, and the publishing Macmillan brothers, entertained their colleagues and clients to saddle of mutton and numerous other courses, they trod the fine line between entertaining, or networking, and actual business or fund-raising.[53] During the twentieth century these dinners, reduced to a few courses, migrated to the small libraries and the picture room, and today it is often impossible to obtain a book from the north or west library at lunchtime because the room is occupied by a private party. The club's banqueting department is very busy, organising not only dinners and lunches, but also drinks receptions, wedding receptions and other large-scale private events.

The high utilisation of the bedrooms to which Nicholson refers, following their refurbishment, has had a similar effect to that of the ballot for diaried events: members have to book well in advance and are often unsuccessful in obtaining a room, not least because of the number of reciprocal members from overseas clubs who take advantage of the facility during their stays in London. The high utilisation of the coffee room also reflects an increase in the number of non-members in the clubhouse, as the private entertainment of groups of guests, sometimes sizeable groups, at lunch or dinner has become common-place in recent years. The proportion of members to guests has diminished, and whereas in the 1830s gales of laughter might have emanated from Theodore Hook's 'Temperance Corner', to the disapproval of other, less outgoing members in the coffee room, today they often come from the friends, families or colleagues of members. Similarly, although the drawing room, originally described by Decimus Burton as 'the Library' and later by Kipling as like a cathedral between services,[54] remains peaceful in the mornings, it can be diffi-cult to read there during post-prandial periods. The author recalls a young family friend of his giggling over coffee when she noticed a member taking a nap on a nearby chaise longue designed by Burton. She was amused by some-body 'sleeping in public', when in fact he was sleeping in private, in his own clubhouse.

The question arises whether the enhancement of the clubhouse's facilities has been for the benefit of the members or their guests, and whether the level of private entertaining that is now a regular feature of club life has changed the tone of the clubhouse. The popularity of Club Table, however, the number of members applying for the various kinds of Talk Dinners and lunches described earlier, the strict rules concerning mobile telephones, the maintenance of an excellent library and archive, and of silence in the south library, all represent continuity of emphasis and practice. Future General Committees will want to consider how a balance can be maintained between the needs of members who wish to entertain in the clubhouse and those of members who regard it as a quiet haven. (In 1823 Sir Humphry Davy encouraged Croker to remember the 'retiring philosophers whom it is always desirable to bring into the living world'.[55])

The first item in a 'policy checklist' approved by the General Committee in October 2002 aimed to achieve this balance: 'The Club exists to provide Members with an agreeable place to relax, to entertain friends, and to enjoy the company of fellow Members with achievements of an intellectual or creative nature and of value to the community.'[56] The wording echoes Brian Gilmore's prophetic comments at the AGM held four months earlier:

With so much going on, the Chairman wants to pay particular attention to an asset of the Club which does not have anyone speaking for it. This is the importance which members attach to being able to walk into the Clubhouse and find a place to relax. There have been various comments recently suggesting that at times the Club is very busy. That's a sign of success and a sign that the Club is doing things which members want; but we are not going to forget the many members who also want to be able to have a place to sit quietly and relax.[57]

For Athenians past and present, sitting quietly and relaxing usually means reading.

So far in this chapter we have considered various kinds of change in the life of the Athenæum. We now turn to the membership and its profile, where the emphasis falls upon continuity and '*la même chose*'. First, however, a word about the staff and another kind of continuity which is reflected in an extraordinary record of retention – a sure sign of job satisfaction for those working in a happy ship. The club has seventy-eight members of staff, twenty-three of whom have served for five to ten years, eleven for ten to fifteen years, ten for fifteen to twenty years, seven for twenty to thirty years, and three for over thirty years.[58] Three of the four assistant managers have worked in the club for more than twelve years, which has done much for the stability and continuity of service to members, who regularly express their appreciation to all the staff. The secretary has served for twenty-two years.

As we have seen throughout the history of the club, the election of candidates is based upon ability and clubbability rather than birth and background. (A distinction made in the 1820s between personal acquaintance with the candidate and 'a knowledge of his works' is retained in the Candidates Book to this day.)[59] Dynasticism is therefore less common at the Athenæum than elsewhere in Clubland; and where it does figure, it tends to take the form of descent from intellectual families or of association with specific centres of intellectual activity. Christopher (Palgrave) Barker, who was born in 1927, elected in 1972 and died in 2017, recalled being taken to the clubhouse at the age of seven by his father to see the Silver Jubilee celebrations for King George V. He described the Athenæum as the 'family club' – his forebears included Dawson Turner (elected in 1824)[60] and Francis Turner Palgrave (1854) – and regarded himself as having been unworthy of election. The musician and author Jeremy Barlow was equally self-deprecating when delivering a Library Dinner talk in 2013 on the extensive Darwin / Barlow connections at the Athenæum.[61] Other current members who have been moved to talk about their Athenian forebears include Anne Chisholm on her grandfather Hugh Chisholm, editor of the renowned 11th edition of *Encylopædia Britannica* (1911); Peter Sabine, formerly deputy director of the Geological Survey, on two original members of the club, General Sir Edward Sabine, who served on the council of the Geological Society, and his brother Joseph, a fellow of the society;[62] and Patience Thomson, an authority of dyslexia, on 'The legacy of the two Braggs', a talk which extended beyond personal associations (both her father and her husband David's father were Nobel laureates) to the club's continuous connection with the Royal Institution since 1824.[63] None of these current members of their families' club is a passive heir, and all 'value particularly the life of the intellect, arts and sciences'.

The Athenæum has always considered itself to be 'more than just another London club',[64] an assessment which has been confirmed by neutral observers.

In 1962 Anthony Sampson reported that, within Clubland, only the Athenæum was 'completely *sui generis*': 'there the bishops are being bishops, the professors are professors, the eccentrics are eccentric, and the dull, distinguished men sit in their deep leather chairs in the silence room [the south library], where no one can disturb them. And they hold to themselves the secret of setting themselves, ostentatiously, at ease, and leaving their interlocutors puzzled, embarrassed, gratified but obscurely discomfited.'[65] Non-members are far less likely to be patronised or embarrassed at today's more informal Athenæum. The bishops are still being bishops, but less grandly. In 2014 Andrew Brown, a commentator on Church affairs, noted that John Habgood (Archbishop of York, 1983–95), the last Etonian to be an archbishop before Justin Welby, 'once told the Synod that one of his ideas had come to him in the bath at the Athenaeum: that was the sort of place where his sort of bishop did his sort of thinking'.[66] Of the five other archbishops who are current members, three were educated at grammar schools, one at a secondary modern and one at a government-aided school in Africa. Four of the six are retired, but none is a trustee, in contrast to earlier eras when this was expected.[67]

Bishops are busy, and although one of their number serves on the General Committee, he is usually retired. (Senior female clerics have yet to be elected.) They are also more embattled, serving a society which is critical of the Church's stance on sexuality and its failures in the area of safeguarding. Today there are fewer bishops in the club, even though the Anglican episcopate has grown in number: thirty-one were elected between 1955 and 1984 (including Roman Catholics), whereas only sixteen have joined the club since 1985. Most of the ten current Anglican diocesans in the club make use of the bedroom facilities when they are on duty in the House of Lords or on national bodies. (More have joined the much less expensive Farmers Club, which must please the Church Commissioners.) Bishops are often to be seen working on papers in the south library, eating at Club Table alongside lay members, or discussing Church matters with clerical colleagues over lunch or dinner in the coffee room, in the tradition of Samuel Wilberforce and William Temple.

If the cost of membership gives the bishops pause, however, this is a greater impediment to most other clergy.[68] A member's suggestion at the 1996 AGM that the clergy rates be lowered was 'not widely supported', and the General

Committee thought that, 'in fairness to other low paid professions, such as certain academic posts, an equitable policy would be difficult to achieve'.[69] The chairman, David Thomson, undertook to discuss the matter with at least three retired archbishops in the club, 'to keep them informed and invite their views'. Although no changes were introduced, sixty-eight non-episcopal clergy of all denominations are current members, and two-thirds of them add other titles to their Reverends: there are seven Very Reverends (Deans), two Prebendaries and twelve Canons, for example, as well as one baronet, two Monsignors and a Reverend and Worshipful diocesan chancellor.[70] More telling, however, is the fact that fifteen Reverends are also doctors and six are professors.

In Sampson's terms, the professors are still professors, but there are now many more of them and they are more varied in subject discipline and demeanour, largely as a result of the rapid expansion of higher education in Britain. In the 1960s, when the number of universities doubled from twenty-two to forty-six, the vice-chancellors of several of the new 'plate-glass' universities were members of the club.[71] In the 1980s, when Lord Quirk was vice-chancellor of London University, he found it 'handy' to have informal contact with virtually all the other V-Cs in the country through the club.[72] By 2016 there were 130 universities in the UK and a central bureaucracy to match.

Academic networking goes on all the time in the clubhouse. It becomes controversial when a member's subscription is covered by a public body that is funded by the tax payer. In 2009, for example, a *Daily Mail* headline screamed of Professor David Eastwood, 'The quango gravy train: £1m expenses bill includes £1,000 membership of exclusive club'.[73] In defence of the historian, chief executive of the Higher Education Funding Council for England, an HEFCE spokesman declared that the board had agreed to his membership of the Athenæum when he was appointed, 'considering it represented value for money', as it was used for 'overnight accommodation and meetings with senior representatives of the higher education sector and business'. (The *Mail's* criticism does not apply to all vice-chancellors.) Some of the most regular users of bedroom facilities include senior academics from the provinces who, like diocesan bishops, have to attend national meetings in London. Dame Janet Finch, for example, formerly vice-chancellor of Keele University, has now taken on a number of public roles such as chairing the Nursing and Midwifery Council, and is often to be seen at Club Table. University chancellors and heads of house at Oxford and Cambridge, not all of whom are academics, have always been well represented at the club. Lord Patten of Barnes, for example, is chancellor of Oxford University and the late Lord Dainton was chancellor of Sheffield; Lord Grabiner is Master of Clare College, Cambridge, Dame Carol Black is principal of Newnham and Lord (Rowan) Williams of Magdalene; Lord Rees of Ludlow is a former Master of Trinity College, Cambridge, Sir Keith Thomas was formerly president of Corpus Christi College, Oxford, and Dame Helen Ghosh is Master of Balliol.

The eminence of its more illustrious learned members has always been a source of pride in the club. Their portraits have not been hung in the major public rooms of the clubhouse, but more discreetly in the morning room, where oil paintings of Victorian heroes such as Darwin and Huxley look down on those taking an aperitif, and in the picture room, where a selection of more recent portraits, somewhat randomly acquired, includes one of Isaiah Berlin, another college head who used the clubhouse for academic business.[74] Yet more discreet is the display of black-and-white photographs of members – a family collection in a home from home – in the bedroom corridors on the second and third floors, and largely unknown to members who never stay overnight. Of the sixty-three members portrayed by Anne Purkiss, all but one was elected after 1960 and eighteen since 2000. Their profiles are similar to those of earlier post-war generations:[75] half were educated at grammar schools and in all they include sixteen peers, twenty knights, and one baroness. But the number of professors – fourteen – is higher than in earlier samples, in a club which currently has over six hundred of them on the roll, almost a third of the membership. Among these photographs, fellows of the Royal Society are strongly represented by the president, Lord Rees (Astronomer Royal), the late Professor Sir Joseph Rotblat (physicist and Nobel peace laureate), Sir Tim Hunt (biochemist and molecular physiologist, Nobel laureate), Professor Dame Kay Davies (molecular geneticist), Professor Sir Walter Bodmer (molecular geneticist), Sir John Pendry (physicist) and Professor Dame Jocelyn Bell Burnell (astrophysicist). In 1960, 28 per cent of fellows of the Royal Society were members of the club, and in 1996 an arrangement whereby the Royal Society Dining Club met at the clubhouse was confirmed.[76] Among several other historical links between current fellows and their Athenian forebears are Pendry's associations with the Blackett Laboratory at Imperial College London and the Cockcroft Institute.

John Wilson Croker and Sir Humphry Davy established strong links between the club and the leading learned societies in 1824, and those connections remain in most cases. Since 1985 four of the seven presidents of the Royal Society have been members: Lord Porter of Luddenham, Sir Michael Atiyah, Lord May of Oxford and Lord Rees. In contrast, only two out of nine presidents of the Society of Antiquaries have been members (Michael Robbins and Professor Sir Barry Cunliffe), and not one of the five presidents of the Royal Academy, a statistic to which we will return. The British Academy, however, founded in 1902 as the national academy for the humanities and social sciences and now housed at Carlton House Terrace, has had nine presidents since 1985, six of whom are current members: Lord Quirk, Sir Anthony Kenny, Sir Keith Thomas, the Baroness O'Neill of Bengarve, Lord Stern of Brentford and Sir David Cannadine.

Engineers were even more active than the scientists in administering the fledgling club in the 1820s, and still have a strong presence today. As the late Sir Frederick Warner pointed out in his millennial essay on 'The engineer in society':

> The British Academy has moved alongside the Royal Society in Carlton House Terrace and the Royal Academy of Medical Studies is joining in. Not far away in Westminster is the Royal Academy of Engineering to complete the close geographical association of Academies. This might provide another focus for the Club in the way that the Cosmos Club in Washington is a necessary complement to the Academies there which operate close to the State Department. A small but diverse group continued by self-selection seems to be a workable and agreeable way of transcending the tendency for specialists to collect in cells, academic ghettoes and institutions for mutual inspection.[77]

The current proximity of the learned societies to the clubhouse encourages just the kind of mutuality that was envisaged in 1824.

Sampson's third category in 1962 was the Athenæum's eccentrics. Like bishops in their purple shirts, eccentrics are noticed, particularly in a clubhouse which has a quiet, even scholarly atmosphere. The Reverend Canon Brian Dominick Frederick Titus Brindley (he added the second and fourth names himself) was never going to be a bishop, but he was certainly noticed. When the Anglo-Catholic Vicar of Holy Trinity, Reading, became a Canon of Christ Church in 1985 he acquired a lavish new clerical wardrobe which included buckled shoes with high heels, which he painted red.[78] It was not as a master of high camp, however, that he was presented for election to the club the following year, but rather as a significant liturgist, a Canon of Christ Church and the newly elected chairman of the Business Subcommittee of the General Synod. Following Brindley's fall from grace in 1989, when taped indiscretions, mainly fantasies about young men, were published by the *News of the World* and reported in the *Independent* by the ubiquitous Andrew Brown, Evangelical enemies are reported to have driven him from his various Anglican posts and Archbishop Coggan, a trustee, is said to have called for his expulsion from the club.[79] If such an attempt was made, it failed, as in other similar cases. It was an ailing Brindley, now a Roman Catholic, who invited a group of friends to celebrate his seventieth birthday at his beloved Athenæum clubhouse in 2001. He collapsed during an elaborate private dinner in the north library, between the dressed crab and the *bœuf en daube*, and was given the last rites by Anthony Symondson SJ. (According to his friend Damian Thompson, then a fellow member, the crab was magnificent.) Brindley's death on the floor of the north library seemed utterly fitting and became legendary. (In reality the paramedics had found movement in the heart, and he was declared dead an hour later in St Thomas's Hospital.)[80]

Soberly suited members of the club like to recount the legend, and more than one admits to having disapproved of Brindley's extrovert behaviour and red heels. Disapproval of another eccentric, elected two years earlier than Brindley, had less to do with his hairstyle than his habit of either brooding in solitary silence in a corner of the drawing room, or barging into private conversations at the smaller tables in the coffee room and talking at length about himself. Jimmy Savile OBE and Knight Commander of the Order of St Gregory the Great, was the nation's most successful 'fund-raiser for charity', as he was described in the Candidates Book.[81] At the time of his election, on 20 February 1984, he had already gained the trust of members of the royal family and of the prime minister, Margaret Thatcher, who made four attempts to secure him a knighthood in the 1980s, against the advice of Sir Robert Armstrong, Secretary of the Cabinet and a member of the club, before she was successful in 1990. Perhaps Sir Robert's veiled warnings were not also passed on to his club. Three days after Savile's election a JAK cartoon entitled 'Jim fixed it for him' appeared in the *Standard*, showing an elderly bishop on the arms of two chorus girls, having successfully applied to the popular television programme *Jim'll Fix It* with an outrageous request. Savile was proud of his membership. (Usually attired in a track suit or shell suit, he kept a formal suit which he wore at the clubhouse, which he used for meetings.)[82] After his death in 2011, and the investigation of over 450 alleged cases of sexual abuse by him, the General Committee of the Athenæum considered whether his membership should be 'expunged from the Club' in order to protect its reputation, and wisely decided against the move on the grounds that history cannot be rewritten.[83]

It would be wrong to assume that Sampson had the club's many civil servants in mind when describing his fourth category of Athenian, the 'dull, distinguished men' sitting in their deep leather chairs. Thanks to the enduring influence of the novels of C.P. Snow and Anthony Powell, however, and of television programmes such as *Yes, Prime Minister*, the club is still assumed to be the place where Sir Humphrey Appleby and his colleagues conduct their most significant business over lunch, as a search of *Hansard* online confirms. Prominent among politicians who refer to the tradition is Charles Clarke MP. In 2003, when he was Secretary of State for Education and Skills, he explained that select committees of the House of Commons had only existed in their current form for the previous twenty years and that this reflected the need for 'increased accountability and scrutiny of modern government'.[84] Six years before the *Daily Mail* article on Professor Eastwood appeared, Clarke went on to say that his department was 'reflecting' on certain kinds of professional relationships and on 'different classes of nods and winks', and that he thought the HEFCE's was 'an Athenæum-type nods and winks operation'. In 2008, when asked about the merits of having a 'strong centre' in government at a meeting of the Public Administration Committee, Clarke said: 'What kind of centre? I would hope that would be interpreted as a stronger Cabinet Office, and a stronger coordination at the top of the Civil Service which went beyond permanent secretaries having lunch in the Athenæum and some process whereby you were able to pull it together.'

In reality the club could claim only one permanent secretary in 2003, Sir Joseph Pilling, a product of Rochdale Grammar School and Kings College, London, who played a significant role in the continuing peace process in Northern Ireland, and who became chairman of the General Committee in retirement.[85] In 2017 the roll also included Sir Martin Donnelly, interim permanent secretary to the Department for International Trade; Sir Alexander Younger, chief of the Secret Intelligence Service (MI6), whose entry in *Who's Who* is one of the shortest in its history; Sir Mark Walport (2011), government chief scientific advisor; and Patrick McGuinness (1992), deputy national security advisor. Of these four, only McGuinness acknowledges his membership of the Athenæum in *Who's Who*, which might suggest that what was once a badge of honour in Whitehall is now regarded by some as an embarrassment.

Other distinguished senior professionals who might be mistaken for dull men on the basis of external appearance include members of the diplomatic service (in 2012 the roll listed six serving diplomats, including the ambassadors to Rome, Belgrade and Athens, and at least sixteen retired) and the legal profession, which has always been strongly represented among the membership. The display of photographs upstairs includes the late Lord Mackay of Clashfern, Lord Denning and Lord Neill of Bladen, and a current legal member, Lord Nicholls of Birkenhead, formerly a trustee and Second Senior Lord of Appeal. Although extrovert barristers tend to prefer the Garrick, a few add colour to the drawing room of the Athenæum, the natural home of the quieter lawyer. The recent increase in the number of financial and insurance experts in the club reflects the expansion of these sectors in modern Britain. Again, however, it is not the contrarian hedge fund manager but the more sober banker or financial legal advisor who is attracted to the Athenæum. The club's oldest and strongest connection in this regard is with the Bank of England, which completed its Grecian remodelling by Soane at the same time that Decimus Burton's clubhouse was built, and whose governors have usually been members, including most recently the late Lord ('Eddie') George and Lord King of Lothbury, an active current member. Paul Tempest, the indefatigable editor of house publications such as *The Wit of the Athenæum, 1824–2016, in Light Verse and Bon Mots*, worked for the bank for many years, and Graham Nicholson, formerly the bank's chief legal advisor, has played leading roles in the governance of the club.

As in other senior clubs, there has always been a sprinkling of bankers and businessmen at the Athenæum. The club has guarded against the intrusion of overt business practices, however, as when dictation to secretaries in the hall and the holding of business meetings were banned in the 1950s, and when access to 'E-Mail, the Internet etc' for business purposes was denied in 1998 on the grounds that supplying these facilities would 'alter the nature of the Club'.[86] Again, changes in the professional world outside Clubland have affected life within it, as the historian of White's noted when commenting on the 'noble lord' who is said to have walked out of his club, never to return, on the day that the first stockbroker was elected: 'The trouble really is not that stockbrokers have become members of White's but that members of White's have become stockbrokers.'[87] London's oldest club is particularly alert to changes in the old order of the British Establishment: as Anthony Lejeune adds in his history, 'That David Lloyd George's grandson can be the Chairman of White's surely says something remarkable about British society and about the Club.'[88] (The 3rd Earl Lloyd George of Dwyfor was a Lloyd's underwriter and became chairman of White's in 1993.) At the Athenæum, whose values are closer to those of the liberal arts and sciences, Professor Cohn-Sherbok warned in a millennial essay that the 'growing army of those who work in the financial services and allied industries' would change the club's identity from 'Bishopsgate', as the cabbies used to call it, to another 'Notting Hill Gate', and that before long these wealthy individuals would be 'the only ones who can afford the pleasures of the Athenæum'.[89] While perhaps not always sharing Cohn-Sherbok's apocalyptic perspective, some current members do sometimes feel that the world is too much with us.

Although Croker's concept of a 'literary' club was broad, it is surprising to see how few creative writers there were among the original members of 1824, and that in *Ballot Day 1892* Andrew Lang was the only 'man of letters', in the sense that writing was his profession.[90] (The major Victorian novelists and poets became members between these dates.) The rise in the number of literary critics and biographers elected to the club in the 1960s and subsequent decades has continued in the present century. Following the deaths of Seamus Heaney in 2013, shortly after unveiling his portrait by Fiona Graham-Mackay (now herself a member), and of P.D. James in 2014, the club's best-known *littérateurs* are now critics, biographers and cultural historians such as the Hon. Victoria Glendinning, Richard Davenport-Hines and Jenny Uglow.[91] Sir Edward Hulton (died 1988) and Lord Weidenfeld of Chelsea (died 2016), both of whom figure in the photographic display upstairs, maintained the club's publishing tradition that was established by the Murrays, Macmillans and Longmans in the nineteenth century, and is continued today by the Hon. Timothy Hely Hutchinson and Michael Fishwick. The club's broader involvement in the book trade has been maintained by the administrator of the Booker Prize, the late Martyn Goff, and by a number of leading literary agents, including Michael Shaw and Bruce Hunter, both of whom were elected in 1986 and later served as trustees, and Georgina Capel. 'Where are the literary salons?' demanded the novelist and journalist Giles Foden in 2008, two years after his election to the club.[92] 'You do still hear intellectual conversation at the venerable institutions of St James's' such as the Reform and the Athenæum, Foden reported, but the membership profile is 'pretty venerable' and the subscriptions 'beyond the pocket of most'.

Judging by the conversation at Club Table and by the subject matter of many of the events that are now held in the clubhouse, the main private passions of today's habitués seem to be music and history, rather than literature in the sense of creative writing. Among the photographs upstairs are members who join a long line of Athenian musicians: Sir Georg Solti, Sir Charles Groves and Lord Menuhin of Stoke d'Abernon, all of whom died in the 1990s, the late Dr John Birch, organist at Chester Cathedral, and Sir Harrison Birtwistle, a current member. Just as there have been more literary critics than creative writers among the membership in recent decades, so the musical interpreters have outnumbered the composers.[93] Another kind of interpreter, the academic historian, is strongly represented at the club, where Professor Jeremy Black, Professor Sir David Cannadine (president of the British Academy), Professor Sir Richard Evans, Professor Sir Michael Howard and Professor Sir Diarmaid MacCulloch are members. The associated worlds of museums and galleries figure prominently in the photographic display, which includes Sir David Wilson, formerly director of the British Museum, Sir Alan Bowness, formerly director of the Henry Moore Foundation, and two former directors of the Victoria and Albert Museum, Alan Borg and Sir Roy Strong. Alongside the arts administrator, Lord Palumbo, are just three practitioners: the artist Bridget Riley, the furniture-maker John Makepeace, and the sculptor Philip Jackson.[94] Among other leading practitioners in the club is Lida Kindersley, the letter cutter.

Although Croker founded a non-partisan literary club in 1824, a hundred of its 'original members' were MPs. Today there are only three: Julian Lewis, Justine Greening (appointed Secretary of State for Education in 2016) and Rory Stewart. When Anthony Sampson reviewed the state of British politics, forty years after the publication of his *Anatomy of Britain* (1962), he commented on the fact that the quality of MPs had been 'widely seen to be declining'.[95] The cabinet, he argued, has been weakened, 'not just by the ambitions of prime ministers, but by the declining quality of their colleagues'.[96] Today, he concluded, 'it is one of the most serious flaws in the British democratic system: that the pool of talent to run the country has become too small to ensure effective government'. Whereas politics is now a separate profession, in the 1960s MPs regarded politics as only part of their activity and were proud of their amateur status.[97] Three of the politicians whose photographs hang upstairs – Enoch Powell, Roy Jenkins and James Callaghan – were of the last generation to regard a major speech in the House of Commons as a momentous rhetorical intervention, and to acknowledge the intellectual excellence of an opponent's speech. Theirs was also perhaps the last generation of MPs to feel at home at the club, where they were 'privileged to be admitted to an academy of letters', in the words of Lord Jenkins of Hillhead,[98] and where unlikely friendships made in the House between political antagonists could be fostered in the clubhouse, as in the case of Enoch Powell and Speaker George Thomas, both of whom were proposed by Patrick Cormack.[99] Margaret Thatcher considered herself to be too busy to take advantage of honorary membership and graciously declined the club's offer;[100] and only Geoffrey Howe among her senior cabinet colleagues was a member.

In a study on club affiliation among members of the House of Lords, published in 2012, Matthew Bond reported that the ten largest clubs, with the number of peers who are members in parenthesis, were the Garrick (49), Pratt's

(43), Beefsteak (41), Athenaeum (39), MCC (36), White's (31), Reform (27), Brooks's (27), Carlton (18), RAC (19), New (15), National Liberal (13), Farmers (12), Royal Commonwealth Society (10) and Oxford and Cambridge (10).[101] Five years later there were forty-four Athenian peers, most of whom were members before their elevation to the Lords. The Athenæum, a society of experts, has more members of what is now largely a House of experts than most other leading clubs. Former cabinet ministers can claim the right to enter the House of Lords. At the Athenæum, however, it is the peers' range of professional backgrounds that is striking: there are eight politicians, eight lawyers, six business people, four academics, three scientists, three medical practitioners, three clergy, three bankers, two diplomats, one police officer, one civil servant, one educationalist and one film producer. The seven Athenian members of the Order of Merit (out of twenty-three) also illustrate this wide professional range: HRH the Duke of Edinburgh, Lord Foster of Thameside, Lord Rees, Sir Magdi Yacoub, Lord Darzi, Lord Eames and Sir Michael Howard.

'For the first time in western democratic history', said George Walden, the former Conservative minister, in 2000, 'society is dominated by an elite of anti-elitists.'[102] In adapting to the age of postmodernity while maintaining a strong sense of its historic identity, the club has in a sense become counter-cultural, flourishing in a society which is suspicious of elites, unless they are of the sporting variety. The membership list, numbering about 2,000, is still impressive. A search of *Who's Who* and *Who Was Who* online by Malcolm Bishop reveals 4,308 entries on members who have died and 969 on living members, 62 of them female. As in earlier generations, most dome-headed Athenians are highly educated specialists whose expertise has some impact in the public domain. Clubbable, they tend to be introverts with social skills. Influential men and women, drawn from a wide range of professional fields, are still attracted to an institution which nurtures civilised conversation and companionship, traditional standards of dress code and etiquette, and access to a great library and high-quality cultural and social events. As Yehudi Menuhin wrote in a short millennial essay:

The wonderful thing about the Athenæum is the setting it offers for productive leisure: the spaces between duties, the borderlines between people, where, perhaps, only antennae become aware of another presence: in silence or behind the protective shield of a book or a newspaper. Then, in conversation, cross-fertilisation occurs quite naturally as the blissful fulfilment of an effortless higher duty – to the future, to our fellow men, colleagues, society. Interest in and information about the most disparate subjects ensue. These are precious fruits which grow from a harmony of differences, a plurality of uniquenesses, if I may invent so unlikely, yet so democratic, a word.[103]

*Plus ça change.*

ᴊᴄ

# NOTES

### Prologue

1. *Illustrated London News*, 102 (11 March 1893), 305–10. See also articles on the Carlton Club, 96 (24 May 1890), 649–52; the Reform Club, 97 (29 Nov. 1890), 676, 681–84; the United Service Club, 104 (24 Feb. 1894), 233–37. The Athenæum group drawing may have been prepared in 1891, the date on the frame in which the original is exhibited in the clubhouse. Waugh was commissioned to write the text in 1892: see COM 13/1, 4 November 1890, p. 113; SEC 1/6, pp. 847, 861; SEC 1/9, pp. 114, 170, 225, 271, 337, 340; SEC 1/10, pp. 288. Waugh used his article as the basis for the first history of the Athenæum, privately printed *c.* 1897 and reprinted for members in 1968.
2. *Punch's* 'Fancy Portraits', which appeared throughout the 1880s, were by Linley Sambourne, who was elected to the club in 1896. Sir Leslie Ward ('Spy' in *Vanity Fair*) was not a member.
3. I am grateful to Malcolm Bishop for this information.
4. See 'Analysis of Athenæum List corrected to 14 July 1884', compiled and hand-written by William Richard O'Byrne, signed and dated 2 February 1885: COM 1/24, pp. 77–78. See also Ward, p. 87.
5. The first thousand or so, listed as 'original members' in 1825: see p. 328, n. 3.
6. See e.g. Francis Caldwell Holland, proposed by Lord Knutsford on 18 June 1888 and elected on 18 April 1904 (MEM 1/1/15). Francis Darwin, son of Charles (1838), was elected under Rule II in 1892: Darwins and Barlows come down to the present day (see p. 314). Early in the life of the club, the General Committee elected three Wilberforces on the same day, 21 September 1824: COM 1/1, pp. 53–54. Among other dynasties are the publishing family of John Murray, the legal Pollocks and the eleven Huxleys, including Thomas (1858), Leonard (1896), Julian (1919), Aldous (1922) and, most recently, the late Professor Sir Andrew (1980), joint winner of the Nobel prize in physiology or medicine.
7. Dr Quain, as the key identifies him, was elevated to a baronetcy in 1891. Sir Rutherford Alcock (50) was a surgeon before he became a diplomat.
8. See p. 42 and Peter A. Sabine, 'Geological science and the early years of the Athenæum', in Fernández-Armesto, pp. 111–26. Sabine has maintained the family connection between the British Geological Survey and the Athenæum that has existed since its inception, when Sir Edward Sabine was an original member.
9. Contrast the Revd Vaughan (38), whose homosexuality was kept secret until 1964: see p. 95.
10. Henry Hart Milman, *Address Delivered at the Opening of the City of Westminster Literary, Scientific, and Mechanics' Institute* (Murray, 1837), p. 6. Milman donated a copy of his pamphlet to the Athenæum library.

11. Lang is described as 'M.A. Oxon, Man of Letters', candidate 7462, elected under Rule II on 17 April 1883: MEM 1/1/15.
12. See Isabella Augusta Gregory, *Seventy Years: Being the autobiography of Lady Gregory*, ed. Colin Smythe (Gerrards Cross: Smythe, 1974), p. 14.

## *1 Croker's London*

1. COM 1/1, copy of a letter pasted into unnumbered pages following the index. Croker donated this document to the club's archive in 1853 as 'a kind of curiosity': COM 1/13, p. 121.
2. See Anthony Lejeune, *White's: The first three hundred years* (Black, 1993), p. 11.
3. The earliest printed lists were of 'the present members', first privately circulated in March 1824 (187) and later published in June 1824 (506) and January 1825 (990). In March 1825 (1,048) the list was of 'the original members', but by May 1826 was simply headed 'List of members'. See Committee notices, 1824–77 (COM 3/1), n.p.; also p. 33.
4. See John Feather, *A History of British Publishing* (Routledge, 2005), p. 81.
5. See e.g. Linda Colley, *Britons: Forging the nation, 1707–1837* (New Haven and London: Yale University Press, 1992), pp. 321, 366–67.
6. See John Timbs, *Club Life of London, with Anecdotes of the Clubs, Coffee-houses and Taverns of the Metropolis during the 17th, 18th, and 19th Centuries*, 2 vols (Bentley, 1866), vol. I, p. 8; vol. II, p. 40.
7. The standard biography is Myron Franklin Brightfield's *John Wilson Croker* (Allen, Unwin, 1951).
8. Later he held five other seats, first in Ireland and then in England. See David Thomson, 'John Wilson Croker (1780–1857), the Club's founder: a littérateur in politics', in Fernández-Armesto, pp. 147–62; Robert Portsmouth, *John Wilson Croker: Irish ideas and the invention of modern Conservatism, 1800–1835* (Dublin: Irish Academic Press, 2010).
9. *The Croker Papers: The correspondence and diaries of the late Right Honourable John Wilson Croker, LL.D., F.R.S., Secretary to the Admiralty from 1809 to 1830*, ed. Louis John Jennings, 2nd rev. edn, 3 vols (Murray, 1885), vol. I, p. 19.
10. At a dinner attended by Lord Hertford and Lord Lowther, London's most notorious courtesan sat next to Croker, whose manner she described as 'starched' and 'pragmatical': Harriette Wilson, *Memoirs*, ed. Lesley Branch (Folio, 1979), pp. 64–65.
11. See Douglas Hurd, *Robert Peel: A biography* (Weidenfeld, Nicolson, 2007), p. 33.
12. See George Jones, *Sir Francis Chantrey, R.A.: Recollections of his life, practice, and opinions* (Moxon, 1849), p. 110.
13. See Joan Evans, *A History of the Society of Antiquaries* (Oxford: Oxford University Press, 1956), p. 225.
14. See *An Auto-biographical Memoir of Sir John Barrow, Bart., late of the Admiralty* (Murray, 1847), p. 272. Barrow was an original member.
15. See *The Croker Papers*, vol. I, pp. 73–74; Barrow, *Memoir*, p. 397. The royal relic was reinterred in 1888: see Henry William Lucy, *The Diary of a Journalist*, 3 vols (Murray, 1920–23), vol. I, pp. 141–42. Captain (later Rear-Admiral Sir John) Franklin was also an original member.
16. John Gibson Lockhart, *The Life of Sir Walter Scott*, 10 vols (Edinburgh: Constable, 1902–3), vol. IX, pp. 41–45. Wellington complained that Croker and Bankes 'talked down' Scott, who was seldom among them: Philip Henry, Lord Stanhope, *Notes on Conversations with the Duke of Wellington, 1831–1851*, 2nd edn (Murray, 1888), p. 100.
17. See David M. Wilson, *The British Museum: A history* (British Museum, 2002), pp. 71–75; Brightfield, *Croker*, p. 145. On the Elgin Marbles and the Athenaeum, see pp. 56–57.
18. The best account of Croker's career and reputation is William Thomas's *The Quarrel of Macaulay and Croker: Politics and history in the age of reform* (Oxford: Oxford University Press, 2000). See also Thomas's article on Croker in *ODNB*.
19. See Brightfield, *Croker*, pp. 235–41, 380–85; Thomas, *The Quarrel of Macaulay and Croker*, pp. 19–22, 26–27, 55–56. In the novel Disraeli refers to Digby's / Croker's forehead:

'Baldness, perhaps, contributed to the spiritual expression of a brow which was, however, essentially intellectual, and gave some character of openness to a countenance which, though not ill-favoured, was unhappily stamped by a sinister cast that was not to be mistaken.' *Coningsby; or, The New Generation*, book 1, chapter 1.

20. See Roger Sharrock, 'The chemist and the poet: Sir Humphry Davy and the Preface to *Lyrical Ballads*', *Notes and Records of the Royal Society of London*, 17, 1 (May 1962), 57–76; David Knight, 'Davy's visions', in James Hamilton, ed., *Fields of Influence: Conjunctions of artists and scientists, 1815–1860* (Birmingham: University of Birmingham Press, 2001), pp. 31–50.

21. See Richard Holmes, *The Age of Wonder: How the Romantic generation discovered the beauty and terror of science* (Harper, 2008). Three of the five volumes of *Lives of the most Eminent Literary and Scientific Men* (1835), by Mary Shelley, Sir David Brewster et al., are listed in Spencer Hall, *Catalogue of the Library of the Athenæum* (Athenæum, 1845), p. 184.

22. Barrow, *Memoir*, p. 334.

23. John Barrow, 'North-west Passage – Parry's second voyage', *Quarterly Review*, 30, 59 (October 1823), 231–72 (231).

24. *OED*, 'literary' (1). See also Gwendy Caroe, *The Royal Institution: An informal history, with a final chapter by Alban Caroe* (Murray, 1985), p. 69.

25. See e.g. Charlotte Klonk, *Science and the Perception of Nature: British landscape art in the late eighteenth and early nineteenth centuries* (New Haven and London: Yale University Press / Paul Mellon Centre for Studies in British Art, 1996).

26. Thomas Andrew Knight (HSL); John Cooke, MD (MCS); William Buckland, John Bostock, MD, William Fitton, MD, and the Revd Adam Sedgwick (GSL); Thomas Telford (ICE), Henry Colebrooke, Francis Baily, Sir John Herschel and Sir James South (ASL); the Right Hon. Charles Williams Wynn (RAS).

27. Charles Lyell, 'Scientific institutions', *Quarterly Review*, 34, 67 (June 1826), 153–79 (153). Sixty-nine learned societies were founded in Great Britain and Ireland between 1815 and 1845.

28. Abraham Hume, *The Learned Societies and Printing Clubs of the United Kingdom: Being an account of their respective origin, history, objects, and constitution* (Brown, 1847), p. 3.

29. Ibid., 20.

30. Ibid., p. 47.

31. Ibid., pp. 42–43.

32. Ibid., p. 21.

33. See *Autobiography of the late Sir Benjamin C. Brodie, Bart.* (Longman, 1865), pp. 68–69; *The Record of the Royal Society of London for the Promotion of Natural Knowledge* (1897), 4th edn (Royal Society, 1940), pp. 61–62. A small dining club within the Royal Society – the Royal Society Club – also originated in the eighteenth century. Bulwer Lytton, elected to the Athenæum in 1825, criticised the Royal Society for being organised like a club, with ballots for membership and with presidents like the wealthy Gilbert Davies, a 'child' when it came to science: *England and the English* [1833], Knebworth edition (London and New York: Routledge, 1874), p. 298.

34. 'Speaking of the Royal Society meetings I said it was dignified dullness or, said Mr Jekyll Junr. "Science under a Pall."' Edward Magrath's Commonplace Book (ST/07), January 1826, unnumbered pages. Magrath was the first salaried secretary of the Athenæum.

35. Twelve painters, including Lawrence, J.M.W. Turner, Wilkie and Mulready; three sculptors, including Sir Francis Chantrey, an active committee man at the Athenaeum; and two architects, Sir John Soane and Sir Robert Smirke. See William Sandby, *The History of the Royal Academy of Arts from its Foundation in 1768 to the Present Time, with Biographical Notices of all the Members*, 2 vols (Longman, 1862), vol. I, pp. 290–91.

36. The earl of Aberdeen did not realise that his trusteeship of the Athenæum was linked to his presidency of the Antiquaries: COM 1/10, p. 79.

37. Sandby, *History of the Royal Academy*, vol. II, p. 29.

38. Ibid., vol. I, p. 333.

39. Ibid., vol. I, p. 385. Rogers described Chantrey as an inferior sculptor: see William Maltby, *Recollections of the Table-talk of Samuel Rogers, to which is added Porsoniana* (Moxon, 1856), p. 156.

40. See *Croker Papers*, vol. I, p. 164.

41. See James Hamilton, 'Artists, scientists and events', in Hamilton, ed., *Fields of Influence*, pp. 1–30; Evans, *History of the Society of Antiquaries*, p. 240.

42. See Hamilton, 'Artists, scientists and events', p. 16; Evans, *History of the Society of Antiquaries*, pp. 231–38.

43. *National Portrait Gallery of Illustrious and Eminent Personages of the Nineteenth century, with Memoirs, by William Jerdan*, 4 vols (Fisher, Jackson, 1830–34), vol. III, p. 5. (Each memoir has individual pagination, indicative of part publication.)

44. Lockhart, *Life of Scott*, vol. IX, pp. 9–10. Rogers is identified as the speaker in Edgar Johnson, *Sir Walter Scott: The great unknown*, 2 vols (New York and Toronto: Macmillan, 1970), vol. II, p. 999.

45. Thomas Campbell, whose main publisher was Longman, edited two volumes of Murray's *Specimens of English Poetry*. The other four poets were published by Murray, as were many other original members of the Athenæum. Murray also published Admiralty material.

46. The standard Victorian account of Murray and his business is Samuel Smiles's *A Publisher and his Friends: Memoir and correspondence of the late John Murray, with an account of the origin and progress of the house, 1768–1843*, 2 vols (Murray, 1891).

47. Thomas, *The Quarrel of Macaulay and Croker*, p. 30.

48. The best modern study of the quarterlies is Joanne Shattock's *Politics and Reviewers: The Edinburgh and the Quarterly in the early Victorian age* (Leicester University Press, 1989).

49. American Philosophical Society, B.D315.1: see www.davy-letters.org.uk.

50. Frank A.J.L. James, 'Davy in the dockyard: Humphry Davy, the Royal Society and the electrochemical protection of the copper sheeting of His Majesty's ships in the mid 1820s', *Physis*, 29 (1992), 205–25 (214). I am grateful to Roger Knight for his guidance on Admiralty matters.

51. This spelling of Sir Humphry's given name was not unusual: see e.g. *Annual Register*, 66 (1824), 260.

52. COM 1/1, copy of a letter pasted into unnumbered pages following the index.

53. David Wilson comments, 'For once Croker did not get his way': 'The British Museum and the Athenæum', in Fernández-Armesto, pp. 229–36 (p. 231). Trustees who were original members of the Athenæum included Davy, Sir Robert Peel, the earl of Ashburnam, Sir Charles Long and George Agar Ellis. A special Saturday meeting of the General Committee in 1826 had to be adjourned in the absence of 'several members' at a meeting of the trustees of the British Museum: COM 1/1, p. 202.

54. Timbs, *Club Life of London,* vol. I, pp. 253–54. The Union may have been founded a year earlier, in 1799.

55. See Seth Alexander Thévoz, *Club Government: How the early Victorian world was ruled from London clubs* (London and New York: Tauris, 2018), p. 27.

56. R.C. Rome, *Union Club: An illustrated descriptive record of the oldest members' club in London, founded circa 1799* (Batsford, 1948), p. 9.

57. Ibid., p. 12.

58. The building is now part of Canada House.

59. London Metropolitan Archives, A/UNC/1, pp. 4, 5, 9. In 1829 Mr Giblet (or Giblett) refused to tender to supply meat to the Athenæum, on the grounds that their carving tradition was unfair to butchers: COM 1/3, p. 55.

60. Sampling of the two membership lists indicates that about 10 per cent of Union Club members became Athenians, at a time when multiple membership was commonplace.

61. London Metropolitan Archives, A/UNC/1, p. 71.

62. The United Universities Club was founded in 1822 and the Oriental Club in 1824.

63. At the Union Club's AGM of 1823 the committee's proposal of a subscription of 6 guineas was discussed in the light of rising costs associated with the new building: London Metropolitan Archives, A/UNC/1, pp. 38–45.

64. *Croker Papers*, vol. I, pp. 255–56.
65. See e.g. *The Annual Register*, 66 (1824), 23, 245.
66. Davy was elected in 1809. In 1828 most of the 34 members of The Club were also Athenians: see Reginald Welby et al., *Annals of The Club, 1764–1914* (The Club, 1914), pp. 47, 54–55. Other small dining clubs included the London Pitt Club, Nobody's Friends and Grillion's.
67. See e.g. James Hamilton, *Faraday: The life* (HarperCollins, 2002), pp. 77–80.
68. See Knight, 'Davy's visions', in Hamilton, ed., *Fields of Influence*, pp. 42–47.
69. See Evans, *History of the Society of Antiquaries*, p. 240.
70. The Astronomical Society of London met in Somerset House and received its royal charter in 1831.
71. The committee met only once, on 15 May 1823: James, 'Davy in the dockyard', 213–14.
72. See *Croker Papers*, vol. I, pp. 256–57 and Royal Institution transcripts of two letters from Davy to Croker, RI HD 26 J6 and J7.
73. John Thomson, '*The Edinburgh, The Quarterly* and the Athenæum', in Fernández-Armesto, pp. 3–18 (p. 12). On Thomson's claims relating to the political impact of the Athenæum see p. 30.
74. Ibid., p. 4.
75. Ibid., p. 16.
76. See *Middlemarch* (1871–72), chapter 15. The novel was the subject of animated discussion in the smoking room of the club: see *The George Eliot Letters*, ed. Gordon S. Haight, 9 vols (New Haven: Yale University Press, 1954–78), vol. V, p. 365.

## 2 'A Committee having been formed'

1. Committee notices, 1824–77 (COM 3/1).
2. Edward Lillie Pierce, *Memoir and Letters of Charles Sumner*, 4 vols (Boston: Roberts, Low, 1881–93), vol. II, pp. 34–35.
3. Various motives, some personal, others tactical within the Royal Society, have been suggested for Davy's opposition: see David Knight, *Humphry Davy: Science and power* (Oxford: Blackwell, 1992), pp. 135–36; James Hamilton, *Faraday: The life* (HarperCollins, 2002), pp. 186–90; Richard Holmes, *The Age of Wonder: How the Romantic generation discovered the beauty and terror of science* (Harper, 2008), p. 402. A convincing argument is that Davy 'did not want to be seen as continuing the Banksian tradition of supporting his friends and opposing his enemies irrespective of their scientific merit': Frank A.J.L. James, 'The military context of chemistry: the case of Michael Faraday', *Bulletin for the History of Chemistry*, 11 (1991), 36–40 (36).
4. After a gap in the diary of experiments, June 1824 was a busy month, following Faraday's resignation as temporary secretary of the Athenæum: see *Faraday's Diary: Being the various philosophical notes of experimental investigation made by Michael Faraday D.C.L., F.R.S. during the years 1820–1862 and bequeathed by him to the Royal Institution of Great Britain*, ed. Thomas Martin, 7 vols (Bell, 1932–36), vol. I, pp. 138–47. Faraday began his discourses at the Royal Institution in his own right in 1825: they proved to be as popular as Davy's lectures.
5. American Philosophical Society, B.D315.1: see www.davy-letters.org.uk.
6. See Frank A.J.L. James, 'Davy in the dockyard: Humphry Davy, the Royal Society and the electro-chemical protection of the copper sheeting of His Majesty's ships in the mid 1820s', *Physis*, 29 (1992), 205–25 (214). James shows that the failure of Davy's 'protectors' by 1825 adversely affected his reputation and those of Croker and Barrow.
7. *The Croker Papers: The correspondence and diaries of the late Right Honourable John Wilson Croker, LL.D., F.R.S., Secretary to the Admiralty from 1809 to 1830*, ed. Louis J. Jennings, 2nd rev. edn, 3 vols (Murray, 1885), vol. I, p. 256.
8. See Ellis Wasson, *Born to Rule: British political elites* (Stroud: Sutton, 2000), pp. 47–48. Cf. David Cannadine, *The Decline and Fall of the British Aristocracy* (New Haven and London: Yale University Press, 1990), pp. 10–15.

9. John Thomson, '*The Edinburgh, The Quarterly* and the Athenæum', in Fernández-Armesto, pp. 3–18 (p. 13).

10. Ibid., p. 4. At a pinch, the 'Celtic Fringe' interest could be said to extend to Wales, the homeland of Joseph Jekyll, and the English West Country: Sir Humphry Davy and Davies Gilbert were born in Penzance, and both Gilbert and Croker were MPs for Bodmin.

11. COM 1/1, fols 1r–1v. (Faraday's minutes were written on loose sheets, later pasted into this book when Magrath took over as secretary.) Three members, Ashburnham, Hopkinson and Palmerston, resigned after a year.

12. Croker was present at meetings of the building committee of the Union Club on 14 and 21 February 1824: see London Metropolitan Archives, A/UNC/1, pp. 84–85.

13. Commons *Hansard* for 16 February 1824, vol. X, cols 167–83. Six years later, on 1 March 1830, Croker wrote to Faraday from the Admiralty asking him to support a candidate that evening: 'the <u>Navy Estimates</u> will detain me and my Admiralty friends in the House of Commons during the hours of ballot'. *The Correspondence of Michael Faraday*, ed. Frank A.J.L. James, 6 vols (Institution of Engineering and Technology, 1991–2012), vol. I, p. 509.

14. See transcript of a sympathetic letter from Davy to Croker the following day. Faraday had been instructed to call on Croker with an account of the meeting. Royal Institution transcript, DD 26J 8 (Ohio State University Library, Spec.Rare.MMS.2.Box 1).

15. Members of the Building Committee were Aberdeen, Chantrey, Croker, Davy, Gilbert, Hatchett, Heber, Jekyll, Lawrence, Long and Smirke.

16. Two names were repeated and two others omitted but added later, giving a true final total of eighty-two. Ward is misleading when he refers to an additional 'large number already elected', but correct when suggesting 'how justly the Athenæum might claim from its earliest days to represent the true *intelligenzia* of the country': Ward, pp. 13–14.

17. His great-great-great-grandson, Christopher Barker (died 2017), was the most recent family member of the Athenæum: see p. 314.

18. Jekyll was a lawyer, an MP and a socialite. Early nineteenth-century chairmen of the club are identified as being the signatories of annual reports. Chairmanship of weekly meetings of the General Committee seems to have been decided on an ad hoc basis, as in other bodies such as the Law Institution (today's Law Society), although the chairman of the club would often preside when major decisions were to be made.

19. Letter dated Portsmouth, 20 February 1824: Royal Institution transcript HD/26/J/9 (Ohio State University Library, Spec.Rare.MSS.2, Box 1).

20. COM 1/1, fol. 5v.

21. Ibid., fols 7r and 13v–14r. Burton joined the General Committee and the Building Committee on 12 April 1824: ibid., fol. 17v.

22. *Croker Papers*, vol. I, p. 257.

23. COM 1/1, unnumbered sheet following Croker–Davy correspondence. Faraday's figure is 390, but two members died before 27 March.

24. Ibid., fol. 8v.

25. See Committee notices, 1824–77 (COM 3/1). The circular contains misprints, which suggests that Faraday may not have had time to check the proofs.

26. See London Metropolitan Archives, A/UNC/1, pp. 84–107.

27. See R.C. Rome, *Union Club: An illustrated descriptive record of the oldest members' club in London, founded circa 1799* (Batsford, 1948), pp. 15–16.

28. See Decimus Burton's letter to Clarke dated 13 April 1824, and lease to the Union Club dated 25 March 1822, in bundle marked 'No. 12 Waterloo Place, 1822–29', Legal Box. The Union paid rent of £1,100 per annum.

29. COM 1/1, fol. 20. Croker's report is reprinted in Ward, pp. 22–25.

30. Specimen articles of solid silver marked 'The Society' were withdrawn from the 'plate stock' for preservation as late as 1932: COM 13/8, p. 54.

31. COM 1/1, p. 14.

32. 'This relic of the club's first home was secured by Mr. T.W. Hill, assistant secretary at the time of the demolition of Waterloo Place in 1912': H. Clifford Smith, 'An inventory and

valuation of the furniture, works of art and general contents of the Athenæum, Pall Mall, S.W.' (typescript), 1939 (BUI 8/10/1), p. 110. The volute, in Roman cement, is painted black.

33. Indenture dated 25 March 1822: Legal Box. The words 'The Society' are scored through and 'The Athenæum' substituted. For a description of the exterior see James Elmes, *Metropolitan Improvements; or, London in the Nineteenth Century* (Jones, 1827), pp. 121–22.

34. Secretary's office records (SEC 1A/1).

35. Report of 8 May 1826, drafted by Croker: COM 20/1.

36. COM 1/1, fol. 17v. See also p. 59. 'Resolved that Mr. Hopkinson's offer be accepted provided the annual rent of the house to be built does not exceed £600' (12 April 1824): ibid., fol. 17v. Hopkinson and Croker were the first two elected trustees.

37. Ibid., fol. 22r.

38. Cf. Rules and Regulations for the Government of the Athenæum, COM 1/1, pp. 1–9; *The Rules and Regulations of the Union Club: With a list of members, &c., &c.* (Pollett, 1868); *Rules and Regulations for the Government of the United Service Club* (Clowes, 1819). See also, 'When the Reform Club was established in 1836, its founding members read aloud the regulations of the Union Club, and voted clause by clause as to whether to adopt each regulation as their own': Seth Alexander Thévoz, *Club Government: How the early Victorian world was ruled from London clubs* (London and New York: Tauris, 2018), p. 28.

39. On 8 March 1825 the General Committee ordered that 'the house be shut up at one instead of two o'clock': COM 1/1, p. 123.

40. At the Athenæum the rule was breached in 1898: see COM 13/1, p. 216.

41. See p. 306.

42. Current facilities include a dining room: see Neville Carrick and Edward L. Ashton, *The Athenæum Liverpool, 1797–1997* (Liverpool: Athenæum Liverpool, 1997), pp. 3, 22.

43. See Tait, p. 204.

44. See the trial reports for 29 October 1829 at www.oldbaileyonline.org/browse. For accounts of Martha Geary's arrest, thefts by other club servants and the dismissal of the steward, see COM 1/3, pp. 35–38. Geary was appointed on 19 October 1824, initially on a month's trial, 'that being the usage of the Club', following receipt of a character reference from 'Miss C. Stapleton': see COM 1/1, pp. 59, 64, and brief for prosecution and other legal documents in Legal Box. Her sentence of transportation was commuted to imprisonment at Newgate, where she conducted herself well, serving as a nurse. At the age of seventy she was given a free pardon on 1 August 1832. (Thanks are due to Dr John Simpson for these last details.) The General Committee resolved to have 'Athenæum' engraved on the plate, instead of 'Society', in December 1824: ibid., p. 97. Silver marked 'The Society' was stolen by the under butler thirty-six years later, see 25 April 1865: COM 1/19, p. 266.

45. COM 1/1, fol. 26v.

46. On Magrath see pp. 49–52.

47. COM 1/1, fol. 23v.

48. Ibid., p. 21.

49. MEM 1/1, pp. 1–25. The first candidate, R.W. Pilkington Esq., Whitehall, Architect, was entered on 30 June 1824 and elected two weeks later, on 13 July, together with another nine members whose names are not in the book. The General Committee further resolved that its members were not to propose or second names entered in the 'Ballotting Book': COM 1/1, p. 28. A bill for 'ballotting boxes' was approved for payment on 11 August 1824: ibid., p. 41. The earliest balloting certificates are lost.

50. On 20 July 1824 it was resolved that there would be no ballot until 'after the 600 Members of which the Club is to consist are nominated by the Committee, and that there shall be a Ballott as vacancies may occur after that Time': ibid., p. 31. Yet even when the membership stood at 900, in December 1824, five new members were elected by the Committee rather than by ballot when five vacancies occurred: ibid., p. 98.

51. Heber had the best attendance record at the General Committee in the twelve months from 16 February 1824: 42 meetings, compared with other leading members such as Colebrooke

(26), Young (25), Burton (24), Locker (22), Lawrence (20), the Bishop of Carlisle (20), Croker (17) and Davy (16). Heber also attended almost every meeting of the Building Committee. Some members of the General Committee attended only once or twice, presumably when their candidates came up for election: COM 1/1.
52. Ibid., p. 47.
53. COM 1/16, p. 28.
54. Among the leading lawyers elected in the 1820s and 1830s were five of the six counsel in the Norton-Melbourne case of 1836: Sir William Follett (elected 1830), Richard Crowder (1826), Sir John Campbell (the Attorney General, 1824), Serjeant Thomas Noon Talfourd (1837) and Frederic Thesiger (1834).
55. Frederick Warner, 'The engineer in society', in Fernández-Armesto, pp. 139–44 (p. 140). Isambard Kingdom Brunel was elected in 1830 and Robert Stephenson in 1840. William Cubitt, elected in 1832 under Rule II, proposed a special swing door between the kitchens and the coffee room, but was turned down on the advice of Burton: COM 1/4, p. 186.
56. Peter A. Sabine, 'Geological science and the early years of the Athenæum', in Fernández-Armesto, pp. 111–26 (p. 112).
57. Lyell donated the second volume of his *Principles of Geology* to the library in January 1832: COM 1/4, pp. 112–13.
58. Ibid., p. 114.
59. *National Portrait Gallery of Illustrious and Eminent Personages of the Nineteenth Century, with Memoirs, by William Jerdan*, 4 vols (Fisher,, Jackson, 1830–4), vol. III, p. 1. (Each memoir has individual pagination, indicative of part publication.)
60. Archibald Geikie, *Life of Sir Roderick I. Murchison, based on his Journals and Letters*, 2 vols (Murray, 1875), vol. I, p. 199.
61. The busy Whewell complained that a club servant 'refused to send for a Coach in less than a quarter of an hour': COM 1/4, p. 235.
62. See George Peacock, *Life of Thomas Young, M.D., F.R.S., &c., and one of the eight Foreign Associates of the National Institute of France* (Murray, 1855).
63. The Library Committee was to build up a fine collection of Egyptology.
64. See David Thomson, 'John Wilson Croker (1780–1857), the club's founder: a littérateur in politics', in Fernández-Armesto, pp. 147–62 (p. 153).
65. See Peacock, *Life of Young*, p. 364.
66. In 2016 Julia Elton, a member, donated an undated letter from South endorsed 'Athenæum'.
67. South also donated his 'charges against the Royal Society': COM 1/3, pp. 251, 259.
68. James South, *Refutation of the Numerous Mistatements and Fallacies contained in a Paper presented to the Admiralty by Dr. Thomas Young (Superintendant of the Nautical Almanac), and printed by Order of the House of Commons, dated 17th March, 1829* (Moyes, 1829), pp. 8–9, 15.
69. See p. 53.
70. *The Life of the Rev. Joseph Blanco White, written by Himself; with Portions of his Correspondence*, ed. John Hamilton Thom, 3 vols (Chapman, 1845), vol. I, p. 431. Philip Bury Duncan, fellow of New College, was an original member. No other Duncan of the period is recorded.
71. Ibid., vol. I, pp. 436–38.
72. In contrast, the compilers of the history of 'The Club', founded by Sir Joshua Reynolds and Dr Johnson, could cite detailed descriptions of discussions there from Lord Carlisle's diary: see Reginald Welby et al., *Annals of The Club, 1764–1914* (The Club, 1914), pp. 59–74.
73. White wrote to a fellow member, John Allen, from the Athenæum, on 11 March 1831, asking him to read his statement to the electors of a fellowship of Dulwich College and the situation of organist for which he had applied: ibid., vol. I, pp. 473–74.
74. John Morley, *The Life of William Ewart Gladstone*, 3 vols (London and New York: Macmillan, 1903), vol. II, p. 248. Like Gladstone's home at Hawarden, St David's is in Wales.
75. *Letters, Literary and Theological, of Connop Thirlwall, late Lord Bishop of St. David's*, ed. J.J. Stewart Perowne and Louis Stokes (Bentley, 1881), p. 54.
76. Ibid., p. 77.

77. Henry Crabb Robinson, *Diary, Reminiscences, and Correspondence*, ed. Thomas Sadler, 2nd edn, 3 vols (Macmillan, 1869), vol. II, p. 275.
78. Ibid., vol. II, pp. 275, 312.
79. Ibid., vol. II, p. 293. Murchison recalled that 'little home dinners of twelve or fourteen were frequent, Heber or Davy often presiding, particularly the former': Geikie, *Life of Murchison*, vol. I, p. 199.
80. 23 November 1824: COM 1/1, p. 78.
81. COM 20/1. Brooks's had 230 MPs in 1832–35, and 109 MPs were members of both the Athenæum and Brooks's, 1832–68: see *Brooks's 1764–2014: The story of a Whig club*, ed. Charles Sebag-Montefiore and Joe Mordaunt Crook (Brooks's, 2013), pp. 41, 45.
82. COM 1/1, p. 151. The ballot was rerun a week later.
83. Ibid., p. 165. This has been attributed to the lateness of the hour, between 9.00 p.m. and 10.30 p.m.: Ward, pp. 28–29. The Rules and Regulations stated that at least twenty members must vote. Ballot certificates for 1826 have survived: voting numbers are rarely under fifty and sometimes over one hundred: see MEM 1/1.
84. Certificates 92 and 93 in MEM 1/1.
85. Ordered by the General Committee on 12 July 1825: COM 1/1, pp. 161–62.
86. Ibid., p. 193.
87. See p. 84.
88. COM 1/1, p. 199.
89. COM 1/2, p. 57.
90. Ibid., pp. 58–59.
91. See pp. 92–93.
92. COM 1/1, p. 42. On 17 June 1825 the committee further ordered that 'the Servants be provided with their new Liveries on the 1st of January and again on the first of June in each year and that they be allowed in addition to the dress Suits already provided a Grey Jacket and Waistcoat and Corduroy Breeches at a cost not exceeding Four pounds fifteen shillings the Suit': ibid., pp. 150–51.
93. Ibid., pp. 97, 113, 150.
94. COM 1/2, p. 16.
95. Ibid., p. 70.
96. Ward, pp. 25, 63.
97. Cowell, pp. 12–13.
98. Maxim Ganci later made a lithograph of the portrait by Eden Upton Eddis. Magrath had four sons: see letters from Elizabeth Magrath (niece) dated 1916/17 (COM 13/4, pp. 121–22, 123–24).
99. Henry Bence Jones, *The Life and Letters of Faraday*, 2 vols (Longmans, Green, 1870), vol. I, p. 58. Dr Jones was an FRS, a Rule II member of the Athenæum from 1854 and secretary of the Royal Institution (1860–73). The City Philosophical Society grew out of the scientific lectures held at John Tatum's house in Dorset Street. It was briefly closed under the Seditious Meetings Act of 1817: see Frank A.J.L. James, 'Michael Faraday, the City Philosophical Society and the Society of Arts', *RSA Journal*, 140 (February 1992), 192–99.
100. Cf. a memorandum of 1835 relating to a pension for Faraday: *Correspondence of Faraday*, vol. II, p. 245. See also loose notes by Magrath concerning Faraday's speech, tipped into his commonplace book (ST 07).
101. *Correspondence of Faraday*, vol. I, p. 422.
102. Ibid., vol. II, p. 435; cf. vol. II, p. 481. For their correspondence on the problem of the air quality in the Athenæum's new clubhouse in 1831, see p. 116. Magrath presented the Royal Institution with a cast of the Athenæum seal: see Royal Institution managers' minutes, 5 February 1827, vol. 7, p. 111. I am grateful to Professor Frank James for this information.
103. The MS was sold to the club for 2 guineas by W.H. Rodger in 1927: see COM 13/7, p. 20.

104. Magrath's commonplace book (ST/07), unnumbered pages. Frederick North, 5th earl of Guilford (1766–1827), a former MP and then governor of Ceylon, founded the Ionian Academy in Corfu in 1823 and became a member of the Athenaeum in 1825.

105. COM 1/1, pp. 151, 152. Magrath's starting salary had been £100, the same as Faraday's salary at the Royal Institution.

106. 'Good God whom shall we trust!', Scott wrote in his journal: 'Here is learning wit gaiety of temper high station in society and compleat reception everywhere all at once debased and lost by such degrading bestiality. Our passions are wild beasts.' Edgar Johnson, *Sir Walter Scott: The great unknown*, 2 vols (New York and Toronto: Macmillan, 1970), vol. II, p. 993. Heber refused to defend himself. Having returned to England in 1831, he resumed his full membership in 1832, but resigned at the end of that year: see *ODNB* and COM 1/4, pp. 105, 245.

107. With Croker in the chair, the General Committee resolved that Magrath 'be allowed a net Salary of Two hundred Pounds a year clear of all deductions and to have free Lodging in the house and his Breakfast but no other allowance whatever': COM 1/2, p. 12. During a review of staff misdemeanours in 1829, Magrath testified that he was being overcharged for food: COM 1/3, p. 36.

108. See note 98 above.

109. See also pp. 120–30.

110. Thomas Frognall Dibdin, *Reminiscences of a Literary Life*, 2 vols (Major, 1836), vol. II, p. 907. His resignation was reported in January 1825.

111. Ibid., vol. I, p. 379.

112. See first unnumbered sheet in COM 1/1.

113. Ibid., p. 14. Rose presented the sixth volume in August 1828: see COM 1/2, p. 180.

114. See COM 1/1, pp. 17, 23, 31, 94.

115. Ibid., p. 56. Purchases included the *Ecclesiastical Register* and the *Law Lists*: ibid., p. 65. Cf. lists of purchases in 1827 and 1829: COM 1/2, pp. 28, 206–7.

116. Ibid., p. 17.

117. Royal Institution transcript HD/26/J/5 of Davy Autograph Letter Signed (hereafter ALS) (Ohio State University Library Spec.Rare.MMS.2, Box 1). The paragraph was not printed.

118. Ibid., p. 181.

119. Ibid., p. 201. On newspapers in the political clubs, see Thévoz, *Club Government*, pp. 148–50.

120. 12 January 1830: COM 1/3, p. 79. An excellent account of the Athenæum's collection of portraiture, cartoons, landscapes, architectural designs, pottery, etc., was published in 2000: see Tait.

### 3 'They have built a perfect palace'

1. See Linda Colley, *Britons: Forging the nation, 1707–1837* (New Haven and London: Yale University Press, 1992), p. 215; Roy Strong, *The Spirit of Britain: A narrative history of the arts* (Pimlico, 2000), p. 502.

2. Decimus Burton's projects in Regent's Park included Cornwall and Clarence Terraces (1820–23), the Colosseum (1823–27) and his father's house, The Holme (1816–18). He also designed the 'Pimlico' arch and screen at Hyde Park Corner (1825–28).

3. See John Summerson, *Georgian London* (1945; reprint, Barrie, Jenkins, 1988), pp. 167–80.

4. See John Summerson, *The Life and Work of John Nash, Architect* (Allen, Unwin, 1980), pp. 85, 131.

5. See Joseph Mordaunt Crook, 'Metropolitan improvements: John Nash and the picturesque', in *London – World City, 1800–1840*, ed. Celina Fox (New Haven and London: Yale University Press / Museum of London, 1992), pp. 77–96 (p. 77).

6. See Ian Jenkins, ' "Athens rising near the pole": London, Athens and the idea of freedom', in Fox (ed.) *London – World City*, pp. 143–53 (p. 148).

7. See Joseph Mordaunt Crook, *The Greek Revival: Neo-classical attitudes in British architecture, 1760–1870* (Murray, 1972), pp. 34, *et passim*.
8. See John Wilson Croker, 'Lord Elgin's collection of sculptured marbles', *Quarterly Review*, 28 (January 1816), 513–47 (514). In 1822 Croker of the Admiralty encouraged any captain in the vicinity to liberate further fragments from destruction by the Turks and to charge the expenses to him: see Cowell, p. 16.
9. Croker, 'Lord Elgin's Collection', p. 513. Cf. William Haygarth, a future original member, who described the sculptures of the frieze, based on Elgin's collection, in *Greece: A poem, in three parts, with notes, classical illustrations, and sketches of the scenery* (Nicol, 1814), p. 70.
10. James Stuart and Nicholas Revett et al., *The Antiquities of Athens*, 5 vols (Nicholas, 1762–1830). Both Decimus and James Burton also subscribed to the fifth volume of this monumental source for architects and interior decorators. A copy is in the Athenæum library.
11. See Crook, *The Greek Revival*, p. 34. Four of Leake's books on Greece and Asia Minor, published before 1830, are listed in Spencer Hall's *Catalogue of the Library of the Athenæum* (Athenæum, 1845), p. 178. Hamilton, who was to be chairman of the club in 1836–37, supervised the shipping of the Marbles to England. Other examples that follow are also from Professor Crook, himself a member of the Athenæum.
12. *English Bards and Scotch Reviewers* (1809), line 509. Byron, who died before the club was founded, complained that Athens was 'infested with English people'.
13. See p. 60.
14. *An Inquiry into the Principles of Beauty in Grecian Architecture, with an Historical View of the Rise and Progress of the Art in Greece* (Murray, 1822), p. 1.
15. On the corner of Regent Street and Charles Street (now Charles II Street), north side, with a Greek Doric portico, this was the first of the post-Waterloo clubs and 'set an example of patrician reserve': Summerson, *Georgian London*, p. 238 and Fig. 128.
16. Aberdeen, *An Inquiry into the Principles of Beauty*, pp. 215–17.
17. *The Complete Poetical Works of Percy Bysshe Shelley*, ed. Thomas Hutchinson (Oxford: Oxford University Press, 1943), p. 447.
18. 'Architectural improvements in London', *Quarterly Review*, 34 (1826), 179–96 (193). Regent Street, 'with all its architectural freaks', is described as 'unquestionably the finest street in Europe': ibid., p. 191.
19. *Metropolitan Improvements; or, London in the Nineteenth Century: Displayed in a series of engravings . . . by Mr. Thos. H. Shepherd . . . with historical, topographical, and critical illustrations by James Elmes, M.R.I.A. Architect* (Jones, 1827), p. iv.
20. Aberdeen, Lawrence and Sir Charles Long (trustees); Chantrey, Hamilton and Westmacott (committee members); Taylor Combe, John Morritt, Charles Rossi and William Wilkins (members). Elgin himself joined in 1825. See Anon., *Report from the Select Committee of the House of Commons on the Earl of Elgin's Collection of Sculptured Marbles; &c.* (Murray, 1816), and Croker's review of it in the *Quarterly Review*.
21. *Short Remarks, and Suggestions, upon Improvements now Carrying on or under Consideration* (Hatchard, 1826).
22. Charles Arbuthnot (1823–27, not on the Committee), the earl of Carlisle (May–July 1827), William Sturges Bourne (1827–28), Viscount Lowther (1828–30) and George Agar-Ellis (1830–31). William Dacres Adams, a co-commissioner from 1810 to 1834, was elected to the club in 1827.
23. See Summerson, *Georgian London*, p. 191.
24. See Myron Franklin Brightfield, *John Wilson Croker* (Allen, Unwin, 1951), p. 119. Croker supported George IV in his marital difficulties and even attended him on Coronation Day in 1821, the king 'dressed in his underclothes' before robing.
25. See Christopher Simon Sykes, *Private Palaces: Life in the great London houses* (Chatto & Windus, 1985), p. 234. The prince incurred large debts improving Carlton House, where he installed Mrs Fitzherbert.
26. William Henry Pyne, *The History of the Royal Residences*, 3 vols (Dry, 1819), vol. III, p. 21.

27. See Shepherd's engraving 'The new Athenæum, Waterloo Place', in James Elmes, *London and its Environs in the Nineteenth Century*, illus. Thomas Hosmer Shepherd (Jones, 1830), vol. II, n.p. Elmes describes it as a 'splendid establishment', vol. II, p. 159.

28. 'Resolved that Mr. Hopkinson's offer be accepted provided the annual rent of the house to be built does not exceed £600' (12 April 1824): COM 1/1, fol. 17v. Hopkinson (1787–1869) married Octavia Burton in 1813. He and Croker were the first two elected trustees.

29. Ibid., p. 31.

30. See Summerson, *Georgian London*, p. 203. Locker, Lord Lansdowne and Sir Charles Long joined later.

31. See Crook, *The Greek Revival*, pp. 119–21. The building had a Greek Doric portico.

32. 21 July 1824: COM 1/1, fols 33–34. Cf. the General Committee's earlier resolutions, pp. 18–19, 26.

33. Ibid., p. 44.

34. I am grateful to Elsie Owusu, a member of the club and a professional architect, for her comments on Burton's elevations.

35. 9 November 1824: ibid., p. 73.

36. 29 November–14 December 1824: ibid., pp. 80, 83, 87–89. Sir Richard was concerned for his heirs and successors. The lowest tender was for £11,612: see 23 November 1824 (BUI 9/1).

37. 14 December 1824: COM 1/1, p. 87. See also letters from the commissioners (BUI 9/2), and Francis Henry Wollaston Sheppard, ed., *The Parish of St. James Westminster, Pt. I: South of Piccadilly*, Survey of London, 29–30 (Athlone / London County Council, 1960), vol. XXIX, pp. 386–99.

38. COM 1/1, p. 89.

39. See John Summerson, *John Nash: Architect to King George IV* (Allen, Unwin, 1935), p. 178. South Africa House, opened in 1933, was designed by Sir Herbert Baker, a member of the Athenæum since 1919. It is tempting to interpret some of the detailing as being in homage to Burton.

40. While praising Regent Street, Long thought that Nash's plan to base the design of the Academy's building on the Parthenon was 'very questionable indeed': see *Short Remarks*, p. 8.

41. 28 December 1824: COM 1/1, p. 95.

42. Photostat of ALS at Ann Arbor, dated 24 Jan. 1825, in Athenæum Library (DA 536 C94).

43. COM 1/1, pp. 118–19. By 1826 the College of Arms site had been reallocated to the Royal Academy of Literature.

44. Burton also used a similar decorative scheme elsewhere. A Panathenaic frieze by John Henning senior and junior, based on the Elgin Marbles, is on the screen at Hyde Park Corner, built shortly after this date. Henning senior had made miniature reproductions of the Marbles between 1816 and 1822: see Tait, pp. 149–56.

45. COM 20/1 (1825).

46. 'Architectural improvements in London', *Quarterly Review*, 34 (1826), 179–96 (187).

47. See Sheppard, *The Parish of St. James*, p. 386.

48. 5 December 1825: COM 1/1, p. 182.

49. February 1826: ibid., pp. 201, 204, 206. The building was later sold to the Junior USC for £15,000.

50. Croker, a regular contributor to the *Quarterly Review*, had time to write only one article for Murray between December 1825 and January 1831.

51. 2 May 1826: COM 1/1, pp. 220–21; COM 20/1 (1826).

52. Milne to Burton, 8 July 1826: BUI 9/2.

53. See Gordon Nares, 'The Athenæum', *Country Life* (6 April 1951), 1018–22. Nash's arrangement of the staircase in his USC clubhouse was unusual, being at a right angle to the entrance, in a comparatively small, almost domestic hallway. Neither the USC staircase nor its portico was from Carlton House: Wilkins's National Gallery later incorporated the portico. See Louis C. Jackson, *History of the United Service Club* (United Service Club, 1937), pp. 20–24.

54. 13 and 20 June 1826: COM 1/1, pp. 235–37. For a detailed account of subsequent events see Sheppard, *The Parish of St. James*, pp. 388–91.
55. 27 June 1826: COM 1/1, pp. 238–39.
56. 24 October 1826: COM 1/2, p. 4.
57. 25 November 1826: BUI 9/2.
58. 12 and 19 December 1826: COM 1/2, pp. 11–13. The Athenæum agreed to make their east front uniform with the USC's west front, subject to centring the entrance, adding 18 inches to the upper storey if Burton wished and having a balcony to each of the windows of the principal floor of the three fronts.
59. 5 May 1827: ibid., p. 52. With the addition of furniture, architect's fees, etc., the total cost was calculated as £34,000, which could be recovered by adding 200 members and taking out a loan to be repaid in 'little more than 5 years'. From January 1827 the Building Committee was made up of Lord Farnborough, Lord Lowther, Croker, Murdoch and William Richard Hamilton. Sir Thomas Lawrence also attended as an *ex officio* trustee.
60. COM 1/2, p. 61. The lithograph is illustrated in Tait, p. xviii.
61. 8 and 28 May 1827: ibid., pp. 55, 65; 14 May 1827 (COM 20/1), signed by Lord Spencer. Two hundred new members would be elected once the clubhouse was built and the annual subscription would rise from 5 guineas to 6 in 1828, the extra guinea going into the 'Building Fund'.
62. 16 July 1827, et seq.: BUI 9/2; COM 1/2, pp. 56–127. Hamilton acted on behalf of the Building Committee in the business. The owner of the other house, the earl of Belfast, was more accommodating, simply requesting that demolition work next door be delayed until he had moved out, on 14 March 1828: see letters of 5 and 8 March 1828 (BUI 9/2).
63. 20 March 1828: BUI 9/5.
64. COM 1/2, pp. 128–32. Nash lied when reporting that Burton had agreed to the omission of the balcony. He also claimed that he had never been consulted by the commissioners on alterations. Waugh, Ward and Cowell all ignore the row in their histories of the Athenæum, perhaps for fear of upsetting the USC, then still their neighbours in Waterloo Place. The USC historian also remains silent: see Jackson, *History of the United Service Club*, pp. 20–29.
65. 19 March 1828: COM 1/2, pp. 137–38.
66. 29 April 1828: ibid., p. 151; 12 May 1828: COM 20/1 (1828), signed by Davies Gilbert.
67. An 'intervening space of blank wall' was created: see letters of May–June 1829 (BUI 9/2).
68. 10 June 1828: COM 1/2, p. 162.
69. 6 January 1829: ibid., p. 204, et seq.; 7 February 1830: COM 1/3, p. 93.
70. 24 June–15 July 1828: COM 1/2, pp. 165–76; letter of 11 July 1828 (BUI 9/7).
71. COM 1/2, p. 168. In the 1890s, however, there is a reference to a 'bath and dressing rooms on the mezzanine storey': Waugh, p. 19.
72. 11 May 1829: COM 20/1, 1829, p. 2. Charles Barry's new Palace of Westminster was also built on shifting sands: see Caroline Shenton, *Mr Barry's War: Rebuilding the Houses of Parliament after the great fire of 1834* (Oxford: Oxford University Press, 2016). See also p. 117.
73. Henning received his second monthly payment on 31 October 1828 (BUI 9/4).
74. 'I'm John Wilson Croker, / I do as I please; / Instead of an Ice-house, / I give you – a *Frieze*': Waugh, p. 7; Cowell, p. 18.
75. 'The United Service Club', in Anon., *London Interiors: A grand national exhibition of the religious, regal, and civic solemnities, public amusements, scientific meetings, and commercial scenes of the British capital . . . with descriptions written by official authorities*, 2 vols (Mead, 1841–44), vol. I, p. 241.
76. January 1828: Letters by Decimus Burton to John Wilson Croker, politician and essayist, 1827–1857, RIBA Library, BuD/1/1/1 – BuD/1/7/13 (photocopies in Athenæum archive). On 23 December 1828 Croker and Magrath were at Belgrave Wharf, Pimlico, viewing 'statuary marble', presumably for the fireplaces: endorsed letter from Hooper to Magrath, 4 December 1828 (BUI 9/9). In January 1830 Burton arranged a meeting with Croker at the Admiralty to consider 'patterns for the cloth on the Vestibule doors': Letters by Decimus Burton to John Wilson Croker.

77. The main manufacturer was Taprell and Holland. See Gordon Nares, 'The Athenæum', *Country Life*, 6 April 1951, 1018–22 (1022). Cf. S.H., 'The Athenaeum Pall Mall, SW1', *The Antique Collector*, December 1972, 287–96. Other furniture would have been brought across from 12 Waterloo Place: see p. 35.
78. Anon., 'Athenæum club house', *Gentleman's Magazine*, 100 (April 1830), p. 351.
79. See pp. 57–58.
80. 11 May 1829: COM 20/1, p. 1.
81. Ibid., pp. 1–2.
82. Henry Crabb Robinson, *Diary, Reminiscences, and Correspondence*, ed. Thomas Sadler, 2nd edn, 3 vols (Macmillan, 1869), vol. II, pp. 416–17. On Robinson, see pp. 45–46.
83. 'Behind Henderson and one or two more there stood Macaulay', Croker's implacable enemy, according to Thomas Hay Sweet Escott in *Club Makers and Club Members* (London and Leipzig: Unwin / Inselstrasse, 1914), p. 184.
84. Robinson, vol. II, pp. 417–18. The minute reads: 'Resolved That it is expedient to leave to the discretion of the Committee the propriety of erecting a more spacious portico': COM 1/2, p. 248. 'There are, in fact, six columns, the middle columns being adjacent pairs': Cowell, p. 17.
85. Edith J. Morley, *The Life and Times of Henry Crabb Robinson* (Dent, 1935), p. 118.
86. Building Committee papers, BUI 9/2. This would allow 'the removal of the Hoard' and thus enable the formation of the 'paved carriage way'.
87. For contradictory interpretations of the portico, see *The Connoisseur's Complete Period Guides to the Houses, Decoration, Furnishing and Chattels of the Classic Periods*, ed. Ralph and L.G.C. Ramsey Edwards (The Connoisseur, 1968), pp. 1064–65, 1272. The Survey of London summarises the contrast between the two clubhouses: 'both favoured the Graeco-Roman style, but Nash inclined to Rome and Burton to Greece' (Sheppard, *The Parish of St. James*, p. 393). The frieze was painted 'parti-colour' in 1950 (COM 20/3). The ground was first painted in November 1845, but only to restore it to the original colour of the stone: BUI 1/1/1, pp. 39–40.
88. See minutes of the General Committee, 27 October 2014, 26 January 2015 (secretary's folder): the spear seems to have been added at the turn of the twentieth century.
89. 'Then opposite the mental club you'll find the regimental one': cited in R.C. Rome, *Union Club: An illustrated descriptive record of the oldest members' club in London, founded circa 1799* (Batsford, 1948), p. 34.
90. COM 1/3, pp. 18–19.
91. Ibid., p. 49.
92. Ibid., pp. 58–60.
93. Some of the club's cellarage was inherited from Carlton House. I am grateful to Tim Gosling, a member of the club and a professional furniture designer, for his comments on the interior of Burton's clubhouse.
94. On the funding of the pavement, supplied by Mr Hakewill of Lisson Grove, see COM 1/3, pp. 28–9.
95. 'Hall of the Athenæum', in *London Interiors*, vol. I, p. 165.
96. A new 'mosaic Flooring' was also laid down in the autumn of 1883: see COM 1/24, p. 41.
97. Smirke had made the same architectural reference in the morning room of the Union Club, but Burton's version is considered to be more successful: see Stanley C. Ramsey, 'London clubs', *Journal of the Royal Institute of British Architects*, 29, 14 (20 May 1922), 417–36 (424).
98. These donations seem to have been regarded as something of an embarrassment: COM 1/4, pp. 152, 181, 183.
99. Captain William Allen refers to the 'now useless ventilating aperture' at each side of the staircase in a letter to the Committee dated 20 July 1854: 'Ventilation and Lighting' folder (BUI 9/7). In March 1846 Lough suggested that the Milo be presented to the Institute of the Fine Arts at Manchester, and this was agreed. In April, Lough and Sotheby's son were approached concerning the Samson, which went to the College of Surgeons: COM 1/10, pp. 31–32, 42, 45, 73.

100. Bill from Sarti dated 24 April 1830 (BUI 9/4). Each cast cost 8 guineas. Cf. Charles Wild, 'The hall of entrance: Carlton House' and 'The lower vestibule', in Pyne, *The History of the Royal Residences*, vol. III, facing pp. 13, 52; cf. also Jenkins, 'Athens rising near the pole', in Fox, p. 146.

101. See Tait, pp. xx–xi, 160–61. These casts were readily available to builders and decorators at the time.

102. *London Interiors*, vol. I, p. 166.

103. See pp. 161–64 and p. 276. Bruce Boucher gives a detailed account in 'Antiquity writ large: Alma-Tadema, Poynter and the redecoration of the Athenæum', in Fernández-Armesto, pp. 55–73.

104. Commentators are equally divided between Athena and Minerva in the identification of Baily's statue over the portico.

105. *London Interiors*, p. 168.

106. New research in 1987 is reported by Boucher in Fernández-Armesto, p. 56.

107. *London Interiors*, p. 125.

108. See Inventory, 1830–39 (BUI 8/1), fol. 15, where twelve mahogany chairs are listed; COM 1/4, p. 101; COM 1/5, p. 134. Also see Anon., 'Athenæum club house', 351.

109. See Second Schedule in the contract between the trustees and the contractors, dated 3 June 1828.

110. *London Interiors*, p. 167.

111. Second Schedule, n.p.

112. Burton and his father also donated fine architectural books in February 1830: COM 1/3, p. 90.

113. January–February 1830 (BUI 9/4), supplementary envelope. It seems to have been Lawrence who favoured the Apollo over an earlier proposal for a Demosthenes. The clock with two number VIIs was added later.

114. COM 1/4, p. 17. The Rennie was later presented to the South Kensington Museum and the space filled with a sofa – 1 August 1865: COM 1/19, p. 294; SEC 1/5, pp.113–15.

115. *London Interiors*, p. 125.

116. Ibid.

117. See Tim Gosling and Emma Crichton-Miller, *London Secrets: A draughtsman's guide* (Endeavour, 2012), p. 154.

118. COM 1/11, p. 78.

119. See General Committee decision on 31 March 1835: COM 1/5, p. 251. The collection of around 10,000 items in 1832 doubled by 1843: see pp. 120–22. Later the continued expansion of the collection led to the installation of larger and less elegant bookcases.

120. COM 1/4, pp. 270, 302; COM 1/5, pp. 129–31. The casts of Newton, Shakespeare, Milton, Locke, Johnson, Harvey, Mansfield, Bacon and Garrick in the drawing room and library each cost between £1. 0s. 0d. and £1. 10s. 0d.; 'Moulding & casting Sir J. Reynolds' cost 3 guineas, and repairing and painting Wren 12 shillings: bill from Sarti, January–February 1830 (BUI 9/4), supplementary envelope. See also John Kenworthy-Browne, *A Temple of British Worthies: The historic busts at the Athenæum*, 2nd edn, (Athenæum, 2013).

121. The decision to 'fit up' this 'South Western Room' as the 'Library and Reading Room' had been made in April 1829: COM 1/2, p. 237. After this the 'Great Room' was no longer called 'The Library'.

122. *London Interiors*, vol. I, p. 126.

123. COM 1/3, pp. 82–87, COM 1/4, pp. 44–46; 'Proceeding relating to the Picture by Sir Thomas Lawrence in the Athenæum Library 1836 & 1834' (BUI 9/7). The unfinished picture was installed in the library. By 1856 it was in the coffee room, but was soon taken down and presented to Brighton Town Council: COM 1/15, p. 196 and Tait, pp. xvii–xix. Today it is on loan to the club and hangs above the main landing.

124. *The Journal of Thomas Moore*, ed. Wilfred S. Dowden, 6 vols (Newark: University of Delaware Press; London and Toronto: Associated University Presses, 1983–91), vol. III, p. 1288.

125. Charles Blomfield, Bishop of London, is not a member: Moore has the wrong See.
126. George Jones, *Sir Francis Chantrey, R.A.: Recollections of his life, practice, and opinions* (Moxon, 1849), p. 222.
127. 'They have built a perfect palace on the site of Carlton House': see Edgar Johnson, *Sir Walter Scott: The great unknown*, 2 vols (New York and Toronto: Macmillan, 1970), vol. II, p. 1128.
128. See pp. 300–6.
129. Charles Lyell, *Life, Letters and Journals*, ed. Katharine Murray Lyell, 2 vols (Murray, 1881), vol. I, p. 263. Cf. Cowell, p. 115. Ladies' visits ended on 20 July.
130. Waugh, p. 10.
131. 'A design for the entrance to St. James Park from Carlton House Street', lithograph by Engelmann (City of London Archive, Solander box 12); Tait gives 'after J. L. Higgins', p. 140. See COM 1/3, p. 129. The source of the petition is not specified.
132. 'There is a staircase to a gallery affording a fine view of the west end of London and the Surrey Hills, but during the last few years no one has been allowed to ascend': Henry Benjamin Wheatley, *London Past and Present: Its history, associations, and traditions, based upon* The handbook of London *by the late Peter Cunningham*, 3 vols (Murray, 1891), vol. III, p. 536.
133. COM 1/3, p. 314.
134. Ibid., p. 208. The final bill was about £40: ibid., p. 221. In 1837 Burton had props placed underneath the balcony to take the weight of members and visitors when the Queen visited the City: COM 1/6, fols 155r, 157r.
135. Ibid., p. 221.
136. Ibid., p. 223.
137. Ibid., p. 225.

## 4 'The most eminent persons in the land'

1. Thomas Walker, 'Clubs', *The Original*, no. 17 (9 September 1835), 253–59 (253). Walker was elected to the Athenæum in 1829.
2. Thomas Hay Sweet Escott, *Club Makers and Club Members* (London and Leipzig: Unwin / Inselstrasse, 1914), p. 188.
3. Waugh, pp. 69–70, 83. In the hall of the National Portrait Gallery are the busts of Lord Stanhope, the driving force behind its foundation, and of Macaulay and Carlyle, who supported him. All were members of the Athenæum.
4. Edward Bulwer Lytton, *England and the English*, Knebworth edition (London and New York: Routledge, 1874), p. 281. First published in 1833, eight years after Bulwer's election to the Athenæum.
5. Annual Reports, 1824–72 (COM 20/1), 1830, p. 1.
6. COM 1/3, p. 174.
7. *The Journal of Thomas Moore*, ed. Wilfred S. Dowden, 6 vols (Newark: University of Delaware Press; London and Toronto: Associated University Presses, 1983–91), vol. III, p. 1304.
8. On Sir Henry (the sole survivor of the committee in 1870) and his son, Lord Knutsford, see p. 4.
9. Henry Holland, *Recollections of Past Life*, 2nd edn (Longmans, Green, 1872), pp. 265–66. (First edition 1870.)
10. *Journal of Thomas Moore*, vol. III, p. 1304. Robert Hunter exhibited Chang and Eng Bunker (1811–84) in 1829 and George Buckley Bolton published an account of them in 1830.
11. Ibid., vol. III, pp. 1307–8.
12. COM 1/3, p. 181. The 'Ballotting Lists' were burnt in the presence of the scrutators.
13. Holland, *Recollections*, p. 265.
14. See MEM 1/1/3. The 'Club at large' spread their votes more evenly than the special committee had done: eight of the successful candidates were proposed in 1827, nineteen in 1828, ten in 1829, twenty-seven in 1830 before 24 May, twenty-six in 1830 from 24 May to 1 June. See ibid. and MEM 1/1/1.

15. COM 1/3, pp. 209–12.
16. On Hook's friends and regular attendance, see Waugh, pp. 28–31. On Hayward, Kinglake and Chenery at the same table, see Isabella Augusta Gregory, '"Eothen" and the Athenæum Club', *Blackwood's Magazine*, 158 (July–December 1895), 797–804.
17. See Waugh, pp. 20–21.
18. See Antonia Fraser, *Perilous Question: The drama of the great Reform Bill 1832* (Weidenfeld, Nicolson, 2013).
19. See Russell Burlingham and Roger Billis, eds, *Reformed Characters: The Reform Club in history and literature – an anthology with commentary* (Reform Club, 2005), p. 12.
20. The fourth was Lord Duncannon: see ibid., p. 62.
21. In Blandford's view, any parliament that could bring in Catholic Emancipation was in need of reform.
22. See e.g. Croker's speech of 21 September 1831, *On the Question that 'The Reform Bill do Pass'* (Murray, 1831), pp. 28–29.
23. General Committee discussion on 29 April 1831: COM 1/4, pp. 15–16. The morning room windows contain forty-eight panes, but rioters are seldom this focused. A man who threw a stone through one of these windows in April 1884 served two months in gaol, with hard labour: see COM 1/24, p. 46. Servants rapidly lit candles during the attack: see eye-witness account by Thomas Courtenay (COL 3/1/2).
24. Ibid., p. 181.
25. When Queen Victoria was due to visit the City in 1837, the committee decided to repeat the illumination it had ordered for the coronation of William IV in 1831: COM 1/6, fol. 157r.
26. Ibid., p. 182.
27. *Memoir and Literary Remains of Lieutenant-General Sir Henry Edward Bunbury, Bart.*, ed. Charles J.F. Bunbury (p.p., 1868), p. 159. Bunbury was an original member of the club.
28. *A Selection from the Correspondence of Abraham Hayward, Q.C., from 1834 to 1884, with an Account of his Early Life*, ed. Henry E. Carlisle, 2 vols (Murray, 1886), vol. I, p. 178.
29. COM 1/11, pp. 33–35, 41.
30. Roy Jenkins argued that 'men of fairly quiet learning' had been 'the core of the Club' since the nineteenth century, and had 'provided the incentive for politicians, often off-shore members, none the less to feel that they were privileged to be admitted to an academy of letters': Fernández-Armesto, p. 168.
31. American visitors tended to write the fullest accounts of the clubhouse, in letters home or in journals. See e.g. George Ticknor, *Life, Letters, and Journals*, ed. George Stillman Hillard, 2 vols (Low, 1876), vol. II, pp. 144–46; Edward Lillie Pierce, *Memoir and Letters of Charles Sumner*, 4 vols (Boston: Roberts, Low, 1881–93), vol. II, pp. 18–19, 35.
32. *Punch*, 14 (January–June 1848), 107 (18 March).
33. Dated 23–24 March 1848, in *Letters of Ralph Waldo Emerson*, ed. Ralph L. Rusk, 6 vols (New York: Columbia University Press, 1939), vol. IV, pp. 42–43.
34. The same was also true of the Travellers Club. On early Athenian MPs see also Seth Alexander Thévoz, *Club Government: How the early Victorian world was ruled from London clubs* (Tauris, 2018), pp. 45–46, 58, 67–69, 74, 78. Thévoz calculates that 320 MPs were members of the Athenæum between 1832 and 1868, and that Liberals outnumbered Conservatives by about 3:2.
35. See p. 47.
36. See *Rules and Regulations for the Government of the Athenæum, with an Alphabetical List of the Members* (Athenæum, 1838): MEM 2/9.
37. 28 June 1831: COM 1/4, p. 49.
38. See ibid., p. 51 and COM 1/6, fol. 146r. The term 'recess' is used in COM 1/14, p. 282; COM 1/16, pp. 298, 351, 372; COM 1/17, p. 12.
39. *Correspondence of Hayward*, vol. I, pp. 178–79. The artist John Gilbert was knighted in 1872 and became a Rule II member of the club in 1877.

40. *George Douglas, eighth Duke of Argyll, K.G., K.T. (1823–1900): Autobiography and memoirs,* ed. Ina, dowager duchess of Argyll, 2 vols (Murray, 1906), vol. I, pp. 326–27.
41. See Waugh, pp. 31–33; Isabella Augusta Gregory, *Seventy Years: Being the autobiography of Lady Gregory,* ed. Colin Smythe (Gerrards Cross: Smythe, 1974), p. 127. Hayward's favourite spot in the drawing room was known as 'Hayward's Heath'. Frederick Locker-Lampson reported that he was 'disliked by the bulk of the members'.
42. *George Douglas,* vol. I, p. 477. Palmerston was elected to the club under Rule XII in 1859.
43. See *Letters of Richard Cobden,* ed. Anthony Howe and Simon Morgan, 4 vols (Oxford: Oxford University Press, 2007–15), vol. III, pp. xxxvii, 316–17, 364–65. Cobden had long admired the 'splendid establishment' (ibid., vol. I, p. 106) and, once elected, often collected his letters from the clubhouse while in London: ibid., vol. III, pp. 435, 447.
44. In 1848 the words 'or for Public Services' were added: COM 1/11, pp. 16–17, 28, 30. A proposal to remove the word 'eminence' was rejected, as was a proposal in 1858 that one black ball should be allowed when the Committee voted: COM 1/16, p. 16. By February 1862, however, a split vote, with a casting vote by the chairman, was followed by a show of hands to enable a 'unanimous' decision: COM 1/17, pp. 32–33.
45. See e.g. pp. 117, 119.
46. COM 1/4, pp. 11, 17. Notice of the special business was sent out to committee members in advance.
47. COM 20/1, 1831, p. 1.
48. 19 and 26 January 1847: COM 1/10, pp. 194, 198.
49. MEM 1/1/7. Ruskin's letter of thanks to Milman was presented to the club in 1942: COM 13/10, p. 215.
50. COM 1/10, p. 157.
51. Ibid., p. 194.
52. Joseph Mordaunt-Crook, 'Locked out of paradise: blackballing at the Athenæum, 1824–1935', in Fernández-Armesto, pp. 19–30 (p. 25).
53. Henry Manning's case was exceptional. He failed to be elected in 1842 when proposed under Rule II as an Anglican Archdeacon, but succeeded in 1870 as Cardinal Archbishop of Westminster: see p. 150.
54. See *The Letters of Sydney Smith,* ed. Nowell C. Smith, 2 vols (Oxford: Clarendon, 1953), vol. II, pp. 620 (Sir Robert Wilmot-Horton, elected 1824), 687, 756, 776, 785 (Dickens, 1838), 687–88 (Grote, 1838), 737 (Elphinstone, 1824), 745 (Murchison, 1824), 751–52 (the earl of Ellesmere, 1825), 762 (Sir George Philips, 1824), 782 (Whewell, 1824), 843 (Dr Arnold, 1825; Stanley, 1838; Horace Twiss, 1824). A member who knew Smith said that he tended to 'strain after effect', whereas Hook's jests were spontaneous: see Waugh, p. 30.
55. See Phyllis Grosskurth, *John Addington Symonds: A biography* (Longman, 1964), pp. 33–37. Her guilty verdict is challenged by Trevor Park in *'Nolo Episcopari': A life of Charles John Vaughan, 1816–1897* (St Bees: St Bega, 2013). Vaughan was originally proposed for membership by Arthur Stanley on 25 March 1854 (MEM 1/1/9) and was elected under Rule II for his eminence in 'classical attainments and for his high ability in conducting the Great Educational Establishment now under his charge': COM 20/1.
56. Dr Vaughan, Dean of Llandaff (1879–97), is no. 38 in *Ballot Day 1892* (see p. xviii).
57. COM 1/15, p. 255. When the ubiquitous Soapy Sam Wilberforce recommended the purchase of a 'Reading Desk invented by the Revd. A. Noel, sold at Messrs Browns, No. 5, Piccadilly, price £4', the idea was approved: COM 1/16, p. 64.
58. Edward Forbes was elected later, in 1845, under Rule II, and served on the General Committee.
59. See the *Hindu,* 2 June 2013 (online). Some of Christie's papers are in the National Library of Scotland (MSS 9, 490–97).
60. 26 April 1831: COM 1/4, pp. 15–16.
61. COM 20/1, 1840, p. 1. Mantell was also an obstetrician.

62. Gideon Mantell, *A Descriptive Catalogue of the Objects of Geology, Natural History, and Antiquity, (chiefly Discovered in Sussex,) in the Museum, attached to the Sussex Scientific and Literary Institution at Brighton*, 6th edn (Relfe, Fletcher, 1836).

63. Lytton, *England and the English*, p. 293.

64. Ibid., p. 298.

65. See p. 17.

66. See Ernest Barker, *The Character of England* (Oxford: Clarendon, 1947), p. 273.

67. See *The Record of the Royal Society of London for the Promotion of Natural Knowledge*, 4th edn (Royal Society, 1940), pp. 349–50.

68. Members of the Athenæum also 'played a significant role in reaching towards and then achieving the Licence in Dental Surgery of the Royal College of Surgeons which gave the profession legal status': Malcolm Bishop, 'The Athenæum Club, the Royal Society and the reform of dentistry in nineteenth-century Britain: a research report', *Notes and Records of the Royal Society*, 71, 1 (March 2017), 61–70 (61).

69. Thomas Joseph Pettigrew, *Medical Portrait Gallery: Biographical memoirs of the most celebrated physicians, surgeons, etc. etc. who have contributed to the advancement of medical science*, 4 vols (Fisher, 1838–40). Each portrait is numbered individually, indicating serial publication.

70. See p. 14.

71. Frank Buckland, son of William and elected in 1854, bequeathed his own father's skull to the Royal College of Surgeons. See Noel Annan, *The Dons: Mentors, eccentrics and geniuses* (HarperCollins, 1999), p. 38.

72. Bransby Blake, *The Life of Sir Astley Cooper, Bart., interspersed with Sketches from his Notebooks of Distinguished Contemporary Characters*, 2 vols (Parker, 1843), vol. II, pp. 385, 444–45.

73. Ibid., vol. II, pp. 322–24.

74. See Philip Henry Stanhope, *Notes on Conversations with the Duke of Wellington, 1831–1851*, 2nd edn (Murray, 1888), p. 271.

75. C.H. Philips, *The East India Company, 1784–1834* (Manchester: Manchester University Press, 1940), p. 290.

76. 20 January 1846: COM 1/10, p. 6.

77. 22 November 1859: COM 1/16, p. 242. Later generations of senior India hands included Sir Bartle Frere (elected 1858 II), Lord Lawrence (1860 II), Major-General Sir Herbert Edwardes (1864 II), Lord Bulwer-Lytton (1874 II), Sir Alfred Lyall (1878 II), Sir Richard Temple (1879) and Sir Mortimer Durand (1896). On Lord Ripon (1862 II), Lord Dufferin (1864 II), Sir Garnet Wolseley (1876 II), Sir William Wilson Hunter (1888), General 'Bobs' Roberts (1881 II) and Lord Lansdowne (1890), see p. 4.

78. See pp. 100–1, 126–27, 128–29.

79. Richard Ford wrote the 'Hand-Book for Spain'; A.H. Layard was 'Commissioner for the Boundary Line between Turkey and Persia' and 'Discoverer of the Ruins in Assyria'; Hugh Falconer, MD, 'in addition to his acknowledged merits as a Botanist', was 'eminently distinguished for his knowledge of the Fossil Zoology of Northern India'; and Lieutenant-Colonel Sir Thomas Livingstone Mitchell was 'eminently distinguished as a Scientific Traveller, and also for his Discoveries in Australia': COM 20/1, 1848, p. 1.

80. Alexander William Kinglake, *Eothen*, ed. H. Gorvett Smith (Dent, 1927), p. 18. Kinglake's inkstand was presented to the club in 1962: see COM 1/35, pp. 27–28.

81. Ibid., p. 155. In Damascus, Kinglake walked on a raised path 'as free and unmolested as if [he] had been in Pall Mall': ibid., p. 257.

82. See p. 175.

83. Kinglake, *Eothen*, p. 178.

84. Spencer Hall, *A Catalogue of the Library of the Athenæum* (Athenæum, 1845), p. 195.

85. 13 July 1830: COM 1/3, p. 209. Cf. Hall, *Catalogue of the Library*, pp. 144–45.

86. See Hall, *Catalogue of the Library*, p. 300.

87. See ibid., pp. 69, 90.

88. See MEM 1/1/1, candidate 343, 1 March 1826. Clapperton was seconded by Denham.
89. See *ODNB*.
90. Lady Franklin and her friends were allowed to watch the inauguration of the statue from the clubhouse balcony on 15 November 1866: COM 1/19, p. 367.
91. For an overview of 'The Athenæum and the military', see Michael Howard's chapter in Fernández-Armesto, pp. 269–79: 33 of the first 506 members elected 'could claim military or naval rank; not a high proportion, but for the most part men of high distinction' (p. 269). The military membership of the club 'thereafter dwindled, although Club lists show that, in addition to naval and military members of the medical profession, some 170 service officers were elected before 1912, and 147 between 1913 and 1945'. Of these some 80 were elected under Rule II (pp. 276–77).
92. See p. 128.
93. COM 1/7, p. 153.
94. See David Alec Wilson, *Carlyle at Threescore-and-ten (1853–1865)* (London: Paul; New York: Dutton, 1929), pp. 32–33.
95. See Ciaran Brady, *James Anthony Froude: An intellectual biography of a Victorian prophet* (Oxford: Oxford University Press, 2013), pp. 210–11.
96. See also p. 138.
97. Lytton, *England and the English*, p. 221.
98. COM 1/7, pp. 7–8. In 1861 Darwin commented that, if the committee were to elect half of the 100 additional members then proposed, the 'standard of Club' would be raised: see *The Correspondence of Charles Darwin*, ed. Frederick Burkhardt, Sydney Smith et al. (Cambridge: Cambridge University Press, 1985–), vol. IX, p. 20.
99. See MEM 1/1/5 and George Philo, 'Dickens and the Forty Thieves', in Fernández-Armesto, pp. 41–51.
100. Ibid., pp. 14–29. Committee members were sent lists on which they were to mark possible candidates. The resulting shortlist was then brought to the special meeting.
101. Sir Thomas Fowell Buxton MP, William Wilberforce's close colleague in the abolition campaign, was also elected in 1825.
102. David Newsome, *The Parting of Friends: A study of the Wilberforces and Henry Manning* (Murray, 1966), p. 244. The book was duly donated, but Samuel's cause was not helped by Robert's name alone being listed as author and donor: COM 20/1, 1839, p. 7.
103. See MEM 1/1/5.
104. John Wilson Croker, 'Life of Wilberforce', *Quarterly Review*, 62, 123 (June 1838), 214–85. Croker considered that the selection of private papers, some of which contained 'twaddle', lacked taste (219).
105. Newsome, *The Parting of Friends*, p. 245.
106. See David Newsome, *Historical Vignettes*, ed. Serenhedd James (p.p., 2011), p. 126.
107. Cooper died on 18 August 1853 from a large haemorrhage caused by cancer of the throat.
108. Philippa Levine, *The Amateur and the Professional: Antiquarians, historians and archaeologists in Victorian England, 1838–1886* (Cambridge: Cambridge University Press, 1986), p. 11.
109. Alan Moorehead, *Darwin and the Beagle* (Hamilton, 1969), pp. 39, 86–87, 153.
110. MEM 1/1/5. Darwin was seconded by Henry Holland. For the impact of Darwin's 'doctrine' on the Club, see pp. 134, 136.
111. *Correspondence of Darwin*, vol. II, p. 97.
112. 26 July 1842: COM 1/8, p. 271.
113. See Philo in Fernández-Armesto, pp. 46–47.
114. Four of the fourteen men whose stories are told in *Men who have Risen: A book for boys*, ed. James Hogg (1859) were members of the Athenæum, elected in 1824–25: Peel, Davy, Franklin and Eldon.
115. COM 1/10, pp. 214–15, 231, 259, 262.

116. See Marion Harry Spielmann, *The History of 'Punch'* (Cassell, 1895), pp. 318–19, and complaints book, 1834–76 (CAT 2/1).
117. *Punch*, 13 (July–December 1847), 193 (20 November).
118. 29 January 1850: COM 1/11, p. 229. Also present were Mahon, Badely, Blore, Broderip, Fellows, Hawkins, Jelf, Charles Edward Long, George Long, Lyell, Macaulay, Milman, Prior, Stanfield and Robert Stephenson.
119. *The Letters and Private Papers of William Makepeace Thackeray*, ed. Gordon N. Ray, 4 vols (Oxford: Oxford University Press, 1945–46), vol. II, p. 636n. Milman's counting was awry.
120. Ibid., vol. II, pp. 636–37.
121. 25 February 1851: COM 1/12, pp. 135.
122. See *Letters of Thackeray*, vol. II, p. 754; MEM 1/1/2.
123. See Peter Ackroyd, *Dickens* (Sinclair-Stevenson, 1990), p. 246; *Dickens's Journalism*, ed. Michael Slater, 4 vols (Dent: 1996–2000), vol. III, pp. 411–12.

## 5 'A score of grave gentlemen'

1. Letter to William Bradford Reed, 14 February 1853: *The Letters and Private Papers of William Makepeace Thackeray*, ed. Gordon N. Ray, 4 vols (Oxford University Press, 1945–46), vol. III, p. 201.
2. *The Works of William Makepeace Thackeray*, 26 vols (Smith, Elder, 1894–98), vol. XXIII, p. 60.
3. See p. 70.
4. 'The Athenæum', in Anon., *London Interiors: A grand national exhibition of the religious, regal, and civic solemnities, public amusements, scientific meetings, and commercial scenes of the British capital . . . with descriptions written by official authorities* (Mead, 1841–44), vol. I, p. 126.
5. Thomas Walker, 'Clubs', *The Original*, no. 17 (9 September 1835), 253–59 (254–55).
6. Ibid., 256–57.
7. See p. 100.
8. 15 February 1831: COM 1/3, p. 296. 145 members voted at the 1866 AGM: COM 1/19, p. 336. The average number voting at each ballot 1859–67 was 188 members: COM 1/19, pp. 433–34, cf. COM 1/20, pp. 21–22.
9. COM 1/16, p. 42. In a chapter on 'Club snobs' (*Punch*, 1847), Thackeray describes how old Brown hogs five newspapers while also demanding *Punch*: *Works of Thackeray*, vol. XIV, p. 161. A shocking report of a member cutting a paragraph out of a newspaper was 'laid before the Committee' on 23 July 1861: COM 1/17, p. 6.
10. See Paul Thompson, *William Butterfield* (Routledge, Kegan Paul, 1971), p. 15.
11. Saba Holland, *A Memoir of the Reverend Sydney Smith, by his Daughter, Lady Holland, with a Selection from his Letters*, ed. Mrs Austin, 3rd edn, 2 vols (Longman, 1855), vol. II, pp. 423, 480; 'Report on Replies to Circular 29th Jan. 1861': COM 1/16, pp. 389–90.
12. The locks were removed in 1869 after two members left for a levée with the keys to two rooms, thus excluding fellow members: COM 1/20, p. 40.
13. 'The United Service Club', in *London Interiors*, vol. I, p. 249.
14. 'A Pailful of Fragments was taken up in the Drawing Room and Balcony the next morning.' 10 July 1838: COM 1/7, pp. 44–45.
15. 3 August 1858: COM 1/16, p. 57.
16. 7 June 1859: ibid., p. 181.
17. 12 July–9 August 1859: ibid., pp. 185, 188, 198, 210.
18. *ODNB*.
19. 16 July 1844: COM 1/9, p. 156.
20. 23 Jul 1833: COM 1/5, p. 22.
21. See e.g. 12 March 1838: COM 1/6, fol. 186r.
22. See e.g. 23 December 1845: COM 1/9, p. 372.

23. In 1859 the Committee received a complaint that the coffee was being filtered through a flannel bag: COM 1/16, p. 114. In 1923 an 'up to date coffee urn' was purchased, following complaints: COM 13/6, p. 15. In 2013 coffee machines of a high specification were introduced.
24. See Waugh, pp. 39, 24; Cowell, p. 95. In 1840 Guizot had dinner with Lansdowne, Aberdeen, Stanhope, Northampton, Houghton, Monteagle, Macaulay, Milman, Holland, Senior, Hallam and Palgrave.
25. Waugh, p. 40.
26. *Works of Thackeray*, vol. XIV, pp. 180–81.
27. 12 April 1831: COM 1/4, p. 9.
28. See Ward, pp. 61–62.
29. See COM 1/3, pp. 117, 181, 201, 230, and on thefts see e.g. COM 1/6, fols 48v–49r (with reward notice), fol. 60r–60v, 62r–62v. West End clubs were vulnerable to thefts: see e.g. *Illustrated London News*, 2 (January–June 1843), 173, and p. 00.
30. See e.g. COM 1/6, p. 119 and COM 1/9, pp. 98–99.
31. See COM 1/16, pp. 367, 374, 398.
32. 26 May 1835: see COM 1/5, p. 278.
33. 24 November 1840: COM 1/7, p. 377.
34. 28 January 1845: COM 1/9, p. 220. William Calcutt died in Lambeth in January 1845. On Mangles, see *ODNB*.
35. COM 20/1, 1855, p. 1, and e.g. 7 December 1841: COM 1/8, p. 154.
36. Walker, p. 258.
37. Denis Smith, 'The building services', in *The Houses of Parliament*, ed. Michael Harry Port (New Haven and London: Paul Mellon Centre / Yale University Press, 1976), pp. 218–31 (p. 218).
38. COM 1/3, pp. 295–96; cf. *The Correspondence of Michael Faraday*, ed. Frank A.J.L. James, 6 vols (Institution of Engineering and Technology, 1991–2012), vol. I, pp. 547–48 for the printed version, with this additional statement: 'I have no hesitation in believing that the cause of these complaints might be removed by extending and adjusting the system of ventilation in those rooms.'
39. 15 February 1831: COM 1/3, p. 297.
40. See COM 1/5, p. 65; cf. drawing no. 22 in Athenæum Plans Miscellaneous; COM 1/5, pp. 114, 276.
41. See ibid., p. 219 and pp. 64 and 68.
42. 19 February 1833: COM 1/4, p. 278.
43. The description of Barry begins, 'The successfull [sic] Candidate for the prize plan of the new house of Parliament': COM 1/6, fol. 44r. Brande, first elected in 1824, resigned on 19 February 1833: COM 1/4, p. 278.
44. 29 March 1836: COM 1/6, fol. 45v.
45. *Questions proposed by the Committee of the Athenæum to Mr. Faraday, on Lighting and Ventilation, with the Answers: Originally printed 14th February, 1831*, dated 26 April 1836: 'Ventilation and Lighting' folder (BUI 9/7).
46. 21 June 1836: COM 1/6, fols 66v–67v.
47. 12 July 1836: ibid., fol. 73r.
48. Ibid.; COM 20/1, 1837, p. 3; paper in Burton's hand, 'Ventilation and Lighting' folder (BUI 9/7).
49. 30 July 1836: *Correspondence of Faraday*, vol. II, pp. 368–69. Cf. 'Messrs Faraday, Gas Fitters to the Club', 22 May 1860: COM 1/16, p. 317.
50. 24 September 1837: COM 1/6, fol. 153v.
51. COM 20/1, 1839, p. 1. Cf. 30 April 1839: COM 1/7, p. 148.
52. Inserted in COM 7/2.
53. Letter to Magrath dated 22 March 1841: ibid.
54. Entered as a candidate on 14 April and elected 24 April: MEM 1/1/5; COM 20/1, 1838, p. 1. Aikin's letter on the impregnation of leather with acid was read to the Library Committee on 26 March 1841: COM 7/2, pp. 62–63.

55. See 30 July 1842: COM 7/2, pp. 93–94; 2 August 1842: COM 1/8, p. 274.
56. Copies are in COM 1/8, p. 274–75 and COM 1/9, pp. 12–13.
57. 12 September 1843: COM 1/8, p. 33.
58. COM 20/1, 1844, p. 1. The cost of Faraday's burners was £359. 19s. 6d. (p. 3).
59. Port, *The Houses of Parliament*, p. 228; cf. also pp. 229–31. In July 1874 the air in the Commons chamber was cooled by passing it over one ton of ice per night at a cost of £20 per week: see *Punch*, 67 (July–December 1874), 33 (25 July).
60. The ventilation system, plus 'necessary repairs' and 'new furniture' and 'alterations', had been projected as £4,500 for the year to 8 May 1837, but actually cost over £8,000: COM 20/1, 1837, p.1.
61. See p. 103.
62. I am grateful to Peter Urbach, lately honorary archivist of the Reform Club, for showing me the furnace area, vents and controls, now disconnected.
63. See George Walter Thornbury and Edward Walford, *Old and New London: A narrative of its history, its people, and its places*, 6 vols (1873–78; reprint, Cassell, n.d.), vol. IV, p. 137.
64. See Cowell, p. 24.
65. 'Ventilation and Lighting' folder (BUI 9/7).
66. Samuel Jones Loyd, Baron Overstone, was a wealthy banker who advised governments on monetary policy. Elected in 1829 and a trustee 1857–83, he was also a member of The Club and the Political Economy Club, founded in 1821 by James Mill and other future members of the Athenæum.
67. 'Ventilation and Lighting' folder (BUI 9/7).
68. COM 20/1, 1859, p. 1.
69. 16 February 1830: COM 1/3, pp. 100.
70. 8 June 1830: ibid., pp. 190–91.
71. Cf. the circular of January 1830, p. 54.
72. The first meeting was on 20 July 1830: see COM 7/1. The committee had five members by 1831 and ten by 1838.
73. COM 20/1, 1835, p. 1.
74. 14 December 1830: COM 1/3, pp. 263, 282–85.
75. COM 20/1, 1832, p. 5.
76. Ibid., 1833, pp. 4–6.
77. 31 January 32: COM 1/4, p. 116.
78. E.g. Henry Hallam, specially thanked for the 'valuable books' that he donated, on 12 October 1841: COM 1/8, pp. 121–23, 128; cf. COM 20/1, 1842, pp. 5–7. John Gould, elected under Rule II in 1854, donated some of his famous and very valuable birds of the world series.
79. 17 January 1832: COM 1/4, p. 108. The grant went down to £400 per annum in the 1860s.
80. See e.g. 11 June 1844: COM 1/9, p. 142. Over 8 cwt of waste paper was sold for 10 guineas.
81. 3 May 1831: COM 1/4, p. 21.
82. 6 March 1832: ibid., p. 135; 20 May 1851: COM 1/12, pp. 188, 194. The librarian of the day, Richard Lambert, was still anxious about the safety of the arrangement in 1926: see COM 13/6, pp. 149–50.
83. 29 April 1834: COM 1/5, p. 129; COM 20/1, 1838, p. 1.
84. See Almeric FitzRoy, *History of the Travellers' Club* (Travellers Club / Allen, Unwin, 1927), p. 136. Cf. George Woodbridge, *The Reform Club, 1836–1978* (p.p., 1978), pp. 102–3.
85. A little after 5 a.m. on 24 October 1850, 'Smith the Groom of the Chambers at the Travellers Club made his way at some risk from the roof of that Club to the roof of the Athenæum and having aroused the Servants, informed them that the adjoining Club was on Fire, & by doing so the inevitable destruction of at least a part of this House was prevented': COM 1/12, p. 66. A 'light Iron bridge' was later constructed as a fire escape.
86. 1 March 1853: COM 1/13, pp. 116–17, cf. p. 138.

87. Anon., *Statement in Elucidation of the Plans for the Enlargement of the Club House, to be submitted to the Consideration of the Extraordinary General Meeting on Thursday, 13th March, 1856* (p.p., 1856), p. 10: see Athenæum Plans Miscellaneous.
88. *Athenæum: A letter to the Committee from Mr. Decimus Burton, on the subject of plans for altering the house* (p.p., 17 July 1854), p. 2.
89. Ibid., p. 6. Both a bookstore and a second reading room were considered.
90. Letter dated 20 July 1854: 'Ventilation and Lighting' folder (BUI 9/7). Members continued to make suggestions in subsequent decades: see e.g. February 1884, COM 1/24, p. 34.
91. *A Letter to the Committee*, p. 15.
92. 29 May 1855: COM 1/14, pp. 138–40; 12 June 1855: ibid., pp. 250–51.
93. Extraordinary General Meeting, 13 March 1856: COM 1/15, pp. 36–37.
94. 1 April 1856: ibid., pp. 47–48.
95. The 'Library Sub-Committee for eliminating Books' was allowed to co-opt any member 'to whom they may think it expedient to depute any given section of the Catalogue', again a practice followed to this day in 'subject reviews' – 30 May 1865: COM 1/19, pp. 278, 280.
96. 9 May 1856: COM 1/15, pp. 73–74. 'The erection of the additional gallery in the South Library has enabled the Committee to carry into effect the long-desired classification of the valuable collection of books possessed by the Club; the number of volumes of which is computed at 31,433': COM 20/1, 1857, p. 1. It would take more than forty years for the clubhouse to get its extra storey: see p. 164–66.
97. COM 7/1. Daly was to be paid an extra £20 a year 'for his services as Librarian', making his wages £80.
98. 9 and 15 January 1833: COM 1/4, pp. 250, 254.
99. 19 March 1833: ibid., p. 273.
100. See 12 March 1838: COM 1/6, fol. 186r.
101. See 17 January 1833: COM 1/4, pp. 257–58; 24 July 1838: COM 1/7, pp. 56–57; 28 June 1842: COM 1/8, pp. 260–61.
102. 12 July 1831: COM 1/4, p. 50.
103. Estimates for 'altering the Bell Pulls in the Library' were examined on 29 November 1831: ibid., p. 90. Cf. also COM 20/1, 1832, p. 1.
104. 18 July 1843: COM 1/9, p. 12.
105. *Works of Thackeray*, vol. XIV, pp. 194–95.
106. Bunbury's obituary in *The Times* recorded that, 'as he got animated and excited he would gasp in his talk, and incident and reminiscence would crowd fast on each other, till he was almost apt to lose himself in a labyrinth of entertaining digressions' (*ODNB*).
107. 11 June 1850: COM 1/12, pp. 5–6.
108. See e.g. 7 February 1832, when 'a List of Books missing from the Library and of those also missing from the circulating Library was laid on the Table': COM 1/4, p. 121. On French novels see e.g. 2 June 1840: COM 1/7, p. 323–24. In *The Book of Snobs*, Tiggs of the Sarcophagus is alone in the 'great library (225 feet long by 150)', reading a French novel by Paul de Kock: *Works of Thackeray*, vol. XIV, p. 189. In 1866 the number of volumes on loan was increased from forty to sixty and Mudie's library replaced Lawthorne and Hutt's: COM 1/19, pp. 330, 336.
109. 6 November 1832: COM 1/4, p. 224.
110. Books Lost (LIB 8/2/1). Cf. also 27 November 1838: COM 1/7, p. 88.
111. 28 January 1840: COM 1/7, pp. 245–46.
112. 11 February 1840: ibid., p. 261; see also p. 364. On book thefts by a member in 1846, see Cowell, p. 77.
113. Henry Holland, *Recollections of Past Life*, 2nd edn (Longmans, Green, 1872), p. 264.
114. 14 February 1832: ibid., p. 124. Cf. a review article on a set of transactions from some of the newly established 'literary and philosophical institutions' by Charles Lyell (1824):

'Scientific institutions', *Quarterly Review*, 34, 67 (June 1826), 153–79. When space for books was tight in 1878 a review of transactions led to the jettisoning of back numbers of only one series, that of the Institution of Civil Engineers, which were considered to be 'specially technical': COM 1/22, pp. 96–97.

115. Spencer Hall, *A Catalogue of the Library of the Athenæum* (Athenæum, 1845), pp. 369–534 ['Tracts'], 1–350 [books].

116. 25 January 1831: ibid., p. 278.

117. See pp. 103–6.

118. See p. 101.

119. On Barrow, see pp. 15, 19, 101, 127.

120. *Memoir and Literary Remains of Lieutenant-General Sir Henry Edward Bunbury, Bart.*, ed. Charles J.F. Bunbury (p.p., 1868), p. 116.

121. See *Life, Letters and Journals of Sir Charles J.F. Bunbury, Bart.*, ed. Frances Joanna Bunbury, 3 vols (p.p., 1894), vol. II, pp. 262–65, 273–76.

122. Hall, *Catalogue*, pp. 250, 349.

123. 1 February 1859: COM 1/16, pp. 122, 134, 162.

124. See Hall, *Catalogue*, pp. 271, 307, 258–60.

125. 7 June 1831: COM 1/4, p. 39.

126. See ibid., pp. 134, 171–72.

127. See Philippa Levine, *The Amateur and the Professional: Antiquarians, historians and archaeologists in Victorian England, 1838–1886* (Cambridge: Cambridge University Press, 1986), pp. 11–12, 23. The fourth variety was the professional who worked on books, antiquities and manuscripts in museums, libraries, etc.

128. See e.g. 'Ecclesiastical History' in Hall, *Catalogue*, pp. 271, 258–60, and Arundel Society publications, 23 July 1850: COM 1/11, p. 32.

129. 'Voyage' occurs 222 times in the modern Online Public Access Catalogue (OPAC), compared to 8,623 hits for 'history'.

130. *Life of Sir Charles Bunbury*, vol. I, p. 519.

131. Ibid., vol. II, p. 180.

132. See pp. 94, 98. Cf. Faraday, for whom note-taking was a natural part of the experimentation process: see James Hamilton, *Faraday: The life* (HarperCollins, 2002), p. 153. In another generation Sir Oliver Lodge, 'when reading seriously', used to 'copy things out in a notebook': *Past Years: An autobiography* (Hodder & Stoughton, 1931), p. 344.

133. Ralph Waldo Emerson, *Complete Works*, Riverside Edn, 11 vols (Routledge, 1883), vol. V, p. 241.

134. See p. 3.

135. *George Douglas, eighth Duke of Argyll, K.G., K.T. (1823–1900): Autobiography and memoirs*, ed. Ina, dowager duchess of Argyll, 2 vols (Murray, 1906), vol. II, p. 5.

136. Eleanor C. Smyth, *Sir Rowland Hill: The story of a great reform* (Unwin, 1907), pp. 237–38.

137. Ralph Nevill and Charles Edward Jerningham, *Piccadilly to Pall Mall: Manners, morals, and man* (Duckworth, 1908), p. 212.

138. Cited in Cowell, p. 58. Tedder is wrong about Eyre Crowe, who was not a member.

139. Smyth, *Sir Rowland Hill*, p. 31.


### 6 Liberal hospitality

1. See Peter Ackroyd, *Dickens* (Sinclair-Stevenson, 1990), pp. 826–27; Edmund Yates, *Mr. Thackeray, Mr. Yates, and the Garrick Club* (p.p., 1859); Patrick Leary, *The Punch Brotherhood: Table talk and print culture in mid-Victorian London* (British Library, 2010), pp. 79–109.

2. Ackroyd, *Dickens*, pp. 923–24. Cf. Percy Fitzgerald's mawkish couplets on the reconciliation in 'Boz's chair' (*St James's Gazette*, 6 March 1899): COL 3/1/1, p. 30.

3. Ackroyd, *Dickens*, pp. 937–38.

4. The other pallbearers were the earl of Carlisle, Sir David Dundas and Sir Henry Holland.

5. Archibald Geikie, *Life of Sir Roderick I. Murchison, Based on his Journals and Letters*, 2 vols (Murray, 1875), vol. II, p. 321. Murchison believed that his own 'geological postulates, if not upset, destroy [Darwin's] whole theory'.

6. See p. 132.

7. George Macaulay Trevelyan, *Sir George Otto Trevelyan: A memoir* (Longmans, Green, 1932), p. 100.

8. *Autobiography of the late Sir Benjamin C. Brodie, Bart.* (Longman, 1865), p. 109.

9. See Reginald Farrar, *The Life of Frederic William Farrar, sometime Dean of Canterbury* (Nisbet, 1904), pp. 109–10; Ruth Barton, ' "An influential set of chaps": the X Club and Royal Society politics, 1864–85', *British Journal for the History of Science*, 23 (1990), 53–81 (78, 81); Ruth Barton, *The X Club: Power and authority in Victorian science* (Chicago and London: University of Chicago Press, 2018), pp. 282–83.

10. See pp. 15–18.

11. COM 20/2, 1876, p. 1. The existing presidents continued to serve as trustees.

12. 14 March 1876: COM 1/21, pp. 461–62. Hooker, elected under Rule II in 1851, wrote to present his apologies to the meeting. He had in fact been president of the Royal Society and a member of the committee without being a trustee since 1874: ibid., p. 348. The text of Sir Michael Palin's talk on Hooker at the Athenæum (13 February 2013) is available at www.kew.org/explore-our-collections/correspondence-collections/joseph-hooker-collections/about-joseph-hooker/michael-palin-on-hooker. See also Palin's *Erebus: The story of a ship* (London: Hutchinson, 2018).

13. See Noel Gilroy Annan, *The Dons: Mentors, eccentrics and geniuses* (HarperCollins, 1999), pp. 121–26. Owens College, Manchester, was also an important scientific centre.

14. See William C. Lubenow, *The Cambridge Apostles, 1820–1914: Liberalism, imagination, and friendship in British intellectual and professional life* (Cambridge: Cambridge University Press, 1998), pp. 230–32.

15. John Kemble (1850), Henry Alford (1856), Charles Merivale (1859), Henry Maine (1862), James Clerk Maxwell (1869), James Fitzjames Stephen (1873), Henry Sidgwick (1879), Francis Balfour (1882), Samuel Butcher (1886), John Hopkinson (1887), Frederick Maitland (1896), George Macaulay Trevelyan (1910), Alfred Whitehead (1923), Lytton Strachey (1931), Maynard Keynes (1942) and Bertrand Russell (1952).

16. See Stefan Collini, *Public Moralists: Political thought and intellectual life in Britain, 1850–1930* (Oxford: Clarendon Press, 1991), pp. 13–15. Rule II elections were announced in the press.

17. Waugh, p. 56.

18. Cf. Lubenow, *The Cambridge Apostles*, pp. 20–21.

19. See p. 9. Lubbock was the eldest son of John William Lubbock, an original member.

20. Candidate 4,178, 5 February 1858, proposed by Hooker and seconded by Falconer, elected under Rule II, 29 March 1859: MEM 1/1/9.

21. Tyndall was candidate 4,325, 17 January 1859, proposed by Murchison and seconded by Thomas Bell, elected under Rule II, 31 January 1860: MEM 1/1/11.

22. Candidate 4,261, 24 June 1858, elected 27 March 1860: MEM 1/1/11.

23. I am grateful to Sir Roland Jackson, a member of the club, for drawing my attention to Hirst's diary, and to the Royal Institution for permission to quote from material in the Tyndall archive.

24. On Liberalism and the X Club, see Ruth Barton, ' "Huxley, Lubbock, and half a dozen others": professionals and gentlemen in the formation of the X Club, 1851–1864', *Isis*, 89 (1998), 410–44 (432–33), and *The X Club*, pp. 170–223.

25. *ODNB*.

26. Buckle had been entered in the Candidates Book on 17 November 1849 as a 'Private Gentlemen': candidate 3,026, MEM 1/1/8.

27. See Alfred Henry Huth, *The Life and Writings of Henry Thomas Buckle*, 2 vols (Low, 1880), vol. I, p. 251.

28. COM 1/15, p. 353; Barton, 'Huxley, Lubbock, and half a dozen others', 420; Barton, *The X Club*, p. 164. Huxley was candidate 3,755, 23 February 1853, proposed by Leonard Horner (factory inspector, geologist and educationalist) and seconded by Murchison, 23 Feb. 1853, elected under Rule II, 26 January 1858 (MEM 1/1/9; COM 1/15, p. 353), following earlier lobbying on his behalf by Hooker and Darwin: see *The Correspondence of Charles Darwin*, ed. Frederick Burkhardt, Sydney Smith et al. (Cambridge: Cambridge University Press, 1985–), vol. VI, pp. 103, 106, 112.

29. MEM 1/3/20.

30. Huth, *Life of Buckle*, vol. I, p. 252.

31. Fawcett, the blind Postmaster General and Liberal MP, who regarded himself as a Radical, was canonised by Leslie Stephen in his *Life of Fawcett*, which went into five editions in 1885.

32. Frederick Temple et al., *Essays and Reviews*, 12th edn (Longmans, 1869), p. 56.

33. See p. 6.

34. Wilberforce was a member of the Committee and chaired the AGM in 1857: COM 1/15, p. 255. See also p. 132.

35. On 1 September 1858 he complained that *Punch* and 'all the infidel and Low Church papers have set on me with full venom': Arthur Rawson Ashwell, *Life of the Right Reverend Samuel Wilberforce, D.D., Lord Bishop of Oxford and afterwards of Winchester, with Selections from his Diaries and Correspondence*, 3 vols (Murray, 1880), vol. II, p. 395. See e.g. *Punch*, 35 (July–December 1858), 87–88 (28 August). In fact he was slippery in his churchmanship: hence his sobriquet.

36. See Frank A.J.L. James, 'An "open clash between science and the Church"? Wilberforce, Huxley and Hooker on Darwin at the British Association, Oxford, 1860', in *Science and Beliefs: From natural philosophy to natural selection*, ed. D.M. Knight and M.D. Eddy (Aldershot and Burlington, VT: Ashgate, 2005), pp. 171–93.

37. See Randall Thomas Davidson and William Benham, *Life of Archibald Campbell Tait, Archbishop of Canterbury*, 2 vols (London and New York: Macmillan, 1891), vol. I, p. 280.

38. '*Essays and Reviews*', *Quarterly Review*, 109 (January–April 1861), 248–305 (248, 251).

39. See John Witheridge, *Excellent Dr Stanley: The life of Dean Stanley of Westminster* (Russell, 2013), p. 215.

40. Davidson, *Life of Tait*, vol. I, pp. 284–87.

41. He considered Temple's essay to be 'written in a truly reverential and religious spirit': *Life, Letters and Journals of Sir Charles J.F. Bunbury, Bart.*, ed. Frances Joanna Bunbury, 3 vols (p.p., 1894), vol. II, p. 218.

42. Ashwell, *Life of Wilberforce*, vol. II, p. 338. He worked in the library at all hours, complaining when there was a delay in the arrival of candles, but also finding time to recommend Rudhall's fountain pens and a special reading stand for 'paralytics': see COM 1/16, p. 64; SEC 1/5, p. 33; COM 1/19, pp. 294, 424.

43. See Edmund Sheridan Purcell, *Life of Cardinal Manning, Archbishop of Westminster*, 2 vols (Macmillan, 1896), vol. II, p. 702.

44. Ashwell, *Life of Wilberforce*, vol. III, p. 22. Cf. a comment on 'Lord Salisbury, Mr. John Bright, the Marquis of Hartington, and Mr. Joseph Chamberlain' making a 'very pleasant party when seated around a table in the club drawing-room': 'nobody would dream of attributing anything of a public nature to a visit from the Premier or a leading member of the Opposition'. 'Ramblings in Clubland, no. 4 – The Athenæum', *Society Herald*, 21 May 1888, p. 19, inserted in COM 1/25, pp. 49–50.

45. See e.g. the duke of Argyll's opinion on Wilberforce: 'Too literally and too much he was "all things to all men," and the life in London did not improve him, or, at least, did not exhibit him at his best.' *George Douglas, eighth Duke of Argyll, K.G., K.T. (1823–1900): Autobiography and memoirs*, ed. Ina, dowager duchess of Argyll, 2 vols (Murray, 1906), vol. I, p. 397.

46. See Rowland E. Prothero, *Life and Letters of Dean Stanley* (Nelson, 1909), p. 481; Witheridge, *Stanley*, p. 288.

47. For a vivid description of the Stanleys' parties, see Witheridge, *Stanley*, pp. 257–58. Stanley was 'the Dean' to the X Club: Adrian Desmond, *Huxley: The devil's disciple* (Joseph, 1994), p. 329.
48. See 'Dr. Punch to Dr. Whateley', *Punch*, 34 (January–June), 18 (9 January).
49. Maurice, whose denial of hellfire had cost him his chair at King's College, London, was elected to the Athenæum in 1860. On Colenso's publications, see Peter Hinchcliff, *John William Colenso, Bishop of Natal* (Nelson, 1964), pp. 74–85.
50. Lyell considered that there would have been 'no sensation' over Colenso if people had read William Rathbone Greg's *Creed of Christendom* (1851): Charles Lyell, *Life, Letters and Journals*, ed. Katharine Murray Lyell, 2 vols (Murray, 1881), vol. II, p. 361. Greg was elected to the Athenæum under Rule II in 1868.
51. Barton, 'Huxley, Lubbock, and half a dozen others', 435; Barton, *The X Club*, p. 190.
52. COM 1/18, pp. 117, 123.
53. 17 February 1863, p. 125. Also present were Sir Roderick Murchison (trustee), Admiral Sir George Back, J.P. Gassiot, Sir Edmund Head, William Sterling, the Comte de Strzelecki, Dean Trench and J.H. Wyatt. Chairmen did not vote if there was a majority in favour.
54. See Ashwell, *Life of Wilberforce*, vol. III, p. 308–9.
55. See *Illustrated London News*, 42 (28 February 1863), 215.
56. Colenso was seconded by Tyndall and the majority in favour was seven (12:5): COM 1/18, p. 135. Attendance was high, as a proposal to expand the membership was on the agenda: also present were Sabine and Murchison (trustees), Back, Carpenter, Chatfield, John Crawford, Francis Galton, Gassiot, Head, Lubbock, Milnes, Richmond, Dr William Sharpey, Sir William Smith, Sterling, Strzelecki, Tyndall and Trench. Dr Gray no longer needed honorary membership at this point.
57. Davidson, *Life of Tait*, vol. I, p. 347. At the height of the controversy over *Essays and Reviews* Tait wrote in a private memorandum, 'The great evil is that the liberals are deficient in religion, and the religious are deficient in liberality': ibid., vol. I, p. 325.
58. Ibid.
59. COM 1/18, pp. 135, 142, 155.
60. Ibid., pp. 183, 184–5, 191, 195.
61. See Owen Chadwick, *The Victorian Church*, Ecclesiastical History of England, ed. J.C. Dickinson, vols VII–VIII (Black, 1966–70), vol. VIII, p. 81.
62. Ibid., p. 83.
63. COM 1/18, pp. 215, 218, 223, 229, 233.
64. In inviting Bishop Gray of Cape Town to be an honorary member in 1867, the committee of the Athenæum maintained the club's tradition of even-handedness. The library collected many of the tracts associated with the controversy and as late as 1874 the club's librarian had to write in search of a missing volume from Colenso's *Pentateuch*. See Athenæum Pamphlets, vols 553, Colenso controversy [11 tracts] (1862–64) and 583, Bishopric of Natal [4 tracts] (1863–67); Tracts from Mills Collection [11 tracts] (1864–67); 30 July 1867: COM 1/19, p. 412; SEC 1/5, p. 259. On Colenso and the club, see also *Punch*, 63 (July–December 1872), 253 (21 December).
65. See candidate 4,562: MEM 1/1/11.
66. Matthew Arnold, *Letters*, ed. Cecil Y. Lang, 6 vols (Charlottesville and London: University of Virginia, 1996–2001), vol. II, p. 347.
67. Ibid., vol. I, p. 331.
68. Ibid., vol. III, p. 54, vol. II, p. 265.
69. See James Fergusson, 'Personal touches', *Times Literary Supplement*, 7 December 2007, p. 23. This copy must have entered the book trade after the club negligently included it in a clearance sale. It was purchased by John Fowles.
70. See F. Max Müller, *Auld Lang Syne* (London and Bombay: Longmans, Green, 1898), pp. 124–25.
71. Matthew Arnold, *Culture and Anarchy*, ed. John Dover Wilson (Cambridge: Cambridge University Press, 1966), p. xxxi.
72. Ibid., pp. 6, 76.

73. See p. 88.
74. *Pall Mall Gazette*, 25 July 1866, pp. 6–7. Ferris was fined 40s. and Philip Mahony, 'a lad of about 15', 5s. Other clubs, including the Reform and the United Service, also received the attentions of the mob: see e.g. *Punch*, 51 (July–September 1866), 3 (7 July).
75. Arnold, *Letters*, vol. III, p. 59.
76. Arnold, *Culture and Anarchy*, pp. 162–63.
77. Ibid., p. 6.
78. Ibid., pp. 7–8.
79. *Pall Mall Gazette*, p. 6.
80. James Fitzjames Stephen, 'Liberalism', *Cornhill Magazine*, 5 (January–June 1862), 70–83 (77).
81. Ibid., p. 80.
82. Leslie Stephen, *The Life of Sir James Fitzjames Stephen, Bart., K.C.S.I., a Judge of the High Court of Justice*, 2nd edn (Smith, Elder, 1895), pp. 184–203.
83. Arnold described Colenso as a scapegoat, sent into the wilderness 'amidst a titter from educated Europe': 'The bishop and the philosopher', in Matthew Arnold, *Complete Prose Works*, ed. Robert Henry Super, 11 vols (Ann Arbor: University of Michigan Press, 1960–77), vol. III, pp. 40–55 (p. 40).
84. Arnold, *Letters*, vol. II, p. 354.
85. Cecil Lang in ibid., vol. II, p. 355.
86. Ibid., vol. III, p. 229.
87. Cf. William C. Lubenow, *Liberal Intellectuals and Public Culture in Modern Britain, 1815–1914: Making words flesh* (Woodbridge and Rochester, NY: Boydell, 2010), pp. 63–64. Stephen was ably assisted by Sidney Lee, whom he proposed for membership of the club in 1891: Lee was elected under Rule II in 1901 (MEM 1/1/16) and knighted in 1911. Stephen collapsed in the clubhouse in 1889 and handed over the editorship the following year: see Noel Gilroy Annan, *Leslie Stephen: His thought and character in relation to his time* (MacGibbon, Kee, 1951), p. 80.
88. George Feaver, *From Status to Contract: A biography of Sir Henry Maine, 1822–1888* (Longmans, 1969), p. 136. Maine was best known as the author of *Ancient Law* (1861).
89. Ibid., pp. 14, 130–31, 246. In a publications order of April 1872, Murray juxtaposed Maine's *Village Communities*, Darwin's *Origin of Species* and *Primitive Culture* by Edward Tylor (1872, Rule II), 'the father of anthropology': ibid., p. 300, n. 19; *ODNB*.
90. Karl Pearson, *The Life, Letters and Labours of Francis Galton*, 4 vols (Cambridge: Cambridge University Press, 1914–30), vol. III, pp. 626–28.
91. David Duncan, *The Life and Letters of Herbert Spencer* (Methuen, 1908), p. 494.
92. Ibid., pp. 501–2.
93. See ibid., pp. 292, 494–96; COM 1/21, p. 454; COM 1/23, p. 202.
94. Spencer may have introduced Tedder to Lord Acton, who employed him as his librarian (1873–74) and recommended him to the Athenæum (*ODNB*).
95. Ironically, the first paper, read by Hutton, was on Spencer's work on hereditary descent: see Alan Willard Brown, *The Metaphysical Society: Victorian minds in crisis, 1869–1880* (1947; reprinted New York: Octagon, 1973), p. 27. See also *The Papers of the Metaphysical Society 1869–1880: A critical edition*, ed. Catherine Marshall, Bernard Lightman and Richard England, 3 vols (Oxford: Oxford University Press, 2015).
96. 13 March 1888: COM 1/25, p. 41; candidate 6,703, MEM 1/1/23.
97. Brown, *Metaphysical Society*, pp. 29, 165.
98. Ibid., p. 9.
99. See ibid., p. 91.
100. Ibid., p. 298.
101. 'The Metaphysical Society: a reunion', *Nineteenth Century*, 13 (1885), 177; reprinted in John Ruskin, *Works*, Library Edition, ed. Edward Tyas Cook and Alexander Wedderburn, 39 vols (London and New York: Allen / Longmans, Green, 1903–12), vol. XXXIV, pp. xxix–xxx. Magee was briefly Archbishop of York in 1891.

102. Brown, *Metaphysical Society*, p. 303.
103. See pp. 91, 132, 134.
104. *ODNB*.
105. Abraham Hayward, *John Stuart Mill*, reprinted from *The Times* (p.p., 1873), p. 6. In the club's copy the name of Odger, a radical union leader, is scored through and replaced by that of Bradlaugh, the controversial propagandist for birth control.
106. *John Stuart Mill*, open letter to Stopford Brooke (p.p, 1873), p. 2.
107. See e.g. George Jacob Holyoake, *John Stuart Mill, as some of the Working Classes knew him*, reprinted from the *Newcastle Chronicle* (Trübner, 1873).
108. *ODNB*. Taylor was elected in 1825 and died in 1849.
109. Collini, *Public Moralists*, p. 313.
110. William Dougal Christie, *John Stuart Mill and Mr. Abraham Hayward, Q.C.: A reply about Mill to a letter to the Rev. Stopford Brooke, privately circulated and actually published* (King, 1873), pp. 9, 27. The Athenæum's copy contains underlinings and marginal marks in pencil.
111. See John Morley, *The Life of William Ewart Gladstone*, 3 vols (London and New York: Macmillan, 1903), vol. II, pp. 543–44.
112. *ODNB*.
113. Arnold, *Culture and Anarchy*, pp. xxxi–xxxii; *ODNB*.
114. See *ODNB*.
115. *ODNB*.
116. See p. 132.
117. 28 August 1888: COM 1/25, p. 65.
118. See p. 101. Burton's letter to Claude Webster, the secretary, dated 28 January 1861 ('When do you think the election will come off? I am anxious to be in England at the time') is pasted into the club's presentation copy of his *The Lake Regions of Central Equatorial Africa, with Notices of the Lunar Mountains and the Sources of the White Nile* (1860). Speke died on 15 September 1864, the day before a public debate with Burton was due to take place: it may have been suicide. He had been elected to the Athenæum under Rule II on 9 February 1864.
119. George James Ivey, *The Club Directory* (Harrison, 1879), p. 82.
120. See Fawn M. Brodie, *The Devil Drives: A life of Sir Richard Burton* (Eyre, Spottiswoode, 1967), p. 190.
121. *The Book of the Thousand Nights and a Night*, 10 vols (Benares: Kamashastra Society, 1885), vol. I, p. x.
122. Ibid., vol. X, p. 253. In the essay Burton discusses subjects such as the nerves of the rectum and genitalia in orgasm (p. 209), sodomy and pederasty, which 'London simply hushes up' (p. 248).
123. See Isabel Burton, *The Life of Captain Sir Richd. F. Burton, K.C.M.G., F.R.G.S.*, 2 vols (Chapman & Hall, 1893).
124. Stevenson was elected under Rule II in 1888, by which time he was living abroad for the sake of his health.
125. See Jane Jordan, *Josephine Butler* (Hambledon: Continuum, 2001), p. 222.
126. COM 1/24, p. 102. Also present were General Sir Henry Lefroy (in the chair), a strong Evangelical, Justine Danvers, George Bradley (the liberal Dean of Westminster), Sir James Hannen (a leading judge), Richard Musgrave Harvey and General (James) Thomas Walker (an army officer and surveyor).
127. William Henry Smith II was Secretary of State for War in 1885, having retired from the firm in 1874. He had been blackballed at the Reform Club in 1862 but elected to the Athenæum in 1877 (*ODNB*).
128. *Pall Mall Gazette*, 13 July 1885, reprinted in www.attackingthedevil.co.uk/pmg/tribute.
129. Sir James Hannen was in the chair: COM 1/24, p. 103. On 23 February 1886, with Pollock in the chair, the General Committee accepted a proposal from the Library

Committee that subscriptions to the *Gazette* be increased from ten to sixteen copies: ibid., p. 121.
130. Stead nominated as potential confidential recipients the Archbishop of Canterbury (Benson, 1877), the Cardinal Archbishop of Westminster (Manning, 1870), Samuel Morley MP, the earl of Shaftesbury (1830), the earl of Dalhousie, as the author of the Criminal Law Amendment Bill, and Howard Vincent, ex-director of the Criminal Investigation Department. Vincent joined in 1893.
131. Elected under Rule II in 1873, Watts regarded membership as his 'only luxury' and gave it up in February 1895: see COM 13/1, p. 153; cf. Veronica Franklin Gould, *G.F. Watts: the last great Victorian* (New Haven and London: Paul Mellon Centre / Yale University Press, 2004), p. 304.

## 7 Strangers and brothers

1. SEC 1/9, p. 114.
2. On the introduction of electric power, generated internally, see BUI 1/12.
3. COM 1/25, p. 88.
4. COM 20/2, 1889, pp. 1–2.
5. COM 20/2, 1890, p. 2.
6. COM 20/2, 1892, p. 2.
7. COM 1/27, pp. 97–98, COM 13/1, p. 173. Sandilands had a breakdown. One of his nine children offered a legacy to the club as reparation and another went into a mental asylum: see COM 15/1.
8. General Committee meetings were sometimes inquorate, even on this monthly cycle: see e.g. COM 1/27, p. 8.
9. In August 1889 Patrick Cumin, head of the Privy Council's Education Department, circulated a printed letter objecting to the Executive Committee's making decisions on room usage without consulting the membership: COM 13/1, pp. 17–18.
10. COM 20/2, 1891, p. 1.
11. 9 June 1890: COM 13/1, p. 71.
12. See William Gaunt, *Victorian Olympus* (Cape, 1952), p. 170.
13. Leighton was an habitué, spending up to £350 a year in the clubhouse: see Mrs Russell Barrington, *The Life, Letters and Work of Frederic Leighton*, 2 vols (Allen, 1906), vol. II, p. 317; Leonée and Richard Ormond, *Lord Leighton* (New Haven and London: Mellon Centre for Studies in British Art / Yale University Press, 1975), p. 64. The sculptor Thomas Brock, a member, executed a duplicate of his bronze bust of Leighton, now on the main landing, at cost in 1907: see COM 20/2, 1907, p. 1; COM 13/2, pp. 130, 140.
14. Richard Jenkins, *The Victorians and Ancient Greece* (Oxford: Blackwell, 1980), p. 313.
15. Gaunt, *Victorian Olympus*, p. 75.
16. Francis Gledstanes Waugh, 'In Clubland, no. III: The Athenæum', *Illustrated London News*, 102 (11 March 1893), 305–10 (306).
17. 'Antiquity writ large: Alma-Tadema, Poynter and the redecoration of the Athenæum', in Fernández-Armesto, pp. 55–73 (p. 59). Boucher's chapter is based upon his article in *Apollo*, 150, 452 (October 1999), 21–29.
18. Fernández-Armesto, p. 66.
19. COM 20/1, 1893, p. 1.
20. Fernández-Armesto, p. 61.
21. Ibid, p. 62.
22. Ibid, p. 63.
23. COM 13/1, p. 100.
24. 12 September 1893: ibid., p. 123.
25. 15 August 1893: SEC 1/10, p. 547. Tedder was so busy that he had 'not a moment to think of holiday making'.

26. Fernández-Armesto, p. 63. The dome was not removed until 1927.
27. Ibid., pp. 65–66. They supervised the external redecoration in 1909, when the figures on the frieze were painted in pure white on a background of yellow ochre. Alma-Tadema died in 1912.
28. Ibid., p. 70.
29. Ibid., p. 56.
30. A mark of the different mores of this group is evident in their deaths. Three of the six were cremated: du Maurier in 1895, creating a stir in London society, Sambourne in 1910 and Stone in 1921. Many members sat to Herkomer and Sargent for their portraits.
31. See COM 1/18, pp. 197–98, 209.
32. See COM 1/21, p. 363.
33. COM 1/23, p. 242.
34. See COM 1/25, inserted pp. 11–12.
35. See COM 20/2, 1890, p. 1.
36. *Report on the Question of Enlarging the Club House . . . 1899*, p. 5, inserted in COM 20/2, 1899.
37. Ibid., p. 13.
38. Charles Barry, *Athenæum Club: Mr. Barry's resignation as 'Architect to the Club': Correspondence 1899*: COL 3/1/1, p. 2.
39. Ibid., p. 10.
40. 26 August 1899: COM 1/26, inserted pp. 17–18. The breach was healed, however, and Sir John returned to the Committee in 1908: see ibid., p. 80.
41. 15 August 1899: COM 13/1, p. 243.
42. *Star*, 23 August 1899 and *Graphic*, 10 March 1900: COL 3/1/1, pp. 37, 41.
43. 'Spoiling the Athenæum Club', the *Builder*, 16 September 1899: ibid., p. 39.
44. 7 April 1898: COM 1/26, inserted pp. 5–6.
45. *Daily News*, 13 December 1894: COL 3/1/1, p. 11.
46. 'London clubs', *Munsey's Magazine*, February 1902: see ww.digitalhistoryproject.com/2012/12/london-clubs.html.
47. Stanley Churchill Ramsey, 'London Clubs – IV. The Athenæum Club', *Architectural Review*, 34 (1913), 54–62 (55).
48. Alcon Charles Copisarow, *Unplanned Journey: From Moss Side to Eden* (Mills, 2014), p. 342.
49. See p. 5. Many believed that Nobel was harshly treated: see *ODNB* entry on Abel.
50. 'These darker aspects of Ross's personality intruded in the satisfaction he might have felt about the honours and fame which came to him: his fellowship of the Royal Society . . . in 1901, the Nobel prize, and decorations by Belgian and British Governments (CB, 1902; KCB, 1911), culminating in his KCMG in 1918' (*ODNB*).
51. Winner of the 1904 Nobel prize for chemistry, Sir William Ramsay, elected 1905; 1908 for chemistry, Lord Rutherford, elected 1917; 1915 for physics, Sir William Henry Bragg, elected 1921 and Sir William Laurence Bragg, elected 1932.
52. See Vern G. Swanson, *The Biography and Catalogue Raisonné of the Paintings of Sir Lawrence Alma-Tadema* (Garton / Scolar, 1990), p. 85; 180 men attended.
53. The other three OMs appointed on 26 June 1902 were General Viscount Kitchener of Khartoum, Admiral of the Fleet the Honourable Sir Henry Keppel and Admiral Sir Edward Hobart Seymour.
54. On Rule II, see p. 48.
55. COM 1/26, p. 37.
56. COM 13/2, p. 20.
57. Dinner to the members of the Order of Merit, July 25th 1902, typescript, p. 10.
58. Ibid., pp. 11–12.
59. Ibid., p. 15.
60. Ibid., p. 14.
61. Ibid., pp. 16–17.

62. *Westminster Gazette*, 7 July 1902: Dinner to the members of the Order of Merit, July 25th 1902, n.p. Of the eighteen OMs elected in the subsequent ten years, thirteen were Athenians: William Holman Hunt, Sir Lawrence Alma-Tadema, Sir Richard Claverhouse Jebb and Sir John Fisher (1905), James Bryce and Joseph Dalton Hooker (1907), Professor Henry Jackson (1908), Sir William Crookes and Thomas Hardy (1910), Sir George Trevelyan and Sir Edward Elgar (1911), Sir Arthur Wilson and Sir Joseph Thomson (1912).
63. Victoria Mary Sackville-West, *The Edwardians* (Hogarth, 1930), p. 43
64. Quoted in George Kennedy Allen Bell, *Randall Davidson, Archbishop of Canterbury*, 2 vols (Oxford University Press / Milford, 1935), vol. I, p. 406. Bell himself was elected in 1926. For an account of Davidson and the Athenæum, see David L. Edwards, 'Archbishop Randall Davidson', in Fernández-Armesto, pp. 185–95.
65. Candidate 6,510, proposed by Bartle Frere on 23 June 1875, but without a seconder when his name was withdrawn on 16 January 1891: see MEM 1/1/13.
66. In his letter to 'Ruddy, my dear', Burne-Jones promised that the newly elected Kipling would soon 'know more of the inner life of bishops than in a hundred biographies of them': see Tait, p. 121.
67. Bell, *Randall Davidson*, vol. I, p. 406. Candidate 6,350, proposed by Dr Vaughan on 27 April 1874 and seconded by Archbishop Tait: see MEM 1/1/13.
68. Bell, *Randall Davidson*, vol. I, p. 406.
69. Roy Jenkins, 'The political waterfront', in Fernández-Armesto, pp. 163–68 (p. 168).
70. Henry William Lucy, *The Diary of a Journalist*, 3 vols (Murray, 1920–23), vol. I, p. 138. The entry is dated 31 May 1899.
71. See Charles Petrie and Alistair Cooke, *The Carlton Club, 1832–2007* (Carlton Club, 2007), p. 116.
72. *Mr. Chamberlain's Speeches*, ed. Charles Walter Boyd, 2 vols (Constable, 1914), vol. II, p. 131; cf. also E.H.H. Green, 'The political economy of Empire, 1880–1914', in *The Nineteenth Century*, Oxford History of the British Empire, vol. III, ed. Andrew Porter (Oxford and New York: Oxford University Press, 1999), pp. 346–68.
73. See Charles Carrington, *Rudyard Kipling, his Life and Work* (1955; reprinted, Harmondsworth: Pelican, 1970), p. 374. After Chamberlain's resignation, Kipling was to write a poem 'In Memoriam', entitled 'Things and the Man'.
74. According to the printed table plan, 'hosts prevented from being present' were the earl of Rosebery, Gladstone's successor as Liberal prime minister, and Sir Oliver Lodge, who became principal of the new University of Birmingham at Chamberlain's invitation in 1900: COL 3/1/1, p. 65.
75. See p. 154.
76. 'Ramblings in Clubland: Ramble no. 4 – The Athenæum', *Society Herald*, 21 May 1888, p. 19, inserted in COM 1/25, pp. 49–50.
77. Unidentified cutting alongside the club's Roll of Honour: COL 3/1/2, p. 1.
78. COM 1/25, p. 128.
79. COM 1/26, pp. 28, 35. Warner and Cunningham were both authors and former India hands.
80. COM 1/26, inserted pp. 33–34.
81. See Cowell, p. 53.
82. In 1904 a German newspaper printed a photograph of the drawing room over the caption 'Bibliothek im Athenäum-Klub': COL 3/1/1, p. 98.
83. Ralph Nevill, *London Clubs: Their history and treasures* (Chatto, Windus, 1911), p. 275.
84. 'Club cameos: The Athenæum', *Pall Mall Gazette*, 29 January 1912, in COL 3/1/2, p. 58.
85. See *Punch*, 131 (July–December 1906), 348 (14 November); cf. also *Punch*, 77 (July–December 1879), 9 (12 July).
86. COM 13/2, pp. 149–60. Sir Edwin was a Liberal Unionist MP until 1906 and a strong advocate for the Baconian authorship of Shakespeare's plays.
87. Ward, p. 93.

88. COM 13/2, pp. 183–84.
89. COM 1/26, p. 85.
90. COM 20/2, 1914, p. 1.
91. COM 1/27, p. 40.
92. COM 13/4, pp. 19–20.
93. COL 3/1/2, p. 74. The new smoking room had been finished in 1901: see COL 3/1/1, p. 103.
94. COM 1/25, p. 16.
95. COM 13/1, pp. 41–42.
96. Cf. a cartoon entitled 'Misunderstood (In the Club Smoking-room)', *Punch*, 104 (January–June 1893), 256 (3 June).
97. 9 December 1903: Lucy, *The Diary of a Journalist*, vol. I, pp. 215–16.
98. A cutting from an unidentified newspaper of around 1914 reads, 'I am glad to see Sir Henry Lucy's story of Herbert Spencer's supposed rudeness to a party of visitors to the Athenæum emphatically contradicted': COL 3/1/2, p. 1.
99. CAT 4/1.
100. *The Gladstone Diaries*, ed. M.R.D. Foot and H.C.G. Matthew, 14 vols (Oxford: Clarendon, 1968–94), vol. XIII, p. 226.
101. Herbert Henry Asquith, *Memories and Reflections, 1852–1927*, 2 vols (Cassell, 1928), vol. I, p. 254.
102. See Roy Jenkins, *Gladstone* (Papermac, 1996), pp. 601–2.
103. See Owen Chadwick, *Acton and Gladstone*, The Creighton Lecture in History 1975 (University of London / Athlone, 1976), pp. 30–31.
104. See e.g. Jenkins, *Gladstone*, p. 603.
105. See John Morley, *The Life of William Ewart Gladstone*, 3 vols (London and New York: Macmillan, 1903), vol. III, p. 421.
106. See p. 4.
107. See Patrick Jackson, *Morley of Blackburn: A literary and political biography of John Morley* (Madison and Teaneck: Fairleigh Dickinson University Press / Rowman, Littlefield, 2012), p. 229.
108. *ODNB*.
109. CAT 4/3.
110. *ODNB*.
111. Candidate 10,033: MEM 1/1/16.
112. Richard Davenport Hines has provided an example of two members arranging a dinner at the club in 1908 to discuss business strategy. John Meade Falkner and Lord Rendel were both directors of Elswick Works, Newcastle-upon-Tyne: Armstrong Whitworth papers 31/7064, Tyne & Wear Record Office.
113. CAT 4/3.
114. Alistair Horne, *Macmillan*, 2 vols (Macmillan, 1988–89), vol. I, p. 61.
115. On the Macmillans' paternalism, see ibid., vol. II, p. 59.
116. Egerton Castle's name is scored through, which suggests that he did not attend. Other Macmillan authors included Hardy and Yeats. John Murray III, son of the founder member of the club, had died in 1892.
117. See e.g. members' dinners on 24 June 1894, 25 March 1901, 19 December 1901, 28 February 1902, 24 October 1905, 5 December 1905, 7 December 1905 and 24 October 1906: CAT 4/1–4.
118. See e.g. dinner on 29 July 1904: CAT 4/4.
119. CAT 4/3.
120. See Andrew Lycett, *Conan Doyle: The man who created Sherlock Holmes* (Weidenfeld, Nicolson, 2007), p. 241.
121. *The Collected Letters of Thomas Hardy*, ed. Michael Millgate, Richard Purdy and Keith Wilson, 8 vols (Oxford: Oxford University Press, 1978–2014), vol. VIII, pp. 36, 42, 74–75. On the Athenæum and literary Clubland at this period see Philip Waller, *Writers,*

*Readers, and Reputations: Literary life in Britain, 1870–1918* (Oxford: Oxford University Press, 2006), pp. 494–500, 510–14, *et passim*.

122. CAT 4/4.
123. See Robert John Strutt, *John William Strutt, Third Baron Rayleigh, O.M., F.R.S.* (Arnold, 1924), pp. 234–35.
124. John Shipley Rowlinson, *Sir James Dewar, 1842–1923: A ruthless chemist* (Farnham: Ashgate, 2012), p. v.
125. William H. Brock, 'Exploring the hyperarctic: James Dewar at the Royal Institution', in *'The Common Purposes of Life': Science and society at the Royal Institution of Great Britain*, ed. Frank A.J.L. James (Aldershot: Ashgate, 2002), pp. 169–90 (p.169). Brock argues that, in reality, this was a world of 'jealous, competing and bloody-minded scientists, engineers and inventors' (p. 188).
126. Of the 103 men depicted, 43 are Athenians and 8 will be elected later.

## 8 Culture wars

1. For images of *Naval Officers of World War I* (1921), *General Officers of World War I* (1922) and *Statesmen of World War I* (1925) see www.npg.org.uk. Admiral Fisher, elected to the club in 1905 and a highly controversial figure by the end of the war, excluded himself, to the relief of those involved in the project.
2. The shaded figure among the seventeen statesmen is Earl Kitchener, who had drowned in June 1916. According to the club's archivist, Jennie de Protani, he did not reply to an invitation to join the Athenæum as a Rule II member in 1909.
3. Hugh Pattison Macmillan, *A Man of Law's Tale: The reminiscences of the Rt. Hon. Lord Macmillan* (Macmillan, 1952), p. 212.
4. Josiah Clement Wedgwood, *Memoirs of a Fighting Life* (London and Melbourne: Hutchinson, 1940), p. 88. Wedgwood, a member of the family of potters, had seven children by a wife who left him in 1913. He was elected to the club in 1909 and served in the Royal Navy Volunteer Reserve during the war.
5. On 4 August *The Times* sold 278,348 copies at the new price of 1d: see Anon., *The History of* The Times, 4 vols (p.p., 1935–52): *The 150th anniversary and beyond: 1912–1948*, Part I, 1912–20 (1952), p. 125. For the first time in its history the club did not include the editor (George Dawson, 1912–19) among its members.
6. Christopher Hussey, *The Life of Sir Edwin Lutyens* (London and New York: Country Life / Scribner's, 1953), p. 333. Lutyens's offices were in Apple Tree Yard, not far from the clubhouse.
7. 5 August 1914: COM 13/4, p. 28.
8. 12 January 1909: COM 1/26, p. 86.
9. 8 September 1914: COM 13/4, p. 31. On opposition to the war among members, see p. 198.
10. See 11 March 1919: COM 13/5, pp. 9–10; *Daily Express*, 17 March 1915 (a 'notable victory for women'), in COL 3/1/2, p. 76; Michael MacDonagh, *In London during the Great War: The diary of a journalist* (Eyre, Spottiswoode, 1935), p. 55. By May 1951 eleven of the twenty-one waitresses had left for better paid jobs elsewhere: COM 1/33, pp. 10–11. Other clubs also employed wartime waitresses: see e.g. Anthony Lejeune, *White's: The first three hundred years* (Black, 1993), p. 159.
11. The board is now stored in the club's archive.
12. 8 September 1914: COM 13/4, p. 31.
13. George Ilsley, for example, 'who was in the service of the Club from 1902 until May 1916 when he left to join the army, engaged as Drawing Room Waiter at £60 p.a.', 4 November 1919: COM 13/5, p. 37. The club also assisted some former members of staff with their demobilisation.
14. 14 August 1915: COM 13/4, pp. 67–68.
15. 30 October 1917: ibid., pp. 157–58.

16. 21 December 1915: ibid., p. 80; 8 December 1915–15 May 1918: COM 7/7, n.p.
17. 14 December 1914: COM 13/4, pp. 39–40.
18. 15 June 1915: ibid., p. 63.
19. 7 March 1916: ibid., p. 91.
20. 13 November 1917: ibid., p. 158.
21. 7 March 1918. Burton J. Hendrick, *The Life and Letters of Walter H. Page*, 3 vols (Heinemann, 1923–25), vol. III, p. 421.
22. COM 13/4, pp. 75–76; cf. pp. 31–33, 35–36, 71.
23. 13 April 1915: ibid., p. 55. Asquith, the prime minister, was the most prominent figure in public life who refused to abstain.
24. Richard Davenport-Hines has transcribed Hensley Henson's frequent references to life in the clubhouse. On 27 April 1915, Henson noted that 'almost everybody dining at the Athenaeum was drinking wine. Clearly, the King's example is not being taken very seriously': Bishop Henson Papers, Durham Cathedral Library (GB-0034-HHH).
25. 23 September 1915: COL 3/1/2, p. 90. For a wartime fictional treatment of a bishop in the north library of the Athenæum, see H.G. Wells, *The Soul of a Bishop* (1917), chapter 6.
26. 26 November 1917: COM 13/4, pp. 161–62.
27. 6 February 1917: ibid., p. 126.
28. 5 February 1918: ibid., pp. 167–68. Milk could only be served with 'tea, coffee, etc.', butter could not be served at lunch or dinner, and no meal could be served after 9.30 p.m.
29. 27 February 1917: ibid., p. 130.
30. 10 May 1920: COM 1/28, pp. 5–6.
31. COM 1/35, inserted pp. 90–91.
32. See Cowell, p. 99.
33. See 13 May 1918: COM 1/27, pp. 75–76.
34. 20 October 1914: COM 13/4, pp. 35–36.
35. 3 November 1914: ibid., p. 36. George Darroch was elected in 1913. On members' contribution to the war, see also the online exhibition, 'World War I and the Athenaeum', by the club archivist, Jennie de Protani: www.athenaeumclub.org.uk (members' section).
36. 23 November 1914: COM 13/4, pp. 39–40.
37. See 16 February 1915: ibid., pp. 48–50; 9 March 1915: COM 1/27: pp. 45–46.
38. Four hundred men and nine officers were killed that day: see Arthur Conan Doyle, *The British Campaign in France and Flanders 1914* (Hodder & Stoughton, 1916), pp. 283–85. See also a drawing in the *Illustrated London News*, 145 (14 November 1914), 672–73. One other member of staff was lost during the war. Private Charles Kennelly, a former cataloguer at the London Library, had moved to a senior post at the club. He was killed in action on 16 April 1917. See COM 13/4, pp. 93–94, 109–10, 142–43; *London Library Magazine*, 26 (winter 2014), 25.
39. 7 September 1914: STA 4/1/1.
40. See cutting from the *Daily Mail*, 2 December 1914: ibid. On Miers see *ODNB*.
41. See *The Times*, 20 November 1914, p. 9; Garen Ewing, 'The funeral of Earl Roberts of Kandahar', www.garenewing.co.uk/angloafghanwar/articles/roberts_funeral.php.
42. See 17 November 1914: COM 13/4, p. 37.
43. See ibid., pp. 37–38, 45–46.
44. *Punch*, 147 (July–December 1914), 438–39 (25 November).
45. David Gilmour, *Curzon* (Murray, 1994), p. 435.
46. *The Letters of Rudyard Kipling*, ed. Thomas Pinney, 6 vols (Houndmills: Macmillan, 1990–2004), vol. IV, p. 253.
47. War grave investigators now believe that the marked grave in a cemetery near the battle site is indeed John Kipling's: see *Daily Telegraph*, 19 January 2016, p. 11.
48. 'In Memory of Major Robert Gregory', published 1919: *The Collected Poems of W.B. Yeats*, 2nd edn (Macmillan, 1950), p. 151. Gregory, a candidate since 1904 (MEM 1/1/19), won the Military Cross with the Royal Flying Corps. He was shot down in error by an Italian pilot on 23 January 1918.

49. *Raymond; or, Life and Death, with examples of the evidence for survival of memory and affection after death*, 6th edn (Methuen, 1916), pp. 395–96. Hensley Henson described it as a 'foolish book' which was becoming 'the Bible of a new religion': Bishop Henson Papers, 13 July 1917. While attracting the interest of some of the most distinguished members of the club, including Arthur Balfour, spiritualism also appealed to the Revd Mildmay: see COM 13/4, pp. 118–19; COM 1/28, pp. 5–6.

50. John Buchan, *Memory Hold-the-door* (Hodder & Stoughton, 1940), p. 58; *ODNB*; John Jolliffe, *Raymond Asquith: Life and Letters* (Collins, 1980), pp. 296–97.

51. On 19 November 1915 he describes how the very numerous rats 'gnaw corpses and then gallop about over one's face when one lies down. Fortunately I was always a lover of animals.' Jolliffe, *Raymond Asquith*, pp. 215–16.

52. See Arthur MacNalty, *Sir Victor Horsley: His life and work*, reprinted from the *British Medical Journal*, 20 April 1957, vol. I, pp. 910–16. Victor Horsley and Mary D. Sturge, *Alcohol and the Human Body: An introduction to the study of the subject, and a contribution to national health*, 5th edn (Macmillan, 1915).

53. *ODNB*.

54. See Royal College of Surgeons website: livesonline.rcseng.ac.uk. Makins left France in July 1917 and chaired a commission to report on the British station hospitals in India. He chaired the club's Executive Committee in the 1920s.

55. *ODNB*. Savage treated Virginia Woolf, who took her revenge in *Mrs Dalloway* with her character Sir William Bradshaw.

56. Taylor Downing, *Secret Warriors: Key scientists, code breakers and propagandists of the Great War* (Little, Brown, 2014), p. 255.

57. Professor Ambrose Fleming in a public lecture at University College London, 10 October 1915: ibid., p. 11.

58. See ibid., p. 7.

59. Bragg was awarded the Military Cross in 1918, mentioned in dispatches three times and rose to the rank of major (*ODNB*). Having returned to Trinity College Cambridge after the war, he soon succeeded Rutherford at Manchester.

60. Downing, *Secret Warriors*, p. 154.

61. *ODNB*.

62. 2 March 1920: COM 1/28, p. 3.

63. MEM 1/1/15, candidate 8019, proposed on 24 November 1887.

64. See *ODNB*.

65. Cochrane was elected in 1923 and Hadcock in 1926. Nel Hichens, chairman from 1910 of Cammell Laird, shipbuilders, steelmakers and armaments manufacturers, was elected in 1928, and Sir Andrew McCance, who worked on armour at William Beardmore & Co., in 1945.

66. See also Henry Tizard, a future member of the club, who had developed new flying techniques and methods of accurately measuring aircraft performance by the end of 1917: see *ODNB* and p. 000. On the romanticisation of flight, see e.g. *Daily Telegraph*, 12 January 1916.

67. *The Times*, 18 March 1914, p. 9; 'Neptune's ally', *Punch*, 146 (January–June 1914), 231 (25 March).

68. 'A Song of Tanksgiving', *Punch*, 151 (July–December 1916), 268 (11 October). Graves was elected to the club in 1902. In October 1919 a Royal Commission on the invention awarded Sir William Tritton and Major Walter Wilson £15,000 jointly and Sir Tennyson d'Eyncourt £1,000.

69. See Downing, *Secret Warriors*, p. 198. Tennyson d'Eyncourt was elected to the Athenæum in 1913. The feud between his and Alfred Tennyson's branches of the family a century earlier is adumbrated in *Maud* (1855).

70. *ODNB*.

71. Downing, *Secret Warriors*, p. 178.

72. *ODNB*.

73. See Richard Burdon Haldane, *An Autobiography* (Hodder & Stoughton, 1929), pp. 284–90. Haig considered him to be the best Secretary of State for War that England ever had.

74. 4 July 1916: COM 13/4, pp. 105–6. Hugh Chisholm, elected in 1911, edited the renowned 11th edition of *Encylopædia Britannica* (1911) and returned to *The Times* as a leader writer in 1913. His grand-daughter Anne Chisholm is a current member. The composer Sir Charles Stanford was elected in 1895. After 1912 his work was largely neglected.

75. 18 July 1916: COM 1/27, pp. 58–59.

76. Ryle had been Bishop of Exeter and of Winchester.

77. Davidson and Ryle met to discuss the Winchester diocese in 1903 and the deanery of Westminster in 1910: see Maurice H. Fitzgerald, *A Memoir of Herbert Edward Ryle K.C.V.O., D.D., sometime Bishop of Winchester and Dean of Westminster* (Macmillan, 1928), pp. 176, 275–76.

78. George Kennedy Allen Bell, *Randall Davidson, Archbishop of Canterbury*, 2 vols (Oxford: Oxford University Press / Milford, 1935), vol. II, p. 736.

79. *ODNB*; see also Hensley Henson's conversations with Lord Bryce at the Athenæum on 16 and 17 July 1915: Bishop Henson Papers.

80. Bell, *Randall Davidson*, vol. II, p. 823.

81. John Grigg, *Lloyd George, War Leader, 1916–1918* (Lane, 2002), p. 363. This and the subsequent quotations are from Henson's diaries, housed at Durham Cathedral Library: see note 24 this chapter.

82. *Punch*, 139 (July–December 1910), 392 (30 November). See also *The Political Diaries of C.P. Scott: 1911–1928* (Collins, 1970), p. 35.

83. *Margot Asquith's Great War Diary, 1914–1916: The view from Downing Street*, ed. Michael Brock and Eleanor Brock (Oxford: Oxford University Press, 2014), p. 255. See also Augustine Birrell, *Things Past Redress* (Faber, 1937), pp. 219–20.

84. In an article on the Athenæum's wartime waitresses, it was claimed that the club had always been 'the hiding-place of the very great': 'Et tu, Brute?', *Daily Express*, 17 March 1915, see COL 3/1/2, p. 76.

85. Herbert Henry Asquith, *Letters to Venetia Stanley*, ed. Michael and Eleanor Brock (Oxford and New York: Oxford University Press, 1982), p. 270.

86. Ibid., p. 313. Edward Phillips Oppenheim, or 'Anthony Partridge', was a prolific popular novelist. In *The Double Life of Mr. Alfred Burton* (1914) magic beans from the East make disreputable estate agents and auctioneers brutally honest.

87. Asquith, *Letters to Venetia Stanley*, p. 363. The amateur detective, Joseph Rouletabille, features in *The Secret of the Night* (translated 1914) by Gaston Leroux, author of *The Phantom of the Opera*.

88. Ibid., p. 484. Like his friend J.M. Barrie (1902), Hewlett, a novelist, poet and essayist, was elected under Rule II (1909).

89. In 1919 the club paid an increased subscription of £20. 5s. 0d. to the Times Book Club: COM 13/5, p. 16.

90. Asquith, Viscount Haldane, the marquess of Crewe, Lloyd George, Sir Edward Grey, Churchill, Birrell and Charles Hobhouse.

91. The *Morning Post* printed Tedder's report on the cable on 9 April. See 17 April 1917: COM 13/4, pp. 63–64. The club's reply reads: 'The Members of the Athenæum cordially appreciate the message of one of its most distinguished honorary members. With all their countrymen they rejoice that the Great Republic has thrown into the scales the sword once crossed with England's in the cause of national Independence, now joined with hers in the cause of Human Freedom.'

92. 'Britain's Destiny and Duty', *The Times*, 18 September 1914, p. 3. Barrie, A.C. Benson, Binyon, Doyle, Haggard, Hardy, Anthony Hope Hawkins, Hewlett, Kipling, Newbolt, Seaman, George M. Trevelyan and George Otto Trevelyan were members. Henry Arthur Jones (1915), Arthur Pinero (1916), Gilbert Parker (1917) and John Galsworthy (1920) were elected later.

93. Masterman, who was not a member of the club, had assistants who were elected later: James Headlam-Morley (1923), Arnold Toynbee (1949) and Lewis Namier (1933).

94. Florence Emily Hardy, *The Later Years of Thomas Hardy, 1892–1928* (Macmillan, 1930), p. 163.
95. *Punch*, 147 (July–December 1914), 185 (26 August); cf. a cartoon of 9 September in which the Kaiser encourages a war artist to 'just get a broad effect of culture', p. 217. On 20 April 1915 Partridge is described in the minutes as principal cartoonist after the death of Linley Sambourne, also a member: COM 1/27, p. 47.
96. *Merriam-Webster Dictionary*.
97. *Punch*, 148 (January–June 1915), 343 (5 May). Seaman quotes from *Macbeth* in the verses that accompany the cartoon. Cf. a lurid treatment of *Kultur* in an American propaganda poster: Jo Tollebeek and Eline van Assche, *Ravaged: Art and culture in times of conflict* (Brussels: Mercatorfonds / Museum Leuven, 2014), p. 19.
98. Arthur Everett Shipley, *The Minor Horrors of War* (Smith, Elder, 1915), pp. ix–x.
99. *Punch*, 148 (January–June 1915), 259 (31 March).
100. See, p. 147.
101. 'When William Comes to Town', *Punch*, 148 (Almanack for 1915), n.p. The German Embassy, referred to in 'His Last Bow', was housed at 8–9 Carlton House Terrace, within sight of the Athenæum.
102. Arthur Conan Doyle, *Danger! and Other Stories* (Murray, 1918), p. v.
103. Arthur Conan Doyle, *The Original Illustrated 'Strand' Sherlock Holmes* (Ware: Wordsworth, 1990), p. 957. Cf. Michael Wheeler, *Heaven, Hell, and the Victorians* (Cambridge: Cambridge University Press, 1994), pp. 83–109.
104. Conan Doyle, *Sherlock Holmes*, p. 958.
105. Charles Waldstein, *What Germany Is Fighting For* (Longmans, Green, 1917), pp. 43–44. Waldstein took British citizenship in 1899, changed his name to Walston in the spring of 1918 and brought a libel case against one of his accusers after the war.
106. Ibid., pp. 42, 115–16. On the definition of a gentleman, see also John Buchan, *Mr. Standfast* (Hodder & Stoughton, 1919), p. 373.
107. Susan Charlotte Tweedsmuir et al., *John Buchan by his Wife and Friends* (Hodder, Stoughton, 1947), p. 87. Buchan would have known that Newbolt and his wife lived in a *ménage à trois*.
108. *ODNB*. Cf. a cartoon entitled 'The Spread of Kultur' in which tennis players capitulate, crying out, 'Kamerad!': *Punch*, 151 (July–December 1916), 185 (13 September).
109. 2 April 1912: COM 1/27, p. 10.
110. *Punch*, 147 (July–December 1914), 387 (4 November), 149 (July–December 1915), 359 (27 October), 151 (July–December 1916), 371 (22 November), 155 (July–December 1918), p. 396 (11 December).
111. Ibid., 148 (January–June 1915), 37 (13 January).
112. See *The Later Life and Letters of Sir Henry Newbolt*, ed. Margaret Newbolt (Faber, 1942), pp. 179–80, 236–37, 245, 250.
113. See MEM 1/1/19. Davidson was in the chair four years later when the committee elected Joseph Conrad.
114. John Hatcher, *Laurence Binyon: Poet, scholar of East and West* (Oxford: Clarendon, 1995), p. 191.
115. Ibid., p. 197.
116. Laurence Binyon, *For Dauntless France: An account of Britain's aid to the French wounded and victims of the war, compiled for the British Red Cross Societies and the British committee of the French Red Cross* (Hodder, Stoughton, 1918), p. 5.
117. See Martin Seymour-Smith, *Hardy* (Bloomsbury, 1994), p. 797; Florence Hardy, *The Later Years*, p. 164.
118. *The Complete Poems of Thomas Hardy*, ed. James Gibson, New Wessex Edn (Macmillan, 1976), pp. 540–41.
119. Ibid., p. 545.
120. David Newsome, *On the Edge of Paradise: A.C. Benson, the diarist* (Murray, 1980), p. 283.
121. *ODNB*.

122. Henry James, *Within the Rim and other Essays 1914–15* (Collins, 1918), p. 119.

123. *Letters of Kipling*, vol. IV, p. 309.

124. Charles Carrington, *Rudyard Kipling, his Life and Work* (1955; reprinted Harmondsworth: Pelican, 1970), pp. 511, 551.

125. Ibid., pp. 513–15.

126. *Punch*, 153 (July–December 1917), 197–98 (12 September). Quatermain survived in later novels.

127. Downing, *Secret Warriors*, p. 306.

128. *ODNB*.

129. 'The Arts in War-time', *Punch*, 152 (January–June 1917), 392 (13 June).

130. The club subscribed to the publications of the Navy Records Society and in April 1914 approved a list of books on naval history for purchase that covered four typed sheets.

131. 26 October 1915 and transcripts: COM 13/4, pp. 73–74.

132. *ODNB*. Galsworthy was elected under Rule II in 1920, after a failed attempt in 1910.

133. M.L. Sanders, 'Wellington House and British propaganda during the First World War', *The Historical Journal*, 18, 1 (March 1975), 119–46 (134, 139). Sir Edward Cook, elected in 1916, had become joint director of the press bureau the previous year; war work undermined his health (*ODNB*).

134. Russell was imprisoned for six months in 1918 for prejudicing Britain's relationship with America. On Russell and Murray see *ODNB*.

135. James Bryce et al., *Report of the Committee on Alleged German Outrages* (HMSO, 1915), p. 3.

136. Downing, *Secret Warriors*, p. 286.

137. Ibid., p. 289.

138. Tweedsmuir, *John Buchan*, p. 8.

139. Ibid., p. 88.

## *9 A roomful of Owls*

1. Jeffrey Williams, *Byng of Vimy: General and Governor General* (Cooper / Secker, Warburg, 1983), pp. 259–60.

2. Ibid., p. 266. Maurois was a liaison officer with the British army during the war.

3. *The Later Life and Letters of Sir Henry Newbolt*, ed. Margaret Newbolt (Faber, 1942), p. 343. After lunch on 14 October 1926 they had 'an enormous talk'.

4. *Punch*, 169 (July–December 1925), 681 (23 December). W.E.F. Macmillan presented the original to the club in 1925: see Tait, p. 112. It was first selected for the club Christmas card in 1956: COM 1/34, p. 24.

5. Morrow was not a member.

6. William Henry Beveridge, *Power and Influence* (Hodder, Stoughton, 1953), p. 3. Beveridge was elected under Rule II in 1924 but resigned in 1927/28. The Reform Club was his true home: see p. 000.

7. COL 3/1/2, p. 16.

8. COM 20/2, 1919, p. 1.

9. Ibid., 1920, p. 1.

10. COM 1/27, inserted pp. 95–96.

11. COM 1/28, inserted pp. 1–2.

12. 18 July 1922: COM 13/5, p. 165.

13. 1 November 1922: COM 1/28, p. 51.

14. COM 13/5, pp. 183–86.

15. See pp. 103–6.

16. See e.g. 26 July 1927: COM 1/29, p. 13; 11 October 1935: COM 13/8, p. 187.

17. 27 October 1904: The Benson Diaries, Magdalene College Cambridge, 61/17. I am indebted to Richard Davenport-Hines for drawing my attention to this comment and that of Falkner (in note 19).

18. See *News Chronicle*, 10 April 1939: COL 3/1/4, p. 6. Cf. also a cutting of 1947: ibid., p. 31.
19. Meade Falkner to Rosemary Noble on club letterhead, 7 February 1918: Armstrong Whitworth Papers 31/7064, Tyne & Wear Record Office. (Falkner was an armaments manufacturer and writer, elected in 1908.)
20. Percy Colson, *White's, 1693–1950* (Heinemann, 1951), p. 121. An incensed Committee extracted an apology from White's, who promised to omit the 'offending remarks' from any future editions of the book (21 January 1952: COM 1/33, p. 27). Ironically a later historian of White's described that club's own reputation for 'fogeydom' in the later nineteenth century: Anthony Lejeune, *White's: The first three hundred years* (Black, 1993), p. 140.) Cf. also a fantasy in the *Sunday Express* (24 January 1937) about the smoking room of the Athenæum full of the bald heads of the deceased, all of whom are clutching copies of *The Times*: COL 3/1/4, p. 1.
21. 6 March 1923: COM 1/28, p. 57.
22. 19 April 1921: COM 13/5, p. 110; 6 March 1923: COM 1/28, p. 57. For details of the scheme see 'Report of the Sub-Committee on the Provision of Bedrooms for Members', signed by Lutyens and dated 8 June 1925: COM 1/28, inserted pp. 107–8.
23. 20 January 1925: COL 3/1/2, p. 32.
24. COM 1/29, p. 9.
25. Ibid., inserted pp. 15–16.
26. *The Graphic*, 18 August 1928, p. 254: COL 3/1/2, p. 103.
27. COM 20/3, 1928, p. 1. The final figure was £28,847 (see ibid., 1929, p. 1).
28. 6 December 1927: COM 13/7, inserted pp. 45–46.
29. Ibid., pp. 66, 75.
30. 19 February 1929: ibid., inserted pp. 103–4.
31. 7 June 1921: COM 1/28, p. 26.
32. Ibid., p. 38.
33. COM 20/3, 1924, p. 1.
34. 23 May 1924: COM 1/28, p. 74. Tedder attended the centenary dinner on 28 May.
35. 4 November 1924: ibid., pp. 93–94. Lord Justice Warr advised that it was legal to pay a fee if the work needed to be done, and by a member, and that the payment was not a secret.
36. Ward, pp. v–vi.
37. 1 March 1927: COM 13/7, inserted pp. 9–10. Remaining copies were offered to members at half a guinea in 1940 and at 2 guineas in 1950: see COM 13/10, pp. 117–18; COM 20/3, 1950, p. 3.
38. 8 September 1925: COM 1/28, p. 108.
39. See e.g. 16 May 1924, 5 Jan 1926: COM 1/28, pp. 86, 114; Tait, pp. xxiv, 1–111.
40. 5 June 1923: COM 1/28, inserted pp. 67–68. The Committee had in fact changed the name of the club on 22 May 1824: see p. 00.
41. See 19 February 1924: COM 13/6, p. 29. In 1928 the Royal Society of St George donated a flag of St George to be flown on the saint's day (see 17 April 1928: COM 13/7, p. 62) and in 1929, having purchased two unidentified flags, the General Committee resolved to follow the lead of government departments 'in all occasions of flying the flag' (22 June 1929: COM 13/7, p. 118).
42. 'Athenæum: Centenary of the Foundation', 28 May 1924, p. 13. The report was by T.W. Hill, deputy secretary.
43. Michael MacDonagh, *In London during the Great War: The diary of a journalist* (Eyre, Spottiswoode, 1935), p. 97.
44. 'Athenæum: Centenary of the Foundation', pp. 14–15. On hostility towards Croker see William Thomas, *The Quarrel of Macaulay and Croker: Politics and history in the age of reform* (Oxford: Oxford University Press, 2000).
45. See e.g. p. 216.
46. See pp. 168, 344n.44.
47. *ODNB*.
48. 'Athenæum: Centenary of the Foundation', p. 17.

49. 1 April 1924: COM 1/28, p. 79.
50. 'Athenæum: Centenary of the Foundation', p. 20.
51. Virginia Woolf's essay on the Georgians, entitled 'Character in fiction', was published in the *Criterion* in July 1924.
52. 'Athenæum: Centenary of the Foundation', p. 23.
53. Ibid., p. 26. On Gladstone see p. 00.
54. 'Report on the Centenary Celebrations 1924': COM 13/6, inserted pp. 43–44.
55. Victorian composers had included Sir William Sterndale Bennett, elected in 1863.
56. See 'In Memoriam', *Punch*, 166 (January–June 1924), 393 (9 April).
57. 'Athenæum: Centenary of the Foundation', pp. 32–33.
58. 'Report on the Centenary Celebrations 1924': COM 13/6, inserted pp. 43–44.
59. See Juliet Gardiner, *The Thirties: An intimate history* (Harper, 2010), p. 190.
60. See Cowell, p. 34. Yeats's election was reported in the *Evening News* (16 February 1937): COL 3/1/4, p. 1. The poet died in 1939.
61. Candidate 10,407, proposed by his father, Leonard Huxley, and seconded by Sir Walter Raleigh: MEM 1/1/19.
62. See Sybille Bedford, *Aldous Huxley: A biography*, 2 vols (Chatto, Windus, 1973–74), vol. I, p. 177.
63. See p. 148.
64. Aldous Huxley, *Proper Studies* (Chatto, Windus, 1957), p. 282.
65. See '"Strange to say, on club paper"', *Roundabout Papers* (*Cornhill Magazine*, November 1863), in *The Works of William Makepeace Thackeray*, 26 vols (Smith, Elder, 1894–98), vol. XXII, p. 292; *Punch*, 83 (July–December 1882), 86 (26 August); *Punch*, 146 (January–June 1914), 105 (11 February); *Punch*, 165 (July–December 1923), 424 (31 October).
66. *Punch*, 159 (July–December 1920), 130 (18 August). Graves was elected to the club in 1902.
67. *ODNB*.
68. Reginald Theodore Blomfield, *Modernismus* (Macmillan, 1934), pp. 116–17.
69. Ibid., pp. 172–73. On Blomfield's attack upon Epstein's *Night and Day* in 1928, see Gardiner, *The Thirties*, p. 328.
70. See p. 291.
71. *ODNB*.
72. Tait, p. xxv.
73. *Since Fifty: Men and memories, 1922–1938: Recollections of William Rothenstein* (Faber, 1939), pp. 34–35. Eight Athenians are among his portraits that are reproduced in this third volume of memoirs.
74. 5 February 1929: COM 1/29, inserted pp. 39–40.
75. See *ODNB*.
76. John N. Hall, *Max Beerbohm: A kind of a life* (New Haven and London: Yale University Press, 2002), p. 56.
77. Ibid., p. 217.
78. Ibid., p. 207.
79. 3 February 1931: COM 1/29, inserted pp. 69–70.
80. *Letters of Max Beerbohm, 1892–1956*, ed. Rupert Hart-Davis (Murray, 1988), pp. 180–81. For Beerbohm's jocular advice on making a first visit to the clubhouse, see pp. 182–83. Strachey died in January 1932.
81. *ODNB*.
82. 15 April 1924: COM 1/28, inserted pp. 85–86.
83. *Punch*, 165 (July–December 1923), 578 (19 December).
84. 4 March 1924: COM 1/28, p. 77
85. 16 November 1920: COM 13/5, inserted pp. 83–84.
86. COM 13/6, inserted pp. 33–36.
87. Ibid.

88. Rothenstein, *Since Fifty*, p. 240. Cf. also Hugh Pattison, *A Man of Law's Tale: The reminiscences of the Rt. Hon. Lord Macmillan* (Macmillan, 1952), p. 101. MacDonald's son, Malcolm, was elected to the club in 1938.
89. COL 3/1/2, p. 24.
90. See Beveridge, *Power and Influence*, pp. 201–9.
91. Richard Davenport-Hines, *Universal Man: The seven lives of John Maynard Keynes* (Collins, 2015), p. 268. Keynes was elected to the club under Rule II in 1942.
92. See *ODNB*.
93. Ian McIntyre, *The Expense of Glory: A life of John Reith* (HarperCollins, 1993), p. 157.
94. 22 November 1932: COM 13/8, pp. 77–78; 8 May 1933: COM 1/29, p. 101.
95. 29 July 1931: COM 13/8, p. 20. In 1953 an offer to lend Hunt's *The Lady of Shalott* was declined: COM 1/33, inserted pp. 73–74.
96. Ibid., pp. 11–12, 83.
97. 22 July 1936: COM 1/30, p. 26; 18 March 1936: COM 13/9, p. 7.
98. *ODNB*.
99. Macmillan, *A Man of Law's Tale*, p. 281.
100. Ibid., p. 307.
101. 29 April 1919, to Brander Matthews: *The Letters of Rudyard Kipling*, ed. Thomas Pinney, 6 vols (Houndmills: Macmillan, 1990–2004), vol. IV, p. 551. A wine bar was discussed in committee and rejected in 1950: COM 1/32, p. 131.
102. 1 June 1926: COM 13/6, inserted pp. 127–28.
103. 16 November 1926: ibid., pp. 147–48.
104. Ibid.
105. See *ODNB*.
106. See 'Athenæum – Monthly Dinners, Monday – Season 1926–27': COM 13/7, inserted pp. 19–20.
107. See *ODNB*.
108. 26 October 1929: SEC 1/69, p. 325. Trevelyan could not accept the invitation.
109. 12 May 1930: COM 1/29, p. 61; 4 November 1930: ibid., p. 67.
110. 5 July 1932: COM 13/8, inserted pp. 69–70.
111. 5 November 1929: COM 1/29, p. 51. Balfour was given honorary membership but died the following year. Copies of his and Randall Davidson's death certificates are preserved in the archive: ibid., inserted pp. 55–58.
112. 14 October 1930: ibid., p. 65. Llewellyn and Rutherford were already *ex officio* members of the General Committee.
113. While Archbishop of York, Temple usually missed meetings of the General Committee, as he had predicted.
114. See *ODNB* and p. 000. On Keynes's influence on Temple see Davenport-Hines, *Universal Man*, pp. 326–27.
115. *The Letters of Sir Walter Raleigh (1879–1922)*, ed. Lady Raleigh, 2 vols (Methuen, 1926), vol. II, pp. 324, 517.
116. 3 June 1935: COM 1/29, p. 146.
117. 3 March 1936: COM 1/30, p. 7; 26 March 1936: ibid., pp. 9–11.
118. See Cowell, pp. 120–21.
119. The annexe's lease ran out in 1961, p. 276
120. COM 1/30, p. 99.
121. COM 1/29, inserted pp. 139–40. In 1900–14 there were over 1,000 candidates and in 1915–21 over 500.
122. 2 July 1935: COM 13/8, inserted pp. 181–82; cf. MEM 1/1/19. The waiting time for candidates was now down to about five years.
123. 7 January 1936: COM 1/30, p.1.
124. G.H. Brown, 'James (Sir) Purves-Stewart' in *Munk's Roll*, vol. IV, p. 477: see munksroll .rcplondon.ac.uk/Biography/Details/3667.

125. See archives.collections.ed.ac.uk/repositories/2/resources/489 (University of Edinburgh archives online). In an Osbert Lancaster cartoon in the *Daily Express* (26 November 1952) a clergyman suggests to a bishop that euthanasia would 'spell the ruin of the Athenæum': see COL 3/1/4, p. 45.
126. See George H.L.F. Pitt-Rivers, *The Clash of Culture and the Contact of Races: An anthropological and psychological study of the laws of racial adaptability, with special reference to the depopulation of the Pacific and the government of subject races* (Routledge, 1927), pp. 11–12. The author donated a copy to the club in 1950.
127. MEM 1/3/63.
128. *ODNB.*
129. See Bradley W. Hart, *George Pitt-Rivers and the Nazis* (Bloomsbury, 2015), pp. 105–6.
130. See COM 13/9, p. 34; Hart, *Pitt-Rivers*, pp. 5–6.
131. *The Czech Conspiracy: A phase in the world-war plot*, 2nd edn (Boswell, 1938), p. 81. Donated to the club in 1950.
132. Ibid., p. 12. On Murray see also p. 210.
133. *The Times*, 6 October 1938. For other members who admired fascist leaders in the 1930s see *ODNB* entries on Lord Sydenham of Combe (George Clarke, elected 1890), Lord Stamp of Shortland (1923, whose earlier *DNB* entry by Beveridge made no reference to Hitler), Sir John Squire (1923), James Strachey Barnes (1928, a British theorist of fascism, seconded by Cardinal Bourne (MEM 1/1/19)), Sir Arnold Wilson (1929), and Walter Starkie (1931).
134. Paul Schwartz, *This Man Ribbentrop: His life and times* (New York: Messner, 1943), p. 199–202.
135. See 18 March 1936, 30 March 1938, 4 May 1938: COM 13/9, pp. 7, 160, 166.
136. *ODNB*; 16 March and 18 May 1942: COM 1/31, pp. 51, 52. In 1936 the Executive Committee had reviewed a complaint that he was wearing 'unconventional attire' in the coffee room (8 July 1936: COM 13/9, p. 34).

## 10 'The secret power of England'

1. Arthur Bryant, 'Our Notebook', *Illustrated London News*, 214 (19 March 1949), 358; cf. COL 3/1/4, p. 39. Bryant inherited this column from G.K. Chesterton, a fellow Athenian.
2. See p. 205.
3. Letter to members concerning the 150th Anniversary Fund: COM 23/4. n.p. Sir Percy was Controller of HM Stationery Office and Queen's Printer of Acts of Parliament in the 1960s.
4. 16 February 1949: COL 3/1/4, p. 38.
5. 19 March 1947: COM 1/32, pp. 45–46.
6. See Charles Petrie and Alistair Cooke, *The Carlton Club, 1832–2007* (Carlton Club, 2007), pp. 161–65. The Carlton established itself at Arthur's old premises at 69 St James's Street, the original home of White's, and is still there.
7. See William Henry Beveridge, *Power and Influence* (Hodder, Stoughton, 1953), p. 275. Beveridge often slept in the basement of the Reform, even when it closed after bomb damage.
8. 14 October 1940: COM 13/10, p. 125. Double-tier bunks were provided for those members occupying bedrooms. Bunks were also available for staff in a separate basement shelter (Interim Report, 18 November 1940: COM 20/3).
9. Interim Report, 18 November 1940: COM 20/3.
10. Annual Report, 1939, ibid.
11. COM 13/10, pp. 45, 51, 55–56.
12. Ibid., pp. 61–62; club Firewatching Records, 1941–1945 (STA 5/4); Air Raid Precautions (ARP), Blitz Feeding, 1941 & 1943 (CAT 6/1).
13. Ibid., pp. 78, 107–8.

14. See COM 20/3.
15. William Sansom, *Westminster at War* (Faber, 1947), pp. 181–82.
16. 16 October 1944: COM 20/3.
17. See 15 April 1940: COM 1/30, p. 124.
18. 17 June 1940: COM 13/10, p. 109.
19. Interim Report, 17 November 1941: COM 20/3.
20. Letter of 13 November 1942: Dispersal of Books during World War II, 1942–1944 (LIB 8/3/2/2, closed).
21. Return of Books, Works of Art and Wine at the End of World War II, 1944–1945 (LIB 8/3/2/3).
22. 13 May 1946: COM 1/32, inserted pp. 13–14.
23. 6 May 1940: COM 1/30, p. 127. Lord Macmillan was chairman from 1936 to 1945. He was 'a collector of the famous, and even though he was personally engaging, those who met him found him increasingly tiresome as the years passed' (*ODNB*).
24. Annual Report, 1944: COM 20/3.
25. 10 February 1940: COM 13/10, p. 86. The 'Indian bison' is the gaur, a large species of ox.
26. *ODNB*; 6 July 1944: COM 13/11, inserted pp. 27–28.
27. Annual report, 1945: COM 20/3. Recipients were the British Museum, the Victoria and Albert Museum, the Science Museum, the London Library, the National Central Library and the Inter-Allied Book Centre.
28. 4 October 1939: COM 13/10, pp. 61–62.
29. 15 January 1940: COM 1/30, inserted pp. 113–14. Mr Norman Daynes KC opened a discussion on 'Need Justice be so Expensive?', with the Hon. Mr Justice Morton in the chair. Morton was a High Court judge and deputy chairman of the contraband committee at the Ministry of Economic Warfare.
30. 17 June 1940: COM 1/30, p. 138; Annual Report, 1949: ibid.
31. AGM 6 May 1940: COM 1/30, p. 129; Annual Report, 1940: COM 20/3.
32. 13 October 1941: COM 1/31, p. 37.
33. See Interim Report, 17 November 1941: COM 20/3; MEM 1/1/21.
34. Interim Report, 21 October 1943: COM 20/3. They also decided to elect a larger proportion of advanced members.
35. 15 March 43: COM 1/31, p. 79. Four years later Sir Findlater Stewart 'called attention to the fact that 7 of the 24 candidates elected at this meeting were members of the medical profession, and reminded the Committee that the question of the large proportion of medical members in the Club had engaged the attention of the Committee in 1943. The Executive Committee were therefore requested to consider the question of limiting particular categories of candidates, in view of the importance of maintaining a balanced membership of the Club.' 17 February 1947: COM 1/32, p. 35. Similar questions were raised in 1963: see p. 291.
36. 15 April 1940: COM 13/10, p. 99; 17 June 1940: ibid., p. 139.
37. Interim Report, 17 November 1941: COM 20/3.
38. Percy Colson, *White's 1693–1950* (Heinemann, 1951), p. 121. On the club's angry response to Colson's disparaging remarks, see p. 000, n. 00.
39. Interim Report, 2 November 1942 (COM 20/3) and anecdotal evidence.
40. Annual Report, 1943: COM 20/3; 4 February 1943: COM 13/10, p. 232; 16 February 1943: COM 1/31, p. 76; Annual Report, 1944: COM 20/3.
41. 6 May 1940: COM 1/30, p. 127; Annual Report, 1941; 17 February 1941: COM 1/31, p. 10.
42. 20 May 1940: COM 1/30, p. 134; 17 June 1940: COM 1/30, p. 145. For an example of a settlement in 1945 see COM 13/11, pp. 68–69, 72.
43. 21 April 1941: COM 1/31, p. 16.
44. See Cowell, p. 54.
45. 14 May 1945: COM 1/31, p. 139.

46. Members' Reminiscences of the Athenæum, 2012.
47. Interim Report, 16 October 1944: COM 20/3.
48. See Harold Perkin, *The Rise of Professional Society: England since 1880* (London and New York: Routledge, 1989), p. 407; Juliet Gardiner, *Wartime: Britain 1939–1945* (Headline, 2004), p. 87.
49. 6 January 1944: COM 13/11, p. 13.
50. Interim Report, 18 November 1940: COM 20/3.
51. For details of these casualties see *ODNB* entries.
52. Rupert Hart-Davis, *Hugh Walpole: A biography* (Macmillan, 1952), pp. 430, 444. Cf. also Sir Anthony Hastings George, who served as British consul-general in Shanghai, never recovered his health after being interned by the Japanese for eight months and defenestrated himself in the United States in 1944.
53. *ODNB*.
54. Andrew Lownie, *Stalin's Englishman: The lives of Guy Burgess* (Hodder, Stoughton, 2015), p. 61; *ODNB*. Macnamara also joined Burgess at homosexual parties held by high-ranking civil servants and members of MI6, and supported his job application to the BBC.
55. See COL 3/1/4, p. 20. Further casualties during the war were Sir Michael O'Dwyer, an administrator in India, who was shot at close range by Udham Singh at Caxton Hall, London, in March 1940, and Lieutenant Ralph Wilson, who was killed in training with the Gordon Highlanders at Warminster in April 1942 (15 April 1946: COM 1/32, p. 11).
56. See p. 192.
57. Michael Sadleir, *Tommy, 1916–1942* (pp. 1943), p. 1. This quotation had been included in a tribute in *The Times*, 10 October 1942.
58. 2 May 1945: COM 13/11, p. 58; 15 August 1945: COM 13/11, p. 69; 3 October 1945: COM 13/11, p. 76. The Victory Dinner was cancelled and the champagne sold when General Eisenhower, a Rule II member, announced that he could not attend (17 September 1945: COM 1/31, p. 143).
59. Hector Bolitho, *My Restless Years* (Parrish, 1962), pp. 2–3. Elected in 1933, Bolitho resigned a few years later, rejoined in 1940 and finally left the club in 1967: MEM 2/27/1, p. 54 and MEM 2/98/1/1, p. 13. On the sale of the Meryon etchings, see p. 000.
60. 6 May 1940: COM 1/30, p. 130; 18 May 1942: COM 1/31, p. 56.
61. Churchill had resigned in 1925/26.
62. 15 September 1941: COM 13/10, p. 179; Philip Ziegler, *London at War, 1939–1945* (Sinclair-Stevenson, 1995), p. 224.
63. 17 December 1942: COL 3/1/4, inserted pp. 16–17; COL 3/1/5, p. 4.
64. He was proposed by Sir Ronald Lindsay, ambassador to the United States: MEM 1/1/21, candidate 12,244.
65. Noël Coward, *Collected Plays* (Methuen, 1999), p. 177.
66. Ibid., p. 239.
67. 3 October 1940: COM 13/10, p. 121; 26 May 1941: COM 13/10, p. 159.
68. 2 October 1941: COM 13/10, p. 182. Knežević was posted to Portugal in June 1943 and remained in exile after the war.
69. 4 December 1941: COM 13/10, p. 189. Other exiles included the Spanish educator and jurist José Castillejo Duarte and Archbishop Stepinac of Croatia: ibid.; 15 June 1942: COM 13/10, p. 211.
70. 19 May 1947: COM 1/32, p. 42. Among other honorary members was Field Marshal Smuts, elected 'during his visit' (19 October 1942: COM 1/31, p. 65).
71. See Tait, p. 182. Barlow was also a prominent member of the Savile Club.
72. See *ODNB*.
73. Ibid.
74. Haining was commissioned in 1901 and retired from the army in 1942. He was present when the Committee elected C.P. Snow (18 February 1946: COM 1/32, p. 5).
75. 12 January 1942: COM 1/31, p. 44; *ODNB*.

76. 14 February 1944: COM 1/31, p. 106; secretary Udal's farewell speech 1951.
77. 14 January 1946: COM 1/32, p. 3; 2 June 1947: COM 1/32, p. 48; 22 January 1951: COM 1/33, p. 1. Slim sat on the General Committee 1960–62. Montgomery donated a redeemable note to the club in the 1960s: COM 1/35, p. 75.
78. See *ODNB*.
79. 13 November 1950: COM 1/32, p. 145.
80. *ODNB*. The son of Sir James Richard Thursfield, naval historian, journalist and a member of the club (elected 1879), Admiral Thursfield took a bedroom in the annexe at a monthly rate after the war (15 October 1945: COM 1/31, p. 147).
81. MEM 1/1/21; 18 January 1943: COM 1/31, p. 74.
82. See *ODNB*. Blackett became an *ex officio* member of the General Committee in 1965, as president of the Royal Society.
83. Fowler was knighted in 1942 for his services on a scientific mission in Washington DC: see *ODNB*.
84. Ronald W. Clark, *Tizard* (Methuen, 1965), p. 371.
85. Richard Davenport-Hines, *Universal Man: The seven lives of John Maynard Keynes* (Collins, 2015), p. 315. Berlin was elected to the club under Rule II in 1962.
86. See MEM 1/1/21. When Wimperis proposed his personal assistant, Albert Rowe, for membership in 1944, Tizard was seconder.
87. Stephen Phelps, *The Tizard Mission: The top-secret operation that changed the course of World War II* (Yardley, PA: Westholme, 2010), p. 19.
88. Clark, *Tizard*, p. 101.
89. Ibid., pp. 116–17. Rowe was proposed by Wimperis in May 1944 and elected in February 1948; his seconder was Wimperis: see MEM 1/1/23.
90. Clark, *Tizard*, pp. 117–18.
91. Lindemann is thought to have been the only professor to have competed at Wimbledon with that title: see *ODNB*.
92. Jones was to be seconded by Tizard in 1948, the year in which his book on scientific intelligence appeared, and was elected in 1952 under Rule II: MEM 1/1/23. Certain senior current members of the club still refer to *Most Secret War* as 'How I Won the War'.
93. See e.g. Clark, *Tizard*, pp. 128–48; C.P. Snow, *A Postscript to Science and Government* (Cambridge, MA and London: Harvard University Press and Oxford University Press, 1962), pp. 18–34.
94. Ibid., p. 130.
95. See MEM 1/1/21 and MEM 1/1/23. Lindemann only seconded one candidate during these years, Sir James Roberts Bt of Stathallen Castle: see MEM 1/1/21.
96. Clark, *Tizard*, p. 164.
97. Ibid., p. 171.
98. For conflicting evaluations of the goodwill mission see ibid., pp. 248–71 and Alan Clark, *The Tories: Conservatives and the nation state, 1922–1997* (Weidenfeld, Nicolson, 1998), p. 195.
99. *The Second World War Diary of Hugh Dalton, 1940–45*, ed. Ben Pimlott (Cape / London School of Economics and Political Science, 1986), p. 62.
100. Churchill's policy of bombing German urban centres was supported by Lindemann and 'Bomber' Harris, but opposed by Tedder, Tizard and Blackett, who favoured attacks on enemy communications.
101. Liddell Hart papers, King's College London Archive, LH1/58/1. Bell was elected to the Athenæum in 1926 and Liddell Hart in 1933.
102. See ibid., LH1/58/7, 16, 24, 32, 36.
103. Fisher also replaced Temple as a trustee of the Athenæum (COM 1/31, pp. 124, 126). In 1959 an 'appeal in memory of the late Bishop Bell' was posted in the Hall: see COM 1/34, inserted pp. 109–10.
104. Snow, *The New Men*, p. 187.

105. Ibid., pp. 269, 271.
106. Clark, *Tizard*, pp. 183–87.
107. Ibid., p. 214.
108. *ODNB.*
109. Ibid.
110. COM 20/3, p. 1. See also p. 000. Among those against unilateral nuclear disarmament was Walter Matthews, Dean of St Paul's, who sat on the General Committee in the mid-1940s.
111. Ibid., LH1/58/46.
112. Tom Lawson, *The Church of England and the Holocaust: Christianity, memory and Nazism* (Woodbridge: Boydell, 2006), p. 150.
113. A meeting at the Athenæum on 22 February 1949 is recorded in the Bell Papers, Lambeth Palace Archive, vol. 48, f. 34. Sir Norman Birkett, a member since 1942, was a judge at Nuremberg.
114. *The Moot Papers: Faith, freedom and society, 1938–1947*, ed. Keith Clement (Clark, 2010), p. 23. Reith signed Oldham's ballot card in 1928: candidate 11,360, MEM 1/3/55.
115. MEM 1/1/21.
116. See also p. 235.
117. See *ODNB.*
118. *The Moot Papers*, p. 343.
119. 17 January 1949: MEM 1/1/23.
120. *The Moot Papers*, p. 350.
121. Paul Addison, *The Road to 1945: British politics and the Second World War* (Cape, 1975), p. 182.
122. Davenport-Hines, *Universal Man*, p. 326.
123. Ibid., p. 327. Both men shortened their lives through overwork.
124. Richard Austen Butler, *The Art of the Possible: The memoirs of Lord Butler K.G., C.H.* (Hamilton, 1971), p. 91.
125. Jeremy Lewis, *Penguin Special: The life and times of Allen Lane* (Viking, 2005), p. 193, and *David Astor: A life in print* (Cape, 2016), p. 88.
126. *The Character of England*, ed. Ernest Barker (Oxford: Clarendon, 1947), p. v.
127. Ibid., p. 122.
128. Ibid. p. 320.
129. Ibid., p. 338.
130. Ibid., pp. 551–52.
131. Ibid., p. 567.
132. 10 March 1937, Liddell Hart papers, King's College London Archive, Athenæum file 5/5. For a partial transcription of the correspondence see Edward Harrison, *The Young Kim Philby: Soviet spy and British intelligence officer* (Exeter: Exeter University Press, 2012), p. 48.
133. Candidate 12,391: MEM 1/1/22. Gaselee was said to be the first clubman in St James's to wear red socks.
134. *ODNB.*
135. Calder Walton believes his colleagues' assessment of Philby to be 'justifiable': *Empire of Secrets: British intelligence, the Cold War and the twilight of empire* (Harper, 2013), p. 70.
136. See pp. 250–51.
137. 10 May 1937, Liddell Hart papers, King's College London Archive, Athenæum file 5/5.
138. Hugh Trevor-Roper, *The Secret World behind the Curtain of British Intelligence in World War II and the Cold War*, ed. Edward Harrison (Tauris, 2014), p. 101. Lord Dacre was elected to the Athenæum in 1978, a year before his peerage.
139. See Anthony Lejeune, *White's: The first three hundred years* (Black, 1993), p. 208. The significance of Philby's intervention has been contested.
140. See p. 000.
141. 3 July 1941: COM 13/10, p. 169.
142. 16 February 1942: ibid. p. 198.

143. 15 May 1944: COM 1/31, p. 111.
144. 18 November 1946: COM 1/32, pp. 27–28.
145. Clark, *Tizard*, p. 386.
146. John Bew, *Citizen Clem: A biography of Attlee* (Riverrun, 2016), pp. 420–21.

## 11 Cultural revolution

1. See Dinners & Celebrations 150th Anniversary 1974/75 (EVE 2/1–3).
2. Cowell, p. 139.
3. See p. 287.
4. See e.g. Peter Hitchens, *The Abolition of Britain: The British cultural revolution from Lady Chatterley to Tony Blair* (Quartet, 1999).
5. Cowell, p. 155.
6. Anthony Powell, *Books Do Furnish a Room* (Fontana, 1972), p. 32. Powell was not a member.
7. Richard Crossman, *The Diaries of a Cabinet Minister*, 3 vols (Hamilton / Cape, 1975–77), vol. I, p. 148. Pannell was Minister of Public Building and Works and a non-member.
8. Ibid., vol. I, pp. 366–67.
9. Ibid., vol. I, p. 496.
10. Matthew Bell, 'Guns, gays and the Queen – a former bishop reminisces', *Spectator* (3 May 2014), 22–23.
11. T.S. Eliot, *Notes towards the Definition of Culture* (Faber, 1948), p. 32.
12. Cowell, p. 157.
13. *ODNB*.
14. See *The Times*, 2 November 1966, p. 23. It was through a chance encounter with Fisher at the Athenæum in 1955 that Arthur Tilney Bassett, the Gladstone family's archivist and a member, set in train the publication of Gladstone's voluminous diaries: see *The Gladstone Diaries*, ed. M.R.D. Foot and H.C.G. Matthew, 14 vols (Oxford: Clarendon, 1968–94), vol. I, p. xxxvi.
15. 14 October 1957: COM 1/34, p. 66. Following Montgomery-Campbell's retirement he was replaced on the General Committee by Dr Stopford, his successor at Fulham Palace. He was still kept as a 'reserve' in 1973, however: COM 1/36, p. 86.
16. See pp. 295, 367n.20, 370n.126.
17. COL 3/1/4, p. 55. See also Peter Simple and a cartoon of Fisher with his mouth taped in the *Daily Telegraph*, 1 January 1957: ibid.
18. 2 January 1957: COM 1/34, inserted pp. 43–44.
19. See Edward Carpenter, *Archbishop Fisher: His life and times* (Norwich: Canterbury Press, 1991), p. 400. The reason given is Fisher's 'not being a particularly clubbable man.'
20. See, p. 229.
21. *Daily Express*, 13 October 1962: see Tait, pp. 113–14. Sir Osbert was a member of the Garrick, the St James's (which was absorbed by Brooks's in 1975), Pratt's and the Beefsteak, but not of the Athenæum.
22. COM 20/3, 1955.
23. 17 December 1951: COM 1/33, inserted pp. 25–26.
24. 21 May 1973: COM 1/36, p. 94.
25. 27 April 1981: ibid., p. 120.
26. See, for example, his report on the accounts at the 1981 AGM and his comments there on the establishment of a 'Way Ahead' working group, a sub-group of the Executive Committee: COM 1/37, inserted pp. 128–29.
27. 17 January 1983: COM 1/38, p. 4.
28. COM 20/4, 1938.
29. See also COM 13/18, p. 121.
30. 15 June 1981: COM 1/37, p. 125. There is also anecdotal evidence of corrupt practices in the club's own catering department.

31. COM 20/4, 1981.
32. 10 May 1948: COM 1/32, p. 77.
33. 2 June 1948: COM 13/11, p. 205.
34. These included the United Service Club, the Guards', the Bath, the Union, the Public Schools, the United University and the Junior Carlton. When the Devonshire Club in St James's Street closed in 1975 its membership merged with that of the East India Club in St James's Square, bringing a dowry of over £1 million as a 'long-term loan': see Anthony Lejeune, *The Gentlemen's Clubs of London* (Stacey, 2012), p. 96.
35. 17 March 1952: COM 1/33, pp. 33–34.
36. 18 July 1955: COM 1/34, p. 1; 17 October 1955: ibid., inserted pp. 7–8; 14 November 1955, ibid., inserted pp. 9–10.
37. 16 January 1956: ibid., inserted pp. 17–18. See Benefactors Book (LIB 8/10/1). A proposal for a Benefactors Book in 1999 indicates that the original had been forgotten and was no longer on display: see COM 1/40, p. 47.
38. 26 August 1968: COM 1/35, p. 156.
39. 14 May 1956: COM 1/34, inserted pp. 27–28; 14 May 1956: COM 20/3.
40. See 1981 AGM: COM 1/37, inserted pp. 128–29.
41. 19 May 1958: COM 20/3.
42. See Cowell, p. 56
43. 14 May 1962: COM 20/3. While some other clubs raised their subscriptions along these lines, the Athenæum delayed raising theirs to 30 guineas until 1966: COM 1/35, inserted pp. 90–91.
44. Malcolm Muggeridge, 'Oh no, Lord Snow', *New Republic*, 28 November 1964. On Muggeridge's further derogatory comments, see *Guardian*, 4 January 1966, in COL 3/1/5, p. 6.
45. Members' Reminiscences of the Athenæum, 2012. Wilson adds, 'The food, while edible, was pretty awful, but cheap; while the wine even then was excellent. The wine-waiter was not. He wore tails, the coat of which was encrusted with the dregs of a thousand bottles – probably some '29 clarets among them. He was also rude.'
46. 13 December 1954: COM 1/33, inserted pp. 131–32. Several members petitioned for retention of the current scheme in the Suggestions Book.
47. COM 20/3, 1956. The tiles were removed in 1987: see COM 1/39, pp. 113, 118. The dining room of the Ladies' Annexe in the basement received the same treatment in 1966: COM 1/35, pp. 108–9.
48. See COM 1/35, p. 1.
49. Cf. p. 236.
50. 7 March 1962: COM 13/15, inserted 46–47; 1 August 1962: ibid., inserted pp. 60–61.
51. 4 April 1962: ibid., inserted pp. 48–49.
52. 24 May 1965: ibid., inserted pp. 152–53.
53. 25 March 1966: COM 13/16, inserted pp. 16–17.
54. 31 May 1966: ibid., p. 24.
55. Candidate 13,566: MEM 1/3/69. Among his friends and mentors were Sir Max Beerbohm, Arthur (later Sir Arthur) Bryant, Lord David Cecil, his proposer Roy (later Sir Roy) Harrod, Frank Pakenham (later Lord Longford), his seconder John (later Sir John) Rothenstein and John (later Sir John) Summerson.
56. 16 December 1932: John Betjeman, *Letters*, ed. Candida Lycett Green, 2 vols (Methuen, 1994–95), vol. I, p. 110.
57. Ibid., vol. II, p. 64. Betjeman's support caused a reaction against Comper (who was not a member): see Anthony Symondson SJ and Stephen Arthur Bucknall, *Sir Ninian Comper: An introduction to his life and work with complete gazeteer* (Spire / Ecclesiological Society, 2006), p. 219. *Ghastly Good Taste* was published in 1933.
58. Betjeman, *Letters*, vol. II, p. 330.
59. Ibid.

60. 18 November 1968: COM 1/36, p. 2; MEM 2/100/1/1, p. 12; 18 March 1974: COM 1/36, p. 114; MEM 2/104/1, p. 13; MEM 2/105/2, p. 16. On his first readmission, the statutory fine of £3 was waived; on the second he was fined £10.
61. The cost of the work was covered by an anonymous donation of £1,000 (19 May 1969: COM 1/36, p. 14).
62. AGM 14 May 1962: COM 1/35, inserted pp. 56–57.
63. AGM 17 May 1971: COM 1/36, inserted pp. 51–52.
64. See COM 1/37, pp. 31, 34, 51, 92.
65. 27 February 1951: COM 7/9, n.p. Over two thousand volumes were 'eliminated' in the early 1950s.
66. 19 November 1958: COM 7/10, pp. 103–4.
67. AGM 1961: COM 1/34, inserted pp. 147–48.
68. 25 February and 25 July 1960: COM 7/10, pp. 124, 131–32.
69. 1962 AGM: COM 1/35, inserted pp. 16–17; 'Reduction of Stock, July 1960', LIB 8/9, includes first editions of Tennyson, a former member.
70. 1964 AGM: ibid., inserted pp. 70–71; 1971 AGM: COM 1/36, inserted pp. 51–52. In the 1970s it took two members many hours to count the 75,000 volumes in the library, using the long cane of a feather duster to deal with the upper shelves: Cowell, p. 66.
71. 22 June 1953: COM 1/33, inserted 83–84; papers relating to sales, 1953–66: LIB 8/9, n.p.
72. 13 July 1953: LIB 8/9, n.p.
73. 13 April 1964: COM 1/35, p. 66.
74. *Evening Standard*, 30 April 1964, in COL 3/1/5, p. 3. The purchase of a facsimile meant that the club would not be 'entirely without Principles'.
75. 19 January 1970: COM 1/36, p. 22.
76. 15 November 1982: COM 1/37, p. 152.
77. 25 April 1983: COM 1/38, p. 11.
78. See Tait, p. xxiv and p. 252.
79. 25 July 1983: ibid., p. 21.
80. 19 January 1948: COM 1/32, p. 65 and report of February 1948 inserted pp. 65–66.
81. 4 February 1948: COM 13/11, pp. 185–86. He also referred to having some 'mainly decorative' names. In 1824 Croker had wanted some 'good names' on the founding Committee: see p. 29.
82. 2 February 1949: ibid., inserted pp. 237–38. See pp. 266–67 for Carr's letter of 1937 to Liddell Hart concerning Philby.
83. See p. 1.
84. Blackett, Chadwick, Cockcroft and, Eliot (Nobel); Attlee, Berlin, Blackett, Cockcroft, Eliot, Penney, Priestley (OM); Attlee, Blackett, Bowra, Chadwick, Hill, Snell (CH).
85. See pp. 12, 110, 267. Grammar schools did not increase in number after 1944, but Butler's Education Act made them available to a wider social range of bright children through the state-funded 11-plus system. 'Rab' Butler became a member in 1954.
86. See *The Macmillan Diaries: The cabinet years, 1950–1957*, ed. Peter Catterall (Macmillan, 2003), p. 615. Macmillan's background was Eton, Oxford and the Guards. Professor Alan Ross's neologisms of 1954 had been gleefully adopted by Mitford in 1955 and were the subject of John Betjeman's commentary on 'fish-knives' and 'serviettes' in 'How to Get On in Society': *A Few Late Chrysanthemums* (Murray, 1954), pp. 94–95.
87. See *High Relief: The autobiography of Sir Charles Wheeler, sculptor* (Country Life, 1968), p. 23.
88. See Harold Perkin, *The Rise of Professional Society: England since 1880* (London and New York: Routledge, 1989), p. 269.
89. Michael Dunlop Young, *The Rise of the Meritocracy, 1870–2033: An essay on education and equality* (Thames & Hudson, 1958; reprinted Penguin, 1961).
90. Anthony Sampson praised Young and adopted the term 'meritocracy' in *Anatomy of Britain* (Hodder, Stoughton, 1962), pp. 185–86.

91. Peter Hitchens, *The Abolition of Britain: The British cultural revolution from Lady Chatterley to Tony Blair* (Quartet, 1999), p. vi.
92. Members' Reminiscences of the Athenæum, 2012.
93. Harold Wilson, *Labour's Plan for Science*, nottspolitics.org/wp-content/uploads/2013/06/Labours-Plan-for-science.pdf. Sir Alcon Copisarow, later a chairman and trustee of the club, was chief scientific officer of Wilson's new Ministry of Technology.
94. 14 December 1964: COM 1/35, p. 79.
95. Ben Pimlott, *Harold Wilson* (HarperCollins, 1992), p. 267.
96. Ibid., p. 274.
97. C.P. Snow, *The New Men* (Macmillan, 1954), p. 98; see also p. 000. See also Philippa Moody, 'In the lavatory of the Athenæum: post-war English novels', *Melbourne Critical Review*, 6 (1963), 83–92, where Snow's *jeu d'esprit* becomes a heavily freighted cultural sign in the hands of a fervent Leavisite.
98. Crossman, *Diaries*, vol. III, pp. 206–7.
99. Perkin, *The Rise of Professional Society*, p. 390.
100. *The Queen*, April 1969, in COL 3/1/5, p. 25.
101. *Alfred Gilbey: A memoir by some friends*, ed. David Watkin (Russell, 2001), p. 142. Members could not occupy a club bedroom for more than ten consecutive nights, yet the Hon. Steven Runciman also 'lodged' in the clubhouse, 'like a nice old fashioned hotel, a little shabby but perfectly comfortable – and by present standards rather cheap', and left the club a legacy: see Minoo Dinshaw, *Outlandish Knight: The Byzantine life of Steven Runciman* (Lane, 2016), p. 559; COM 1/40, p. 185. Gilbey had hoped to die on his seventieth birthday, 'while carrying his suitcases up the steps at the entrance to the Athenæum' (p. 121).
102. Cowell, p. 174.
103. Sampson, *Anatomy*, p. 124.
104. Captain Barnabe Rich, 'The last club man', *Evening Standard*, 3 June 1939, in COL 3/1/4, p. 9.
105. David Anderson, 'Club of the British immortals', *The New York Times Magazine*, 2 April 1944, typescript in ibid., p. 25.
106. The book's publication by Heinemann was arranged by a member who was a director of the firm (19 November 1973: COM 1/36, p. 102). The club owned the copyright.
107. See pp. 145, 266. I am indebted to Adrian Cowell, also a member of the club, for his comments on his late father and the 1975 history.
108. Two years earlier the General Committee shortened a meeting because a power cut was expected (14 February 1972: COM 1/36, p. 67).
109. Cowell, pp. 59–60.
110. Peter Hitchens wrote, 'So many features of this country's life crumbled at once, that the new culture had to take the place of patriotism, faith, morality and literature': *Abolition of Britain*, p. ii.
111. Cowell, p. 149.
112. Almeric FitzRoy, *History of the Travellers' Club* (Travellers' Club / Allen, Unwin, 1927). Travellers no longer adopt the possessive in their title.
113. Cowell, p. 61.
114. Adrian Bingham, *Family Newspapers? Sex, private life, and the British popular press, 1918–1978* (Oxford: Oxford University Press, 2009), p. 257.
115. Phillip Knightley and Caroline Kennedy, *An Affair of State: The Profumo case and the framing of Stephen Ward* (Cape, 1987), p. 209.
116. See Richard Davenport-Hines, *An English Affair: Sex, class and power in the age of Profumo* (Harper, 2013), p. 328.
117. See ibid., p. 323.
118. Ibid., p. 329, where the report is described as being 'awash with the spite of a lascivious, conceited old man'.
119. See p. 267.

120. Edward (later Sir Edward) Heath was elected to the club under Rule IV on 19 October 1970: MEM 1/1/27, candidate 16,563.
121. John le Carré (David Cornwell), *The Pigeon Tunnel: Stories from my life* (Viking, 2016), p. 14.
122. See Martin Pearce, *Spymaster: The life of Britain's most decorated Cold War spy and head of MI6, Sir Maurice Oldfield* (Bantam, 2016), p. 136.
123. See COM 1/39, p. 193; MEM 1/1/29, candidate 19,820.
124. Ivan Yates, 'The man who runs the Secret Service', *Observer*, 12 August 1973, in COL 3/1/5, p. 42.
125. See Pearce, *Spymaster*, p. 21, *et passim*.
126. *Reformed Characters: The Reform Club in history and literature – an anthology with commentary*, ed. Russell Burlingham and Roger Billis (Reform Club, 2005), p. 138, citing a table from Richard Rose, *Policy Making in Britain* (1969). The Carlton had no senior civil servants.
127. *The Art of the Possible: The memoirs of Lord Butler K.G., C.H.* (Hamilton, 1971), pp. 156–57. A cold buffet was available in the coffee room: see e.g. COM 13/18, p. 147, 151.
128. Armstrong resigned by 1977: see MEM 2/103/1.
129. 6 November 1963 (COM 13/15), inserted pp. 98–99. The paper was marked 'confidential'.
130. See p. 247.
131. 16 November 1964: COM 1/35, p. 77; cf. pp. 32, 47.
132. MEM 1/1/27, candidate 17,365.
133. Patrick White, *Flaws in the Glass: A self-portrait* (Cape, 1981), p. 237. Nolan was appointed OM in 1983.
134. See *The Times*, 7 April 1970, and James Stourton, *Kenneth Clark: Life, art and Civilisation* (Collins, 2016), p. 271. Fraser's daughter, Rosalind Gilmore, is a current member.
135. On Eliot and Betjeman see pp. 000 and 000.
136. Cecil resigned in 1950 (MEM 2/77/3) and rejoined in 1975.
137. 20 October 1975: COM 1/36, p. 147.
138. 18 October 1976: COM 1/37, p. 13. On the Century Club, see p. 000.
139. 18 May 1981: COM 1/37, p. 121.
140. 20 October 1969: COM 1/36, p. 18.
141. 17 May 1976: COM 1/37, inserted pp. 6–7.
142. 19 November 1979: COM 1/37, p. 87; 3 April 1979: ibid., p. 73.
143. COM 1/38, p. 108.
144. In a letter to *The Times* (30 December 1983), HM Coroner for Westminster, Dr Paul Knapman, lamented the absence of a philosopher at Club Table during a lunchtime conversation to which a scientist and a lawyer contributed: see COL 3/1/5, p. 69.
145. See John Charlton, 'The Sofa', in Fernándo-Armesto, pp. 237–40 (p. 237).
146. See Members' Reminiscences of the Athenæum, 2012.
147. See *The Times*, 28 January 1982, in COL 3/1/5, p. 56.
148. Dinners & Celebrations 150th Anniversary 1974/75 (EVE 2/1–3); cf. Cowell, p. 156, where a few words are added for clarification.
149. 18 March 1974: COM 1/36, p. 113.
150. 13 May 1974: ibid., inserted pp. 119–20; COM 23/4, inserted typescript.
151. Watkin is listed in 1980 but not in 1984: see MEM 2/105/2.
152. Roger Scruton, *Gentle Regrets: Thoughts from a life* (Continuum, 2005), pp. 63–71; *Alfred Gilbey*, ed. Watkin, *passim*; see also p. 000.
153. See Tait, p. 114.

### 12 *Plus ça change*

1. *Daily Mail*, 21 April 2011.
2. Robert Tombs, *The English and their History* (Allen Lane, 2014), p. 791.

3. See p. 280.
4. 14 October 1985: COM 1/38, p. 75.
5. 18 November 1985: ibid., p. 79.
6. 16 December 1985, 20 January 1986: ibid., pp. 82, 85.
7. Tait, p. 83. In 1940 the bust had been the first item to be stored in the basement for protection from bombing: see p. 246.
8. AGM 13 June 1988: COM 1/38, inserted pp. 163–64.
9. See e.g. the architectural survey of 1999: COM 1/40, pp. 73–74. The secretary, Richard Smith, left for Boodles in 1998 and was succeeded by John Stoy of the East India Club, with Jonathan Ford initially as assistant secretary.
10. AGM 15 June 98: COM 1/40, p. 28.
11. COM 23/4, 2003
12. Ibid., 2016.
13. Ibid., 2010. The plan was approved by the General Committee, chaired by the ebullient Dr Henry Kinloch, an investments specialist.
14. Lesley Knox, Ann Chant, Jane Barker and Dr Ann Limb.
15. MEM 1/1/29, candidate 18,253.
16. 23 January 1984: COM 1/38, p. 29.
17. Papers relating to Debate concerning Admission of Women Members, 1984–2003: COM 4/8/7.
18. 18 June 1984: COM 1/38, inserted pp. 47–48.
19. 23 January 1985: COM 1/39, inserted pp. 61–62.
20. Papers relating to Debate: COM 4/8/7.
21. Professor Sir Richard Evans, a member of the club, does not mention Hobsbawm's membership in *Eric Hobsbawm: A life in history* (Little, Brown, 2019).
22. 20 May 1985: COM 1/38, p. 69.
23. 13 June 1994: COM 1/39, inserted pp. 128–29.
24. 11 July 1994: ibid., p. 132.
25. Cuckney's entry in *ODNB* records that he was the 'one obvious winner' in the Westland affair, for example. During his work resolving the Maxwell pensions scandal he met Jane Newell, now his widow, a dame in her own right and a trustee of the club. He was not well during his chairmanship, which lasted only two years.
26. 22 February 1999: COM 1/40, p. 48.
27. Papers relating to Debate, appendix O: COM 4/8/7.
28. See COM 1/40, inserted pp. 113–14.
29. Papers relating to Debate, appendix T: COM 4/8/7.
30. COM 1/40, inserted pp. 203–4.
31. See COM 1/40, pp. 171–72.
32. *First Ladies: Reminiscences of the first women members of the Athenæum*, ed. Victoria Glendinning and Cecil Cameron (Athenæum, 2013).
33. 17 December 2001: COM 1/40, p. 178.
34. 16 June 2003: COM 1/41, p. 43.
35. 28 April 2008: COM 1/42, p. 29. The late John Grieves was in the chair.
36. COM 1/42, inserted pp. 179–80. Henry Kinloch was in the chair.
37. See p. 293.
38. COM 1/38, inserted pp. 133–34. The Chairman, Judge Paul Baker, 'remarked particularly that it was a pleasure to see the Coffee Room frequently full for dinner'.
39. Ibid., p. 106.
40. See p. 233. A parallel series of Dinner Talks was arranged at the Ladies Annexe from 1937.
41. COM 1/39, inserted pp. 102–3.
42. COM 1/40, inserted pp. i–ii.
43. 1998 AGM: ibid., inserted p. 28.
44. See p. 274.

45. COM 23/5, 2014.
46. Ibid.
47. Ibid., 2016.
48. See e.g. the X Club, pp. 142–44.
49. I am grateful to Dr Christopher Wright for this information.
50. See www.studyofparliament.org.uk/hist2.htm.
51. See Members' Correspondence in Favour of the Admission of Lady Members, 1990–2000: COM 4/8/3.
52. 2016 AGM: COM 23/5.
53. See pp. 180–81.
54. See p. 175.
55. See p. 54.
56. 14 October 2002: COM 1/41, inserted pp. 11–12.
57. COM 1/40, inserted 203–4.
58. Figures provided by the Secretary, Jonathan Ford, in May 2019.
59. See p. 48. 'Works' has become 'work', however.
60. See p. 32.
61. 'Networking, nepotism, and gongs galore: seven generations of Athenaeum membership', 13 March 2013. See also p. 00.
62. Peter A. Sabine, 'Geological science and the early years of the Athenæum', in Fernández-Armesto, pp. 111–26 (p. 118). See also pp. 41, 42.
63. Informal library talk, 21 October 2015. Directors of the Royal Institution, a post created in 1965, have all been Athenians: Sir William Lawrence Bragg (elected to the club in 1932), Baron (George) Porter (1966), Baron (David) Phillips (1986, acting director), Sir John Meurig Thomas (1986), Professor Peter Day (1991) and Baroness (Susan) Adele (2001). For early connections see pp. 00, 00.
64. See p. 243.
65. Anthony Sampson, *Anatomy of Britain* (Hodder, Stoughton, 1962), p. 74.
66. Andrew Brown, 'Turning vestments into frocks', *The Oldie*, 313 (September 2014), 12.
67. See pp. 171, 235, 271.
68. For a new member over forty the annual subscription is £1,430, with an entrance fee to match; bedrooms are priced at £127 per night, single.
69. 17 June 1996: COM 1/39, p. 177.
70. Dan Cohn-Sherbok exaggerated when stating that in 2001 the number of clergy had 'dwindled to a handful': see Fernández-Armesto, pp. 197–204 (p. 202).
71. See p. 283.
72. Ibid.
73. *Daily Mail*, 31 October 2009. Professor Eastwood became vice-chancellor of Birmingham University in 2009 and was knighted in 2014.
74. See Tait, pp. 1–109.
75. See p. 281.
76. See Peter Collins, *The Royal Society and the Promotion of Science since 1960* (Cambridge: Cambridge University Press, 2016), p. 103n; COM 1/39, pp. 164–65.
77. Fernández-Armesto, p. 144.
78. Anthony Symondson SJ, 'Renovating heaven and adjusting the stars', in *Loose Canon: A portrait of Brian Brindley*, ed. Damian Thompson (London and New York: Continuum, 2004), pp. 65–122 (p. 94).
79. Ibid., pp. 103–4.
80. Ibid., p. 116.
81. Candidate 18,216, MEM 1/1/29.
82. See Dan Davies, *In Plain Sight: The life and lies of Jimmy Savile* (Quercus, 2014), p. 388, 390, 394.
83. 26 November 2012: Confidential Minutes of the General Committee.

84. Select Committee on Education and Skills, 19 March 2003: www.publications.parliament .uk/pa/cm200203/cmselect/cmeduski/425/3031902.htm. Clarke is not a member of the Athenæum.
85. Sir Anthony Hammond was of equivalent rank, as director general of legal services at the Department of Trade and Industry, 1992–97.
86. See p. 273; 20 July 1998: COM 1/40, p. 31.
87. Anthony Lejeune, *White's: The first three hundred years* (Black, 1993), p. 223.
88. Ibid., p. 225.
89. Dan Cohn-Sherbok, 'Clergy', in Fernández-Armesto, pp. 197–204 (p. 204).
90. See p. 7.
91. Sir William Golding, elected in 1976, died in 1993.
92. *Guardian* Books Blog, 1 April 2008.
93. Among the conductors in the club, Sir Colin Davis died in 2013, Sir John Eliot Gardiner was a member in the noughties and Dr Christopher Seaman was elected in 2013. Choir directors have included Sir David Willcocks (died 2015) and David Trendell (died 2014 aged fifty), a popular habitué who has been described as a 'unifier in affability'.
94. Photographs of two of the club's architects, the late Sir Geoffrey Jellicoe and Lord Foster of Thamesbank, a current member, are also on display.
95. *Who Runs This Place? The anatomy of Britain in the 21st century* (Murray, 2004), p. 11.
96. Ibid., p. 90.
97. Ibid., p. 8.
98. Roy Jenkins, 'The political waterfront', in Fernández-Armesto, pp. 163–68 (p. 168).
99. Patrick Cormack, 'Two parliamentary members', in ibid., pp. 169–81.
100. See Alcon Charles Copisarow, *Unplanned Journey: From Moss Side to Eden* (Mills, 2014), p. 344. Sir Alcon died in 2017.
101. Matthew Bond, 'The bases of elite social behaviour: patterns of club affiliation among members of the House of Lords', *Sociology*, 46 (2012), 613–32 (620).
102. Cited in Sampson, *Who Runs This Place?*, p. 351.
103. Yehudi Menuhin, 'Athenæum spaces and wishes', in Fernández-Armesto, pp. 297–99 (p. 297).

# INDEX

INDEX